BN 0848714 6

THE CIA, THE BRITISH LEFT AND THE COLD WAR
Calling the Tune?

CW00820195

HUGH WILFORD
University of Sheffield

Foreword by
DAVID CAUTE

 Routledge
Taylor & Francis Group
LONDON AND NEW YORK

First published in 2003 by
FRANK CASS PUBLISHERS

Published 2013 by Routledge
2 Park Square, Milton Park, Abingdon, Oxfordshire OX14 4RN
711 Third Avenue, New York, NY, 10017

First issued in paperback 2014

Routledge is an imprint of the Taylor & Francis Group, an informa business

British Library Cataloguing in Publication Data

Wilford, Hugh, 1965–
   The CIA, the British Left and the Cold War: calling the
tune?. – (Cass series. Studies in intelligence)
   1. United States. Central Intelligence Agency 2. Socialism –
Great Britain – History 3. Communism – Great Britain –
History 4. Cold War 5. Great Britain – Politics and
government – 1945–
I. Title
320.5'31'0941'09045

Library of Congress Cataloguing-in-Publication Data

Wilford, Hugh, 1965–
   The CIA, the British left, and the Cold War: calling the tune?/Hugh Wilford.
      p. cm. – (Cass series–studies in intelligence, ISSN 1368-9916)
   Includes bibliographical references and index.
      1. United States. Central Intelligence Agency–History–20th century.
   2. Labour Party (Great Britain)–History–20th century. 3. Cold War.
   4. Great Britain–Politics and government–1945–1964. I. Title. II. Series.

UB271.U5W55 2003
327.1273041'09'045–dc21   2002041758

ISBN 13: 978-0-714-65435-5 (hbk)
ISBN 13: 978-1-138-01118-2 (pbk)

Contents

In Loving Memory of My Father

Co-Series Editor's Preface

Hugh Wilford's remarkable analysis of the relationship between agencies of the United States and the British left during the early Cold War represents the first serious and exhaustively documented study of a subject that has long been surrounded by speculation and rumour. It also forms part of a wider re-assessment of this period, which has highlighted the importance of ideology and culture, rather than power, in American foreign policy.

A significant new wave of writing about America and the world of intellectuals and cultural organisations has increasingly sought to develop the concept of the 'state-private network'. This has emphasised the way in which Washington pursued its Cold War objectives in partnership with private groups and independent organisations embedded in a free society. The Soviet Union had blazed a similar trail in the 1930s, making ingenious efforts to dominate the world of international conferences, festivals, exhibitions and social movements. After the Second World War, the United States sought to emulate its rival in a dynamic display of organised spontaneity and cultural largesse. Some groups were deliberately created, but the majority were co-opted, into a struggle for intellectual hearts and minds. By the 1960s, many organisations across Europe were receiving sponsorship from one Cold War agency or another, and indeed the basic facts were widely understood by numerous participants.

Wilford's study is amongst the very best of this new writing about 'state-private networks'. Scholars working in this area offer one of the most important challenges to the orthodox conceptions of United States foreign policy in the postwar world. Conventional perspectives have tended to see American behaviour as defensive, pragmatic and uninterested in ideology. New writings located in the realm of culture and ideas are questioning these assertions and seeking to examine the way in which social movements and intellectual organisations formed a central element in a deliberate American effort to extend the Cold War to all levels of society. The Central Intelligence Agency was significant in this process. By 1951, Tom Braden, perhaps the most insightful pioneer of the American Cold War, had set up the International Organizations Division of the CIA for precisely this purpose.

Wilford's impressive study, which draws out the many clandestine aspects of this subject, has extended its research beyond the familiar

vii

diplomatic files, to cover a bewildering range of repositories that hold the papers of innumerable private bodies, many of which are only recently declassified. He concludes that discreet 'arm's-length' CIA covert operations involving intellectuals and trade unionists affected the whole spectrum of the British left during the early years of the Cold War. American activities touched many leading figures including senior Labour Party politicians, union leaders and even Bloomsbury *literati*.

The CIA, together with American information officers, sought to push the British left towards the centre and a degree of success accompanied the political dimensions of these operations. American support for such ventures as the Congress for Cultural Freedom and its London-based magazine *Encounter* subtly transformed the political culture of the British left, making it less socialist and more Atlanticist. Close cooperation with elements in the Labour Party formed a highlight of American activities in Britain.

By contrast, in other areas, such as trade union politics and left-wing attitudes towards European unity, the CIA proved less successful. British trade unionists were never enamoured of American ways in the work-place and here – like the Marshall Plan – it failed to influence its left-wing British friends in favour of American industrial practices. For that matter, amongst trade-unionists, even the CIA's agents on the American labor left proved unreliable and rebellious, asserting that they had been in the anti-communist game much longer than the 'johnny-come-lately' officials who merely funded them. Wilford's nuanced study shows us how union elements in both Britain and America were barely coordinated and rarely controlled.

Another major American project was support for the idea of a 'United States of Europe', built in the American image. CIA support for a federal united Europe went hand in hand with the Marshall Plan. Although the CIA pursued a successful programme of support of European federalism on the continent, this initiative never flowered in Britain. Some British MPs received subventions from the CIA in their pro-European work, but cross party-suspicions of European federalism were too strong in Westminster and Whitehall and they made little headway.

This is a careful and scholarly study, revealing much that is new about the place of culture and ideas in the complex Cold War relationship between Britain and the United States. The story of American influence in Britain also has a resonance with more recent American initiatives that have involved the promotion of democracy and free market philosophies in other parts of the world in the 1980s and 1990s. As such, its judicious observations about overt and covert action in the cultural realm, and the slippery nature of support operations, contain lessons that travel far beyond the immediate historical subject.

Professor Richard J. Aldrich, March 2003

List of Illustrations

Foreword

The diplomatic and military crisis known as the Cold War was simultaneously a moral and ideological confrontation. Both Soviet communism and Western liberal democracy were contesting the heritage of the rationalist Enlightenment from which Marxism sprang. Given the extravagant cruelties of the Stalinist autocracy, its contempt for the fundamental freedoms we cherish, we may be tempted to dismiss the Soviet promise of utopia much as Orwell did in *Animal Farm*. But the communists and fellow travellers despised by Orwell stubbornly refused to believe reports of false trials, forced labour, and mass deportations in the USSR – or excused them as transitional responses to 'capitalist encirclement' and fascist aggression.

The question for historians, then, is why did leading western intellects, sharing a common cultural heritage, arrive at such irreconcilable conclusions? Were some of them bribed, bought or simply unwittingly manipulated? As Hugh Wilford points out, 'Moscow gold' was a familiar accusation before 'Washington gold' arrived on the scene with a series of revelations in the mid-1960s. Focusing on the covert political and cultural operations of the CIA and allied American agencies in western Europe and Britain, where the new Congress for Cultural Freedom received concealed subsidies, Wilford in effect asks, 'Conspiracy or genuine conviction?'

This puts his book at the heart of an ongoing debate. His (by no means fashionable) emphasis on conviction rather than conspiracy is welcome, although he is justly cautious in his conclusions. But the issue has been professional as well as ideological. Although the investigative impulse is indispensable, and exposure of sacred cows entirely healthy, there is no gainsaying that revelations of conspiracy make more of a splash than reflective explorations of sincere conviction. Hugh Wilford admirably resists the prevalent temptation to offer exaggerated claims about the role of the secret services in controlling the cultural production of the Cold War. Here is a scholar who had lifted his head above the archival tunnel and wisely taken note of the wider culture of the mid-twentieth century.

David Caute, January 2003

Acknowledgements

Many participants in the events described in this book kindly gave up their time to answer my questions in person or in writing. For this I am very grateful to Daniel Bell, Tony Benn, Tom Braden, Geoffrey Goodman, Denis Healey, Myron Kolatch, Irving Kristol, Melvin Lasky, Mitchel Levitas, Cord Meyer, Paul Sakwa, Arthur Schlesinger Jr., Jasper Ridley, Adam Watson, Herbert Weiner and David Williams.

Numerous fellow researchers have commented on draft chapters or provided other valuable assistance. My heartfelt thanks to Nathan Abrams, Pertti Ahonen, Valerie Aubourg, Paul Buhle, Leonard Bushkoff, Richard Carwardine, Robert Cook, Nina Fishman, Scott Lucas, David Martin, Ray Monk, Ted Morgan, James Oliver, Maurice Pearton, Patrick Renshaw, Dominic Sandbrook, Giles Scott-Smith, Victor Silverman, Melvyn Stokes, Jack Stuart, Robert Taylor, Andrew Thorpe, Richard Thurlow, Nick Tiratsoo and Michael Warner.

There are certain individuals to whom I owe a particularly heavy debt of gratitude: Richard Aldrich, for his instruction in intelligence history and faith in the project; Tony Carew, for guiding me through the labyrinth of Cold War labour diplomacy; Richard Fletcher, for laying the groundwork in the 1970s and granting me access to the 'Fletcher archive' preserved by Paul Lashmar; Brandon High, for his superb bibliographical knowledge and constantly insightful comments; and Frances Stonor Saunders, for her exemplary generosity to other researchers in her field – and for stirring up so much interest in the Cultural Cold War!

A number of institutions have defrayed the financial costs of transatlantic research: the Arts and Humanities Research Board; the Council for the International Exchange of Scholars; the Eisenhower Foundation; the Fulbright Commission; the Gilder Lehrman Institute of American History; the Harry Ransom Humanities Research Center, the University of Texas at Austin (which awarded me a Fleur Cowles Fellowship);

Middlesex University (where John Annette's early interest in the project deserves special mention); and my current institution, the University of Sheffield, whose Department of History, under the leadership of, successively, Ian Kershaw and Edmund King, has provided a most supportive research environment. I am also indebted to my referees, in particular the late Peter Parish, a great British Americanist who is sorely missed by his friends and colleagues.

Many libraries and record centres have assisted me in my archival research and, in some cases, granted permission to quote from documents in their possession. These include the Walter P. Reuther Library, Wayne State University; the Dwight D. Eisenhower Library; the Firestone Library, Princeton University; the George Meany Memorial Archives; the Ford Foundation; the Harry S. Truman Library; the Harry Ransom Humanities Research Center, University of Texas at Austin; the Hoover Institution, Stanford University; the John F. Kennedy Library; the Joseph Regenstein Library, University of Chicago; the Lauinger Library, Georgetown University; the Mugar Memorial Library, Boston University; the Seeley G. Mudd Library, Princeton University; the Sterling Memorial Library, Yale University; the Tamiment Institute Library, New York University; the British Library of Political and Economic Science, London; Durham County Record Office; Edinburgh University Library; the Modern Records Centre, Warwick University; the National Museum of Labour History, Manchester; the Polish Library, London; and University College London. I am particularly grateful to the following archivists: Barbara Constable, Phil Dunn, Lee Sayrs, Mike Smith, Gail Malmgreen, Idelle Nissila, Nicholas Scheetz and Christine Woodland. Daniel Bell and Ernest Hook kindly granted individual permissions to quote from manuscript collections (the American Committee for Cultural Freedom and Sidney Hook Papers, respectively).

At Frank Cass, Lisa Hyde has overseen each stage of the editorial process with great professionalism and good humour.

My family has, as ever, been a constant source of emotional support and pleasant distraction, particularly my wonderful nephews and nieces. My wife, Heidi Wilford, graciously put up with the project over an eight-year period. My father-in-law, Mervyn Hodgkin, provided much of the office furniture and computing equipment on which the manuscript was eventually composed. My own father, Frederick Albert Wilford (1917–2000), did not live to see the book completed, but his personal and professional example remains a powerful inspiration in my life.

List of Abbreviations

ACCF	American Committee for Cultural Freedom
ACUE	American Committee on United Europe
ADA	Americans for Democratic Action
AEU	Amalgamated Engineering Union
AFL	American Federation of Labor
AIF	Americans for Intellectual Freedom
BBC	British Broadcasting Corporation
CCF	Congress for Cultural Freedom
CCNY	City College of New York
CDS	Campaign for Democratic Socialism
CIA	Central Intelligence Agency
CIO	Congress of Industrial Organizations
CPUSA	American Communist Party
DCI	Director of Central Intelligence
EAG	Europe–America Groups
ECA	Economic Cooperation Agency
ECLC	Emergency Civil Liberties Committee
EEC	European Economic Community
EIU	Economist Intelligence Unit
ELEC	European League for Economic Cooperation
EM	European Movement
EPU	European Parliamentary Union
ERP	European Recovery Program
ESU	English-Speaking Union
EYC	European Youth Campaign
FBI	Federal Bureau of Investigation
FO	Foreign Office
FRF	Friends of Russian Freedom

FTUC	Free Trade Union Committee
HICOG	US High Commission for Germany
ICFTU	International Confederation of Free Trade Unions
IFTU	International Federation of Trade Unions
ILGWU	International Ladies Garment Workers Union
ILO	International Labour Organisation
IOD	International Organizations Division
IRC	International Rescue Committee
IRD	Information Research Department
IRIS	Industrial Research and Information Services
ISS	Institute of Strategic Studies
IUS	International Union of Students
JICMEU	Joint International Committee of the Movement for European Unity
JLC	Jewish Labor Committee
LIO	Labor Information Officer
LLY	Labour League of Youth
MI5	Security Service
MI6	Secret Intelligence Service
NCCL	National Council for Civil Liberties
NCFE	National Committee for a Free Europe (also Free Europe Committee)
NCL	Non-Communist Left
NEC	National Executive Committee
NL	*New Leader*
NSC	National Security Council
NUS	National Union of Students
NYU	New York University
OPC	Office of Policy Coordination
OSR	Office of the Special Representative
OSS	Office of Strategic Services
PCA	Progressive Citizens of America
PPS	Policy Planning Staff
PR	*Partisan Review*
PRO	Public Record Office
PSB	Psychological Strategy Board
PWE	Political Warfare Executive
SDF	Social Democratic Federation
SIS	Secret Intelligence Service
SOE	Special Operations Executive

SPA	Socialist Party of America
SPG	Special Procedures Group
THF	Trust-House Forte
TUC	Trades Union Congress
UAW	United Automobile Workers
UDA	Union for Democratic Action
UEM	United Europe Movement
ULR	*Universities and Left Review*
USIA	United States Information Agency
USIE	US International Information and Educational Exchange Program
WFTU	World Federation of Trade Unions
YPSL	Young Peoples Socialist League

Introduction

At the turbulent 1960 Labour Party conference, during the same speech in which he famously announced he would 'fight, fight and fight again' to defeat advocates of unilateral nuclear disarmament within the British labour movement, Party leader Hugh Gaitskell lashed out angrily at what he called 'fellow travellers' on Labour's left wing, thereby equating opposition to his multilateralist position with support for the Soviet Union.[1] Standing near the back of the conference hall, one of the putative fellow travellers, left-wing intellectual Michael Foot, turned to his neighbour and muttered darkly, 'But who are *they* travelling with'?[2]

In posing this question, Foot was articulating a belief widely held on the British left in 1960: that right-wing leaders of the Labour Party and trade unions, in their enthusiasm for bringing about the defeat of the Soviet Union in the Cold War, had forged too intimate an alliance with non- and anti-socialist forces, in particular the United States government. Indeed, there were even rumours that pro-American anti-communists within the British labour movement were covertly receiving financial support from the US secret service, the Central Intelligence Agency (CIA). Gaitskell and his allies might throw around allegations of 'Moscow Gold', but what of their own record on '*Washington* Gold'?

This book will show that Foot and his fellow left-wingers were right to suspect secret US interest in the Cold War British labour movement. During the late 1940s and 1950s, American officials, responding to a concerted anti-US propaganda offensive by the Soviet Union, launched a massive, clandestine effort to win the Cold War allegiance of the European left, a category they defined broadly to include socialist politicians, trade unionists and leftist intellectuals. Although this campaign of 'psychological warfare' was targeted mainly at continental Europe, it also embraced Britain, where the position of right-wing Labour politicians such as

Gaitskell and his supporters was secretly strengthened at the expense of leftists like Foot and their leader, Aneurin Bevan. There were, moreover, covert attempts to combat communist penetration of British trade unions, stimulate support within the Labour Party for European unification (a key strategic aim for the US in the early years of the Cold War) and even influence the political opinions of Bloomsbury *literati*. In short, CIA operations affected every section of the Cold War British left.[3]

As well as using previously inaccessible primary sources to document these operations in detail, the book will also attempt the necessarily more speculative task of assessing their impact on the British left. In the small amount of literature on the subject published to date, the tendency has been to assume that the CIA's Cold War campaign in Britain was immensely successful. Right-wing labour leaders such as Gaitskell, whether as a consequence of having been hoodwinked or through a deliberate decision on their part to betray their followers, became, in effect, stooges of American capitalism; thanks to the right's growing dominance over the labour movement during the early years of the Cold War, the result was that the British left was reduced to a state of tame ideological obedience to the US. Such was the argument advanced in a pioneering piece of investigative journalism by Richard Fletcher published in the mid-1970s, 'How CIA money took the teeth out of British socialism'.[4] A similar verdict is implied in the title of a much more recent study of the CIA's efforts to influence European intellectual life in the so-called 'Cultural Cold War', Frances Stonor Saunders's enterprisingly researched *Who Paid the Piper?*, with its tacit suggestion that the Agency called the tune of those intellectuals who received its secret patronage.[5]

The evidence presented here tends to contradict this interpretation. The British response to CIA operations, it suggests, was in fact much more complex than talk of teeth-pulling or tune-calling would lead one to expect. Far from feeling themselves to be the victims of aggressive ideological colonisation, many on the British left positively welcomed the US intervention because they naturally shared its values and goals. In other words, this was, in part at least, an example of a phenomenon historians of continental European countries in the same period have termed 'self-colonization' or 'empire by invitation'.[6] By the same token, there is also evidence of members of the British left, including even strongly anti-communist Atlanticists, *resisting* aspects of the US campaign with which they did not happen to agree. The Labour leadership's position on Europe is perhaps the most obvious instance of this. A third response

2

which needs to be taken into account is *appropriation*, that is local groups or individuals adapting the apparatus and rhetoric of the American intervention to serve domestic purposes which had little or nothing to do with the Cold War. To suppose, then, that those British leftists who became involved in the CIA's operations were dupes or slaves of American foreign policy is to repeat the mistake made by Gaitskell and his followers when they identified all critics of their defence policies as puppets of the Kremlin.

The other major problem with the existing interpretation of the CIA's campaign on the British left – such as it is – is that it oversimplifies the nature of the campaign itself. The Agency did not, as a rule, intervene directly in Britain; the operations described here were carried out at 'arm's-length', that is by private citizens on the American 'non-communist left' (or 'NCL', to use an abbreviation favoured in Washington at the time) in a tactic directly imitated from the 'front' organisations created by the Soviets. The assumption has been that the NCL was a faithful and unquestioning instrument of the CIA's will, but newly available documents indicate a more problematic relationship. Anti-Stalinist intellectuals and unionists had been waging their own war on communism long before intelligence professionals appeared on the scene and, even after they became 'agents' in the US Cold War effort, were determined to have a say in the planning and conduct of anti-communist operations. Moreover, relations between the American NCL and British left in this period were not simply a function of official strategy; rather, they need to be viewed in the context of a long-standing and ongoing Anglo–American leftist dialogue. Indeed, it will be argued here that western commitment to the Cold War was itself prompted to a significant degree by members of the left, on both sides of the Atlantic.

This is not to deny that there are serious ethical questions raised by the CIA's secret sponsorship of the American NCL or that the US campaign did have an important effect on the postwar development of British socialism.[7] Indeed, one aim of the book is to show how the Cold War foreclosed various 'postwar possibilities' for the left, in America as well as in Britain, while another is to show how the US intervention artificially strengthened certain tendencies within the British left, not only political but cultural as well, at the expense of others. However, in assessing the impact of the CIA's covert operations on Britain, it is vitally important to acknowledge the *agency* of both the British and American lefts. Not to do so is to risk lapsing into discredited notions of American 'cultural imperialism' or even cruder forms of conspiracy theory.

The following chapters, then, trace the origins of the US's Cold War campaign on the non-communist left, describe those CIA operations which impacted particularly on Britain and examine the British response to the American intervention. Chapter 1 concerns the years immediately after the Second World War – a historical moment described by left-wing American intellectual, Dwight Macdonald, as 'the grey dawn of peace' – when socialist politicians, anti-communist literary intellectuals and trade unionists on both sides of the Atlantic engaged in various attempts to create a new, leftist international order, a project whose initial promise was quickly destroyed by the escalation of the Cold War in the late 1940s.[8] The next two chapters document the first official attempts to mobilise the non-communist left in the Cold War. Chapter 2 examines links between the Information Research Department (IRD), a secret Foreign Office propaganda unit created in 1948, and the British left, in particular the Labour Party, the Trades Union Congress and such literary intellectuals as George Orwell. Although originally charged with publicising the socialist foreign policy of the 'Third Force', IRD rapidly developed instead into an anti-communist political warfare agency. With Chapter 3, the focus shifts across the Atlantic, to the relationship which formed during the late 1940s between elements of the American NCL – anti-communist activists in the labour movement and literary ex-communists – and the CIA (or, to be more precise, the CIA's semi-autonomous covert operations arm, the Office of Policy Coordination). Far from being a 'puppet-on-a-string' affair, the chapter shows this was a partnership initiated and dictated to a significant degree by the NCL. The following chapter expands on this theme in a case study of the curiously neglected NCL American publication, *The New Leader*, arguing that the *NL* played an important role in the creation during the 1940s of 'Cold War consciousness', both in the US and abroad.

The remaining chapters all deal with specific American operations on the Cold War British left during the 1950s. Chapter 5 analyses the impact on Britain of US 'labor diplomacy', that is American attempts to eliminate communist influence in the British labour movement and spread the so-called 'productivity gospel' amongst industrial workers. Chapter 6 documents the activities in Cold War Britain of the Congress for Cultural Freedom (CCF), an international organisation of NCL intellectuals secretly subsidised by the CIA. Chapter 7 examines covert American measures to increase Labour Party support for European unification as well as investigating Labour participation in the semi-secret, Atlanticist forum known as the Bilderberg Group. Finally, Chapter 8 presents a further case study of a leading NCL publication of the period, the CCF's English-language, London-based organ, *Encounter*. In each chapter, emphasis will be placed on the complex and even contradictory nature of the US campaign, the variety of British responses to it and the uneven impact on Britain of the CIA's covert operations.

Before attempting any of this, however, it is necessary to give a brief, comparative account of the historical development of the non-communist left in Britain and America prior to the Cold War. There were, it will become clear, important Anglo–American differences: the absence in the US of a powerful socialist party to compare with Labour, the relative strength of American Trotskyism as an ideological and organisational focus for anti-Stalinist literary intellectuals and US unions' generally 'non-political' character. However, there were marked similarities as well: convergences between British socialism and American 'social liberalism', the sense of a common political fate shared by ex-communist literary intellectuals, the fierce anti-communism of many labour leaders and idealistic internationalism of much rank-and-file. These meant that there was a surprising amount of left-wing, transatlantic contact and collaboration in the years leading up to the end of the Second World War. Hence, to understand the Anglo–American encounters of the early Cold War era properly, we must first turn our attention to this earlier period.

SOCIALISTS

Although New Labour has represented itself as a radical departure from a continuously socialist past, in fact the British Labour Party's relationship with socialism has always been contingent and problematic. Formed in 1900 by a group of unionists and socialists seeking to ensure the representation of the labour 'interest' in Parliament, the Party was from the outset a 'contentious alliance' of pragmatists seeking piecemeal solutions for the problems of industrial workers – an approach often referred to by historians as 'labourism' – and visionaries hoping to transform capitalist society.[9] This is to say nothing of the intellectual incoherence of the British socialist movement itself, which comprised a bewildering variety of often contradictory ideas and impulses, including Christian nonconformity, Marxist doctrine and Fabian managerialism. During the economic crisis of the 1930s many Labour socialists moved leftwards, urging the Party to become a force for radical change in British society. Among them was the Welsh former miner, Aneurin 'Nye' Bevan, who during the war years, assisted by Jennie Lee and Michael Foot, would help transform the weekly newspaper *Tribune* into an influential mouthpiece of the 'Labour left'.[10] Other socialist intellectuals in the Labour Party, however, young intellectuals such as Hugh Gaitskell, Evan Durbin and Douglas Jay, were impatient with what they perceived as left-wing dogma and, under the guidance of their patron Hugh Dalton, sought to synthesise traditional Fabian ethical concerns with promising new practical ideas, in particular the economic proposals of Liberal John Maynard Keynes. Dalton's experimental, modernising influence would live on in the postwar period, not only through early protégés such as Gaitskell and Jay (Durbin, widely considered the most brilliant mind of his generation, died tragically young, in 1948), but also a second generation of social democratic 'revisionists' who began rising through the Party's ranks during the 1950s, among them Anthony Crosland, William Rodgers and Roy Jenkins.[11] That said, the revisionist project would continue to meet determined, vocal opposition from such left-wingers as Bevan, Lee and Foot, as well as the less articulate but more obdurate resistance of labourism.

Although it suffered from even worse doctrinal disputes than Labour, the Socialist Party of America (SPA) never enjoyed the compensation of national power. Apart from two periods when it seemed poised to break out of its local bases of support, under the leadership of Eugene Debs in the early 1900s and, during the 1930s, under Norman Thomas, the unresponsiveness to its message of American organised labour (of which more below) condemned it to historical marginality. This is not to say that American socialism was entirely ineffectual. For one thing, it functioned as one of several foci on the American left for anti-communist thought and activity: those exiled Russian social democrats or 'Mensheviks' who sought refuge from Bolshevism in the US tended to gravitate towards it, while many of the most effective anti-Stalinist activists in the 1930s American labour movement came from the ranks of the SPA.[12] More positively, during the late 1930s, the right wing of the socialist movement blurred with the left wing of Franklin D. Roosevelt's New Deal to produce what has been dubbed 'social liberalism' – a distinctive blend of liberal activism and social democracy which was to prove a powerful tendency in mid-twentieth century American political life.[13] The most obvious organisational expression of this socialist–liberal alliance was the Union for Democratic Action (UDA), a political action committee formed in 1941 to agitate for a continuation of New Deal reform at home and democratic intervention abroad, against both communist and fascist depredations. Amongst those involved were such left-liberals as Freda Kirchwey of *The Nation* (the organisation's first chair), the former socialist James Loeb (its director and organiser) and the distinguished Protestant theologian Reinhold Niebuhr (who later succeeded Kirchwey). When the UDA was reconstituted as Americans for Democratic Action (ADA) in 1947, it attracted an even more impressive array of political talent, making it the foremost anti-communist, liberal pressure group in postwar America.[14]

Despite their contrasting fortunes, there was considerable contact between British and American socialists in the years before the Cold War, especially during the 1930s. Labour intellectuals interested in revising Party doctrine, such as the social democrat Evan Durbin, looked to New Deal 'Brain Trusters' like A. A. Berle for theoretical and practical inspiration.[15] Even the Labour left, which had long been fascinated by America, with its confusing mix of social egalitarianism and untrammelled capitalism, was impressed by aspects of the Roosevelt experiment. Jennie Lee visited the US frequently during this period, while Harold Laski, the most influential interpreter of American affairs to the British left, befriended the President personally.[16] That said, British socialists never fully reconciled themselves with the US, Laski, for example, remaining a doctrinaire Marxist despite his affection for things American. For their part, American socialists and left-liberals were equally disparaging about aspects of Britain, particularly its history of colonialism. However, there was also great respect and admiration on the American left for the British Labour Party, which many regarded as a model of successful socialist organisation. Indeed, the UDA was partly based organisationally on the example of the Labour think-tank, the New Fabian Research Bureau. Consequently, the unexpected Labour victory in the 1945 General Election aroused considerable interest in left-liberal circles in the US.[17]

EX-COMMUNISTS

A second important element of the non-communist left, on both sides of the Atlantic, was that made up of literary intellectuals who had been attracted to communism during the crisis of the Great Depression, but then were violently repelled by it as a result of one or other of the 'shocks' of the late 1930s: the Moscow 'show trials', Stalinist persecution of Trotskyists and anarchists fighting in Spain and the Nazi–Soviet non-aggression pact of 1939. The archetype of the anti-Stalinist man of letters was George Orwell, who formed the centre of a reasonably distinct community of non-communist left *literati* in Britain, made up mainly of such émigrés as the publisher Fredric Warburg, journalist T. R. Fyvel and novelist Arthur Koestler.[18] Together these intellectuals perceived themselves as an embattled ideological minority, bravely struggling against a massive *trahison des clercs*, symbolised most powerfully by the Popular Front alliance between communists and fellow-travelling leftists.

However, it would be a mistake to exaggerate the group identity and political purpose of the British literary non-communist left. The comparative weakness of the Trotskyist movement in Britain meant that anti-Stalinist Marxists like Orwell lacked an alternative organisational base when they began their retreat from communism. Hence Orwell's increasing attraction to *Tribune*-style socialism during the early 1940s, and the influence of other ideologies on the British non-communist left in this period, such as anarchism and, most importantly, aestheticism. The latter, arguably only partially submerged during the 'Red Decade', came roaring back in the late 1930s and war years, subduing the commitment of 'MacSpaunDay' (the group of Oxford-educated poets Louis MacNiece, Stephen Spender, W. H. Auden and Cecil Day Lewis) to radical politics. Consequently, while the main organ of Britain's literary intellectuals, Cyril Connolly's *Horizon*, (which, incidentally, Stephen Spender helped to edit), published several important political statements by Orwell, Koestler and other anti-Stalinist writers in this period, its main preoccupation was with the preservation of high cultural standards in wartime Britain, a fact which earned it charges of irresponsible bohemianism and *belle-lettrism*.[19]

Anti-Stalinist Marxists were rather better organised in America. To the right of the American Communist Party (CPUSA) were the 'Lovestoneites', named after Jay Lovestone, a former Party leader deposed by Stalin in 1929 for ideological 'deviationism'. Aided by his lieutenants Benjamin Gitlow and Bertram D. Wolfe, Lovestone led the Communist Party (Opposition) throughout the 1930s, taking an increasingly anti-Stalinist line until eventually abandoning Marxism–Leninism altogether in 1939.[20] To the CPUSA's left was a predominantly Trotskyist group of factions, including the Cannonites, Shachtmanites and Musteites, whose combined membership never amounted to more than a few thousand, yet which counted among their supporters a number of soon-to-be influential anti-Stalinist thinkers.[21]

The single most important institution for literary intellectuals on the American NCL, however, was not a political party but a magazine. Under the editorship of William Phillips and Philip Rahv, *Partisan Review*, originally the cultural organ of the New York Communist Party, became a rallying point for American intellectuals who were revolted by Stalinism but still thought of themselves as Marxists, such as writers Dwight Macdonald and Mary McCarthy.[22] Although *PR* devoted increasing attention to culture, in particular literary Modernism, it did not go as far down the path of aestheticism as its British counterpart, *Horizon*.[23] Anti-Stalinism remained the editors' ruling passion, as was shown by their enthusiastic participation in the Committee for Cultural Freedom, an organisation created in 1939 by former Trotskyist philosopher, Sidney Hook, to protest 'totalitarian' – meaning communist as well as fascist – acts of 'cultural dictatorship'.[24] Indeed, so great was their abhorrence of Stalinism that it gradually overwhelmed other more positive leftist impulses: the Trotskyism they espoused immediately after their defection from the CPUSA was gradually replaced by a rather vague, Marxist 'hyper-radicalism'. Eventually this process of 'de-radicalisation' led to a major editorial dispute in 1942, specifically over the issue of the magazine's position on the Second World War, with Dwight Macdonald eventually quitting the magazine to launch a publication of his own devoted to the exploration of new forms of political radicalism, *politics*.[25] Despite this and other internal disagreements, the 'New York intellectuals', as they were later designated, remained for the most part a remarkably cohesive group, united by an intense hatred of Stalinism.

A number of factors predisposed literary anti-Stalinists to international collaboration: their self-perception as beleaguered minorities, allegiance to universalist ideologies such as Marxism and Modernism, even the simple fact that so many of them were immigrants or émigrés. Internationalism was a particularly strong characteristic of *Partisan Review*, which functioned as an important point of transatlantic intellectual contact from the first. During the 1940s, George Orwell and Arthur Koestler contributed regular 'London Letters', as well as maintaining a private correspondence with the editors.[26] There was also a 'special relationship' between *PR* and *Horizon*, with the latter even helping to publish a short-lived special London edition of the American magazine.[27] Dwight Macdonald's *politics* was another channel of Anglo–American communication, especially with such British anarchists as George Woodcock, although again Orwell featured prominently.[28]

9

Their ideological sympathy and solidarity notwithstanding, there were also significant differences between the American and British literary non-communist lefts. The New York intellectuals were mainly from immigrant, proletarian backgrounds; if they had received any university education at all, it was probably from the low-prestige City College of New York (CCNY). Most of the British, in contrast, were from at least middle-class families, educated at public school and Oxbridge; those who were not were quickly absorbed into the dominant, aristocratic intellectual culture, with its carefully cultivated air of languid elegance. Whereas for most of the Americans their engagement with communism had been the defining intellectual experience of their lives, for the British (excepting émigrés like Koestler, who had worked as an officer of the Comintern), it had tended rather to be a brief flirtation at university. Consequently, while the anti-communism of the British NCL was undoubtedly intense, it lacked some of the fervour of its American counterpart. This difference would haunt Anglo–American literary collaborations during the Cultural Cold War of the 1950s.

LABOUR

There were several major divergences between the development of national trade union centres in Britain and the US. Whereas the Trades Union Congress (TUC) was strongly associated with socialism from the late nineteenth century, the American Federation of Labor (AFL), under the leadership of the English immigrant cigar-maker, Samuel Gompers, practised a form of 'trade unionism, pure and simple', whose sole aim was procuring practical benefits – principally, higher wages – for skilled workers. Following on from this denial of a broader, social purpose was a marked reluctance on the part of the AFL to identify itself with any political party – Gompers believed that political entanglements would lead inevitably to the domination of labour by more powerful economic interests – which again contrasted sharply with the TUC's involvement with Labour. Finally, although British labour leaders were on the whole strongly anti-communist – Ernest Bevin, first General Secretary of the powerful Transport and General Workers Union (and later Labour Foreign Secretary), detested communism with an almost religious zeal – they generally avoided direct confrontation with communists in their ranks, preferring instead a positive policy of working to improve the poor working and living conditions on which communism thrived. Britain's wartime

10

alliance with the Soviet Union, which swelled the numbers of communists in union posts and strengthened internationalist impulses amongst the rank-and-file, dampened the TUC leadership's anti-communism still further.[29] The AFL, in contrast, was fanatically anti-communist in deed as well as word. Hence, during the Second World War, while the TUC took the initiative in launching a new labour international, the World Federation of Trade Unions (WFTU), the AFL refused membership of a body in which Soviet trade unions played a prominent role. Instead, the Federation established its own independent foreign policy unit, the Free Trade Union Committee (FTUC), one of whose main purposes was to counter Soviet designs on postwar Europe. The running of the FTUC was entrusted to the ex-communist Jay Lovestone, who had by this point earned a reputation within the AFL leadership as a supremely effective anti-communist activist and expert on world affairs.[30]

Despite these differences, there were strong bonds between the AFL and TUC which dated back to the late 1800s and were reinforced in the early twentieth century by the exchange of fraternal delegates at annual conferences, joint participation in the International Labour Organisation (ILO) and such symbolic gestures of international solidarity as the presentation by the Congress to the Federation in 1918 of a bronze panel depicting 'The Triumph of Labour' to adorn its new Washington offices.[31] If anything, the relationship grew closer in the 1930s and early 1940s as the AFL, partly under the influence of the determinedly internationalist David Dubinsky, head of the New York garment workers' union, (ILGWU), and his foreign affairs adviser Lovestone, abandoned its traditional isolationism and began pressing for more vigorous American intervention in European affairs, particularly to assist the victims of totalitarianism. Underpinning the alliance were links between the ILGWU's Educational Department, which was headed by a former Labour Party parliamentary candidate who had emigrated to America, Mark Starr, and the TUC's Publicity Department, run by Herbert Tracey.[32] Another organisation associated with Dubinsky's ILGWU, the Jewish Labor Committee (JLC), constituted a second bridge between the American and British labour movements, hosting visits to the US by TUC General Secretary Walter Citrine and, after Britain's declaration of war against Nazi Germany, helping create the American Labor Committee to Aid British Labor. The JLC had originally been created in the wake of a stirring speech by Citrine to the 1934 AFL convention about the plight of European victims of fascism.[33]

11

Moreover, after 1935 the AFL was no longer America's sole national labour centre. The Committee of Industrial Organizations (CIO), formed in the wake of the breakthrough National Labor Relations Act of that year, represented an ambitious attempt to organise the factory workers in mass industries previously regarded as untouchable by the AFL. In contrast with the latter's ethos of wage consciousness, the Committee (after 1938, the Congress) had a strong tinge of democratic socialism. Indeed, several of its leading figures, such as the dynamic Detroit autoworker leader, Walter Reuther, had earlier belonged to the Socialist Party. In addition, the CIO made no attempt to disguise its interest in politics, occasionally calling for the formation of a new political organisation to represent labour, but mainly campaigning on behalf of Roosevelt's Democratic Party, in the process becoming an important element of the New Deal electoral coalition. Later, such CIO leaders as Reuther would form an even more vital component of the alliance between New Deal left-wingers and socialist right-wingers which found organisational expression in, first, the UDA, then the ADA. Finally, while Reuther and the majority of his colleagues were firmly anti-communist, the CIO displayed a more pragmatic attitude towards communism than the AFL. When the WFTU was established at the end of the Second World War, the Congress became a member, along with the TUC and Soviet unions, leaving the Federation on the sidelines.[34] Combined with its much-vaunted history of industrial militancy and its social democratic complexion, this evidence of the CIO's internationalism greatly appealed to rank-and-file British unionists, as well as members of the Labour left: during the mid-1930s Walter Reuther struck up a close friendship with Jennie Lee and, through her, her soon-to-be-husband, Nye Bevan. In short, the TUC had more ideological sympathy with the new American labour centre than it did with the AFL.

Historical scholarship has tended to represent both the British and American lefts as peculiar, insular and exceptional. Certainly, both did possess their own distinctive features due to the different historical environments which shaped them and which they sought to shape. It would be foolish to deny the relative weakness of the American socialist movement, coherence of its literary non-communist left and conservatism of its union movement. However, equally it would not do to overstate the contrasts between the British and American lefts, or ignore the interaction which took place between them. Shared values, concerns – and an enduring mutual fascination – created a distinct transatlantic community

12

of left-wing discourse and bred a desire to create an international leftist order which would transcend national boundaries. This ambition did not die out with the Second World War; rather it intensified, as Chapter 1 will show.

NOTES

1. Quoted in Brian Brivati, *Hugh Gaitskell* (London: Richard Cohen Books, 1996), p. 374.
2. Quoted in Richard Fletcher, 'How CIA money took the teeth out of British socialism', in Philip Agee and Louis Wolf (eds), *Dirty Work: The CIA in Western Europe* (London: Zed Press, 1978), p. 200.
3. As Richard Aldrich has shown, the 'hidden hand' of the CIA also reached into areas of British life other than the political left, such as student organisations and news agencies. Such ventures, however, lie outside the scope of this study. See Richard J. Aldrich, *The Hidden Hand: Britain, America and Cold War Secret Intelligence* (London: John Murray, 2001).
4. See Fletcher, 'How CIA Money', pp. 188–200.
5. Frances Stonor Saunders, *Who Paid the Piper? The CIA and the Cultural Cold War* (London: Granta, 1999).
6. Reinhold Wagnleitner, *Coca-Colonization and the Cold War: The Cultural Mission of the United States in Austria after the Second World War* (Chapel Hill: University of North Carolina Press, 1994), p. 2; Geir Lundestad, 'Empire by invitation: The United States and western Europe, 1945–52', *Journal of Peace Research* 23 (1986), 263–77.
7. For a judicious discussion of the harmful consequences for the American left of its Cold War alliance with the CIA, see Eric Thomas Chester, *Covert Network: Progressives, the International Rescue Committee and the CIA* (New York: M. E. Sharpe, 1995), chap. 15.
8. Quoted in Neil Jumonville, *Critical Crossings: The New York Intellectuals in Postwar America* (Berkeley: University of California Press, 1991), p. xi.
9. Lewis Minkin, *The Contentious Alliance: Trade Unions and the Labour Party* (Edinburgh University Press, 1991). John Saville has defined labourism as 'a theory and practice which [accepts] the possibility of social change within the existing framework of society ... [and emphasises] the unity of Capital and Labour'. Quoted in Peter Weiler, *Ernest Bevin* (Manchester University Press, 1993), p. viii.
10. On the origins and early history of *Tribune*, see Ben Pimlott, *Labour and the Left in the 1930s* (Cambridge University Press, 1977), pp. 107–8.
11. See Radhika Desai, *Intellectuals and Socialism: 'Social Democrats' and the British Labour Party* (London: Lawrence and Wishart, 1994), pp. 57–60. Desai generally gives a very useful account of the relationship between social

democratic intellectuals and the Labour Party. See also Elizabeth Durbin, *New Jerusalems: The Labour Party and the Economics of Democratic Socialism* (London: Routledge and Kegan Paul, 1985) and Edmund Dell, *A Strange Eventful History: Democratic Socialism in Britain* (London: HarperCollins, 2000).

12. See chap. 4.
13. Sean Wilentz, 'Socialism', in Richard Wightman Fox and James T. Kloppenberg (eds.), *A Companion to American Thought* (Cambridge, MA: Blackwell, 1995), p. 639.
14. For a brief history of the UDA and more detailed accounts of the origins of the ADA, see Steven M. Gillon, *Politics and Vision: The ADA and American Liberalism, 1947–85* (Oxford University Press, 1987), ch. 1.
15. See Stephen Brooke, 'Atlantic Crossing? American views of capitalism and British socialist thought, 1942–62', *Twentieth Century British History* 2 (1991), 112–18.
16. See Henry Pelling, *America and the British Left: From Bright to Bevan* (London: Adam and Charles Black, 1956), ch. 8.
17. See Douglas Richard Ayer, 'American liberalism and British socialism in a Cold War world, 1945–51', Ph.D. thesis, Stanford University (1983), ch. 2.
18. See T. R. Fyvel, *George Orwell: A Personal Memoir* (London: Weidenfeld, 1982) and Fredric Warburg, *All Authors are Equal: The Publishing Life of Fredric Warburg, 1936–71* (London: Hutchinson, 1973). Warburg, Orwell and Fyvel collaborated on a series of short books on British war aims called 'Searchlight Books'. The first work to be published in this series was Orwell's *The Lion and the Unicorn* (1941). Stephen Spender also contributed (*The Life and the Poet*). See John Newsinger, 'George Orwell and Searchlight: A radical initiative on the home front', *Socialist History* 9 (1996), 55–81.
19. Bernard Bergonzi, *Wartime and Aftermath: English Literature and its Background, 1939–60* (Oxford University Press, 1993), p. 6. For a detailed description of the *Horizon* circle, see Michael Shelden, *Friends of Promise: Cyril Connolly and the World of Horizon* (London: Hamish Hamilton, 1989).
20. See Ted Morgan, *A Covert Life. Jay Lovestone: Communist, Anti-Communist and Spymaster* (New York: Random House, 1999).
21. See Alan M. Wald, *The New York Intellectuals: The Rise and Decline of the Anti-Stalinist Left from the 1930s to the 1980s* (Chapel Hill: University of North Carolina Press, 1987), chap. 6.
22. For a detailed account of *Partisan Review*'s early history, see Terry A. Cooney, *The Rise of the New York Intellectuals: Partisan Review and Its Circle* (Madison: University of Wisconsin Press, 1986).
23. See Hugh Wilford, *The New York Intellectuals: From Vanguard to Institution* (Manchester University Press, 1995), chaps. 2 and 3, for a discussion of the New York intellectuals' engagement with Modernism.
24. See Cooney, *Rise of New York Intellectuals*, pp. 141–5. Around the same

time Dwight Macdonald, concerned that Hook's group placed insufficient emphasis on positive, radical goals, formed a rival organisation called the League for Cultural Freedom and Socialism. This split prefigured the later divisions in *PR*'s editorial board and Europe–America Groups, which are described below.

25. See Gregory D. Sumner, *Dwight Macdonald and the Politics Circle: The Challenge of Cosmopolitan Democracy* (Ithaca, NY: Cornell University Press, 1996).
26. See John Newsinger, 'The American connection: George Orwell, "literary Trotskyism" and the New York intellectuals', *Labour History Review* 64 (1999), 23–43.
27. See Wilford, *New York Intellectuals*, p. 51.
28. See Newsinger, 'American connection', 33–5.
29. See Nina Fishman, 'The phoney Cold War in British trade unions', *Contemporary British History*, 15.3 (2001), 83–104.
30. See Federico Romero, *The United States and the European Trade Union Movement, 1944–51* (Chapel Hill: University of North Carolina Press, 1992), pp. 12–17.
31. File on 'American Federation of Labor, 1918–34', Trades Union Congress Papers, 973/17, Modern Records Centre, Warwick University.
32. See Pelling, *America and British Left*, p. 140.
33. Walter Citrine, *Men and Work: The Autobiography of Lord Citrine* (London: Hutchinson, 1964), p. 346.
34. On Reuther and the CIO, see Anthony Carew, *Walter Reuther* (Manchester University Press, 1993); Nelson Lichtenstein, *The Most Dangerous Man in Detroit: Walter Reuther and the Fate of American Labor* (New York: Basic Books, 1995); and Robert H. Zieger, *The CIO, 1935–55* (Chapel Hill: University of North Carolina Press, 1995).

1

Postwar Possibilities

For members of the non-communist left on both sides of the Atlantic, the end of the Second World War appeared a historic moment of opportunity. The defeat of fascism and a widespread expectation of change, both domestic and international, stimulated an unprecedented sense of political possibility. The most dramatic expression of this mood was the election in Britain of a Labour government. It was not the only one, however: the mid-1940s witnessed a proliferation of other, albeit less conspicuous, left-wing projects, including several which built on the transatlantic contact and collaboration of previous decades. For example, American social liberals established new links with the left wing of the British Labour Party in an attempt to create a 'Third Force' in international politics; ex-communist literary intellectuals collaborated on the reformulation of leftist ethical principles and the construction of organisational forms appropriate for the postwar environment; and union leaders joined in a common effort to create a new world order based on the values of labour 'internationalism'. There were, of course, big differences between the values and practices of these socialists, ex-communists and unionists. Nevertheless, all three of the principal components of the transatlantic non-communist left were united in 1945 by an unusual sense of optimism and idealism.

All of them were also to suffer a similar fate. In each case, the sense of optimism and idealism which had prevailed in the immediate postwar period gave way to feelings of disillusionment and realism as the western world divided into hostile ideological blocs after 1947. By the end of the decade the non-communist left had abandoned its attempt to occupy a third-camp position and thrown in its lot with the American cause in the Cold War. Although the polarising effect of the superpower conflict was clearly the main factor involved here, the causation of this development

17

was highly complex. It was not a simple case of the left being 'co-opted' by Cold War governing élites, or of US influence subduing impulses towards independence in the British left. The left itself – British as well as American – played an important role in the process, with its more anti-communist, 'right-wing' elements gradually squashing the positive, constructive intentions of those who retained a greater sense of leftist possibility. In other words, the left made a major contribution to the onset of Cold War in the west during the late 1940s. One sign of this is that all three of the ventures described below directly anticipated the organisational weapons with which the US government would wage its anti-Soviet campaign after the mid-century.

INTERPRETING BRITAIN TO AMERICA

The Union for Democratic Action – the amalgam of American socialists and left-wing New Deal-ers created in 1941 – had always regarded the British Labour Party as its leading foreign ally. It campaigned on Labour's behalf in the US throughout the war years, drumming up progressive support for the Party's domestic programme and contribution to the British war effort.[1] With peace and electoral victory in 1945, the UDA's enthusiasm for Labour increased further still, as did its determination to extend a helping hand across the Atlantic. According to James Loeb Jr., the organisation's ex-socialist National Executive Secretary, the election result constituted 'the most significant event of this generation from the point of view of democratic progressives'. Not only did the new British government represent 'the first great chance of democratic socialism in a major world power'; it was also 'the last chance', the squandering of which would have disastrous consequences, leaving Europe and the world to be fought over by 'two rival totalitarian systems'.[2] The UDA must therefore do all in its power to make the experiment a success. In America, where British foreign policy was prone to 'misunderstanding' and the Party lacked any 'public relations' apparatus, this meant stepping up efforts to give Labour favourable publicity.[3]

In the winter of 1946, Bruce Bliven, editor of the liberal magazine, *The New Republic*, and the British-born educational director of New York garment workers union, ILGWU, Mark Starr, carried across the Atlantic a memorandum from Loeb proposing that the UDA send to Britain an American who would act 'as the unofficial ambassador of American progressives and as a competent and sure source of

18

information'.[4] When this proposal met with a positive response from Michael Young, Secretary of the Labour Party's Research Department, Loeb immediately set about raising funds and selecting a suitable candidate for the role. His first choice was another former socialist, the CIO publicist William Dufty, who had recently spent several years in Britain in the company of Aneurin Bevan and Jennie Lee.[5] Shortly before he was due to leave, however, Dufty fell seriously ill. Into the breach stepped David C. Williams, an engineering professor with union experience who had developed an intense interest in British socialism while studying at Oxford as a Rhodes Scholar during the 1930s. Williams arrived in London in June 1946 eager to see for himself an experiment he believed to be 'unprecedented in world history'.[6]

Williams soon proved himself extremely effective at, as he later put it, 'interpreting Britain to America'.[7] His duties as the UDA's representative in Britain included sending a bi-weekly 'London Letter' to a select group of American 'opinion-formers'; preparing a monthly 'London Labor Report' for the Labor Press Associates, a Washington DC-based news agency, for dissemination to American labour publications; and organising lecture tours by Labour politicians in the US.[8] Although unimpressed by the Labour Party's own publicity efforts,[9] Williams was grateful for the assistance he received during his first months in London from Michael Young, who provided him with a desk in the headquarters of the London Labour Party until he acquired his own offices in Queen Anne's Gate. Young also helped him secure some much-needed financial support from the Elmgrant Trust (the main benefactor of which was the mother of Michael Straight, publisher of *The New Republic*, who helped channel additional funds to Williams via the New York-based Whitney Foundation).[10] Thanks to his relationship with the Labour Research Department, Williams was able to fill his London Letters to élite American liberals with first-rate intelligence about the affairs of the British left.

However, his main source of knowledge about internal Labour politics was not the Party's official machinery. From the moment of his arrival in London, Williams enjoyed a surprisingly close rapport with the group of young left-wingers associated with *Tribune*, particularly Jennie Lee, Michael Foot and the maverick intellectual Richard Crossman. In this respect he was following a trail blazed by Bill Dufty, who viewed Lee and her husband Bevan with admiration verging on veneration.[11] Williams was not quite this starry-eyed about the Labour left. For example, he regarded Crossman's politics as 'confusing', even 'unintelligible',

19

referring in a voluminous correspondence with James Loeb to 'Tricky Dick' and 'double Cross-man'.[12] For the most part, though, he found the *Tribune* group personally as well as politically sympathetic, praising Lee as 'the conscience of the Labour Party in Parliament', Foot as its 'ablest journalist' and Crossman as displaying 'intelligence and aggressiveness' in his opposition to aspects of Labour foreign policy. Indeed, his under-standing of Crossman's complex role in Labour politics was more acute and nuanced than that of most British observers.[13]

This helps explain the, on the face of it, somewhat surprising fact that Williams sided with the Labour left when, in November 1946, it attacked the Party leadership's foreign policy as excessively pro-American. This back-bench rebellion was linked to the notion of the Third Force, a vision of the postwar international order in which democratic socialist Britain would lead a coalition of western European and Commonwealth countries along a *via media* between capitalist America and communist Russia. According to such advocates of the Third Force as Richard Crossman, the Labour leadership, in particular Foreign Secretary Ernest Bevin, was siding too closely with the US, a power basically hostile to British socialism, and thereby helping to foster a sphere-of-influence politics in Europe which would surely lead to another world war.[14] In his 'London Letter' of 1 December 1946, Williams lauded the foreign policy dissidents 'as men whose belief in democracy is genuine' and declared that:

> In the main, the rebellion has as its object exactly what the last UDA London Letter suggested – the taking by Britain of an independent line in world policy, giving leadership to those forces in the world dedicated to effecting basic and progressive social changes through democratic means.[15]

Similarly, when in May of the following year the rebels published a pamphlet urging the Labour Party to '*Keep Left*' in its foreign and domestic policies, Williams again was supportive, describing Crossman's criticisms of the US as 'almost benevolent'.[16]

In adopting this line on the *Keep Left* group, Williams was not entirely representative of the UDA leadership's position. His American-based boss Loeb, for example, was strongly disapproving of aspects of the back-bench rebellion.[17] This is not to say, however, that Loeb necessarily rejected the Third Force concept or disagreed with the Labour left's criticisms of Bevin's foreign policy. Indeed, the same memorandum he had written in the winter of 1946 depicting Labour as an alternative to two rival totalitarianisms also identified 'younger and more vigorous progressives' in the Party who shared 'the distaste of Americans for certain aspects of British foreign policy' as particularly worthy of cultivation by the UDA.[18] The 'certain aspects' Loeb probably had in mind were Labour policies regarding Indonesia, Greece and Palestine; pronouncements by Bevin on this last issue in the summer of 1946 caused outrage amongst Jewish-Americans and cast a shadow over the first days of Williams's mission to London.[19] In other words, the UDA leadership's deference to the anti-colonial and pro-Zionist beliefs of many American liberals meant that it was just as inclined as its London spokesman to sympathise with the rebellious tendencies of the Labour left. In Loeb's case, this inclination was reinforced by his own personal friendship with Jennie Lee, with whom he corresponded regularly throughout this period.[20] When it came to choosing a representative of British Labour to go on a lecture tour of the US in the autumn of 1946, Lee was Loeb's automatic first choice. This was due not only to her considerable speaking skills, already demonstrated during an earlier UDA-sponsored tour in October 1942; Loeb also believed that Lee's dissenting line on British foreign policy would play well in liberal America.[21] In sum, the immediate postwar years, 1945–1947, witnessed the forging of what in retrospect seems an improbable alliance between the left wing of the British Labour Party and what would soon become America's leading liberal anti-communist organisation, around a shared commitment to progressive social ideals and a Third Force foreign policy. As Loeb explained to Lee in October 1946, 'We still believe that Britain is the one hope of sanity in this insane world and we are anxious to convince others'.[22]

INTERPRETING AMERICA TO BRITAIN

In the remaining years of the 1940s, however, the relationship between the UDA and the Labour left was to undergo a subtle transformation, as the concept of the Third Force was slowly abandoned in favour of that of an American-led, transatlantic progressive alliance. The chief cause of this development was, of course, the Cold War. The polarisation of international politics which occurred during the late 1940s gradually eroded the Third Force position, forcing British leftists to 'choose sides' between two apparently irreconcilable ways of life. Moreover, events seemed to be conspiring to render the choice an obvious one. The Soviet Union's every action seemed hostile, expansionist, even imperialistic, the US, in contrast, appeared liberal and humane. In particular, the Marshall Plan, announced in June 1947, was welcomed by even the most obdurate left-wingers as an enlightened and benign attempt to solve the economic crisis facing war-ravaged Europe, while the Soviet response – the creation of the Cominform to coordinate communist insurgencies around the globe and denounce alleged acts of 'war-mongering' by the western democracies in the name of 'peace' – appeared retrograde and sinister. In these circumstances, the Cold War axiom that the American–Soviet rivalry was not a conventional geo-political power struggle, but rather a momentous, even apocalyptic confrontation between the forces of good and evil, acquired ever greater plausibility.

The American left, too, felt its hand forced by the Cold War. One of the many domestic consequences of the breakdown in Soviet–American relations was an end to the Popular Front politics which had prevailed in left-wing circles for much of the 1930s and undergone a revival during the Second World War. As discussed earlier, there were leftist elements in the US which had always opposed the united front strategy. During the late 1940s, against the backdrop of deepening Cold War, these activists at last achieved a clear majority on the non-communist left and helped purge it of its remaining traces of communism, thereby enabling it to join in the anti-communist consensus then achieving ideological dominance in American society (and at the same time leaving the communists isolated and exposed to the attentions of conservative 'red hunters').

For present purposes, the most significant aspect of this development to note is the splitting of New Deal-style liberalism into two organisational wings. One of these was the Progressive Citizens of America (PCA), a united front-style political party which supported the presidential candidacy in 1948 of Roosevelt's former Vice-President, Henry Wallace, who, uniquely amongst mainstream American politicians, advocated a policy of friendly coexistence with the Soviet Union. Although Wallace at first enjoyed considerable prestige in liberal circles, regarded by many as Roosevelt's true heir, his pro-Soviet stance and a growing communist presence amongst his supporters turned anti-communist liberals of the sort who belonged to the UDA against him. In January 1947 (a month after the formation of the PCA) the UDA transformed itself into the larger and more militant Americans for Democratic Action and joined in a battle for the soul of Cold War American liberalism.[23]

22

The Progressive uprising had major repercussions for David Williams and the UDA London mission. James Loeb was deeply worried not only that Henry Wallace might be mistaken in Britain for the true voice of American liberalism, but also that the Labour left might be misidentified in the US as the British equivalent of the Wallace movement. His concerns on both scores increased as a result of the 1946 back-bench rebellion over Labour foreign policy which, as he explained to Williams, was commonly interpreted in America 'as identical with the Wallace position'.[24] While quick to reassure his boss that this was not in fact the case, and pointing out the problems for the London operation which might result from campaigning too openly against Wallace due to the latter's recent appointment as editor of Michael Straight's *New Republic*,[25] Williams did nonetheless set about quietly educating his friends at *Tribune* about the issues involved in the recent split of American liberalism. When, for example, Richard Crossman received a cable from Wallace congratulating him on his leadership of the foreign policy revolt, Williams intervened in the ensuing Labour left discussions about how to respond, individually advising Lee, Foot and Crossman to ignore Wallace's overtures.[26] Meanwhile, Loeb informed Lee by letter of the communist influence on the PCA and, when Michael Foot visited Washington DC, gently impressed on him the fact that Wallace was 'not the only liberal leader in the country'.[27]

After the influential left-wing journal, *The New Statesman and Nation*, invited the former Vice-President to visit Britain in early 1947, the UDA's campaign moved up a gear. Loeb liaised with the Head of British Information Services in Washington to ensure that BBC coverage of the event made it clear 'Wallace does not speak for all American liberals', and Williams sought assurances from Michael Young that the Labour Party 'did not plan to do anything official for him'.[28] Judging by the Labour reaction to Wallace's visit, these efforts paid off. Following his return from Washington, Foot wrote a series of articles for the *Daily Herald* praising the newly-formed ADA and criticising the Wallace movement ('You did a good job on Michael Foot, and he's done well for us', Williams reported to Loeb); after extensive briefings by Williams, Lee had 'the various political and trade union groups sorted out sufficiently to be able to tell Parliamentary colleagues something of the American background' and prevent 'the Wallace visit being used against the ADA'; and the young Labour MP, Patrick Gordon-Walker, who in early 1947 undertook a speaking tour of the US arranged by Williams, generally did what he could 'to dish' Wallace for the ADA (although a *Tribune* article by Gordon-Walker on the subject embarrassed Williams by referring critically to *The New Republic* as 'Wallace's organ').[29]

A desire to proselytise on behalf of the UDA's particular version of American progressivism had been present in the London project from the start, but the celebration of British socialism had taken priority. Now, however, under the impact of the creation of ADA and the Wallace campaign, the missionary impulse became dominant, and what had begun as (in the well-chosen words of historian Douglas Richard Ayer) an experiment in 'ideological diplomacy', became instead a Cold War 'crusade for allies'.[30] This is not to say that the London bureau began churning out crude pro-American and anti-Soviet propaganda. Indeed, Williams was extremely careful to avoid the appearance of partisanship in the Cold War, so sensitive was he to conditions on the ground in Britain, in particular the sensibilities of the young intellectuals on the Labour left, who even at this stage were reluctant to identify wholeheartedly with the ADA.[31] Hence he was exasperated when the anti-communist New York weekly, *The New Leader*, sent a cable to Ernest Bevin signed by a long and politically heterogeneous list of prominent US citizens attacking Wallace and assuring the Labour government of American support for its foreign policy. The effect of this 'ill-judged and ill-timed' intervention, Williams complained to Loeb, was to 'multiply my difficulties, identify ADA more and more firmly with Bevin or even further right, and distress people like Jennie Lee'.[32] Similarly, when Bill Dufty, now recovered from his illness and in charge of *ADA World*, suggested that the London mission enlist Arthur Koestler and George Orwell in the anti-Soviet struggle, Williams objected that many British socialists found their brand of dark, brooding anti-communism off-putting. It was telling, he thought, that both writers had recently 'retired to the wilds – Wales in one case, the Highlands in the other'.[33] Williams's reluctance to avoid ruffling British feathers earned him the occasional mild rebuke from Loeb, who thought him 'over-sensitive' on the issue.[34] He did not alter his approach, however, pointing out to Loeb that he was in a better geographical position to judge what was appropriate for a British audience.[35] This pattern of Americans in London 'going native' and disobeying orders from home was to be repeated later in the Cold War.

Williams, then, was no propagandist. Still, during his time in London he did place increasing importance on the task of, as he phrased it, 'interpreting American progressivism to British Labour'.[36] His most important achievement in this regard was his input into the American coverage of the Labour left's organ, *Tribune*. He and Loeb had long been disappointed by the left-wing British press's reporting of US politics. *The New Statesman and Nation*, in particular, was, in their view, guilty of persistent misrepresentation and distortion.[37] Williams's friendship with *Tribune*'s editors, therefore, seemed to offer an ideal opportunity for putting the other side of the story. At first, Loeb entertained hopes of the paper taking on prominent American columnist and liberal, James Weschler, as its Washington correspondent.[38] When this deal failed to come off, Williams (who in any case had doubts about an American-based journalist coming up with stories suitable for a British readership) volunteered his services, contributing US material with increasing frequency throughout 1947, until by the end of that year he had become, for all intents and purposes, '*Tribune*'s American editor'.[39] In January 1948, following a reshuffle of the editorial board which put Michael Foot and Evelyn Anderson in charge, Williams was involved even more closely in the running of the paper, attending weekly conferences of the editors and generally 'moulding [its] American policy'.[40] This placed him in an excellent position from which to promote the political vision to which he was now drawn, that of a transatlantic coalition of democratic progressives or 'non-communist left' seeking to influence the domestic and foreign policies of the western powers as they confronted the threat of the Soviet Union. In other words, Williams had now begun to distance himself from the Third Force position to which he had originally subscribed.

He was not alone in this. By 1949 even those British leftists who had invented the Third Force in the first place were abandoning it in favour of the notion of the transatlantic non-communist left associated with the ADA. There were various signs of this. A major statement of the non-communist left strategy issued by the ADA in December 1947, 'Towards Total Peace', which stressed such positive features of US Cold War diplomacy as the Marshall Plan, was hailed by no less a Labour rebel than Richard Crossman, writing in the *New Statesman*, as by 'far the best outline of a progressive American foreign policy that I have read'.[41] A year later, Crossman embarked on an ADA-sponsored tour of the US from which he returned convinced that the time had come to 'stop giving patronising advice to our friends in America, and assume that we have at least as much to learn from them as they from us'.[42] (For Crossman, it was not merely in the realm of foreign relations that the British left stood to gain from listening to American liberals: his 'Socialist Stocktaking' series written around this time, and again published in the *New Statesman*, reflected the influence of US economic prescriptions in its move away from a *Keep Left* emphasis on nationalisation towards an acceptance of the mixed economy.)

However, the most spectacular proof of the allure of the non-communist left strategy for British Labour – as well as the crowning success of Williams's London mission – came in July 1949, when Jennie Lee and Michael Foot organised a reception in the House of Commons for an ADA study group led by James Loeb which was attended by, amongst others, Aneurin Bevan, Hugh Dalton and Clement Attlee.[43] As the ideological diversity of this company testifies, mid-century found the left, right and centre of the British Labour Party united in admiration of ADA-style American liberalism.

It would be a gross simplification to give all the credit for this development to David Williams and his London bureau. Major historical events played a crucial role in changing Labour attitudes: Harry Truman's surprise election victory in November 1948, which raised the prospect of a new liberalisation of American politics; the Cold War shocks of the same year, including the Communist coup in Czechoslovakia and Berlin crisis, which further tarnished the image of the Soviet Union; and the launching of various anti-communist initiatives at home, such as the covert propaganda campaign of the Information Research Department (IRD, of which more below). Equally, it would be a mistake to exaggerate the Labour left's conversion to the concept of an American-led coalition of Atlantic powers. Indeed, 1950 witnessed a shift back towards the rebellious attitudes of 1946, as the outbreak of war in Korea, the German rearmament issue and the first stirrings of McCarthyism contributed to an outburst of anti-Americanism and the rise of 'Bevanism'. After 1949, the ADA and the Labour left drew apart, and the American organisation began to associate instead with the young revisionist intellectuals on the right wing of the Party, who were soon to become known, after their leader Hugh Gaitskell, as the 'Gaitskellites'. The ending of the alliance between American liberal anti-communists and the Labour left was symbolised by David Williams's departure for Washington in 1951 and the termination of the London mission.

Equally, though, it would not do to underestimate the significance of the UDA's presence in postwar London. True, Williams's original objective of conveying the influence of British socialism to American progressivism was not realised: the Third Force failed to materialise. Indeed, after the onset of the Cold War, the short-lived alliance between the UDA and the Labour left came to appear, in retrospect, a curious historical aberration. However, the impact of the London bureau's other mission, 'interpreting'

26

American liberalism to British Labour, was considerable. Williams succeeded in discrediting the Wallaceite campaign in the eyes of the *Keep Left* group; the 'dramatic' transformation of *Tribune*'s American coverage after he took it over was, according to a leading historian of the Labour left, a vital factor in the fragmentation of the Third Force movement;[44] and Richard Crossman's shift towards a proto-revisionist stance on matters of domestic political economy as well as foreign relations was due in part to his exposure to ADA-style liberalism at the hand of Williams. The American would have accomplished none of these things if he had not displayed such exemplary knowledge and understanding of the complexities of left-wing British politics. In this respect, his London mission would serve as kind of model for later official representatives of the US government in Cold War Britain.

THE LEAGUE FOR THE FREEDOM AND DIGNITY OF MAN

The transformation of the UDA's London mission was roughly mirrored by developments on another important section of the transatlantic non-communist left, that constituted by literary ex-communists. In the mid-1940s, many left-wing British and American intellectuals evinced a strong desire to reformulate the ethical bases of political action – hardly surprising, considering the still very recent horrors of the Second World War, from the Nazi death camps to Hiroshima and Nagasaki. In particular, leftists on both sides of the Atlantic, such as George Orwell in Britain and Dwight Macdonald in America, set about trying to create new political organisations which would help individuals in all countries achieve the maximum degree of human freedom possible – again an understandable objective, considering the outrages against the individual recently perpetrated by the modern state. In both cases, however, the proposed organisation had barely got off the ground before it was abandoned, the chief problem in Britain being the institutional incoherence of the non-communist left and, in America, the growing preoccupation of the New York intellectuals with fighting the Cold War. Indeed, in much the same way as David Williams's performance in London anticipated the tactics of American diplomats who would later follow him to Britain, so it is possible to trace a direct line of continuity between the ex-communist intellectuals' organisational experiments of the mid-1940s and the weapons with which the US would wage the Cultural Cold War during the 1950s, in particular the CIA-sponsored Congress for Cultural Freedom.

It was in Britain that anti-Stalinist literary intellectuals first attempted to organise themselves for the postwar period. In July 1945, George Orwell became Vice-Chairman of the Freedom Defence Committee, a civil liberties body whose aims were 'to uphold the essential liberty of individuals and organisations, and to defend those who are persecuted for exercising their rights to freedom of speech, writing and action'.[45] The organisation, whose sponsors included Harold Laski, Cyril Connolly and Bertrand Russell, was clearly of the non-communist left. Indeed, it had been set up in the first place partly in opposition to the increasingly communist-dominated National Council for Civil Liberties (NCCL), which had failed to come to the defence of a group of anarchists suffering government harassment. Moreover, with Herbert Read as its Chairman, and George Woodcock its Secretary, the Committee had a distinctly anarchist tinge to it.

Before long, though, Orwell had begun to feel that the anarchist-dominated Committee's focus was too 'narrow'. While staying with Arthur Koestler in North Wales over Christmas 1945, he and his host discussed the possibility of creating a universal human rights organisation similar to the pre-war League for the Rights of Man 'that would be proof against Communist infiltration'.[46] In January, after returning to London, Orwell sent Koestler a rough, two-page draft of a manifesto for the proposed body.[47] This document painted a grim picture of political conditions in the western democracies, especially Britain, where organisations such as the NCCL had succumbed to communist influence and 'a considerable section of the intelligentsia has set itself almost consciously... to hold totalitarian methods up to admiration'. The situation demanded not only urgent political action but also an effort to redefine the concept of democracy itself. According to Orwell, the truly democratic state guaranteed the individual equality of opportunity, freedom from economic exploitation and protection against any 'fettering or mis-appropriation of his creative faculties and achievements'. The manifesto then proposed such practical measures as the launching of a new magazine and further lobbying on behalf of political prisoners.[48]

Koestler thought Orwell's draft 'very good' and showed it to Russell, who at the time was living nearby in Wales, hoping for his approval and participation (the first of many attempts that would be made in this period to enlist the support of the grand old man of British philosophy). Russell, however, was sceptical. 'He thinks it is too late to start any sort of ethical movement', Koestler told Orwell, 'that war will be on us soon and that more directly political action is necessary to prevent it.' What Russell proposed specifically was a conference of various experts on world politics who might 'work out a programme of action'.[49] Meanwhile, in London, Orwell described the plan to Tom Hopkinson and Barbara Ward, and met with objections of a different sort. The two journalists were 'timid', he explained to Koestler, 'because they realise that an organisation of this type would in practice be anti-Russian…and they are going through an acute phase of anti-Americanism'.[50]

Despite this lukewarm response, the two men pushed ahead with the proposal, organising a conference of the kind envisaged by Russell to take place near Koestler's Welsh home around Easter, 1946. In the run-up to this gathering, they carried on discussing the projected organisation, now named the 'League for the Freedom and Dignity of Man', with various left-wing acquaintances (among them Michael Foot), revising its manifesto in light of their comments.[51] Orwell also established tentative links with some American organisations, including the UDA and the International Rescue Committee, a Lovestoneite refugee relief agency which during the 1950s would be absorbed into the CIA's 'covert network'.[52] Koestler, meanwhile, secured the involvement of his friend, the novelist and former Comintern agent, Manès Sperber, telling him that the purpose of the meeting was:

> to lay the foundations of a new, broader and more modern League for the Rights of Man, with the primary aim of coordinating those at present isolated movements, people and groups from America to Hungary, which have a common outlook.[53]

However, with the conference only a few weeks away, the project suffered a blow from which it never recovered. Humphrey Slater, who had promised the backing of his magazine *Polemic*, got cold feet about associating himself with an anti-Soviet venture and withdrew his support.[54] Immediately afterwards, Koestler's main financial sponsor, Rodney Phillips, a wealthy Australian member of the *Polemic* circle, announced that he was going to sink his money instead in, of all things, a night-club revue.[55] Not surprisingly, the conference collapsed.

Even at this stage, Koestler was still hopeful of bringing his and Orwell's plans to fruition. In June, after revising the manifesto, he petitioned the left-wing publisher, Victor Gollancz, a recent convert to anti-communism, for financial and administrative backing, telling him:

> I know a number of people in France, Italy and the States who are only waiting for the initial spark to come in whole-heartedly.... I believe that the time is ripe for such an initiative and that the league would quickly have a considerable international echo.[56]

Although initially enthusiastic, Gollancz eventually declined to take any leading role in the proposed organisation.[57] Koestler also kept up a desultory and often bad-tempered dialogue with Russell, trying to dissuade him from his belief that intellectuals were better working on an individual basis than in groups.

> The whole history of the last decades seems to me to show that organised collective action through groups, cliques, leagues, petitions, etc. is a form of propaganda which cannot be dispensed with. It is my conviction that the so-called intellectuals have to try to influence the politicians by concerted action, as a chorus and not as solo voices.[58]

This ringing statement, which harked back to Koestler's experience as an officer of Willi Muenzenberg's Comintern, and looked forward to his part in the planning of the Congress for Cultural Freedom in 1950, failed to sway Russell from his conviction that intellectuals were best left to their own devices,[59] and Koestler was at last forced to concede the defeat of his and Orwell's plans. However, he never fully abandoned his hopes of creating an organisation of anti-communist intellectuals dedicated to the promotion of individual freedom, as was demonstrated four years later at the CCF's founding conference in Berlin, by which time a more reliable patron than Rodney Phillips had been found to foot the bill. That said, the Congress for Cultural Freedom never possessed the independent, third-camp dimension of the organisation envisioned in 1946, and was concerned less with human freedom conceived in a universal sense than with the particular threat posed to intellectual freedom by Stalinism.

EUROPE–AMERICA GROUPS

Koestler and Orwell's discussions about launching a new international political movement in the wake of the Second World War found a strong echo in America. During the summer of 1945, while on holiday in the resort town of Truro on Cape Cod, Dwight Macdonald, Mary McCarthy and their friend, Italian journalist Nicola Chiaromonte, set about trying to construct a new, non-Marxist code of ethical radicalism out of elements of anarchist and communitarian doctrine.[60] As McCarthy later explained, the postwar political environment 'looked free'.

> At least there was still hope of small libertarian movements. Even Koestler was writing at that period about the possibility of founding oases.... It seemed possible still, utopian but possible, to change the world on a small scale.[61]

Following conversations between Chiaromonte and the French existentialist, Albert Camus, a plan emerged for 'the formation of groups of individuals in various countries "committed" to some statement of principles'. On learning of this proposal, Macdonald wrote to Camus recommending that they begin by issuing a 'pamphlet stating ... our ideas of how to make a new approach from ... the level of personal relations and issues'. Macdonald could barely contain his enthusiasm: these were 'the first practical suggestions for activity which seem to me to offer some possibility of taking us where we want to go'.[62]

Little followed in the way of concrete action, however. Camus appears to have lost interest in the venture, while Macdonald fell into a deep personal depression caused partly by the increasing hopelessness of the international situation for independent radicalism and partly by the unresponsiveness to his proposals of most of his fellow New York intellectuals, who regarded his non-Marxist ideas as frivolous and *jejune*.[63] There are parallels here with the disappointing reaction of left-wingers in London to Orwell and Koestler's League for the Freedom and Dignity of Man (indeed, it is tempting to read some significance into the fact that both projects were originally conceived in geographically remote, rural locations, and were abandoned after unsuccessful attempts to transplant them to urban environments). In any case, it was not until three years later that Macdonald, now recovered from his depression, revived the Camus/Chiaromonte plan. In March 1948 a meeting held at his Manhattan apartment appointed McCarthy Chair and Chiaromonte European Representative of a new organisation, Europe–America Groups (EAG).[64] The purpose of EAG, a manifesto explained, was 'to provide some center of solidarity with and support for intellectuals in Europe who find themselves outside the mass parties'. By restoring communication between such intellectuals, EAG would, it was hoped, aid the emergence of 'that new force on the democratic left whose absence is so acutely felt everywhere'.[65]

These hopes were destined to be disappointed. Apart from providing money to some scattered individuals and groups in Europe, EAG actualised little of its programme. Practically moribund for most of its short existence, it was eventually dissolved formally at a meeting in spring 1949 (about the same time that Macdonald's magazine *politics* folded due to lack of funding). EAG's failure can partly be attributed to the inability of its officers to agree as to precisely what function the organisation was supposed to perform. McCarthy appeared to favour an interpretation of its purpose along the lines of the libertarian movements idea originally proposed in 1945, but was unsure as to how this was to be realised in practice and, in any case, was preoccupied with finishing her novella *The Oasis*, a fictionalised account of her experiences in the Chair of EAG.[66] Macdonald stood somewhat to McCarthy's right, holding a fairly limited conception of the organisation's role. This stance reflected his growing confusion about political events in Europe and disenchantment with 'absolute' political positions, including pacifism.[67] Meanwhile, Chiaromonte, who was largely absent in Europe at this time, discharging his duties as EAG's European Representative, occupied a position somewhere in between Macdonald and McCarthy, urging realism on the one and idealism on the other.[68] As intellectuals on the left wing of the Labour Party were discovering simultaneously on the other side of the Atlantic, the rising Cold War tensions of the late 1940s were making third-camp politics practically impossible.

While not arguing amongst themselves, EAG's officers were in almost constant conflict with a large and powerful faction of the organisation's membership, composed of *Partisan Review* editors William Phillips and Philip Rahv, Sidney Hook (whom Phillips and Rahv regarded as their political mentor) and their supporters. By this stage the anti-Stalinism of many New York intellectuals had hardened into a state of mind that some observers referred to as 'Stalinophobia'.[69] That is, they had become so preoccupied with the threat of Soviet expansion into Europe that they had almost entirely lost interest in other political issues, including suggestions for new, positive leftist activity. Indeed, it would seem that the only reason the *PR*/Hook faction had joined EAG in the first place was that its members entertained hopes of converting it into a weapon with which to fight Stalinism. At an early meeting Rahv suggested that members picket the Soviet Embassy in Washington to protest at communist violations of cultural freedom.[70] Later, in the spring of 1948, the *PR*/Hook faction hatched a plot to take over EAG by packing a meeting due to take place at Rahv's house. A suspicious Mary McCarthy alerted members of the organisation who did not normally go to meetings and persuaded them to attend on this occasion. Years later, McCarthy still remembered 'the faces of Hook and company when they looked around Rahv's living room and realised they were not in the majority'.[71]

Although Hook and the *PR* editors failed to turn EAG to their own purposes, they did succeed in wrecking most of the organisation's more positive aims, thereby ensuring that, rather than being remembered as a significant experiment in new forms of radicalism, its principal historical legacy would be that of precursor of the Cultural Cold War committees of the 1950s. As EAG stumbled towards its demise in the winter of 1949, Macdonald, McCarthy, the *PR*/Hook faction and Nicolas Nabokov, an exiled Russian composer (and cousin of novelist Vladimir), began to talk over the possibility of creating a new non-communist left organisation along more practical lines. These talks were to bear fruit in early March 1949, when the organising meeting of the Friends of Russian Freedom (FRF) was held in New York.[72] Although Macdonald sought to reassure Chiaromonte that FRF's principles were consistent with those of EAG,[73] it soon became clear that the new organisation's primary purpose was fighting Stalinism. After electing Hook Chairman, the March meeting discussed a 'Preliminary Statement' drafted by the Lovestoneite Bertram Wolfe.

This document began by stating the principle that 'a minimum of political freedom is necessary for any decent social order', then went on to note that this minimum was denied to Soviet citizens by their government. FRF, it explained, viewed Stalin's 'régime, and the social institutions it has created, with uncompromising hostility'. However, as ordinary Russians were victims rather than accomplices of Stalinism, they were 'potential allies' of the freedom-loving peoples of the west. FRF's purpose, therefore, was 'to encourage these potential allies, by every means of political enlightenment, in their struggle for freedom – with the aim of driving a wedge between the Kremlin and the Russian people'. The main practical proposal contained in the 'Preliminary Statement' was the setting up of a 'Russian institute' in the US, to be staffed by displaced Soviet citizens, 'so that they can make their rich store of knowledge ... available to the world', and in this way 'carry on ... the fight against the Kremlin'. FRF, using data provided by this institute, would wage a publicity campaign against the Stalin régime employing every available

33

medium. Throughout it would remain 'entirely independent' of the US government.[74]

While there was nothing intrinsically wrong with these proposals – indeed, in many respects they constituted a humane and imaginative response to the perceived communist threat – FRF did nonetheless signify the abandonment of EAG's positive aims in favour of a limited and essentially negative anti-Stalinist programme. Moreover, despite its insistence on its independence of government control, the new organisation showed an almost eerie prescience in anticipating several of the key elements in the CIA's covert campaign against the Soviet Union: the mobilisation of eastern bloc émigrés, the emphasis on anti-communist 'psychological warfare' behind the Iron Curtain and the rhetorical centrality of the concept of 'freedom'. Despite his absence in Europe, Chiaromonte, the theoretical architect of EAG and himself a wartime political refugee, appreciated the dangers of such an organisation being co-opted by the US government's Cold War effort, warning Macdonald to 'oppose the very obvious State and War Department plans to use the refugees from Russia as ... agents and quislings'.[75]

In the event, FRF proved even shorter-lived than EAG, for it was rapidly overtaken by a startling new development. In March 1949, former members of the American Popular Front began gathering in New York's Waldorf-Astoria hotel to attend a conference modelled on the same lines as the peace rallies the Cominform had been orchestrating in various European cities since the announcement of the Marshall Plan two years earlier. At a meeting of the FRF, a horrified Sidney Hook proposed the formation of a committee 'to expose and counteract the work' of the Waldorf gathering.[76] In the rush of events, FRF was replaced by the far more aggressive, militant organisation, Americans for Intellectual Freedom (AIF), whose actions – as a number of historical accounts have demonstrated – directly inspired the creation of the Congress for Cultural Freedom the following year, as well as laying the foundations of the CCF's American affiliate, the American Committee for Cultural Freedom (ACCF).[77] Much as Arthur Koestler's attempts to launch a new organisation in 1946 prefigured his own later involvement in the founding of the CCF, Dwight Macdonald's EAG – originally intended as an international vehicle for a new kind of independent, ethical, anti-statist radicalism – eventually mutated into a Cold War front for the CIA.

LABOUR INTERNATIONALISM

A third form of leftism which was to experience a surge of energy and creativity during the mid-1940s, only to suffer frustration and 'recuperation' later in the decade, was labour internationalism. Workers of many nationalities had long believed that they had more in common with working people in other countries than they did with the governing classes of their own. International working-class solidarity was a powerful feature of pre-1914 socialism and the Second International. However, the post-First World War split between communist and non-communist unions undermined attempts to give institutional expression to this internationalist impulse, so that, for example, the International Federation of Trade Unions (IFTU), re-founded in 1919, included neither Soviet labour organisations nor the American Federation of Labor. This situation was to change during the 1930s, when the united front against fascism temporarily healed the rift in the ranks of international labour (the AFL joined the IFTU in 1937). Working-class solidarity was strengthened further by the wartime Grand Alliance, which raised hopes of a new, all-inclusive labour international. 1945, therefore, discovered many unionists expecting to play a leading role in the postwar settlement, which they envisioned as an unprecedented opportunity to construct a new world order based on the principles of labour internationalism.

Nowhere was this hope nursed more fondly than within the leadership of the US national confederation of industrial unions, the Congress of Industrial Organizations. Economic considerations and organisational self-interest undoubtedly played their part here – the prospect of industrial reconversion and fears of a possible conservative resurgence caused all American unionists to consider means of securing the massive advances they had made in the past decade and ensure future prosperity by facilitating international trade[78] – but there was genuine idealism at work as well. The social democratic convictions of many CIO leaders stimulated a (perhaps somewhat paternalistic) desire to see the gains recently won by American labour enjoyed by workers of other nationalities, especially in the colonial and less industrialised regions of the world. Similarly, the organisation's genesis in the experimental corporatism of the New Deal had bred a faith in the possibility of bureaucratic global institutions – the United Nations was an obvious model and inspiration – brokering peaceful relations between states. Finally, the experience of participation in the united front against fascism caused even anti-communists in the CIO to place a premium on the continuation of cooperation with the

35

Soviet Union (a policy naturally popular with the few communists who still held leadership positions in the organisation). The essential features of the CIO's almost 'mystical' vision of the postwar world were summed up by its most ardent advocate, the garment-worker leader Sidney Hillman, thus:

> Speedy and uncompromising victory over the enemy; an enduring peace; an economy which will fully utilise the rich resources of the world for the benefit of its people, yielding employment with rising standards of living and real security to the men and women of all nations; a democratic society which will assure political and civil equality and full cultural opportunity for all the people of the earth.[79]

Outside the US, these sentiments found their strongest reverberation in the pubs and working-men's clubs of Britain. In no other country had the war against fascism done more to increase working-class internationalism. Military service overseas and greater contact with foreigners at home had widened mental horizons traditionally bounded by the forces of localism and xenophobia. At the same time, few sections of the world population had suffered more in the service of the anti-fascist cause than the British working class. The heroic sacrifices of the war years bequeathed not only a powerful desire for a more peaceful world order, but also a fierce conviction that workers deserved a better deal in the postwar settlement. The Soviet Union – the one place where workers had sacrificed more to defeat fascism than Britain – seemed to many a model for the kind of society they were hoping to create, both domestically and internationally, when war ended. Among numerous signs of popular enthusiasm for the Anglo–Soviet alliance was a groundswell of working-class support for a unitary international labour organisation.[80]

In November 1943 the British Trades Union Congress responded to this pressure by issuing invitations to a World Trade Union Conference to be held in London in June of the following year. The purpose of this event, the invitations explained, was to discuss union attitudes towards the forthcoming peace, ensure the representation of labour in the postwar settlement and identify the likely problems of peacetime reconversion, 'including the reconstruction of the International Trade Union Movement'.[81] The Soviet unions accepted enthusiastically; the AFL declined, predicting that the conference would become 'part of the popular front apparatus'.[82] The CIO, in contrast, which had been excluded from the

36

IFTU due to a rule forbidding membership to more than one national representative, spotted an opportunity to increase its international standing and simultaneously take a giant stride towards realising its 'mystical vision'. Answering a call for the submission of agenda items, CIO president Philip Murray suggested that discussion of postwar reconstruction centre on such objectives as economic development, anti-fascism, welfare provision, full employment, international unity, the destruction of cartels and the creation of a new labour international.[83] Having been moved from its original date due to the Allied landings in Normandy, the World Trade Union Conference eventually convened in London in February 1945, at the same time as the 'Big Three' were meeting at Yalta. Inspired by a desire to extend the unity and cooperation of the Grand Alliance into peacetime, representatives of the Soviet unions, the TUC and the CIO (the latter led by Hillman) agreed to a set of resolutions which included a proposal to bring together 'in one World Federation, the Trade Union bodies of freedom-loving nations, irrespective of considerations of race or creed or of political, religious or philosophical distinctions'.[84]

Events moved rapidly during the remaining months of 1945. The World Conference had established a Conference Committee, which in turn created an Administrative Committee, based in Paris, to lay the foundations of a permanent body. A meeting of the latter took place in the US over three weeks in late April and early May, at which representatives of all the national centres except for the AFL hammered out a constitution for the new organisation. Reconvened in Paris in early October, the World Conference ratified this document with only a few, minor amendments, thereby transforming itself into the first constituent Congress of the World Federation of Trade Unions (WFTU). In language reminiscent of that used by Sidney Hillman and Philip Murray, the constitution conjured up a vision of a 'World Order in which all the resources of the world will be utilised for the benefit of all its peoples'. The WFTU would help build this order by fostering trade unionism in all countries of the world, especially the 'less developed' ones; work to eliminate any remaining traces of fascism; and seek 'a stable and enduring peace'.[85] Officers were elected, including a General Secretary (Louis Saillant of the French Confédération Générale du Travail) and a President (Walter Citrine of the TUC). Eleven resolutions were adopted, including calls to the Allied governments to end diplomatic relations with Franco's Spain and Peron's Argentina, a protest at the Greek and Iranian governments' refusal to allow delegates to attend the conference and a blanket denunciation of racism. The final resolution described the World Federation as 'a firm monument to the aspirations of the working classes to freedom and democracy'.[86] The hour of labour internationalism, it seemed, was at hand.

THE SCHISM

As with internationalist projects conceived on other sections of the Anglo–American non-communist left at this time, the vision proved illusory. The WFTU was handicapped from the first by tensions and conflicts between its constituent national centres, which culminated in 1949 when both the CIO and TUC quit the organisation and joined with the AFL in launching a new, anti-communist labour international, the International Confederation of Free Trade Unions (ICFTU). The main causes of the schism within the WFTU – the growing tendency of the Soviet Union to employ the organisation for propaganda purposes, the profoundly divisive effect on international labour of the Marshall Plan and the problematic status of the international trade secretariats – have been analysed in detail elsewhere, and therefore will not be recounted here.[87] Instead, attention will focus on the consequences of the breakdown for the four principal western parties involved, beginning with the most enthusiastic exponent of labour internationalism in 1945.

The CIO's walk-out from the WFTU cannot be properly understood without reference to the organisation's domestic history during the late 1940s. The Cold War-driven split of New Deal-style left-liberalism symbolised by the rift between the ADA and Henry Wallace's PCA had profound consequences for American industrial unionism. Before 1947 the anti-communist majority of the CIO leadership had coexisted relatively peacefully with communists. Indeed, Sidney Hillman's internationalist vision of continuing Great Power cooperation had, if anything, brought the right and left wings of the organisation into closer alliance. However, the escalation of the diplomatic Cold War from 1947, in particular the unveiling of the Marshall Plan, combined with mounting evidence of the dreaded conservative revival at home, such as the overtly anti-labour Taft-Hartley Act of 1947, to make a continuing united front policy increasingly undesirable to the anti-communists, leading eventually to a swingeing purge of communist elements in 1949.[88] Abroad, the death of Hillman in the summer of 1946 had robbed CIO internationalism of its most persuasive advocate. His replacement as the organisation's 'point-man' in the WFTU was the youthful and volatile anti-communist James Carey.[89] Although broadly supportive of the Soviet position until 1947, after the inauguration of the Marshall Plan Carey began looking for ways of extricating the CIO from the Federation. The walk-out of January 1949 signified the end of the Grand Alliance on the international labour front much as the domestic purge of a few months later would signal the final agony of the American Popular Front. This is not to say, though, that 1949 witnessed the utter extinction of the CIO's early postwar internationalist, corporatist, social democratic vision. Rather it underwent a kind of ideological mutation, reformism and anti-communism merging to create a labour variant of Cold War liberalism personified by the newly dominant personality in the CIO on both the domestic and international fronts, the United Automobile Workers' (UAW) president, Walter Reuther.

The complex ideological contortions of the CIO during the late 1940s contrasted sharply with the stark consistency of the AFL's anti-communism in the same period. Indeed, AFL foreign policy personnel in the immediate postwar years generally displayed an unrivalled degree of political purposefulness and *élan*, as they set about hastening the end of the experiment in labour internationalism that was the WFTU. It has already been noted that a growing interest in combating European 'totalitarianism' and influencing the postwar international order had led the AFL leadership in 1944 to establish the Free Trade Union Committee, under the charge of the fanatical anti-communist activist Jay Lovestone. As soon as hostilities had ceased, Lovestone's lieutenant Irving Brown, a battle-scarred veteran of factional infighting in the UAW, was roaming the European continent dispensing aid to anti-communist unionists and sabotaging the alliance between communists and socialists which underpinned the WFTU. The announcement of the Marshall Plan and the Soviet Union's hostile response to it gave the AFL operatives the opportunity they had been looking for to kick-start a new labour international which would exclude the communist unions. In November 1947 Brown, now officially the AFL's 'European Representative', travelled to London in order to try and persuade TUC and Labour Party leaders to break away from the WFTU. Rebuffed by the British, Brown complained to his boss Lovestone about their lack of political courage; the CIO was, as far as he was concerned, beyond the political pale altogether. By 1949, however, 'Lovestone diplomacy' had paid off, as both the TUC and CIO walked out of the WFTU and joined the ICFTU.[90] Whereas, then, the CIO came to the anti-Soviet struggle late and then only with considerable misgivings, the AFL had fought it enthusiastically from the start. Indeed, Brown had been one of the first American combatants in the conflict actually on the ground in Europe.

The TUC's role in this series of events was distinctly ambiguous. As discussed above, the rank-and-file of the British labour movement was for the most part strongly internationalist and supportive of the WFTU. Its leadership, however, did not altogether share this outlook. Indeed, a combination of anti-communism, loyalty to the AFL and jealousy of British colonial interests had made the likes of Walter Citrine extremely cautious about launching the WFTU in the first place (the TUC General Secretary had constantly stressed the 'advisory and consultative character' of the World Trade Union Conference, and sought AFL involvement right up to the last moment).[91] At first Citrine and his successor as WFTU president in 1946, Arthur Deakin, submerged their differences with the Soviet unions in the interests of international harmony. Gradually, however, a number of grievances, including the performance of General Secretary, Louis Saillant, the quality of WFTU publications and the thorny problem of the international trade secretariats, combined with the pressures of Cold War to create a determination on the part of the British representatives to quit the Federation.[92] Nevertheless, it was not until rank-and-file opinion, expressed in the rousing reception given to an anti-communist oration by Deakin at the 1948 TUC Congress, had caught up with the leadership that the decision to walk out was eventually taken.[93] Moreover, as with the CIO, this act did not signify a complete reconciliation with the AFL's position. Irritation with what was perceived as excessive American anti-communism remained, as did a reflexive defensiveness where British national interests were concerned. Similarly, although most British workers now shared their leaders' cynicism about the Soviet Union, they had not abandoned their wartime dreams of international cooperation altogether.[94]

The final party whose role in the WFTU's break-up requires some attention is, strictly speaking, two parties, that is the governments of the United States and the United Kingdom. On both sides of the Atlantic, the years of the Second World War had witnessed surprisingly close co-operation between government officials and trade unionists. In Britain, for example, TUC officers, who during the late 1930s had established close relations with the Colonial Office, 'offered to help establish British-oriented, non-communist trade unions in liberated territories'; in America, the labour desk of the wartime intelligence agency, the Office of Strategic Services (OSS) supported covert operations involving Lovestoneite agents in occupied parts of Europe.[95] As the Grand Alliance disintegrated in 1946 and 1947, this somewhat unlikely partnership was revived. The main cause of this development in the US was the Marshall Plan. American unionists performed a crucial part in the administration of Marshall aid, especially the massive publicity campaign which accompanied it, thereby winning themselves a powerful position in the vast new apparatus of US 'labor diplomacy'.[96] Meanwhile, in Britain, Foreign Secretary Ernest Bevin helped broker a close working relationship between the mandarins of the Foreign Office (FO) and his former colleagues in the trade union movement. For example, a new labour specialist in the FO liaised closely with the head of the TUC's International Department (H. G. Gee and Ernest Bell, respectively).[97]

In both the American and British cases, the campaign against the WFTU was a pivotal moment in the emerging public–private axis. Although neither Whitehall nor Washington appeared to be particularly hostile to the labour international at first, the deterioration of great power relations in 1946 and 1947, and a growing awareness of the strategic importance of labour in the Cold War, caused a burst of hostile interest in the organisation. The State Department orchestrated a covert propaganda campaign against the Federation, secretly collaborating with the AFL's Lovestoneite foreign relations staff and pressurising the CIO to end its membership. In like manner, the Foreign Office attempted to reinforce the anti-communist resolve of the TUC leadership and clear the path to British withdrawal. Finally, and most significantly from the point of view of this study, the newly formed CIA, the peacetime reincarnation of the OSS, got in on the act by covertly financing the anti-communist operations of the Free Trade Union Committee (an arrangement described at greater length below).[98] Once again, the spontaneous actions of the non-communist left had merged with US government operations as the Cold War took hold.

By 1950 the internationalist and third camp impulses of the Anglo–American left had not been eliminated altogether – they would remain a source of nagging irritation for the CIA throughout the following decade – but they had weakened considerably. How realistic such ambitions ever were is, of course, very much open to question: the domestic political marginality of the UDA following Roosevelt's death in 1945, the lack of popular support shown for the radical programmes of such intellectuals as Orwell and Macdonald, and the isolationist tendencies of American unions' rank-and-file members, all would have seriously hampered any attempt to substantiate an independent, leftist position in the postwar world, regardless of other developments in international politics. Above all, though, it was the Cold War which wrecked the leftist possibilities of the period, confusing and demoralising those still trying to carve out a space for a humane socialism in between the great powers, and emboldening those whose main concern was fighting communism. Both these factors – the overwhelming effect of the Cold War and the contribution to the conflict's genesis of left-wing anti-communists – were evident in the irony that many of the CIA's Cold War covert operations were based on networks created by the would-be third campists and internationalists of the mid-1940s. The most spectacular manifestation of this phenomenon, however, occurred not in America but on the other side of the Atlantic, in Whitehall, where in 1948 a secret, official organisation linked to the British security services revived the Labour left's concept of the Third Force as its slogan in the UK government's propaganda war with the Soviet Union.

NOTES

1. For more information about the UDA's links with British Labour during the war years, see Frank A. Warren, *Noble Abstractions: American Liberal Intellectuals and World War II* (Columbus: Ohio State University Press, 1999), pp. 162–71.
2. James Loeb to Reinhold Niebuhr and Mortimer Hays, no date [probably 1945], Americans for Democratic Action Papers, microfilm edition, 1.125.
3. James Loeb, memorandum on 'Special project on British–American relations', 13 February 1946, ADA Papers, 1.130.
4. Michael Young to the Secretary, UDA Educational Fund, Inc., no date [probably early 1946], ADA Papers, 1.83.
5. James Loeb to Reinhold Niebuhr, 23 January 1946, ADA Papers, 1.130.
6. David Williams, 'London Labor Report', 20 July 1946, ADA Papers, 1.63.
7. David Williams, 'London Bureau, UDA Educational Fund Inc., Final Report: July 1, 1946–January 31, 1951', ADA Papers, 2.332.
8. Loeb, 'Special project'. Williams's official title was Director of the London Bureau of the Union for Democratic Action Educational Fund, Inc..
9. See, for example, David Williams to James Loeb, 28 June 1948, ADA Papers, 1.63. Throughout this period there was desultory discussion of the possibility of the Labour Party imitating the UDA's London mission by placing its own representative in the US. This scheme was never realised. See, for example, David Williams to James Loeb, 1 January 1948, ADA Papers, 2.165.

10. On funding and office arrangements, see David Williams to James Loeb, 28 June 1948, ADA Papers, 1.63; also James Loeb to Alfred Baker Lewis, 7 December 1948, ADA Papers, 2.165.

11. Dufty 'would rather bend paper clips for Ni [sic] Bevan', he once confessed, 'than be Senator from Michigan'. William Dufty to James Loeb, 29 January 1945, ADA Papers, 1.130.

12. David Williams to James Loeb, 18 December 1946, ADA Papers, 1.63; David Williams to James Loeb, 9 October 1946, ADA Papers, 1.63.

13. David Williams, 'London Letter', 31 August 1946, ADA Papers, 1.308. See, for example, David Williams to James Loeb, 27 September 1946, ADA Papers, 1.63, in which he suggested that Crossman represented the best hope of keeping *The New Statesman and Nation* 'out of the hands of the Stalinists'; or David Williams to James Loeb, 27 May 1947, ADA Papers, 2.332, wherein he described Crossman 'as a life-preserver to gather young intellectuals just as they are about to plunge into a straight pro-communist position'.

14. See Jonathan Schneer, 'Hopes deferred or shattered: The British Labour left and the Third Force movement, 1945–49', *Journal of Modern History 56* (1984), 197–226.

15. David Williams, 'London Letter', 1 December 1946, ADA Papers, 1.308.

16. David Williams to James Loeb, 16 May 1947, ADA Papers, 2.332.

17. See, for example, James Loeb to David Williams, 26 November 1946, ADA Papers, 1.63; and James Loeb to David Williams, 10 May 1947, ADA Papers, 2.332.

18. See Loeb, 'Special project'.

19. See, for example, James Loeb to David Williams, 19 June 1946, ADA Papers, 1.63. According to Loeb, Williams was 'starting this project at a time when opinion on Britain is at low ebb in America'.

20. One of the subjects of this correspondence was Lee's project of sending aid packages to Austrian women socialists, in which she enlisted Loeb and the UDA's help. See, for example, Jennie Lee to James Loeb, 26 February 1946, ADA Papers, 1.81.

21. See, for example, James Loeb to Jennie Lee, 9 September 1946, ADA Papers, 1.130.

22. James Loeb to Jennie Lee, 11 October 1946, ADA Papers, 1.40.

23. On ADA's birth and its struggle with the PCA, see Steven M. Gillon, *Politics and Vision: The ADA and American Liberalism, 1947–85* (Oxford University Press, 1987), chaps. 1–2.

24. James Loeb to David Williams, 26 November 1946, ADA Papers, 1.63.

25. David Williams to James Loeb, 29 November 1946, ADA Papers, 1.63.

26. David Williams to James Loeb, 8 December 1946, ADA Papers, 1.63.

27. James Loeb to Jennie Lee, 11 October 1946, ADA Papers, 2.40; James Loeb to David Williams, 15 January 1947, ADA Papers, 2.165.

28. James Loeb to David Williams, 4 February 1947, ADA Papers, 2.165; David Williams to James Loeb, 22 February 1947, ADA Papers, 2.165.

29. David Williams to James Loeb, 31 January 1947, ADA Papers, 2.165; Jennie Lee to James Loeb, 25 April 1947, ADA Papers, 2.40; Patrick Gordon-Walker to James Loeb, 23 April 1947, ADA Papers, 2.47.
30. Douglas Richard Ayer, 'American liberalism and British socialism in a Cold War world, 1945–51', Ph.D. thesis, Stanford University (1983), p. 472.
31. Jennie Lee, for example, found the ADA too supportive of official British foreign policy and 'sharp in its Soviet criticism'. Jennie Lee to James Loeb, 25 April 1947, ADA Papers, 2.40.
32. David Williams to James Loeb, 5 February 1947, 2.332; David Williams to James Loeb, 7 August 1947, 2.332. See chap. 4.
33. David Williams to William Dufty, 13 August 1947, ADA Papers, 2.332.
34. James Loeb to David Williams, 31 July 47, ADA Papers, 2.332.
35. David Williams to James Loeb, 24 May 1948, ADA Papers, 2.165.
36. David Williams to James Loeb, 2 December 1948, ADA Papers, 2.165.
37. See, for example, David Williams to James Loeb, 5 February 1947, ADA Papers, 2.332.
38. See, for example, James Loeb to Jennie Lee, 7 May 1947, ADA Papers, 2.47.
39. See Ayer, 'American liberalism and British socialism', p. 204. Williams wrote to Bill Dufty, 'As I prepare much of the American stuff [for *Tribune*], this gives me the opportunity for literary masturbation. I write in the London Letter, "as *Tribune* says", and quote myself.' David Williams to William Dufty, 2 January 1948, ADA Papers, 2.165.
40. David Williams to James Loeb, 7 February 1948, ADA Papers, 2.165.
41. Quoted in Ayer, 'American liberalism and British socialism', p. 235.
42. Quoted in ibid., p. 310.
43. Ibid., p. 315.
44. Schneer, 'Hopes deferred', 218.
45. 'Constitution of the Freedom Defence Committee', no date, Victor Gollancz Papers, Modern Records Centre, Warwick University. See Peter Davison (ed.), *The Complete Works of George Orwell, Volume 17: I Belong to the Left, 1945* (London: Secker and Warburg, 1998), p. 264, fn. 2.
46. Iain Hamilton, *Koestler: A Biography* (London: Secker and Warburg, 1982), p. 105. See also David Cesarani, *Arthur Koestler: The Homeless Mind* (London: William Heineman, 1998), pp. 252–6.
47. George Orwell to Arthur Koestler, 2 January 1946, Arthur Koestler Papers, Edinburgh University Library.
48. See Hamilton, *Koestler*, pp. 105–6.
49. Arthur Koestler to George Orwell, 9 January 1949, Koestler Papers.
50. George Orwell to Arthur Koestler, 10 January 1946, Koestler Papers.
51. George Orwell to Arthur Koestler, 11 February 1946, Koestler Papers.
52. George Orwell to Arthur Koestler, 16 March 1946, Koestler Papers. For more on the International Rescue Committee, see Eric Thomas Chester, *Covert Network: Progressives, the International Rescue Committee and the CIA* (New York: M. E. Sharpe, 1995).

53. See Cesarani, *Arthur Koestler*, p. 254.
54. Humphrey Slater to Arthur Koestler, 19 March 1946, Koestler Papers.
55. Bernard Crick, *George Orwell: A Life* (London: Secker and Warburg, 1980), p. 345.
56. Arthur Koestler to Victor Gollancz, 20 June 1946, Koestler Papers.
57. Victor Gollancz to Arthur Koestler, 18 June 1946, Koestler Papers.
58. Arthur Koestler to Bertrand Russell, 6 May 1946, Koestler Papers.
59. Bertrand Russell to Arthur Koestler, 13 May 1946, Koestler Papers.
60. For an excellent extended analysis of this venture, see Gregory D. Sumner, *Dwight Macdonald and the Politics Circle: The Challenge of Cosmopolitan Democracy* (Ithaca, NY: Cornell University Press, 1996). See also Hugh Wilford, *The New York Intellectuals: From Vanguard to Institution* (Manchester University Press, 1995), chaps. 5–6, and Hugh Wilford, 'An Oasis: The New York intellectuals in the late 1940s', *Journal of American Studies* 28 (1994), 209–23.
61. Quoted in Elisabeth Niebuhr, 'An interview with Mary McCarthy', *Paris Review* 27 (1962), 77.
62. Dwight Macdonald to Albert Camus, 17 May 1946, Dwight Macdonald Papers, Sterling Memorial Library, Yale University.
63. See Wilford, 'Oasis', 213–14. In 1948–49, Camus engaged 'in his own, equally abortive experiment in third-campism, *Group de Liaison Internationale*'. See Sumner, *Dwight Macdonald and the Politics Circle*, pp. 209–10.
64. EAG calendar and minutes, no date [probably 28 March 1948], Macdonald Papers.
65. EAG manifesto, no date [probably March 1948], Macdonald Papers.
66. Mary McCarthy to Dwight Macdonald, no date [probably July 1948], Macdonald Papers.
67. Dwight Macdonald to Mary McCarthy, 30 July 1948, Macdonald Papers.
68. Nicola Chiaromonte to Dwight Macdonald, 3 September 1948, Macdonald Papers.
69. In 1947, for example, the literary critic Irving Howe, still at this stage a Trotskyist, accused *Partisan Review* of suffering from 'Stalinophobia' – 'a disease common among intellectuals who were once radicals; its major symptom is that regular tired feeling'. Irving Howe, 'How *Partisan Review* goes to war', *New International* 13 (1947), 109.
70. EAG calendar and minutes, no date [probably 11 April 1948], Macdonald Papers.
71. Carol Gelderman, *Mary McCarthy: A Life* (New York: St Martin's Press, 1988), p. 141.
72. Friends of Russian Freedom minutes, 4 March 1949, Macdonald Papers. For more on this organisation, see Chester, *Covert Network*, pp. 77–9.
73. Dwight Macdonald to Nicola Chiaromonte, 10 December 1948, Macdonald Papers.

74. Sidney Hook et al., 'Friends of Russian Freedom: Preliminary statement', Macdonald Papers.

75. Nicola Chiaromonte to Dwight Macdonald, 15 December 1948, Macdonald Papers.

76. Friends of Russian Freedom minutes, 4 March 1949, Macdonald Papers.

77. See, for example, Frances Stonor Saunders, *Who Paid the Piper? The CIA and the Cultural Cold War* (London: Granta, 1999), pp. 54–6.

78. See Federico Romero, *The United States and the European Trade Union Movement, 1941–51* (Chapel Hill: University of North Carolina Press, 1989), pp. 8–12.

79. Sidney Hillman, 'Basis for a World Trade Union Federation', no date, Trades Union Congress Papers, 918/05.3, Modern Records Centre, Warwick University. See Victor Silverman, *Imagining Internationalism in American and British Labor, 1939–49* (Urbana: University of Illinois Press, 2000), chap. 9.

80. See Silverman, *Imagining Internationalism*, chap. 3.

81. Walter Citrine to various recipients, 2 November 1943, TUC Papers, 910.1/5.

82. Matthew Woll, quoted in 'Reuter' to TUC, 6 January 1944, TUC Papers, 910.1/5.

83. Philip Murray to Walter Citrine, 5 April 1944, TUC Papers, 910.11/1.

84. Quoted in TUC memorandum, 'World Federation of Trade Unions', 17 February 1948, TUC Papers, 981/6.

85. Constitution, World Federation of Trade Unions, 3 October 1945, TUC Papers, 918/5.

86. Resolutions of WFTU Conference-Congress, Paris, 25 September–8 October 1945, TUC Papers, 918/1.

87. See, for example, Peter Weiler, *British Labor and the Cold War* (Stanford University Press, 1988), chap. 3; Anthony Carew, *Labour under the Marshall Plan: The Politics of Productivity and the Marketing of Management Science* (Manchester University Press, 1987), chap. 5; and Jon V. Kofas, 'US foreign policy and the World Federation of Trade Unions, 1944–48', *Diplomatic History* 26 (2002), 21–60.

88. See Harvey A. Levenstein, *Communism, Anticommunism and the CIO* (Westport, CT: Greenwood, 1981), chap. 16. On the ideological implications of the domestic postwar settlement for the CIO, see the extremely suggestive essay by Nelson Lichtenstein, 'From corporatism to collective bargaining: Organized labor and the eclipse of social democracy in the postwar era', in Steve Fraser and Gary Gerstle (eds), *The Rise and Fall of the New Deal Order, 1930–80* (Princeton University Press, 1989), pp. 122–52.

89. Ronald L. Fillippelli, *American Labor and Postwar Italy, 1943–53* (Stanford University Press, 1989), p. 111.

90. On the AFL's international activities during the late 1940s, see Carew, *Marshall Plan*, chap. 4; Weiler, *British Labor*, ch. 3; and Denis Macshane, *International Labour and the Origins of the Cold War* (Oxford: Clarendon Press, 1992), chap. 6.

91. Walter Citrine, speech to World Trade Union Conference, 13 February 1945, TUC Papers, 918/05.3.
92. See TUC memorandum, 'World Federation of Trade Unions', 17 February 1948, TUC Papers, 981/6.
93. TUC to all affiliated organisations, 27 October 1948, TUC Papers, 918/2.
94. See file entitled 'Replies from tus in response to a TUC circ. outlining its proposed course of action re the WFTU; and re its decision to leave WFTU' in TUC Papers, 918/05.1; also 'Protests from tu branches and TCs re TUC and WFTU, espec. the decision to withdraw', TUC Papers, 918.05/2, for various expressions of dismay at the schism within the WFTU.
95. See Weiler, *British Labor*, p. 84; Fillippelli, *American Labor*, p. 20.
96. See Carew, *Marshall Plan*, chap. 6.
97. See Weiler, *British Labor*, pp. 75–7. Gee helped Bell, for example, keep watch on the sometimes mysterious movements of Louis Saillant. See Ernest Bell, memorandum on Louis Saillant, 4 February 1948, TUC Papers, 918/1.
98. See chap. 3.

2

The Third Force Revisited: The British Left and IRD

As the history of the World Federation of Trade Unions shows, the United States was not the only western government to respond to the Soviet peace offensive by mounting its own front operations involving anti-communist leftists; indeed, it was not even the first. Although still shrouded in official secrecy, the nature and extent of Britain's Cold War propaganda campaign have recently been partially illuminated by the declassification of hundreds of files from the late 1940s and 1950s documenting the early history of a covert unit in the Foreign Office devoted to producing anti-communist 'publicity' (the term preferred at the time to propaganda) called the Information Research Department.[1] These records show that IRD was created in January 1948, fully six months before the US government acquired a similar secret anti-communist agency in the shape of the Office of Policy Coordination. The newly available files also reveal that distribution of the Department's 'grey' (that is factually accurate, but selective or slanted) publicity was not limited to official channels abroad. The FO also employed a vast network of ostensibly private or independent institutions and bodies at home in order to disseminate its 'unattributable' anti-communist output to a domestic as well as an international audience. These fronts included the BBC, several mass-circulation daily newspapers and – most significantly from the point of view of this study – all three major sections of the British non-communist left, that is, the Labour Party, leftist literary intellectuals and trade unions.

Not surprisingly, the involvement of prominent British left-wingers in secret government propaganda attracted a great deal of media attention when it was revealed during the late 1990s. Broadly speaking, two explanations of this apparently paradoxical situation were advanced. According to some commentators, IRD's leftist collaborators were the victims

48

of 'hoodwinking' by the British secret state: the episode was merely another chapter in the ongoing story of Labour politicians' 'manipulation' by the security services.[2] The other theory hinged on the well-worn leftist trope of 'betrayal'. By cosying up to the Whitehall mandarins and spies, the Labour leaders and socialist writers who cooperated with IRD dishonoured their political convictions and sold out the labour movement.[3] Hence, while one explanation tended to exonerate the left of moral blame by suggesting it had been duped by secret 'puppet-masters', the other assigned it a full share of political opprobrium by accusing it of wittingly betraying its principles.

While there are doubtless elements of truth in both the 'hoodwinking' and 'betrayal' theses, the following examination of the newly available FO records documenting the relationship between the Information Research Department and British left suggests that they both oversimplify what was in fact an extremely complex phenomenon. For one thing, the suggestion that the leftists involved were dupes ignores evidence that, to a certain extent, they initiated the alliance with the IRD themselves and then turned it to their own limited advantage: in short, it underestimates their *agency*. For another, talk of betrayal fails to take into account the different attitudes prevailing in this period about the left's relationship to government and, more importantly, the possibility that the decision to cooperate with IRD might itself have been principled in the sense that it was consistent with previously and strongly held anti-communist convictions. Indeed, in some cases such convictions were probably stronger than those held by FO officials. Finally, and following on from this last point, most writing about IRD to date has neglected to note an undercurrent of tension and even conflict running throughout the Department's dealings with 'private' anti-communists. This tendency would later prove to be an even more significant factor in CIA covert operations on the non-communist left.

BEVIN AND THE THIRD FORCE

The Information Research Department was called into existence on 4 January 1948 when Ernest Bevin presented a memorandum to Cabinet entitled 'Future Foreign Publicity Policy'. Noting that the Soviet Union had, since the end of the War, 'carried on in every sphere a vicious attack against the British Commonwealth', Bevin proposed that His Majesty's Government abandon its previous publicity policy of merely 'supporting and explaining' its actions and 'pass over to the offensive', making the 'enemy ... defend themselves'. His main practical recommendation was the establishment in the Foreign Office of a new department 'to collect information' about communism and 'provide material for our anti-communist publicity through our Missions and Information Services abroad'. Such material would also be made available to ministers, British delegations to conferences and – 'on an informal basis' – Labour Party and trade union representatives. This policy would ensure not only the effective rebuttal of 'Russian misrepresentations about Britain' but also help expose communist human rights abuses, the 'poverty and back-wardness' of Soviet society and the imperialistic intent of Stalin's foreign policy.

However, the new publicity policy was not confined to negative attacks on the Soviet Union. A much stronger theme in Bevin's memorandum was the positive projection of Britain as representing a superior way of the life to communism. In part, this superiority was 'spiritual': with its heritage of 'Democratic and Christian principles', Britain clearly embodied the ideals of 'Western civilisation' better than the godless tyranny of the Soviet régime. Furthermore, British social democracy offered a higher material living standard to the 'broad masses of workers and peasants' – the main target of the new publicity offensive – than did communist Russia, where 'privilege for the few' was increasingly the rule. In this as in the spiritual aspect, social democracy was also superior to communism's opposite, that is 'unrestrained capitalism', which suffered from 'inefficiency, social injustice and moral weakness'.

As this last comment suggests, Bevin was not proposing that the Labour government simply join in the anti-communist offensive launched the previous year by the US government, with the proclamation of the Truman Doctrine and the Marshall Plan. Rather, he envisioned an inter-national role for Britain similar to that prescribed by advocates of the Third Force foreign policy on the Labour Party's left wing. Indeed, this equation was made explicit in a passage of his memorandum worth quoting in full:

> It is for us, as Europeans and as a Social Democratic Government, and not the Americans, to give the lead in spiritual, moral and political sphere [sic] to all democratic elements in Western Europe which are anti-Communist and, at the same time, genuinely progressive and reformist, believing in freedom, planning and social justice – what one might call the 'Third Force'.[4]

Within weeks of Bevin's announcement in Cabinet, the Information Research Department – the deliberately anodyne name given to the new section in the FO in order to disguise its true anti-communist purpose – was up and running, for example, furnishing the British Embassy in Rome with materials to help combat the communist campaign in the April 1948 Italian elections.[5] Even at this early stage, however, it was evident that the Department's negative anti-communist function was taking precedence over its positive, Third Force mission. In fact, social democracy barely featured as a theme in IRD output during 1948 and, on the occasions it did, its purpose was merely to reinforce the anti-Soviet message. In those geographical regions where it was deemed to possess no instrumental value in the Cold War, such as the Middle East, it was not mentioned at all. Indeed, as researcher James Oliver has pointed out, British publicity in the Middle East actually backed reactionary governments *against* socially progressive movements.[6] By 1949 IRD had abandoned the Third Force altogether, leaving the promotion of 'the virtues and advantages of our system' to its sister organisation, the Information Policy Department, so that it could concentrate on the business of exposing 'the machinations of the Soviet bloc and the evils of communism'.[7]

This development has led several historians to conclude that Bevin only launched IRD because he had been tricked into doing so by permanent officials in the Foreign Office who desired a new anti-Soviet propaganda unit and were prepared to pay lip-service to the Third Force ideal in order to gain one from the Labour government.[8] Fiercely anti-communist, determined not to repeat the mistakes of the 1930s by appeasing another totalitarian dictator and increasingly appreciative of the potential utility of political warfare to an economically and militarily enfeebled Britain, FO officials such as Christopher Warner, head of the Northern Department, had long been campaigning for the development of a more effective propaganda capability. Initially, Bevin had resisted such pressure, for example rejecting a proposal by Assistant Under-Secretary in charge of information, Ivone Kirkpatrick, for a specialist anti-communist publicity unit in the summer of 1946.[9] It was only when his Parliamentary Under-Secretary, the young anti-communist intellectual, Christopher Mayhew, joined in the calls for such a body – and, crucially, linked the proposal to the positive notion of the Third Force – that Bevin came on board, giving Mayhew the go-ahead to meet with FO officials in November 1947 and draw up plans for the establishment of IRD (it was, incidentally, Mayhew who drafted Bevin's memorandum of 4

January 1948).[10] Just how sincere the likes of Warner and Kirkpatrick ever were in their commitment to promoting a social democratic foreign policy is highly questionable. The patrician personal backgrounds of senior FO officials – many had known each other at Eton – hardly predisposed them to support social democracy.[11] They also had qualms about the possible repercussions for Anglo–American relations of an explicitly anti-capitalist publicity policy.[12] Finally, there are IRD links with the military and secret services to consider. According to intelligence historian Stephen Dorril, the impetus for the new department's creation came, at least in part, from surviving elements of the disbanded wartime clandestine organisation, the Political Warfare Executive (PWE) – a claim born out by the fact that IRD's first head was an old PWE operative, Ralph Murray.[13] Hardly surprising, then, that the new department should have been closely allied with both the Secret Intelligence Service (MI6) and the Security Service (MI5). This clandestine tendency was further reinforced by the fact that, in order to conceal its existence, IRD was funded from the Secret Service budget, the Secret Vote.[14]

All these considerations, then, count in favour of the 'hoodwinking' thesis. However, there are other pieces of evidence to weigh against them. Most important of these is Christopher Mayhew's later admission that in linking the projected anti-communist offensive with social democracy his main intention had been to defuse potential opposition to government policy from Labour's left wing. 'We only dealt with the Third Force idea frankly', Mayhew told James Oliver in an interview shortly before his death, 'because I was Parliamentary Under-Secretary and I didn't want Bevin to be defeated and humiliated inside the Labour Party.'[15] It is arguable that this claim was merely a ploy to conceal Mayhew's embarrassment at having been deceived by the Foreign Office. However, there is contemporaneous documentary evidence to support his statement in the form of assurances to American government officials that Bevin's apparent leftwards turn was tactically motivated.[16] Indeed, the British Embassy in Washington 'very secretly' passed to US Secretary of State, General George C. Marshall a summary of Bevin's memorandum which strongly hinted that the new British publicity policy would, despite the hostile talk about capitalism, in fact complement American propaganda efforts.[17] In this connection, historian Dianne Kirby has argued that, in much the same way as the allusion to the Third Force served as a rhetorical device designed to placate the Labour left, Bevin's (or, to be more accurate, Mayhew's) invocation of western spiritual unity in the face of the communist threat was mainly intended to flatter American religious sensibilities and tacitly imply British support for the Truman Doctrine.[18] Mayhew's appropriation of the Labour left's foreign policy slogan might not have been quite as cynical as he later made out, but it did undoubtedly have a tactical dimension to it.

This is not to deny the possibility that Bevin himself did entertain genuine hopes of Britain leading an independent bloc of social democratic powers in western Europe backed by their colonial possessions. However, his definition of the 'Third Force' was different from the socialist vision of Labour foreign policy favoured by the *Keep Left* group. Rather, his main objective was the more traditional one of preserving Britain's imperial power and prestige in the world – not much different, in fact, from that of his permanent officials in the Foreign Office.[19] Moreover, there can be no doubting the intensity of the Foreign Secretary's anti-communism, which dated back to his earliest days as a trade unionist and was exacerbated during the late 1940s by fiery personal confrontations with his Soviet opposite number, Molotov. Bevin's reluctance to commit himself wholeheartedly to an anti-Soviet publicity offensive prior to late 1947 was probably less the result of ideological uncertainty, as has been suggested by some historians, than a fear of alienating rank-and-file opinion in the British Labour movement.[20] In the end, it was not so much the wiles of Whitehall mandarins which scuppered Bevin's imperial version of the Third Force as the pressure of world and domestic events in 1948. The escalation of the Cold War, the increasing economic weakness of Britain and, ironically, Labour objections to greater involvement in Europe, all combined to throw Bevin back on the Atlantic alliance as the chief means of securing Britain's status as a Great Power. Perhaps the key to understanding the character of Bevin's foreign policy is to view it as an extension of his earlier practice of trade unionism, that is a corporatist strategy of cooperating with the state in order to gain the best deal possible for his followers.[21] This would explain why, despite his proletarian origins, Bevin was so at ease in the company of old Etonians, and they in his.

IRD AND THE LABOUR PARTY

A similar spirit pervaded the relationship between the Information Research Department and the Labour government as a whole. Right from the first, Labour politicians proved themselves willing recipients of IRD propaganda. One example of this kind of material was a series of

'Speaker's Notes' prepared by the Department at the suggestion of Christopher Mayhew. These briefing sheets, 'containing facts and debating points on the familiar Communist themes', were designed to help ministers and 'friendly' Labour MPs resist 'Communist-inspired opposition at Labour Party and Trade Union meetings'. The range of topics covered included '"American imperialism", Soviet expansion, Soviet intransigence', and so on.[22] These and similar documents were not forced on individuals, but (as Mayhew later explained to researcher Lyn Smith) 'if some anti-Stalinist MP wanted information or briefing on some subject, then we were only too happy to send him the facts'.[23] Ministers were singled out as particularly effective channels for IRD propaganda. In July 1948, Mayhew wrote to a number of senior members of the government, including the Prime Minister himself, urging them to utilise the Department's output. Ministerial speeches were, he explained, an invaluable medium for British publicity abroad, 'far better' than 'explanations by Heads of Missions or the work of our Information Officers'.[24] Indeed, Mayhew counted his own performance at the United Nations General Assembly in October 1948, when he used IRD data to mount a fierce retaliatory attack on the Soviet Union for its use of forced labour, as the new department's first major propaganda coup.[25]

Relations between IRD and Labour were not entirely harmonious. In addition to the element of tension always present in dealings between permanent officials and elected representatives – it is possible, for example, to detect some bureaucratic friction in correspondence between Mayhew and Ralph Murray during the former's attendance at the UN Assembly in 1948[26] – there was the instinctive ideological hostility felt by a predominantly conservative Foreign Office towards a Labour administration and vice versa. Despite the early abandonment of the Third Force in IRD output and Bevin's growing Atlanticism, FO staff continued to feel embarrassed by negative perceptions of British socialism in the US.[27] On Labour's side, there were repeated calls for a purge of obstructive Whitehall mandarins and the democratisation of civil service recruitment procedures at annual conferences and local meetings. Interestingly, the charge that Bevin was a captive of duplicitous permanent officials first surfaced during the late 1940s, with Harold Laski describing the Foreign Secretary as falling 'an immediate victim to the worst gang in the FO'.[28]

Laski's sentiments were not, however, shared by the majority of Labour leaders and officers, who appear to have had no hesitation at all in cooperating with the IRD. Perhaps the most remarkable example of this tendency was that provided by a young party official, Denis Healey. Since taking over as Secretary of Labour's International Department in 1945, Healey – himself an ex-communist – had rapidly earned a reputation as not only a leading expert on foreign affairs but also a skilful practitioner of anti-communist political warfare.[29] When his friend, J. H. Adam Watson, began working for IRD in the autumn of 1948, Healey became the Department's chief point of contact in the Labour movement. In addition to receiving and disseminating large amounts of unattributable material,[30] Healey also became an important source of inside information for the Foreign Office on international labour affairs. On one occasion, for example, he passed on to Watson suggestions from various émigré socialists living in London, such as the Czech social democrat Walter Kolarz, about 'our propaganda etcetera [sic] to Eastern Europe'.[31] On another, he provided a list of names of European socialists to whom IRD might begin sending its publications.[32] Watson followed up this lead, arranging for papers to be sent via Information Officers to the individuals concerned.[33] Healey also reciprocated the flow of documents from the Foreign Office by furnishing Watson with *Talking Points* and other Labour publications for possible use overseas.[34] Early in 1949, IRD even began sending copies of *Tribune* to British missions abroad for distribution to sympathetic foreign contacts, explaining to perhaps somewhat puzzled British diplomats that, 'Many articles in it can be effectively turned to this Department's purposes'.[35] In other words, this was very much a two-way exchange of anti-communist intelligence and propaganda.

How to explain this spectacle of a socialist political party cooperating so readily with a secret government agency? Part of the answer to this question lies in many Labour politicians' still recent experience of service in one or other of the numerous clandestine organisations which had flourished during the Second World War. The Special Operations Executive (SOE), the most prestigious of these, had been under the charge of none other than Hugh Dalton, patron of the postwar generation of Labour revisionists known as the Gaitskellites. Amongst the young Labourites assisting Dalton in his duties as Minister of Economic Warfare was Christopher Mayhew.[36] The PWE – the organisational precursor of the IRD – counted amongst its staff the future Labour Commonwealth Secretary Patrick Gordon-Walker.[37] Even Richard Crossman, left-wing scourge of the Labour leadership for much of the postwar period, had served in the PWE, earning himself a reputation as an expert on 'psychological warfare' in the process (and, incidentally,

1 Denis Healey, the Labour Party's international secretary and key
contact with the Information Research Department.
(By Permission of People's History Museum)

developing a close relationship with the American C. D. Jackson, later President Eisenhower's principal adviser on the subject of 'psy-war').[38] There was, in short, a powerful precedent for collaboration between the British left and the secret state – not to mention the strong personal bonds of friendship and mutual loyalty forged in the heat of war.

There is also the potential *utility* of the Information Research Department to the Labour Party to consider. IRD's unattributable propaganda made excellent ammunition for use by the right wing of the Labour movement in its ongoing civil war with British communists and their sympathisers, just as intelligence passed from the security services via the Foreign Office could help the Party leadership maintain discipline by identifying undesirable members and organisations for expulsion or proscription. By the same token, the Department's willingness to distribute such publications as *Tribune* abroad through official British diplomatic channels offered the prospect of enhancing Labour's international influence. Finally, by joining in the FO's anti-communist campaign Labour politicians were able to demonstrate their ideological bona fides to permanent officials perhaps sceptical about a socialist party's claim to custodianship of the national interest. In other words, IRD functioned as a convenient meeting place between the Labour Party and Whitehall. Labour had good reason to back the Information Research Department, Third Force or no Third Force.

IRD AND LITERARY INTELLECTUALS

In addition to Labour politicians, literary intellectuals on the non-communist left were also on hand to assist IRD. In February 1949, for example, the émigré novelist Arthur Koestler, whose sister-in-law Celia Kirwan worked for the Department, met with Healey's contact Adam Watson and discussed with him 'the need for combating Communist penetration in Israel and Mapam'.[39] The former Comintern officer's advice to the Foreign Office ran along the same lines as that he had given Bertrand Russell a few years earlier: the west had to take the communists on at their own game, turning the front tactics they had pioneered during the 1930s back against the Soviet Union. Hence, when IRD officers were debating entering the publishing field for the first time, Koestler 'forcibly' pointed out to Ralph Murray 'the crying need' for cheap publications of the kind produced by the Left Book Club during the 1930s, to 'tackle the themes on which public opinion needs to be enlightened'. Indeed, it was desirable, Koestler continued, that 'such publications should be sponsored by publishers with known left affiliations'. Following this advice rather literally, IRD considered approaching the Left Book Club publisher himself, Victor Gollancz, 'putting to him that the national interest required the organisation of publications of this sort', and offering 'to intervene unobtrusively to cause them to appear in suitable cheap editions'.[40] Subsequently, however, the FO appears to have developed cold feet about this scheme, judging by IRD deputy head Leslie Sheridan's remark in June 1949 that, 'I have given up any hope of co-operation with Gollancz, of whom every one seems apprehensive'.[41] By October the idea of cultivating left-wing publishers as IRD fronts had been dropped, at least for the time being. 'This has now been overtaken', it was noted, 'by other arrangements' (a reference, presumably, to the launch of IRD's own dummy publishing house, Ampersand).[42]

IRD was also interested in the fiction produced by anti-communist literary intellectuals as a form of Cold War propaganda. For example, thousands of copies of Koestler's powerful fictional exposé of Stalinist political terror, *Darkness at Noon*, were purchased by the Foreign Office in 1948 and distributed in Germany.[43] The most remarkable example of this phenomenon, however, was IRD's exploitation of George Orwell's anti-communist fictions, *Animal Farm* and *1984*. The latter was translated into a multitude of foreign languages and distributed widely overseas. Burmese rights to the novel, to cite just one example, were bought by IRD at the request of its Regional Information Office in Singapore.[44] *Animal Farm*, described in a Department circular as 'a brilliant satire on the Communist régime in the USSR, in which the scene is transferred from Russia to a farmyard', was considered a particularly 'effective propaganda weapon, because of its skilful combination of simplicity, subtlety and humour'.[45] An Arabic edition was prepared by the Information Department at the British Embassy in Cairo, where one official noted the happy coincidence that 'both pigs and dogs are unclean animals to Muslims', and distributed throughout the Middle East.[46] A Chinese translation 'had quite a success in South East Asia'.[47] IRD even commissioned a strip-cartoon version of Orwell's fable, the production of which was attended to with considerable interest by Sheridan, for dissemination in South America, the Middle East and Far East. The resulting images reinforced the allegorical elements of the tale – presumably for the benefit of the 'uneducated' audiences at which they were targeted – by depicting Major, the pig who inspires the animals' revolution, with a Lenin-like spade beard, and his despotic successor

2 A strip-cartoon version of George Orwell's *Animal Farm*, commissioned by the Information Research Department. Note Major's Lenin-like beard and Napoleon's Stalin-esque moustache. (Public Record Office, London)

Napoleon sporting a Stalin-esque moustache.[48] Another graphic version of *Animal Farm*, a CIA-financed animated cartoon, was exhibited in the 'backward' areas of the British Commonwealth by mobile film units paid for by IRD.[49] This exhaustive milking of the propaganda potential of Orwell's novel lends credence to historian Susan L. Carruthers's contention that fictional representations of communism were at least as important as 'factual' accounts in establishing Cold War constructions of the Soviet Union in the western imagination.[50]

That said, Orwell's utility to IRD was not confined to the realm of fiction: he was also a valuable source of anti-communist intelligence. In March 1949, Celia Kirwan visited him at a sanatorium in Gloucestershire, where he lay fatally ill from tuberculosis. As she reported to her superiors the following day: 'I discussed some aspects of our work with him in great confidence, and he was delighted to learn of them, and expressed his whole-hearted and enthusiastic approval'. Although too sick to contribute to the Department's publicity work himself, Orwell suggested the names of other intellectuals whom he thought might be prepared to do so. These included the *Manchester Guardian* correspondent D'Arcy Gillie, the scientist C. D. Darlington, and the German historian of the Comintern, Franz Borkenau. He also drew on his earlier experience as a colonial policeman to offer advice about publicity work in Burma and India, and echoed Koestler by recommending Gollancz as a possible publisher of IRD material, expressing a willingness 'to act as a go-between if he had been well enough'.[51] Shortly after Kirwan's visit, Orwell wrote her a follow-up letter suggesting further writers the Foreign Office might contact, including his non-communist left allies in the US, that is 'the hordes of Americans, whose names can be found in the (New York) *New Leader*, the Jewish monthly paper *Commentary* and the *Partisan Review*'. He also volunteered to send Kirwan 'a list of journalists and writers who in my opinion are crypto-Communists, fellow-travellers or inclined that way and should not be trusted as propagandists'.[52] Kirwan accepted this offer on behalf of IRD, promising to treat the information 'with the utmost discretion', and Orwell duly furnished her with a list of 35 names.[53]

When the IRD files containing this correspondence were released to the Public Record Office in 1996, there was a blaze of negative publicity. 'Orwell is revealed in role of state informer', proclaimed one newspaper headline; 'Orwell offered blacklist', announced another.[54] Various luminaries of the postwar British left declared their shock at this revelation. 'There's a lot of argument about him deserting his socialism at the end of his life', explained one of Orwell's *Tribune* colleagues, Michael Foot. 'I don't think that's true, but I am very surprised that he was dealing with the secret service in any form.'[55] The fact that the list itself was not included among the documents declassified by the Foreign Office appeared only to heighten media interest. 'Orwell's little list leaves the left gasping for more', exclaimed the *Independent on Sunday* breathlessly, above a story quoting historian Christopher Hill's opinion that, 'There was something fishy about Orwell'.[56] When the list – or, to be more accurate, the contents of a notebook listing 135 names from which Orwell culled the 35 he handed to Celia Kirwan – was eventually published in 1998, the story flared up again. 'Socialist icon who became Big Brother', was how the *Daily Telegraph* trailed its publication of a transcript of the notebook.[57] The fact that the longer list contained remarks about individuals that could easily be interpreted as homophobic or anti-Semitic, thereby lending weight to recent scholarly claims that Orwell was a racist and chauvinist, only compounded the damage to his reputation.[58] Final judgement was pronounced in two books published shortly after the appearance of the longer list. For Frances Stonor Saunders, author of *Who Paid the Piper?*, Orwell's actions in naming radicals to a secret government agency with links to the security service 'demonstrated that he had confused the role of the intellectual with that of the policeman'.[59] In their history of IRD, *Britain's Secret Propaganda War*, Paul Lashmar and James Oliver delivered the following verdict:

> For many years after his death some in the left had often argued that Orwell had never meant *Animal Farm* or *1984* as anti-Soviet parables and claimed that the books had been hijacked by Cold War Warriors of the right. These files show that this was not the case.[60]

Why did Orwell cooperate so readily with IRD and what do his actions tell us about the state of his politics shortly before his death? Clearly the idea of a list of suspected subversives is an extremely troubling one, not least because the following year Senator Joseph McCarthy was to launch his notorious career as a 'red-baiter' by brandishing just such a document. Yet the 35 names Orwell handed over were not intended as a blacklist for McCarthyite action by the security service. Rather, as he explained in his letter to Kirwan, they were merely meant to warn IRD whom it should avoid when seeking contributors to its anti-communist campaign. In common with his non-communist left literary colleagues in New York, Orwell had long regarded western governments as disastrously relaxed in their attitudes towards communism. Indeed, he strongly suspected (with, it later emerged, good reason) that a Soviet agent working in the Ministry of Information during the Second World War had been involved in an attempt to suppress publication of *Animal Farm*.[61] In the absence of purposeful official action, it was, Orwell believed, up to the minority of informed anti-Stalinists such as himself to expose concealed communist influence. Hence his denunciation of scientist J. D. Bernal in the anti-Stalinist, left-wing *Polemic*, and his attack on Labour MP Konni Zilliacus in the New York intellectuals' flagship, *Partisan Review* (which resulted in a noisy controversy in the pages of *Tribune*).[62] The notebook from which the 35 names were extracted was the product of several years' updating and reworking, carried out in collaboration with fellow anti-communist literary intellectual Richard Rees and, in all probability, Arthur Koestler.[63] Moreover, the transaction with Kirwan occurred at a time when, along with many other observers, Orwell believed that a Soviet invasion of western Europe was imminent (the Berlin blockade, after all, was still in progress). In sum, 'the list' needs to be read in the context not only of a perceived immediate political crisis but also of Orwell's long-standing, principled and public opposition to communism.[64] It is finally worth pointing out that Orwell was on record as explicitly rejecting calls for the suppression of the Communist Party and a political purge of the civil service on civil liberties grounds.[65] His actions in 1949 should not therefore necessarily be interpreted as a repudiation of the tenderness for the rights of political minorities which had prompted his membership of the Freedom Defence Committee in 1945.

It should also be taken into account that Orwell did not hand the 35 names to some faceless bureaucrat. He had known Celia Kirwan since 1945, when they had met at Koestler's house in Wales. Indeed, he had briefly been in love with her (she and her sister Mamaine were celebrated society beauties) and had even proposed marriage. Although she turned him down, they had remained close friends.[66] This fact is significant here for two reasons. First, it points towards a wider truth: that the lines between the worlds of government officials and private citizens – the state apparatus and civil society – were extremely blurred in early Cold War Britain. Like many Labour Party politicians, such left-wing literary intellectuals as George Orwell had recent experience of working for an official, or semi-official, agency – in his case, the BBC's Indian Service – as part of Britain's total effort in the Second World War. Even for someone as sensitive to the intrusions of state power as himself, the notion of cooperation with government did not appear as problematic to Orwell as it would to later generations of leftists. Following on from this, there is less reason than might at first appear to interpret the handing over of the list as evidence of a creeping 'right-wing' bias. IRD was the creation of a Labour government which Orwell supported strongly. Its declared purpose was to oppose communism in the name of social democratic values – a point no doubt emphasised by Celia Kirwan, who only a few years previously had helped edit *Polemic*, a journal with which Orwell was closely associated and which was, as just noted, very much of the literary left. (Nor was Kirwan the only member of Orwell's circle to work for IRD: so too did T. R. Fyvel, a member of the 'Searchlight' group during the Second World War.)[67] In short, Orwell was given no reason to doubt IRD's socialist credentials.

This is not to defend Orwell's decision to entrust his list to the Foreign Office. Given his opposition to political persecution, his naming of suspected security risks to a covert government agency with links to the secret services appears surprisingly naïve. It is also a sad truth that the notebook from which the names were culled betrays his worst ethnic and sexual prejudices (although it is perhaps worth stating in mitigation that he never allowed his racism or, for that matter, his hatred of Stalinism to overwhelm his anti-imperialism, as was demonstrated by his refusal to join the anti-communist League for European Freedom, due to its failure to denounce British colonialism).[68] However, allegations that Orwell's actions reveal him to have been a pioneer of the blacklist or political turncoat are simply not born out by the evidence. Even less warranted is the suggestion that the IRD documents demonstrate that *Animal Farm* and *1984* were originally conceived as right-wing tracts. Records showing that these works were posthumously employed by western governments as Cold War propaganda in no way constitute proof of conservative authorial intention. To claim that they do is seriously to misread both Orwell's personal political history and the fictions themselves. The readiness with which some contemporary leftists have conceded neo-conservative claims to Orwell's literary reputation begs the question succinctly phrased by his biographer, Bernard Crick: 'Why are radicals so eager to give up one of their own?'[69]

Returning briefly to the larger theme of the Information Research Department's relationship with left-wing literary intellectuals, it is worth noting the limits on this collaboration. While prepared to consult such intellectuals and utilise their fiction for propaganda purposes, IRD was not ready to mobilise them as a fighting force in the Cold War. This is not to say that such a course of action was never considered. In May 1949, Christopher Mayhew met with Ralph Murray, Christopher Warner and R. L. Speaight, head of the Information Policy Department, to discuss the need to 'rally the forces of freedom and inspire a crusading spirit in all our peoples in defence of the civilisation, liberties and values which Europe has given the world and which are threatened by totalitarianism'.[70] In the course of discussions, Speaight suggested the recruitment of 'a body of leading figures working together ... and without evident Government sponsorship, but with the Foreign Office in the background to give advice and guidance'.[71] These figures should possess considerable 'intellectual appeal, for we feel that one part of the job to be done is to influence the intellectuals in this country and on the Continent'.[72] Speaight then came up with a number of names, including those of Bertrand Russell, Harold Nicolson, Arnold Toynbee, Michael Foot and Michael Oakeshott. To this list Mayhew added Arthur Koestler, Barbara Ward and Denis Healey, that is those who were 'rather younger and less orthodox'.[73]

The proposal, however, never got past the Minister. 'I am very chary', declared Hector McNeil on June 20. 'The people who are on fire with this theme ... do not need help from us. They are impelled.' In any case, poets, including 'even political poets, make bad committee men'.[74] A second meeting of FO information officers reached the conclusion that intellectuals were in fact 'extremely woolly-minded about totalitarianism and true democracy' and agreed merely to survey foreign posts asking whether a 'positive digest' of intellectual items would be any use.[75] A series of negative responses from the missions surveyed finally killed off the plan. When tackled by the *New Statesman* many years later, the surviving intellectuals on Speaight and Warner's list denied ever having been approached by the Foreign Office and insisted that, if they had been, they would not have agreed to the proposal.[76] The idea of opening an intellectual front in the Cold War had been rejected by British government officials. That tactic would have to await development by the Americans.

IRD AND THE UNIONS

Considering the cooperation between the Foreign Office and Trades Union Congress which had already taken place in regard to the WFTU, it is perhaps not surprising that there should have been close links between the TUC and the new Information Research Department. The principal point of contact during the first year of the latter's existence was an anti-communist action group spontaneously formed by right-wing members of the Congress's General Council, known as the Freedom and Democracy Trust. In June 1948 Christopher Mayhew met with TUC Publicity Officer Herbert Tracey, who was responsible for editing the Trust's newsletter, *Freedom First*, and put to him the possibility of producing an international edition of this publication with the discreet assistance of the Foreign Office. Such an arrangement would, it occurred to Mayhew, address the perennial problem facing IRD, that is how to distribute 'anti-communist propaganda abroad in a manner which is, on the one hand, authoritative and, on the other, non-official'.[77] Tracey received the idea 'warmly' – he was already using IRD materials in *Freedom First*'s domestic edition, which was sent to between 200 and 300 leading British unionists – and, following approval by Christopher Warner, agreed to edit 'an anti-communist periodical addressed to foreign trade unionists' with material supplied by IRD 'on a strictly confidential basis'.[78] Although purportedly the organ of a non-official body called 'The Defence of Democracy Trust against all Forms of Totalitarianism', the international *Freedom First* was effectively to be an IRD publication. Warner, who had some reservations about the quality of Tracey's journalism, demanded that it 'should be written in close contact with us', while Tracey himself wanted IRD to 'do as much as possible of the editing'.[79] The venture was to be subsidised by the simple expedient of the Foreign Office buying up copies at inflated prices for distribution via British information officers abroad (who themselves were not informed about the source of the newsletter's contents).[80]

This venture was dogged by difficulties. Despite Tracey's pliability, IRD continued to nurse misgivings about his abilities as an editor, drafting in Denis Healey later in 1948 to give him some journalistic tips.[81] Doubts were also expressed about the TUC's effectiveness as a conduit of anti-communist publicity to individual unions and 'the man in the street'.[82] Then, in October 1948, disaster struck. A financial backer of the Freedom and Democracy Trust, by the name of Sidney Stanley, was exposed in the course of a high-profile official inquiry into government corruption as having bribed a junior minister at the Board of Trade. Soon afterwards, he fled to Israel to escape prosecution.[83] It did not matter that his only donation to the Trust had been a dud cheque for £50.[84] According to a 1951 IRD minute, 'references to Freedom First' made during the trial had been 'picked up by the Communists'.[85] This breach

65

of security demanded swift and drastic action. IRD 'immediately ceased showing any interest' in *Freedom First*, writing to British missions in January 1949 to inform them that the international edition of the newsletter had been dropped.[86] Simultaneously, the direct supply of confidential information to Tracey was cut – although steps were taken to ensure that his sources in the TUC were 'kept fully briefed ... through Mr Denis Healey'.[87] This 'dismal experience' appears to have disillusioned IRD staff considerably about its relations with the TUC. In April 1949, a gloomy Ralph Murray described the organisation as 'too cumbersome, too un-publicity minded and too short-staffed to make a significant contribution in practical publicity'.[88]

Still, IRD did not burn all its bridges to the TUC. In the course of 1949 there was frequent liaison over such matters as the Congress's withdrawal from the WFTU and the Department's campaign to discredit the communist-penetrated National Council for Civil Liberties.[89] This reflected the fact that the Foreign Office had discovered a more effective contact person in the TUC than its Publicity Director in the shape of its clever young Deputy General Secretary, Vic Feather. A shrewd backroom operator with 'a well-earned reputation for being a hammer of the communists', Feather had orchestrated a successful internal campaign against trade union communism in October 1948, consequently winning himself an introduction to Ralph Murray in January 1949.[90] Most of his subsequent dealings with the FO, however, appear to have been with deputy head Sheridan, with whom he evidently developed a close working relationship. In August 1950, for example, Sheridan raised with Feather IRD's disappointment in the quality of the publicity being generated by the new anti-communist labour international, the International Con-federation of Free Trade Unions. Subsequently, the TUC officer and Denis Healey arranged for the 'reliable and useful' Edward Thompson, head of the ICFTU's Publications Department, to begin receiving IRD material.[91] On another occasion, following the visit of a British trade union delegation to Hungary from which the delegates returned extolling the freedom of Hungarian workers, Sheridan suggested to his TUC opposite number the possibility of, in future, 'briefing selected Trade Unionists ... before they leave'. Feather welcomed the suggestion and proposed the preparation of specially tailored briefing notes for each delegation which would include 'awkward questions to ask'.[92] Feather was not the only friend of the Information Research Department in the British labour movement. Others included the zealously anti-communist leader of the Transport and General Workers Union, Arthur Deakin, arguably a more powerful figure in this period than the TUC General Secretary himself; the 'very sound' Durham miners' leader Sam Watson, tipped as a future Labour Foreign Secretary, who contributed to a 'Background Book' (one of IRD's secret publishing imprints) on *Why I Am an Anti-communist* (at, incidentally, Feather's recommendation);[93] and the Labour MP Woodrow Wyatt, who became 'a prime journalistic outlet for the MI5/IRD material' and led a covertly-sponsored campaign against alleged communist ballot-rigging in the Electrical Trades Union.[94] Nonetheless, Feather remained IRD's point-man in the unions, performing a similar role to that played by Denis Healey in the Labour Party. Perhaps it was no coincidence that both men were ex-radicals whom some critical observers perceived as retaining vestiges of the communist mindset.[95]

The collapse of Freedom First in the wake of the Stanley scandal had deprived right-wing trade unionists in Britain of an organisation capable of waging effective political warfare against communism (at least on a national basis: individual unions still contained powerful anti-communist cliques, such as the Amalgamated Engineering Union's [AEU] 'Club'). This lack was remedied in November 1951 by the launch of a body called Common Cause, an extremely militant anti-communist action group whose leadership included several members of the old Freedom and Democracy Trust, such as John Brown, former General Secretary of the Iron and Steel Trades Confederation, and Tom O' Brien, Labour MP and General Secretary of the Theatrical and Kine Employees. Common Cause was not simply a reincarnation of Freedom First, however. Indeed, its origins were highly complex. In part it had grown out of the one-man anti-communist crusade of the maverick leftist, C. A. Smith. A former chairman of both the Independent Labour Party and Commonwealth Party, Smith had during the late 1940s forged a network of alliances with various industrialists and aristocrats who shared his hatred of communism. The latter included the Duchess of Atholl (founder of the British League for European Freedom, the organisation Orwell had refused to join), the Conservative MP Lord Malcolm Douglas-Hamilton, and the Hungarian-born Judith, Countess of Listowel, editor of the journal *East Europe and Soviet Russia*. Common Cause also had strong American antecedents. An organisation with that name had been launched in 1947 by Natalie Paine, who earlier had run the wartime 'Bundles for Britain' programme, and attracted a distinguished membership which overlapped with that of the National Committee for a Free Europe (NCFE), the CIA front for the organisation of eastern European exile groups. A third distinct ideological strand feeding into Common Cause was religiously motivated anti-communism. Catholics featured disproportionately in leadership positions, and the organisation had ties to the fiercely anti-communist Association of Catholic Trade Unionists.[96]

Although Common Cause embraced an extremely wide ideological spectrum extending far beyond the unions, its main concern was organised labour. As a letter announcing the organisation's launch explained, 'It is a matter of extreme urgency to recover the ground lost in several fields – notably within the Trade Unions – a number of which are already officered and controlled by avowed communists'.[97] The importance attached to the anti-communist battle in the unions was evidenced by the make-up of Common Cause's governing councils. John Brown sat in one of its two chairs (the other being occupied by Douglas-Hamilton); its 'Advisory Council' was stuffed with unionists, including Bob Edwards, Vic Sullivan and Henry Solomons; so too was an 'industrial committee'.[98] The subject of communism in the unions was a regular feature of the organisation's publicity. Vic Feather lectured on the theme in October 1952, while an information officer from the US Embassy, William C. Gausmann, covered it from an American perspective in March 1955.[99] A list of 'hostile organisations', which included several British unions, was circulated widely, as was a publication entitled 'Trade Union Facts' detailing incidents of alleged communist entryism (and provoking anxious protestations of innocence from several of the unions named to Transport House).[100] Most important – although, unfortunately, least documented – was Common Cause's covert work in combating communist campaigns in union elections, for example in the AEU.[101]

IRD watched these developments with considerable interest. Here was precisely the sort of non-official anti-communist body whose absence the Department had earlier lamented. However, what stands out most from the newly available Foreign Office files concerning Common Cause is not the official encouragement offered the organisation – although there was plenty of that[102] – but rather the strong sense of apprehension felt by professional Cold Warriors about this incursion into their territory by amateur enthusiasts. To begin with, FO officials perceived Common Cause as, to some extent, an unwelcome American intervention in British internal affairs. The organisation was only inaugurated formally in Britain after persistent agitation by the head of Common Cause USA, Natalie Paine who, it was noted somewhat uneasily, was 'a close friend' of high-ranking State Department officials and the Director of Central Intelligence, Walter Bedell Smith.[103] IRD sympathised with Paine's desire to improve Britain's image in the US by stimulating public displays of British anti-communism. However, there were fears that what she had in mind – a 'splash' such as a mass rally at the Royal Albert Hall – might do more harm than good to the western Cold War effort by arousing British anti-Americanism (fears which can hardly have been allayed when long-time MI6 asset Christopher Emmet resigned as Chairman of Common Cause USA citing Paine's 'well-known exuberance and tendency to go dashing off in several different directions at the same time').[104] Small wonder, then, that British diplomats in the US should have been instructed to keep a close eye on Paine and try as far as possible to exercise a restraining influence on her.[105]

Such concerns were not confined to the American dimension of Common Cause. IRD staff assigned to deal with the organisation's British founders also feared the potentially counter-productive effects of excessive private anti-communism. 'We have been occupied here in trying to keep the infant Common Cause-England on the rails', explained Mollie Hamilton, the Department's contact with the Countess of Listowel, to an American-based colleague. 'Nothing could be less useful to anybody but the Communist Party than an entry by us on the witch-hunt.' The unexpectedly inconspicuous nature of the organisation's launch in Britain must have reassured IRD: it is possible to detect a note of relief in Hamilton's observation that 'the establishment of Common Cause here has passed practically unnoticed'.[106] She would presumably have been less gratified by the fact that the organisation soon attracted left-wing allegations of engaging in, precisely, a communist witch-hunt; or by its robust response to these charges, contained in only its second *Bulletin* (July 1952), that its activities 'would be better termed a rat-hunt – save that this is unfair to the quadrupeds'.[107] Such name-calling would soon become a staple of Common Cause publicity, which alluded to the British Communist Party as the 'Muscovites' and 'the Red Army (British Non-Uniformed Section)'.[108] This red-baiting tendency reflected the growing influence over the organisation of C. A. Smith, now its General Secretary, described by IRD officer J. H. Peck as 'a fanatic who sometimes comes dangerously near to advocating witch-hunts and also appears to be vain and indiscreet'.[109] Peck attempted to rein Smith in by secretly liaising with Douglas-Hamilton and, after the latter had resigned the Chair of Common Cause (around which time he also married Natalie Paine), appealing to another Conservative MP, Tufton Beamish.[110]

Finally, IRD was concerned by the ideological heterogeneity of Common Cause, and the potential for instability this posed. In a somewhat satirical minute of December 1954, Department staff member J. Manchip White described a fund-raising cocktail party for the body he had just attended as incognito representative of the FO. Most of his fellow guests were, he noted, financiers or captains of industry: J. Arthur Rank, J. O. Barclay and W. H. Whitbread were among those present. The evening went well until the organisation's new Chairman Peter Crane (a Catholic barrister) gave a brief speech 'larded with references to the "enemy" and "anti-Christ"'.

> He persisted in referring to the stony-featured audience in front of him as the apostles of good, righteousness, decency, and just dealing. They didn't seem to be at all impressed....

This display of 'restrained fanaticism' was followed by a far more effective talk by Jack Tanner of the AEU. According to the sardonic White, 'Mr Tanner obviously didn't like the people to whom he was talking, but he liked the Communists much less'. Following this public demonstration of the tensions within Common Cause between its labour, conservative and Catholic elements, the party dispersed in a desultory fashion.[111]

Two years later, the organisation as a whole suffered a similar fate. Its labour elements broke away to launch an arguably much more effective anti-communist operation specialising in union affairs, the Industrial Research and Information Services Ltd. (IRIS), chaired by Tanner and managed by Charles Sonnex. Although the relevant FO papers have yet to be released, it would seem reasonable to assume that IRD had links to IRIS (indeed, there has been speculation about covert sponsorship by the CIA).[112] In short, a strong, corporatist partnership continued to exist between the right-wing leadership of the labour movement and the British secret state in what was a joint front against communism in the unions. This was, however, a relationship plagued by operational difficulties, of a sort which would also beset covert American activities on the non-communist left.

IRD AND THE AMERICANS

In addition to illuminating the Cold War collaboration between the Information Research Department and the British left, the recently declassified Foreign Office files also throw some revealing light on the shifting balance of power in Anglo–American relations during the early Cold War period. At first, IRD approached US anti-communist propaganda efforts with a mixture of caution and diffidence. Christopher Warner was highly circumspect in his dealings with staff at the US Embassy in London; British representatives in Washington were instructed to avoid entering any 'general agreement' which might lead to an 'undesired collaboration'.[113] This attitude was produced by a number of factors. To begin with, the Foreign Office's publicity experts appear to have had a rather poor opinion of the work produced by their American counterparts, viewing it as 'ham-handed', doubting its 'reliability' and fearing that it might 'commit some costly blunder'. Greater experience and, it was often implied, superior intellect gave the British a natural advantage in the field. There was even talk of 'educating' the Americans in the propaganda arts by influencing them 'imperceptibly in the direction of greater subtlety' and guiding their 'feet onto surer ground'.[114] Linked to this instinctive feeling of national superiority was an important strategic consideration. Whereas the Americans perceived the Soviet bloc as being highly susceptible to 'penetration by cultural and psychological weapons', in particular broadcasting, IRD was bound by ministerial decision not to incite subversion in countries behind the Iron Curtain.[115] Bound up with this rejection of 'rollback' was a general determination on the part of the Foreign Office to stake a unique territorial claim for its Cold War campaign. Representatives abroad were instructed not to give up 'any important geographical area or field of activity in favour of United States publicity', and to ensure that British and American propaganda were not 'identified in the minds of local inhabitants'.[116] Finally, there was the fact that IRD output was supposed to follow a different 'line' from that of the Americans with regard to 'social problems'.[117] In practice, as already noted, the Department tended to de-emphasise social democracy and avoid criticism of capitalism, so this was rarely a problem. Indeed, there was, as a number of British officials remarked, positive benefit to be gained from both sides 'shooting into the same target from different angles'.[118]

As this last comment suggests, IRD was not averse, in spite of its misgivings about aspects of the US Cold War campaign, to entering into occasional cooperation with the Americans when circumstances called for it. As early as February 1948, the Foreign Office had agreed arrangements for the exchange of information with the State Department, as well as between British and American representatives in the field.[119] The approach of the crucial Italian elections in April brought the two sides still closer together, with IRD sending copies of the seven 'Basic Papers' it had produced so far to Washington, and British and American personnel in Italy attending 'weekly inter-Embassy meetings'.[120] In October Warner travelled to Washington and held 'detailed and satisfactory conversations' with various State Department officials.[121] Even more successful was a visit by Adam Watson in January 1950, which raised the 'initial stage of cooperation to a new and promising level'.[122] A series of high-level meetings followed in the summer of 1950 during which it was agreed that Watson should be posted permanently to the US as IRD liaison with the various American information services.[123] This meant regular dealings not only with the State Department, but also the Central Intelligence Agency (coyly referred to by Watson as 'Joyce's Friends' – a reference presumably to the State–CIA liaison, Bob Joyce – or 'the other side of the House'), C. D. Jackson, and an array of such 'para-private' bodies as the NCFE.[124] Indeed, the range of contacts identified in Watson's correspondence with the IRD during the early 1950s suggest that his importance as a linchpin of Cold War Anglo–American relations has been underestimated by diplomatic historians.[125]

There were several reasons for IRD's increased willingness to co-operate with the Americans. One was to avoid duplication of activities, which would not only lead to waste but might also result in 'kick-back' from target populations. There were particular concerns on this score about the impact of American publicity on India.[126] Another was a continuing desire to exert British influence on the US Cold War effort: reservations about the quality of American propaganda remained, as did jealousy of IRD's freedom of manoeuvre.[127] London's hopes in this respect do not appear to have been entirely unfounded. There is some evidence of the Americans deferring to the FO's views about the conduct of Cold War propaganda in south-east Asia during the early 1950s due to Britain's greater experience and knowledge of that region.[128]

However, the main reason for increased Anglo–American liaison was the Foreign Office's gradually dawning realisation of the US's growing dominance in the field of psychological warfare. By the end of 1948, at the same time that Britain had abandoned any notion of pursuing a non-Atlanticist foreign policy, IRD was being overtaken in the anti-communist propaganda field by a number of American initiatives. The Economic Cooperation Agency (ECA) was engaged in a massive publicity effort to smooth the path of the Marshall Plan in Europe. The Office of Policy Coordination, called into existence in June 1948, had already initiated a number of covert political warfare measures in support of the ECA's overt information campaign. Even the State Department, which had at first been reluctant to join in the anti-communist crusade, was stepping up its publicity programme. At first, IRD was only vaguely aware of these developments, but knew enough to understand that the Americans were developing an unprecedented propaganda capability. Hence, when Warner departed for Washington in October 1948, he was interested less in the possibility of 'educating' the State Department than acquiring fresh research material from the rapidly expanding US publicity network.[129] Watson had a similar brief when he was dispatched to Washington in January 1950.[130] By 1954, thanks in large part to the intelligence about American operations transmitted to London by Watson, the British could be in little doubt as to where the balance of power now lay. In that year the British Ambassador in Washington, Sir Roger Makins, testified frankly to the 'enormous scale' of American research into Soviet and communist affairs, conducted by a vast range of government and 'quasi-private concerns'. In addition to this research, which formed the basis of 'most of what we know' about the eastern bloc, there was the 'enormous stream of what might be called psychological warfare ammunition' flowing from US sources. This was, Makins observed, 'of considerable value to the Information Research Department'.[131]

As leadership of the anti-communist crusade passed to the Americans, IRD's sights gradually widened from the Soviet Union to any and all targets deemed 'anti-British'. During the 1950s the Department would help defend British interests in various countries and regions, including Africa, Indonesia and, especially around the time of the Suez crisis, the Middle East. Later, during the 1970s, it was even rumoured to be active in Northern Ireland.[132] At the same time, it increasingly engaged in 'black' propaganda, the deliberate spreading of disinformation, as opposed to the grey publicity it had produced originally. Eventually, an easing of Cold War tensions, combined with growing concerns about the unit's accountability, led to its closure in 1977 at the command of – ironically enough – the then Labour Foreign Secretary, David Owen.

The fact that IRD had wandered so far from its original brief – the promotion of Britain as a social democratic Third Force in world politics – would appear to lend credence to suggestions that the Labour ministers who helped create it in 1948 were the victims of hoodwinking by their permanent officials. Yet this interpretation both exaggerates the mandarins' sway over the politicians and underestimates the pressure of

Cold War events: by 1949, even the *Keep Left* intellectuals who had invented the Third Force were backing the Atlantic alliance. Similarly, the charge that the various leftists who supported the new Department in the early years of its existence were so many political turncoats ignores the principled nature of their anti-communism and the historical precedent for cooperation with secret government agencies established during the Second World War. The fact that none of IRD's left-wing collaborators ever stopped to question the moral propriety of their actions is surely telling. Also suggestive is the fact that the professional anti-communists of the Foreign Office sometimes felt the need to dampen the Cold War fervour of their amateur allies. This last problem would prove to be an even more pronounced characteristic of the relationship between the CIA and the American non-communist left.

NOTES

1. Document releases have occurred annually since 1995. Although a considerable amount of material has therefore been declassified, much has been retained by the Foreign Office, and even those files available at the Public Record Office contain lengthy deletions.
2. See Stephen Dorril, 'The puppet masters', *Guardian* 18 August 1995. See also the same author's impressive, *MI6: Fifty Years of Special Operations* (London: Fourth Estate, 2000), chap. 3.
3. Allegations of betrayal arose mainly in relation to the revelation in 1996 that George Orwell had cooperated with IRD. See below.
4. Ernest Bevin, memorandum on 'Future Foreign Publicity', 4 January 1948, FO 1110/1, Public Record Office (PRO), London.
5. For more details of IRD's early output and its dissemination abroad, see Hugh Wilford, 'The Information Research Department: Britain's secret Cold War weapon revealed', *Review of International Studies* 24 (1998), 358–9.
6. See James Oliver, 'Britain and the covert war of words: The Information Research Department and sponsored publishing', MA thesis, University of Kent (1995), p. 14.
7. Christopher Mayhew to Secretary of State, no date, FO 1110/277, PRO.
8. See Dorril, *MI6*, chap. 3, and Raymond Smith, 'Ernest Bevin, British officials and British Soviet policy, 1945–47', in Anne Deighton (ed.), *Britain and the First Cold War* (London: Macmillan, 1990), pp. 32–52.
9. See Smith, 'Ernest Bevin', pp. 41–2.
10. See Christopher Mayhew, *Time To Explain* (London: Hutchinson, 1987), pp. 105–7. For more detail on the origins of IRD, see W. Scott Lucas and C. J. Morris, 'A very British crusade: The Information Research Department

and the beginning of the Cold War', in Richard J. Aldrich (ed.), *British Intelligence, Strategy and the Cold War, 1945–51* (London: Routledge, 1992), pp. 88–96; and Peter Weiler, *British Labor and the Cold War* (Stanford University Press, 1988), pp. 191–207.

11. See John Saville, *The Politics of Continuity: British Foreign Policy and the Labour Government* (London: Verso, 1993), chap. 1.

12. See Dianne Kirby, 'Divinely sanctioned: The Anglo–American Cold War alliance and the defence of Western civilization and Christianity, 1945–48', *Journal of Contemporary History* 35 (2000), 402–3.

13. See Dorril, *MI6*, pp. 71–2.

14. Richard J. Fletcher, 'British propaganda since World War II: A case study', *Media, Culture and Society* 4 (1982), 98.

15. Quoted in Paul Lashmar and James Oliver, *Britain's Secret Propaganda War, 1948–77* (Stroud: Sutton, 1998), p. 27.

16. Ibid., pp. 27–8.

17. See Kirby, 'Divinely sanctioned', 401.

18. Ibid., 385–412.

19. See Peter Weiler, *Ernest Bevin* (Manchester University Press, 1993), chap. 5.

20. See Saville, *Politics of Continuity*, chap. 2.

21. See Weiler, *Bevin*, p. 147.

22. Christopher Mayhew to Christopher Warner, 24 March 1948, FO 1110/41, PRO.

23. Quoted in Lyn Smith, 'Covert British propaganda: The Information Research Department, 1947–77', *Millennium: Journal of International Studies* 9 (1980), 70.

24. Christopher Mayhew to Herbert Morrison, 17 July 1948, FO 1110/41, PRO.

25. See Mayhew, *Time To Explain*, pp. 110–11.

26. In a letter of 28 September, Mayhew requested that IRD provide him with 'crisp debating points' as opposed to 'the more scholarly papers' produced to date, drew Murray's attention to propaganda items that IRD appeared to have overlooked and suggested that the Department send a representative to Paris to assist the British United Nations delegation. In a highly defensive reply, Murray pointed out that the delegation 'did not in fact consult us at all before they went', complained that last-minute requests for material 'had loaded my Department with a frantic amount of work' and stated that the 'weakness' of IRD's current resources meant it could not spare any staff for Paris. Christopher Mayhew to Ralph Murray, 28 September 1948, FO 1110/14, PRO; Ralph Murray to Christopher Mayhew, 1 October 1948, FO 1110/14, PRO.

27. See Caroline Anstey, 'The projection of British socialism: Foreign Office publicity and American opinion, 1945–50', *Journal of Contemporary History* 19 (1984), 417–51.

28. Quoted in Kevin Theakston, *The Labour Party and Whitehall* (London: Routledge, 1992), p. 27.

29. In May 1948, for example, Healey attended a meeting of senior ministers 'to discuss the possibilities of increasing the influence of the Labour Party in countering Communism in other countries'. Christopher Mayhew to Christopher Warner, 6 May 1948, FO 1110/10, PRO.

30. There is a considerable amount of IRD publicity material amongst the papers of the International Department, Labour Party Archive, National Museum of Labour History, Manchester. The friendly relationship between IRD and the International Department continued with Healey's successor, Saul Rose. See Lashmar and Oliver, *Propaganda War*, p. 111.

31. Denis Healey to Adam Watson, 2 November 1948, FO 1110/15, PRO.

32. Denis Healey to Adam Watson, 8 December 1948, FO 1110/15, PRO. Healey performed a similar service for IRD with regard to socialists in Burma.

33. Adam Watson to Denis Healey, 10 December 1948, FO 1110/15, PRO.

34. Denis Healey to Adam Watson, 17 December 1948, FO 1110/15, PRO.

35. IRD to Information Officers, 4 March 1949, FO 1110/221, PRO.

36. Lashmar and Oliver, *Propaganda War*, p. 12.

37. Ibid., p. 14.

38. The IRD papers for 1949 contain a long paper by Crossman entitled 'The Principles of Psychological Warfare', FO 1110/220, PRO.

39. Adam Watson, minute, 11 February 1949, FO 1110/215, PRO.

40. Ralph Murray to Christopher Warner, 28 January 1949, FO 1110/221, PRO.

41. Leslie Sheridan, minute, 16 June 1949, FO 1110/221, PRO. IRD approached several other publishers in 1949, including Odhams, Oxford University Press and Penguin. Leslie Sheridan to Allen Lane, 2 June 1949, FO 1110/221, PRO; Ralph Murray to Christopher Mayhew, 10 April 1949, FO 1110/221, PRO.

42. Anonymous, minute, 12 October 1949, FO 1110/221, PRO. See Lashmar and Oliver, *Propaganda War*, chap. 11, for a discussion of IRD's publishing activities in the 1950s.

43. Frances Stonor Saunders, *Who Paid the Piper? The CIA and the Cultural Cold War* (London: Granta, 1999), p. 60.

44. 'Editorial Adviser', minute, 21 February 1955, FO 1110/738, PRO.

45. IRD to Information Officers, 11 December 1950, FO 1110/365, PRO.

46. Ernest Main to Ralph Murray, 4 April 1949, FO 1110/221, PRO; Roderick Parkes to Ralph Murray, 25 October 1950, FO 1110/319, PRO.

47. H. A. H. Cortazzi to Douglas Williams, 28 January 1955, FO 1110/740, PRO. However, a Ukranian version 'came to grief', IRD worker Celia Kirwan told Charles Thayer of the US government radio station, Voice of America, 'because ... most of the copies were seized by American Military Government in Munich and handed over to the Russian Repatriation Commission'. The same letter refers to a Russian translation being 'undertaken by an impoverished but respectable group of Russian refugees in West Germany'. Celia Kirwan to Charles Thayer, 4 November 1949, FO1110/221, PRO.

48. See FO 1110/392, PRO. Following the success of the graphic version of *Animal Farm*, Leslie Sheridan considered other proposals for cartoon outlines, such as 'Greenhorn's travels – in Stalinovia', a story 'based on Voltaire's *Candide*' and '*Gulliver's Travels*'. Leslie Sheridan, minute, 18 June 1951, FO 1110/392, PRO.

49. H. A. H. Cortazzi to Douglas Williams, 28 January 55, FO 1110/740, PRO; H. A. H. Cortazzi to W. T. A. Cox, 19 February 1955, FO 1110/740, PRO. For an excellent discussion of the CIA's involvement in film productions of Orwell's novels, see Tony Shaw, *British Cinema and the Cold War: The State, Propaganda and Consensus* (London: I. B. Tauris, 2001), chap. 4.

50. Susan L. Carruthers, 'Cold War captives: Narratives of captivity and early Cold War culture in America', unpublished paper, workshop on 'Cold War Cultures and Societies', 25 March 2000, Warwick University.

51. Celia Kirwan, minute, 30 March 1949, FO 1110/189, PRO.

52. George Orwell to Celia Kirwan, 6 April 1949, FO 1110/189, PRO.

53. Celia Kirwan to George Orwell, 30 April 1949, FO 1110/189, PRO; George Orwell to Celia Kirwan, 2 May 1949, in Peter Davison (ed.), *The Complete Works of George Orwell, Volume 20: Our Job is to Make Life Worth Living, 1949–50* (London: Secker and Warburg, 1998), p. 103.

54. Richard Norton-Taylor and Seumas Milne, 'Orwell offered blacklist', *Guardian* 11 July 1996; Tom Utley, 'Orwell is revealed in role of state informer', *Daily Telegraph* 12 July 1996.

55. Quoted in Norton-Taylor and Milne, 'Orwell offered blacklist'.

56. Ros Wynne-Jones, 'Orwell's little list leaves the left gasping for more', *Independent on Sunday* 14 July 1996.

57. Michael Shelden and Philip Johnston, 'Socialist icon who became Big Brother', *Daily Telegraph* 22 June 1998. Despite the sensational headline, this article was a serious and fair treatment of the subject.

58. One interesting thing to note about 'the list' is the large number of Americans who featured on it. These included Paul Robeson (whom Orwell described as, 'Very anti-white. Wallace supporter'); John Steinbeck ('Spurious writer, pseudo-naif'); and Henry Wallace himself ('Very dishonest [i.e. intellectually].') For the list in full, see Davison (ed.), *Complete Works, Volume 20*, appendix 9. Davison, noting that 35 of the entries in the notebook have asterisks next to them, plausibly conjectures that these were the names sent to Kirwan. Ibid., p. 242.

59. Saunders, *Who Paid the Piper?*, p. 300

60. See Lashmar and Oliver, *Propaganda War*, p. 98.

61. See Davison (ed.), *Complete Works, Volume 20*, p. 103, fn. 3.

62. Ibid., p. 240.

63. Bernard Crick, 'Why are radicals so eager to give up one of their own?', *Independent on Sunday* 14 July 1996.

64. Christopher Hitchens makes this point very effectively in 'Was Orwell a

snitch?', *The Nation* 14 December 1998. See also his *Orwell's Victory* (London: Penguin, 2002).

65. John Newsinger, 'George Orwell and the IRD', *Lobster* 38 (1999), 12.
66. See Davison (ed.), *Complete Works, Volume 20*, p. 318.
67. See Lashmar and Oliver, *Propaganda War*, p. 119.
68. See chap. 1.
69. See Crick, 'Why are radicals?'.
70. Quoted in Weiler, *British Labor*, p. 366, fn. 145.
71. Quoted in ibid., fn. 147.
72. Quoted in Duncan Campbell, 'The FO and the eggheads', *New Statesman* 27 February 1981.
73. Quoted in Weiler, *British Labor*, p. 366, fn. 147.
74. Quoted in Campbell, 'FO and eggheads'.
75. Quoted in ibid.; Weiler, *British Labor*, pp. 210–11.
76. See Campbell, 'FO and eggheads'.
77. Christopher Mayhew to Christopher Warner, 3 June 1948, FO 1110/11, PRO.
78. Christopher Mayhew to Christopher Warner, 17 June 1948, FO 1110/11, PRO.
79. Christopher Warner to Christopher Mayhew, 16 June 1948, FO 1110/11, PRO; Christopher Mayhew, minute, 8 September 1948, FO 1110/13, PRO. Mayhew went on, 'We should agree to do this as far as possible without compromising IFF [International *Freedom First*] as an independent T. U. paper ... I shall expect the greatest discretion to be observed.'
80. Information Officers were told by the IRD that 'The Defence of Democracy Trust' was acting 'entirely unofficially'. IRD to Information Officers, 30 July 1948, FO 1110/11, PRO.
81. Ralph Murray, minute, 3 September 1948, FO 1110/13, PRO.
82. J. H. Peck, minute, no date, FO 1110/521, PRO.
83. See Weiler, *British Labor*, pp. 217–18; Christopher Mayhew, *A War of Words: A Cold War Witness* (London: I. B. Tauris, 1998), p. 41.
84. Christopher Mayhew to Ernest Bevin, 6 January 1949, FO1110/213, PRO.
85. T. S. Tull, minute, 3 May 1951, FO 1110/380, PRO.
86. IRD to Information Officers, 31 January 1949, FO 1110/213, PRO.
87. T. S. Tull, minute, 3 May 1951, FO 1110/380, PRO.
88. Ralph Murray to Christopher Mayhew, 10 April 1949, FO 1110/221, PRO. Discussion about the possibility of producing an international labour newsletter in collaboration with the TUC continued throughout 1949. At one point Hector McNeil suggested involving the AFL's European representative Irving Brown in the venture and recommended his *Free Trade Unions News* as a possible model for such a publication. In response, Ralph Murray advised strongly against 'Brown having anything but an invisible hand in things'. Hector McNeil to Christopher Mayhew, 13 January 1949, FO1110/213, PRO; Ralph Murray, minute, 25 January 1949, FO1110/213, PRO.

89. See Lashmar and Oliver, *Propaganda War*, p. 109.

90. Robert Taylor, *The TUC: From the General Strike to New Unionism* (Basingstoke: Palgrave, 2000), p. 167; John S. Beamish to Vic Feather, 17 January 1949, TUC Papers, 770/5, Modern Records Centre, Warwick University.

91. Leslie Sheridan, minute, 12 August 1950, FO 1110/380, PRO; J. H. Peck, minute, 19 January 1951, FO 1110/380, PRO.

92. Leslie Sheridan, minute, 24 November 1952, FO 1110/521, PRO.

93. F. J. C. Mennell, 'Report on 53rd annual conference of the Labour Party, Scarborough, September 21–October 1', 4 October 1954, FO 1110/704, PRO. IRD operative Mennell also reported from Scarborough, 'It was useful to renew contact with Sam Watson, Philip Noel-Baker, Hugh Gaitskell, John Hynd and many other MPs and Party officials'. On IRD commissioning the miners' leader to contribute to its Background Books series, see correspondence between Watson and Stephen Watts in Box 55, Sam Watson Papers, Durham County Record Office, Durham.

94. See Lashmar and Oliver, *Propaganda War*, pp. 106, 111.

95. Geoffrey Goodman, interview with author, 1 September 2000, London. Fellow unionist Len Murray described Feather as 'very effective, very knowledgeable. [He] shared some of the qualities of the CP (from [his] own ILP background) – perseverance, attention to detail.' Quoted in Richard Stevens, 'Cold War politics: Communism and anti-communism in the trade unions', in Alan Campbell, Nina Fishman and John McIlroy (eds), *British Trade Unions and Industrial Politics, Volume 1: The Postwar Compromise, 1945–64* (Aldershot: Ashgate Press, 1999), p. 172.

96. See Robin Ramsay, 'The clandestine caucus: Anti-socialist campaigns and operations in the British labour movement since the war', *Lobster* special issue, 7-11; Dorril, *MI6*, pp. 436–7.

97. Lord Malcolm Douglas-Hamilton and John Brown to 'Mrs Hamilton', November 1951, FO1110/374, PRO.

98. 'Common Cause' publicity pamphlet, TUC Papers, 770.2/3.

99. P. Clavell Blount to Vic Feather, 16 November 1952, TUC Papers, 770.2/3; Common Cause *Bulletin* 34 (March 1955), TUC Papers, 770.2/3.

100. Common Cause's other publicity work included: publishing leaflets and pamphlets; holding regular meetings and lectures; supplying speakers and a mobile film unit; and providing 'a small but efficient Information Service increasingly used by anti-communist lecturers, journalists, etc.'. 'Common Cause' publicity pamphlet, TUC Papers, 770.2/3.

101. J. Manchip White, minute, 16 December 1954, FO1110/704, PRO.

102. For example, J. H. Peck met regularly with Lord Douglas-Hamilton and kept him supplied with IRD publicity materials. See J. H. Peck to Lord Malcolm Douglas-Hamilton, 3 December 1951, FO 1110/374, PRO.

103. Desmond Morton to J. H. Peck, 28 November 1951, FO 1110/374, PRO. Paine visited Britain in the summer of 1951, when she met J. H. Peck

and was introduced to Denis Healey. Anonymous, memorandum on 'Information Research Department's Dealings with Common Cause', 27 February 1953, FO1110/547, PRO.

104. Desmond Morton to J. H. Peck, 28 November 1951, FO 1110/374, PRO; C. B. Ormerod, 'Aide Memoire' about Common Cause, 20 November 1951, FO 1110/374, PRO.

105. Adam Watson to A. C. E. Malcolm, 5 November 1951, FO 1110/374, PRO; Mollie Hamilton to D'Arcy Edmonson, 6 December 1951, FO 1110/374, PRO. Similar jurisdictional concerns arose when a possible merger between Common Cause and a CIA-funded French anti-communist organisation, Paix et Liberté, was discussed. See J. H. Peck, 'Paix et Liberté and Common Cause', 1 March 1953, FO1110/547, PRO.

106. Mollie Hamilton to D'Arcy Edmonson, 6 December 1951, FO 1110/374, PRO.

107. Common Cause *Bulletin* 2 (July 1952), TUC Papers, 770.2/3.

108. Common Cause *Bulletin* 8 (January 1953), TUC Papers, 770.2/3.

109. J. H. Peck, 'Paix et Liberté and Common Cause', 1 March 1953, FO1110/547, PRO.

110. J. H. Peck to Sir Anthony Meyer, 20 March 1953, FO1110/547, PRO. Beamish was also involved in discussions about the possible merger of Common Cause and Paix et Liberté.

111. J. Manchip White, minute, 16 December 1954, FO 1110/704, PRO.

112. See Ramsay, 'Clandestine caucus', 10-11. There is material relating to IRIS in the TUC Papers, 770.2/6.

113. Christopher Warner to Sir John Balfour, 16 February 1948, FO 1110/1, PRO.

114. Ibid.; IRD to Information Officers, 12 May 1948, FO 1110/6, PRO; Sir John Balfour to Christopher Warner, 25 February 1948, FO 1110/24, PRO.

115. Sir John Balfour to Charles Bateman, 14 February 1948, FO 1110/24, PRO.

116. IRD to Information Officers, 12 May 1948, FO 1110/6, PRO.

117. Christopher Warner to Sir John Balfour, 16 February 1948, FO 1110/1, PRO; IRD to Information Officers, 12 May 1948, FO 1110/6, PRO.

118. Christopher Warner to Sir John Balfour, 26 February 1948, FO 1110/1, PRO.

119. Christopher Warner to Sir John Balfour, 16 February 1948, FO 1110/1, PRO; Christopher Warner to Sir John Balfour, 26 February 1946, FO 1110/1, PRO; Bill Edwards to Christopher Warner, 19 February 1948, FO 1110/24, PRO; Sir John Balfour to Christopher Warner, 25 February 1948, FO 1110/24, PRO.

120. Sir Victor Mallet to Christopher Warner, 18 March 1948, FO 1110/3, PRO; Christopher Warner to Sir Victor Mallet, 28 March 1948, FO 1110/1, PRO; Christopher Warner to Sir John Balfour, 12 April 1948, FO 1110/5/196, PRO; Sir John Balfour to Christopher Warner, 20 April 1948,

FO 1110/7, PRO; Sir Victor Mallet to Christopher Warner, 30 April 1948, FO 1110/8, PRO.
121. Ralph Murray to C. Holt, 23 November 1948, FO 1110/122, PRO.
122. Llewellyn E. Thompson to Derick Hoyer Millar, 20 February 1950, FO 1110/305, PRO.
123. Christopher Warner, 'Publicity in, and about, South East Asia and the Far East: Liaison with the State Department', no date [presumably about August 1950], FO 1110/305, PRO.
124. Adam Watson to J. H. Peck, 6 July 1951, FO 1110/383, PRO.
125. See, for example, Adam Watson to J. W. Nicholls, 17 July 1953, FO 1110/587, PRO, which communicates the gist of personal conversations with George Kennan, Walter Bedell Smith and Charles Bohlen.
126. Christopher Warner to Sir Frederick Hoyer-Millar, 31 December 1949, FO 1110/236, PRO.
127. Christopher Warner to Denis Allen, 3 November 1949, FO 1110/236, PRO; Christopher Warner to Sir Frederick Hoyer-Millar, 31 December 1949, FO 1110/236, PRO; P. A. Wilkinson to Emile P. Lecours, 14 August 1951, FO 1110/400, PRO.
128. See Tony Shaw, 'The Information Research Department of the British Foreign Office and the Korean War, 1950–53', *Journal of Contemporary History* 34 (1999), 263–81.
129. Christopher Warner to Sir Frederick Hoyer-Millar, 22 September 1948, FO 1110/14, PRO.
130. Christopher Warner to Sir Frederick Hoyer-Millar, 31 December 1949, FO 1110/236, PRO. It was perhaps significant that the US did not station an officer corresponding to Watson in London. Plans to post an American called 'Frye' were not executed, leaving Watson to oversee Anglo–American liaison single-handedly. Adam Watson to Christopher Warner, 6 June 1951, FO 1110/ 374, PRO.
131. Sir Roger Makins to Anthony Eden, 31 July 1954, FO 1110/684, PRO. For more detail on IRD's relations with the Americans, see Richard J. Aldrich, *The Hidden Hand: Britain, America and Cold War Secret Intelligence* (London: John Murray, 2001), especially chaps 5 and 20.
132. See Lashmar and Oliver, *Propaganda War*, chap. 17.

3

CIA and NCL

The Central Intelligence Agency did not, as a rule, intervene directly in the European left. Rather, as with so much of the American Cold War effort, it did so indirectly, by proxy, in highly sophisticated covert operations involving those elements of the American non-communist left with most experience of combating communism and the best links with their European counterparts. Indeed, these CIA operations tended to be based on initiatives that had originally been developed by American leftists. Therefore, in order to understand fully the US intervention in left-wing British politics which took place in the early years of the Cold War, we need a prior understanding of the relationship between the CIA and American non-communist left, or 'NCL', as it was designated by Agency officers.

Before the CIA's covert operations were exposed in public, the tendency was to view the left-wing American anti-communists active in Cold War European politics as disinterested, even heroic, defenders of political freedom.[1] After the late 1960s, when a series of newspaper reports revealed the basic facts of the Agency's secret sponsorship of the NCL, this view was exchanged for that of a puppet-on-a-string, with the unionists and intellectuals involved now portrayed as so many stooges or 'patsies' of the American national security establishment.[2] In recent years, with the opening of new archival collections (all, admittedly, on the non-communist left's side of the equation – the CIA still refuses to release the relevant records from its files), a third picture has emerged. This depicts a far more complex and problematic relationship than was previously supposed, involving an ongoing struggle for control of covert operations. While it is true that the CIA usually got the better of the NCL in this struggle, the leftists nonetheless remained in the picture – the secrecy in which the Agency was forced to operate meant that it needed them as 'fronts' – a contradiction which created a profound tension at the heart of the US's covert Cold War network.

The fact that the Information Research Department was first in the field of secret anti-communist propaganda testifies to the hesitancy with which the Americans undertook covert operations after the Second World War. In September 1945, President Harry Truman abolished the Office of Strategic Services (OSS), the civilian intelligence agency established in the wake of Pearl Harbor, explaining he wanted no part in the creation of an 'American Gestapo'.[3] 'Psychological warfare' – the term used by Americans for measures designed to undermine enemy morale and foster resistance movements in occupied territories – was also discarded as un-American, with US information services abroad being gradually wound down (except in areas of special significance such as Germany).[4] As cracks began appearing in the Grand Alliance, support did gradually grow in official circles for the establishment of a peacetime secret service. However, even after the creation of the CIA by the National Security Act of July 1947, the prejudice against 'dirty tricks' remained. Director of Central Intelligence (DCI) Admiral Roscoe K. Hillenkoetter strongly opposed calls that the new Agency undertake covert operations, preferring to stick with what was deemed in military circles to be the more respectable business of intelligence collection and analysis.[5]

The fact that the US did eventually engage in anti-communist political warfare was thanks in no small part to persistent agitation by specific groups of individuals located both within and outside government, usefully identified by historian Sallie Pisani as the 'determined interventionists'.[6] As in Britain, where former officers of the Political Warfare Executive were among those pressing for the creation of an anti-communist agency in the Foreign Office, wartime covert operatives were in the vanguard of this movement. OSS chief, General William 'Wild Bill' Donovan and his deputy, Allen W. Dulles, now reluctantly back on 'civvie street' (or, to be more accurate, Park Avenue – both men were corporate lawyers practising in New York), constantly lobbied the Truman administration to revive covert political and psychological warfare, while at the same time carrying out their own private operations in postwar Europe.[7] Joining these espionage luminaries in their calls for more determined intervention was a cadre of anti-communist intellectuals in the State Department disaffected from what they perceived as the excessively pro-Soviet outlook of post-New Deal Washington, men like future Ambassador to France, Charles 'Chip' Bohlen and Moscow Embassy official, George F. Kennan (again, there are parallels here with the British situation, and the crucial presence of strongly anti-Soviet officials in the FO). Kennan, installed as Director of the powerful Policy Planning Staff (PPS) in 1947 after his return to Washington, has long been recognised as the chief architect of the US Cold War policy of 'containment'. Recently released documents have revealed the great extent to which his definition of containment anticipated the more aggressive strategy of 'rollback' usually associated with John Foster Dulles and the Eisenhower administration.[8]

The first significant victory for the determined interventionists came in December 1947, when the National Security Council (NSC) directed DCI Hillenkoetter to undertake 'covert psychological operations to counteract Soviet and Soviet-inspired activities which constitute a threat to world peace and security, or are designed to discredit and defeat the United States in its endeavors to promote a world peace and security'.[9] This resulted in the creation of the Special Procedures Group (SPG), which was soon setting up 'black' radio stations and dropping propaganda by balloon into the 'occupied' countries of eastern Europe. [10] However, the interventionists were not satisfied: continuing obstructionism by Hillenkoetter combined with the demonstrable success of psychological warfare campaigns in France and Italy in early 1948 to create pressure for a more responsive and offensive clandestine unit in place of SPG. On 4 May 1948, against a background of mounting Cold War tension caused by the beginning of the Berlin blockade, Kennan's PPS presented a plan for 'the inauguration of organized political warfare' involving 'the creation of a covert political warfare operations directorate within the Government'.[11] Kennan, who believed that the SPG had operated too 'freely', wanted this body under the control of the State Department. This last proviso was resisted by Allen Dulles, then seconded to Washington to carry out a review of CIA operations, who, supported by Defense Secretary James V. Forrestal, insisted that covert operations should be located in the CIA's Office of Special Operations. After a period of bureaucratic infighting, a compromise was reached whereby the new organisation was to be quartered and rationed by the CIA but accept policy guidance from the Secretary of State (which meant, in effect, Kennan's PPS).[12] NSC directive 10/2, approved on 18 June 1948, ratified Kennan's proposals of May by replacing SPG with a new body authorised to conduct 'any covert activities related to',

> propaganda; economic warfare; preventive direct action, including sabotage, anti-sabotage, demolition and evacuation measures; sub-version against hostile states, including assistance to underground resistance movements, guerrillas and refugee liberation groups, and support of indigenous anti-communist elements in threatened countries of the free world.[13]

The Office of Policy Coordination (OPC), as the new unit soon became known (a deliberately opaque appellation reminiscent of IRD's), was placed under the charge of one of Dulles's 'Park Avenue cowboys', former head of OSS intelligence and New York lawyer Frank G. Wisner (Dulles himself had passed up the job in the belief that he would become DCI in a Republican administration following the presidential election of 1948).[14] As the Assistant Director for Policy Coordination, the extra-ordinarily energetic and driven Wisner inherited SPG's budget and acquired access to the 'counterpart funds' set aside for administrative expenses connected with the Marshall Plan. He lost no time in recruit-ing to the OPC staff rather like himself, former OSS officers and profes-sionals with European experience, in the process creating (in the words of one recruit from Princeton who later would become DCI, William Colby), 'the atmosphere of an order of Knights Templars, to save Western freedom from Communist darkness'.[15] The new recruits were either assigned to headquarters in Washington (then housed in a collection of huts strewn along the Mall) or placed undercover in diplomatic posts and military bases abroad. The Washington-based personnel were split into five 'Functional Groups' – psychological warfare, political warfare, economic warfare, preventive direct action and 'miscellaneous' – and, in imitation of the Marshall Plan, six geographical divisions, whose heads controlled the field-staff.[16] In practice, however, OPC officers abroad, who were usually second-in-command at their embassy, enjoyed a large measure of autonomy, often initiating their own opera-tions or 'projects', as they were called.[17] The independence of individual officers was mirrored by that of the organisation as a whole, which, although housed by the CIA and guided by State, was, thanks to its access to the 'unvouchered' Marshall Plan funds, which amounted to more than $2 million a year, practically non-accountable.[18] The determined interventionists had triumphed: covert operations, including psychological warfare, had now acquired truly effective organisational form.

However, creating the official machinery was only one stage of the process. Much as the new political warfare task-force had partly originated in the actions of individuals outside government, so now the determined interventionists turned to the private sphere in order to execute the covert operations they were proposing. As in Britain, the mobilisation of supportive elements in civil society was necessary not only to conceal the fact that the US government was engaging in propaganda and other practices associated with 'totalitarian' states – in short, to preserve secrecy – but also to gain access to institutions and groups which would otherwise be outside operational reach. This strategy would have the additional advantage of creating the appearance that private American citizens were acting spontaneously to defend the independence of those countries under threat from Soviet annexation. The much-vaunted voluntarism and associationalism of the American people would make this impression all the more plausible. As George Kennan observed in his memorandum of May 1948:

> What is proposed here is an operation in the traditional American form: organized public support of resistance to tyranny in foreign countries. Throughout our history, private American citizens have banded together to champion the cause of freedom for people suffering under oppression.... Our proposal is that this tradition be revived specifically to further American national interests in the present crisis.[19]

The first priority of this 'State-private network' (to use historian Scott Lucas's helpful phrase) was to deal with the political leadership of the thousands of refugees who had fled to the west from the 'satellite countries' in eastern Europe.[20] Exile groups had been regarded as a valuable source of information about the Soviet Union since the end of the Second World War: one of the unstated aims of the so-called 'de-Nazification' programme operated by the American Military Government in western Germany was to extract anti-communist intelligence from displaced Nazi collaborators. As the Cold War intensified, the determined interventionists became increasingly aware of the refugees' value as 'a potential secret army'.[21] To this end, Kennan's memorandum on the inauguration of political warfare proposed the formation of 'Liberation

Committees' amongst national groups to increase refugee morale, inspire resistance within eastern bloc populations and 'serve as a potential nucleus for all-out liberation movements in the event of war'. To encourage this process, Kennan proposed the establishment of a public committee by 'trusted American citizens' which would give practical assistance to exile leaders. This committee 'should receive covert guidance and possibly assistance from the government'.[22]

The outcome of this proposal was the prototypical state–private organisation, the National Committee for a Free Europe. The NCFE (later the Free Europe Committee) was a private corporation chartered by the State of New York in May 1949 after Allen Dulles's law firm had drawn up the necessary legal papers. The post of Executive Secretary was assumed by DeWitt C. Poole, who during the Second World War had been in charge of the OSS Foreign Nationalities Branch.[23] The organisation's expenses, including the lease on its Empire State Building office suite, were paid for by the OPC, although this fact was revealed only on a 'need-to-know' basis: when the question of funding came up at Executive Committee meetings, Poole would refer mysteriously to 'our friends in the South'.[24] Soon the NCFE had set up a radio station to broadcast behind the Iron Curtain (Radio Free Europe), founded a Free European University in Exile in Strasbourg and launched a domestic information campaign called the 'Crusade for Freedom', under the leadership of General Dwight D. Eisenhower.[25] By this point it had been joined by a sister organisation, the American Committee for the Liberation of the Peoples of Russia, designed to cater for defectors from the Soviet Union itself, which also operated a radio station, Radio Liberty.[26] Both in terms of inspiration and membership, all these groups were coterminous with the élite band of Park Avenue cowboys who had helped create the OPC in the first place.

Encouraging the disintegration of the eastern bloc was the ultimate objective of Kennan's containment strategy, but it was also imperative that the US do what it could to prevent further communist incursions into western Europe. In addition to the Cold War mobilisation of émigré groups, Kennan's memo of May 1948 had identified as a priority for the new covert operations directorate the 'support of indigenous anti-communist elements in threatened countries of the Free World'.[27] In Europe, this would mean secretly assisting the non-communist left, that is socialist and social democratic politicians, centrist or right-wing trade union leaders and ex-communist literary intellectuals. The European right, after all, had its own resources and, in any case, its anti-communism could be taken for granted. Moreover, the forces of conservatism were on the retreat throughout the continent, discredited as they were by their association with fascism, and the left in the political ascendancy, most spectacularly, of course, in Labour Britain. It would therefore be on the terrain of the European left that the battle for 'hearts and minds' would be at its most intense; and anti-communist leftists were potentially Washington's most valuable allies in this fight. 'The trend in Europe is clearly toward the left', explained one State Department official. 'I feel that we should try to keep it a non-Communist left and should support Social Democratic governments.'[28]

This tactical ploy chimed in with the natural ideological preferences of the other main grouping of determined interventionists besides the Park Avenue cowboys, anti-communist diplomats like Kennan and Chip Bohlen. During the war years, the latter's Georgetown house had become a salon for various intellectuals who shared his fascination with Russia and hatred of communism. These included the influential Washington journalist, Joseph W. Alsop, his brother Stewart, and the Russian-born Oxford philosophy don, then working in the Washington British Embassy, Isaiah Berlin. According to Joe Alsop's later recollection, Bohlen and Berlin were 'too astute and farseeing to believe that the brittle, right-wing, anti-Soviet sentiment that some early Soviet and eastern European émigrés to the West had begun to advocate could have much future'.[29] Instead, they viewed the democratic socialist elements of European politics, which they adumbrated in the phrase 'non-communist left', as the most effective bulwark against Soviet expansion. Before long the NCL was catching on in State Department circles, not merely as shorthand for European social democrats but also their counterparts in the US, liberals and former socialists of the kind who would shortly form the anti-communist rival to Henry Wallace's Progressive Party, Americans for Democratic Action. Harvard historian and OSS intelligence analyst, Arthur M. Schlesinger Jr., already developing into the leading theoretician of ADA-style liberal anti-communism, first heard the initials when a fellow guest at a dinner party thrown by Joe Alsop, State Department consultant and former OSS-er Charles Thayer, turned to him saying, 'So, you're NCL as well'.[30] Later in the decade Schlesinger would give the concept its classic formulation in his seminal political tract, *The Vital Centre* (1949), in which he described the non-communist left as 'the standard to rally the groups fighting to carve out an area for freedom'.[31]

How, though, was the NCL strategy to operate in practice? This is where the advice of leftist intellectuals who were not part of Kennan and

Bohlen's Georgetown salon came in. 'The feeling was we had to fight fire with fire', explained Arthur Cox, a CIA officer who specialised in psychological warfare during the early 1950s, 'to use communist methods to fight communists.'[32] Who better to advise the OPC, then, than ex-communists like Arthur Koestler? Shortly before he departed Europe for the US on a 1948 speaking tour intended to alert American liberals to the danger of Soviet expansionism, Koestler met with Chip Bohlen to discuss possible western responses to the launch of the communist 'peace' offensive. While crossing the Atlantic he talked about Cold War strategy with a fellow passenger, Allen Dulles's brother and future Secretary of State, John Foster Dulles. Arrived in New York, he lunched with Bill Donovan, noting afterwards in his diary, 'Discussed need for psychological warfare. First-rate brain.'[33] After delivering a lecture in Washington in which he satirised the American fellow traveller as 'the Left Babbitt', Koestler held a series of meetings at which various government officials picked his brains about Soviet propaganda techniques. He was, according to his biographer, Iain Hamilton, 'exasperated to the point of anger by the extraordinary naivety he encountered'.[34] The author of *Darkness at Noon* was not only in demand in Whitehall: his inside knowledge of the communist camp was prized on both sides of the Atlantic.

However, the OPC's most valued consultant amongst the ranks of ex-communist intellectuals was an American, the former Trotskyist and future 'godfather' of American neo-conservatism, James Burnham. Judging by various clues scattered throughout his personal papers at Stanford University, Burnham's professional relationship with the OPC began in the summer of 1949, when a Princeton classmate by the name of Joseph Bryan, who had been recruited to the organisation only a few months earlier to run its Psychological Warfare Workshop, approached him in the hope of engaging him 'as an expert consultant'.[35] Evidently Burnham himself must have raised the matter of his Trotskyist past, because in a subsequent letter Bryan felt the need to reassure him that 'the chief of my branch' (presumably Frank Wisner) did not share his 'apprehension about possible embarrassment to the administration'.[36] In any event, by July Burnham had obtained the necessary security clearance to begin his consultancy with the OPC.[37] In the years that followed he was to provide advice on, in the words of E. Howard Hunt (a CIA officer before achieving notoriety as one of Richard Nixon's White House 'plumbers'), 'virtually every subject of interest to our organization'.[38] A particular area of expertise in the early 1950s was eastern European politics: Burnham played a crucial part in the OPC's attempts to organise political refugees from Iron Curtain countries into an anti-Soviet resistance movement. He was, for example, the organisation's main point of contact with the group of Polish exiles associated with the Paris-based journal *Kultura*, a tendency he considered representative of what 'the liberation movement as a whole ought to be', that is 'irreconcilably anti-Bolshevik but at the same democratic', 'activist ... but also intellectually sophisticated' and, finally, willing to accept 'American leadership'. One of the leaders of this group, Joseph Czapski, proposed to Burnham the creation of 'an East European "institute" or "university" located in Europe ... financed and directed by the US'.[39] This proposal was eventually to develop into the NCFE's Free Europe University in Strasbourg.

This was not simply a case of the American intelligence service 'using' a left-wing intellectual. If anything, Burnham was performing a role like that played by the 'determined interventionists', attempting to impose his anti-communist agenda on the US government. Something of his attitude towards American officialdom and the Cold War can be gleaned from correspondence between him and his colleague in New York University's (NYU) Philosophy Department, Sidney Hook. In an August 1946 letter to Hook, Burnham gave voice to his conviction that 'either western civilization is going to be ... literally destroyed ... or the United States will have to take the leadership in the destruction of communism and the organization of some kind of workable world political system'.[40] His *Struggle for the World*, published the following year, was an attempt to awaken the American people to the scale of the Soviet threat and their duty to combat it. Despite the Truman Doctrine and other signs of awakening official resolution to resist Soviet expansion, Burnham's own anti-communism continued to outstrip that of government's. 'The only morsel of hope that I've swallowed during these months is from my southern excursion', he told Hook in December 1948, in an oblique reference to his recent sallies to OPC headquarters in Washington. 'The people there seem to understand what is, and what should be done better than any other group of which I know.'

However, Burnham's enthusiasm about America's new covert action agents was qualified. 'They do not', he remarked to Hook, 'know how to implement their knowledge and willingness. We ought to be able to find some way to help them – and ourselves – there.'[41] With this in mind, Burnham attempted to put Hook in touch with OPC. He also tried to arrange a meeting in Washington between Arthur Koestler and 'a dozen or so persons to which you might be a severe and needed teacher' (adding, in case Koestler was in any doubt about whom he meant, 'I am *not* referring to editors of the *Partisan Review*').[42] Still, Burnham's Cold War commitment continued to exceed that of the Truman administration. A paper presented to OPC in or about 1950, 'The Strategy of the Politburo and the Problem of American Counter-Strategy', echoed his book of the same year, *The Coming Defeat of Communism*, by urging an aggressive campaign 'on the most massive scale' designed to bring about 'the disintegration of the communist élite'.[43] Burnham's advocacy of rollback, soon to find its most famous expression in his 1953 *Containment or Liberation?*, was associated with a growing political conservatism, which manifested itself in a populist identification with 'the masses' and – ironically, considering his radical background – increasing dissatisfaction with the OPC's NCL strategy (of which more below). In short, Burnham was not merely advising official opinion – he was actively trying to shape it.

Much the same was true of the third major ex-communist intellectual in the CIA's 'stable' of consultants, Burnham's NYU colleague, Sidney Hook. The evidence concerning Hook's relationship with the intelligence services is less clear than in Burnham's case. Certainly he performed consultancy work for the CIA after Walter Bedell Smith became DCI in 1950. The general was a great admirer of the professor, recommending him to Edward W. Barrett, Assistant Secretary of State with special responsibility for overt anti-communist psychological warfare, as in possession of 'a profound and accurate knowledge and appreciation of Communist political philosophy'.[44] Hook also consulted with the Psychological Strategy Board, the body created in 1951 to oversee and coordinate official anti-communist propaganda work, corresponding with its first director, Gordon Gray, and writing to his successor, Raymond B. Allen, even before he had taken up the position, to offer his advice on psychological warfare. 'This subject has interested me for years', Hook told Allen, 'and I have watched despairingly as we have lost one round after another to the Kremlin.'[45]

However, Hook's relations with the OPC were, judging by the available evidence, less happy. Correspondence with Burnham from the late 1940s suggests a certain reluctance on the part of the new covert operations agency to contact the philosopher. In January 1949, for example, Burnham expressed surprise that Hook had not yet 'heard from my friends', interpreting this as 'a very bad sign'.[46] OPC's diffidence possibly resulted from the fact that, whereas Burnham had escaped investigation by the FBI, Hook was the subject of an Internal Security Case in 1943 after J. Edgar Hoover had spotted a *Daily Worker* article describing him as 'the chief carrier of Trotskyite bacilli' at NYU.[47] Another possibility is that Hook had already earned a reputation in government circles as being too zealous an anti-communist and too plain a speaker. In April 1948, for example, he had blasted the State Department for its 'utter ineptness' in failing to adopt an 'aggressive approach' in its radio broadcasting, fulminating:

> Whoever formulated this policy doesn't understand the world he is living in, is abysmally ignorant of Central Europe, and ought to be retired to some field where he can do less damage to the fight for democratic survival.[48]

Like his fellow professor Burnham – although possessing fewer social graces – Hook's attitude to government officials was distinctly didactic. In September 1948, after spending a week consulting with General Lucius D. Clay and other administrators of the American occupation zone in Germany, he wrote to Burnham informing him, without any apparent irony, that 'they have accepted my diagnosis of the situation in Europe'.[49]

The involvement of ex-communists like Koestler, Burnham and Hook in the planning of the covert American campaign was to have momentous consequences. For one thing, it helped ensure that the OPC's operations on the non-communist left would basically imitate those of the Soviets. As Burnham (whose own analyses of the Soviet system and proposals to destroy it always had a slightly Marxian flavour – ex-communist Louis Fischer once described him as 'communistically anti-communist') put it in one of his memoranda to OPC, 'The basis and aim of Soviet strategy imply the basis and aim of the only feasible American counter-strategy'.[50] For another, it would cause a host of operational problems for the OPC, not so much because of the security risk involved in employing people who had once been communists – these converts were amongst the most fanatical devotees of the American cause in the Cold War – but because they thought they knew better than government officials how to fight the Soviet threat. The extent of the problems facing the OPC is graphically demonstrated by a closer examination of the two principal organisational vehicles of its campaign on the non-communist left, Jay Lovestone's Free Trade Union Committee and the Congress for Cultural Freedom.

92

THE FREE TRADE UNION COMMITTEE

The collaboration between the OPC and FTUC got underway in December 1948 when Lovestone, who was already friendly with DCI Hillenkoetter, was formally introduced to Frank Wisner by Committee Chairman Matthew Woll.[51] Lovestone received his first payment from Wisner the following month. This and subsequent OPC subsidies were disguised in the FTUC's accounts as donations from generous individuals (and referred to in the code language Lovestone soon evolved for his secret dealings with Wisner as 'books' or 'volumes' from the OPC's 'library').[52] Meanwhile, Irving Brown, the FTUC's Paris-based European representative, (who had earlier forged a close relationship with Bill Donovan while carrying out secret work for the OSS's labour desk),[53] received payments directly from the Marshall Plan 'counterpart funds'. These he and his wife Lillie Brown 'piggy-backed' to non-communist labour elements all over Europe: in France the Force Ouvrière (Lovestone talked of Brown's budget for 'French perfume'); in Italy the LCGIL ('spaghetti'); and in Finland the socialist majority in the SAK ('lumber').[54] Although the most visible, Brown was not the only FTUC field agent now handling covert US government subsidies: Lovestone had a network of operatives, mainly ex-communists like himself, spanning the world, some of whom, such as Willard Etter in China, were involved in para-military activities.[55] OPC expenditure on the Lovestoneite network rose steadily: in 1950 FTUC account books listed individual donations amounting to $170,000.[56] This was a classic US Cold War front operation, Lovestone turning the tactics pioneered by the Comintern back on the Soviets.

That said, the FTUC was no mere tool of American government policy. Indeed, the American Federation of Labor had been funding its own programme of assistance to non-communist unionists in Europe for several years before the OPC was even invented. In part this reflected the intense anti-communism of such AFL leaders as Woll and David Dubinsky, not to mention the particularly bitter hatred of Stalinism felt by the Lovestoneites. The destruction of the World Federation of Trade Unions was as important an objective of the AFL's in this period as was positive support for the forces of democratic trade unionism. Also significant, however, was the powerful tradition of internationalist labour solidarity most evident amongst members of the New York garment unions which earlier had found organisational expression in such bodies as the Jewish Labor Committee. It is perhaps telling that one of the conduits for OPC funds employed by the FTUC in 1949 was the JLC's

93

3 Irving Brown, European representative of the American Federation of Labor and CIA agent, George Meany, AFL president, and Arthur Deakin, powerful general secretary of the Transport and General Workers Union. (Jay Lovestone Papers, Hoover Institution, Stanford University)

European bank account.[57] In any event, the fact is that the leaders of the AFL had spontaneously spent as much as $35,000 a year out of the Federation's own purse on the FTUC's overseas activities.[58] Moreover, since first touring postwar Europe in October 1945, Irving Brown had been acting more or less on his own in conveying American support to European 'free' trade unions. This was indeed Lovestone's 'finest hour', before the injection of large sums of secret government money began, arguably, to corrupt his foreign operations.[59]

Considering that the AFL had the field of overseas labour operations pretty much to itself in the immediate postwar period – the Congress of Industrial Organizations was still trying to make a go of the WFTU – it is not surprising that the FTUC should have regarded the OPC's sudden interest in its activities with mixed feelings. On the one hand, Lovestone and Brown were naturally glad of the extra funding: it had been clear for some time now that the AFL's subsidies were not enough by themselves to support the sort of operations that would be necessary to defeat communist influence in European trade unions. On the other, their expertise in anti-communist warfare – combined with their chronic factionalism – meant that they were bound to resent any official attempts to control their activities. Lovestone adopted a simple definition of his new patron's duties: providing money in large quantities, while leaving the actual job of covert anti-communist warfare to himself and his agents. Indeed, Lovestone's attitude towards the professional covert operatives with whom he dealt was condescending, even disdainful, not unlike that he displayed towards ex-socialists in the American labour movement. The code-name he employed for these raw novices in the anti-communist struggle was indicative: they were the 'Fizz kids'.[60]

Unfortunately for Lovestone, the OPC did not share his minimalist interpretation of its patronage function. Although generous, its subsidies were not indiscriminate. Rather, they were carefully targeted, reflecting the US government's strategic priorities in the Cold War. For example, when the focus of international tension in south-east Asia shifted from China to Korea, support for Willard Etter's anti-communist insurgency operations dried up, with the result that several of his agents were left stranded, captured and executed.[61] Meanwhile, Brown's operations in Europe were constantly stymied by the irregularity of OPC funding. 'Volumes' for 'the lumber people' were promised then withheld; delays to the 'French budget' meant Brown was unable to purchase any 'perfume'; having assured Lovestone 'that there would be five cook books for the spaghetti chefs', the Fizz kids 'backwatered and doublecrossed'

95

him.[62] In addition to regulating the flow of money to the FTUC 'on a drip-feed basis', the OPC also demanded that Lovestone give a fuller account of his expenditure than he had with AFL monies, CIA security chief Sheffield Edwards even opening the Committee's mail to monitor its outgoings.[63] Lovestone was infuriated by what he perceived as 'petty snooping' and 'insolent bookkeeping'.[64] Nor did he respond well to the OPC reneging on its financial pledges. In April 1951, for example, he told his CIA liaison Samuel D. Berger that he was on the verge of instructing his field agents to 'pack their grips, close their shops and come home'.

> You see, I am not a nylon merchant – black market or otherwise. ... I do not intend to lend aid and comfort to any attempt of second-class bookkeepers determining the policies of our organization.[65]

Worse still from Lovestone's point of view was growing evidence that the OPC was attempting to usurp his control of FTUC field operatives. Etter, for example, was approached with an offer of a large salary if he performed 'extra-curricular' activities or took full-time employment with 'another organization'.[66] Similar efforts were made 'to drive a wedge' between Lovestone and his most valuable asset, Brown, but the latter loyally resisted the OPC's blandishments.[67] When the co-option of Lovestoneite personnel failed, the OPC went outside the apparatus of the FTUC altogether, using other Americans in the field, such as Rome Labor Attaché, Tom Lane, as agents instead.[68] The secret service's motivation here is understandable: not only did it want greater control over operations, it was also concerned about the security risks involved in funding a private covert network run by a notorious intriguer like Lovestone. The fact that Wisner assigned immediately responsibility for OPC labour operations to Carmel Offie, a well-known Washington 'fixer' and flamboyantly open homosexual, can have done little to assuage such concerns. (The 'Monk', to give Offie his Lovestoneite code-name, was removed from the OPC payroll in June 1950 when Senator Joseph McCarthy began investigating him, and transferred onto that of the FTUC; he appears to have transferred his personal allegiance from Wisner to Lovestone at the same time, henceforth siding with the FTUC boss in his faction fights against the OPC.)[69] Lovestone, however, did not care about the OPC's security fears. Indeed, he thought that unchecked spending on European labour by government officers such as Lane actually increased the possibility of exposure or 'blowback'. 'In view of the type of rich dishes that Uncle Tom has been serving up, a number of my friends will not touch any spaghetti shipment', he complained to Lillie Brown in March 1951. 'They don't want to be involved in such filthy kitchens.'[70] What was even worse was that the OPC occasionally invoked the name of the AFL in operations that had nothing to do with the FTUC. Brown in particular objected to this practice, as it threatened to damage his personal reputation in Europe. The FTUC retaliated against the unauthorised use of its brand-name by withholding intelligence from the OPC and terminating its involvement in non-labour operations such as the Congress for Cultural Freedom.

However, the most disquieting implication of the OPC's evident intention of expanding its labour operations beyond the purview of the FTUC was the possibility of it forging a relationship with the AFL's rival labour federation, the CIO. Since finally giving up on the WFTU in 1949, the CIO had been looking for new ways to make its influence felt abroad, for example, opening an office in Paris in 1951 under the charge of Walter Reuther's younger brother, Victor. It had also succeeded in winning considerable influence within the Marshall Plan's European administration, the Economic Cooperation Agency, whose head Milton Katz favoured the notion of a 'dual-track' labour foreign policy involving the two American labour organisations on an equal footing.[71] For Lovestone and Brown, whose enmity towards the Reuther brothers dated back to faction fights within the United Automobile Workers during the 1930s, the CIO's tie-in with the ECA opened up the unpleasant prospect of the 'YPSLs', as they sneeringly referred to the Reuthers (a reference to the Young Peoples Socialist League), gaining access to the Marshall Plan counterpart funds (or 'Cat nip' in Lovestoneite code – a reference, presumably, to Katz). The suspicion that the OPC approved of the foreign ambitions of the CIO took hold in November 1950, when under questioning from Lovestone, Wisner admitted he was interested in the possibility of funding operations by the AFL's competitor on a project-by-project basis.[72] By April of the following year Lovestone was 'convinced that Victor and his friends are operating not only with a lot of Cat nip but also with the aid of substantial injections from Dr. Fizzer'.[73] This was, he felt, an example of 'the cheap opportunist and petty political patronage so characteristic of the behavior of certain political machines since the American trade union movement was split in two'. As he explained to Sam Berger,

> Victor Reuther might be a very nice guy. If I had an eligible daughter and she was in love with him, I would not interfere with her desire to marry him. But to put Victor Reuther and Irving Brown on a par in carrying on the frontal struggle against totalitarian Communism and its machinations ... is enough to make, as Stalin said, a horse laugh.[74]

Whether or not Lovestone's views of the Reuthers were passed on to the CIA is not known. What is clear is that Lovestoneite opposition did not deter the Fizz kids from pursuing their interest in the CIO. Among the details of the CIA's front operations publicised in the late 1960s was the fact that both Walter and Victor Reuther had personally handled secret Agency subsidies during the early 1950s (although neither with the same frequency nor in the same quantities as Lovestone and Brown).[75]

At the same time that Lovestone was protesting the entry of the CIO into the field of covert operations, major organisational changes were occurring within the CIA which would further queer relations with the FTUC. In January 1951 the new DCI Walter Bedell Smith, determined to assert his authority over Wisner's freewheeling OPC, appointed Allen Dulles Deputy Director of Plans with overall responsibility for covert operations.[76] Spotting an opportunity for a power play, Lovestone went to Dulles in March 1951 to renegotiate the terms of the FTUC's relationship with the CIA, proposing that the Committee receive block grants to fund specific projects – a measure clearly intended to increase the Lovestoneites' operational independence. Dulles, however, would have none of it. In April he put his protégé Thomas W. Braden, a particularly dashing former OSS officer, in charge of the International Organizations Division (IOD), thereby removing direct control of labour affairs from Wisner, a move correctly interpreted by the AFL as indicating a desire on the part of the CIA to step up its 'extra-curricular' activities. Dulles also insisted on the removal of Offie from the FTUC payroll as a condition of continued CIA funding.[77] By now, AFL leaders such as David Dubinsky were advocating a complete cessation of relations with the CIA. Tensions came to a head at a meeting between the FTUC and Bedell Smith ('the super-duper Fizz kid') on 9 April 1951, which 'degenerated into a shouting match'.[78] According to Dubinsky's later account:

> We told them they would ruin things [in Italy], but they wouldn't stay out. General Smith kept sounding more and more dictatorial

at our conference. Finally, Lovestone said to him: 'You're a general, but you sound like a drill sergeant'. When he protested, I told Smith, 'You're not telling us what to do; we are from the labor movement'.[79]

This angry exchange neatly captures the contradictions at the heart of the CIA–FTUC partnership. On one side there were professional spies wanting to exert the maximum degree of control possible over the operations they were paying for and uninhibited by loyalty to any one private group – but at the same time constrained by their need for concealment and, in this particular instance, access to non-communist elements in the European labour movement. On the other side were representatives of American labour entirely confident of their own ability to carry out covert operations, indeed, positively jealous of their independence in the field, yet bound to the CIA by the purse-strings of covert patronage. Nor were these the only strains in the partnership. Underlying the organisational frictions were simmering social and even ethnic tensions. The CIA, after all, recruited most of its entry-level staff from the Ivy League universities, while its higher echelons were dominated by military top-brass and corporate lawyers. It is clear that there were conservative elements in the Agency who never felt comfortable working alongside the ex-radical, immigrant-stock proletarians who staffed the FTUC; indeed, there were some who positively opposed the relationship on security grounds.[80] 'In general, the Fizz kids are continuing their marked anti-labor and anti-Semitic tendencies in addition to their incompetence', Lovestone once told Brown.[81] This instinctive suspicion was reciprocated. When James Burnham's Polish contact, Joseph Czapski, was introduced to the head of the FTUC, he was immediately struck by the fact that Lovestone's remarks 'expressed a "class line" that had nothing to do with political and ideological issues. Specifically, L[ovestone] was expressing the fact that he is a plebeian and a Jew'.[82] In his dealings with the CIA, Lovestone articulated his grievances about the Agency's behaviour in language permeated with class consciousness. For example, an FBI wiretap once picked him up complaining to Bill Donovan that the CIA was made up of 'Park Avenue socialites and incompetents and degenerates'.[83]

The relationship between the CIA and FTUC was an unnatural one of New York and Washington, Lower East and Upper West Side, CCNY and Princeton, that only the strange circumstances of the secret Cold War crusade against communism could have brought into existence. It is even

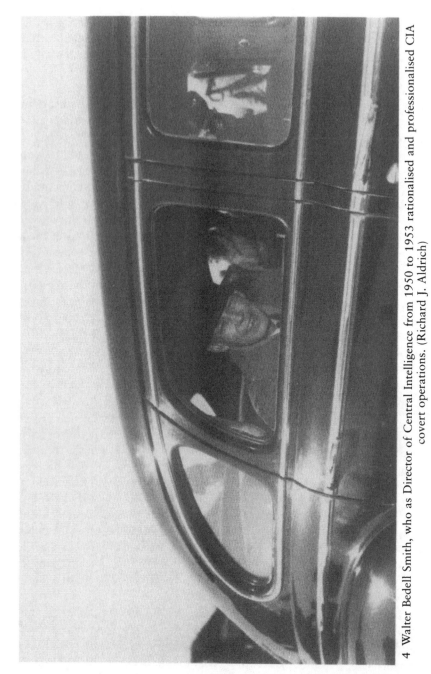

4 Walter Bedell Smith, who as Director of Central Intelligence from 1950 to 1953 rationalised and professionalised CIA covert operations. (Richard J. Aldrich)

possible to detect a whiff of labour militancy in the meetings between the AFL leadership and the CIA directorate, which the former rarely displayed in industrial relations. The meeting described above might as easily have been an unsuccessful wage negotiation. Certainly the Lovestoneites did evince a conception of a labour 'interest' in their dealings with the CIA, which they thought was being harmed. 'These people have done labour in general and the AF of L in particular', Lovestone told Brown, referring to the Fizz kids, 'an enormous amount of damage'.[84] Indeed, labour-management relations are arguably a more appropriate paradigm for conceptualising relations between the FTUC and the CIA than the puppet-on-a-string image deployed by many earlier writers on the subject.

The climactic meeting of April 1951 did not bring an end to FTUC–CIA relations: joint operations carried on into the mid-1950s, with both parties still struggling to get the upper hand, and several new disputes springing up between them. However, it did signify a turning point. After peaking in 1950, covert subsidies to the FTUC declined steadily, reaching a mere $10,000 in 1958. By that point the Committee's position within the American labour movement had in any case been seriously undermined, thanks to the merger in 1955 of the AFL and CIO, and the creation of a joint International Affairs Committee. In December 1957, the decision was taken to wind down the Committee.[85] Subsequently CIA–AFL covert operations involving Brown continued on a freelance basis. Meanwhile, the focus of Lovestone's work shifted to intelligence-gathering, which he carried out in league with his new controller in the Agency, head of counter-intelligence, James Jesus Angleton.[86] Lovestoneite influence over covert labour operations had been greatly reduced; the professionalising and rationalising drive carried out by Walter Bedell Smith had largely succeeded. That said, the public realm had not colonised the private entirely: Lovestone retained his network of informants and agents dotted around the globe. Indeed, factional American union politics would continue to undermine official efforts by the US government at 'labor diplomacy' throughout the early Cold War period.

THE CONGRESS FOR CULTURAL FREEDOM

The major cooperative venture involving the CIA and intellectuals on the American non-communist left was the Congress for Cultural Freedom

(CCF), an organisation launched in 1950 in response to the Cominform's peace offensive. Briefly – the story of the CCF's launch has already been told in detail several times elsewhere[87] – there were three strands feeding into this initiative. The first of these was the formation in March 1949 by the New York intellectuals under the leadership of Sidney Hook of the Americans for Intellectual Freedom (AIF) as a counter to the communist-orchestrated Waldorf peace conference. (The membership in this organisation of Dwight Macdonald and Mary McCarthy testifies to the irony that it was descended, via Friends of Russian Freedom, from their failed experiment in anarcho-pacifist radicalism, Europe–America Groups.) Second, there were calls from ex-communist intellectuals in Europe, such as Ruth Fischer, former Comintern officer (and sister of Gerhart Eisler, head of Cominform operations in East Berlin), for a mass demonstration by western intellectuals in protest at Soviet political repression, echoing Koestler's words of advice to Bertrand Russell a few years earlier. The involvement of the likes of Fischer and Koestler in the planning of the Congress for Cultural Freedom would ensure that the resulting organisation would bear a strong resemblance to similar communist front bodies. Providing a crucial link between these Europeans and Hook's group was Melvin J. Lasky, a youthful New Yorker who had recently created a centre for anti-communist intellectuals in American-occupied western Germany by helping launch the US military government-sponsored journal, *Der Monat*, the model for later CIA-funded intellectual publications in Cold War Europe. The third strand leading to the Congress for Cultural Freedom was the covert support and sponsorship of Frank Wisner's OPC, provided on the ground in Europe by Michael Josselson, a multi-lingual intellectual of Baltic extraction who had been recruited by the CIA in 1948.

It was Josselson who succeeded in persuading Wisner that the OPC should support a proposal by Lasky for a rally of freedom-loving intellectuals in West Berlin along the lines suggested by Fischer ('giving the Politburo hell right at the gate of their own hell', as she put it), although in Josselson's tactical formulation the plan placed less emphasis on outright political confrontation than the 'softer' theme of intellectual freedom. [88] The Congress for Cultural Freedom met at Berlin's Titania Palast over four oppressively hot late-June days, each of which witnessed, in the words of CCF historian Peter Coleman, 'moments of high drama – defections from the East, political conversions, intellectual confrontations'.[89] Despite the outward appearance of crisis, an impression strengthened by the simultaneous outbreak of war in Korea, the event was carefully stage-managed throughout by an 'unofficial steering committee' led by Koestler, who himself contributed to the raising of the political temperature with a series of stirring speeches, including a ringing declaration on the final afternoon before a 15,000-strong crowd of cheering Berliners: 'Friends, freedom has seized the offensive!'[90]

The Congress delighted its backers in Washington; even President Truman himself was reported to be 'very well pleased'.[91] After the OPC's Project Review Board had given the go-ahead, a permanent organisation was established to defend and promote cultural freedom, with a secretariat strategically located in the citadel of western neutralism, Paris, under the control of Michael Josselson. Soon, a number of national affiliates had sprung up to support the programme of the international Congress. By 1951, following the restructuring of covert operations which had seen the appointment of Allen Dulles as Deputy Director of Plans, responsibility for funding the CCF was transferred from the OPC to Tom Braden's International Organizations Division, which channelled its subsidies via a number of fake private foundations created specially for the purpose. The most important of these was the Farfield Foundation, fronted by the colourful figure of Cincinnati gin millionaire, Julius 'Junkie' Fleischmann. Buoyed by the secret patronage of the CIA, the Congress became a major institutional force in western intellectual life, staging glamorous arts festivals, convening prestigious academic seminars and publishing high-profile literary magazines. It was, in short, the US's principal weapon in the Cultural Cold War, the superpower struggle for the 'hearts and minds' of the world's intellectuals.[92]

However, as with covert labour operations involving the Lovestoneites, this venture into the field of cultural patronage exposed the CIA to a number of risks. Indeed, the scope for conflict over strategy and operational control was if anything greater in this case due to literary intellectuals' notorious unpredictability and fierce sense of independence. The first hint of trouble came shortly after the New York intellectuals' counter-demonstration against the Waldorf conference, when a similar rally held in Paris with secret OPC funding descended into organisational chaos. Dismayed by reports of a stage-invasion by a group of anarchists, Frank Wisner voiced his apprehension that the mooted 'little Deminform' might turn 'into a nuts folly of miscellaneous goats and monkeys whose antics would completely discredit the work and statements of the serious and responsible liberals'.[93] In the event the Congress for Cultural Freedom passed off without any major hitches. Significantly, though, Wisner was deeply unhappy with one aspect of the event, namely the

5 Arthur Koestler, Irving Brown and James Burnham huddle during the Congress for Cultural Freedom, Berlin, 1950. (Congress for Cultural Freedom Papers, Joseph Regenstein Library, University of Chicago)

prominent role played in it by Melvin Lasky. Several months earlier, in April, Wisner had remarked that Lasky, as an employee of the American military government, was generally perceived in Germany as an agent of official US interests and should, therefore, be kept out of sight in Berlin (James Burnham was to be sidelined too, for similar reasons). The boisterous Lasky, however, was not squashed so easily, and featured all too visibly at the Congress. Wisner was 'very disturbed' by the 'non-observance' of his directive and insisted on Lasky's removal as a condition of continued funding by the OPC.[94] Initially, Josselson, who had tactfully remained behind the scenes in Berlin, defended Lasky, claiming that 'no other person here ... could have achieved such success'.[95] When it became clear, however, that Wisner would withhold OPC support if his demand was not met, Josselson backed down. Lasky was advised to take a well-earned holiday; observers assumed that he was not invited to run the new CCF because he could not be spared from the editorship of *Der Monat*.[96] This was not an end, however, to official difficulties in secretly managing so public an operation.

Another early casualty of the gathering conflict between the intellectual and official spheres was Arthur Koestler. After having dominated the Berlin conference (indeed, some observers thought he had been too dominant),[97] the Hungarian-born novelist had signalled his intention of shaping the development of the permanent Congress for Cultural Freedom by hosting further meetings of the informal steering committee at his home just outside Paris.[98] As usual, Koestler had a definite tactical agenda: the Congress should, he believed, concentrate on anti-communist political warfare, staging Comintern-style mass rallies and propagandising behind the Iron Curtain.[99] For this reason he backed Louis Fischer, another former Comintern officer (and a fellow contributor to the classic collection of essays by disillusioned ex-communists, *The God That Failed*) for the post of Secretary-General of the new organisation. Fischer's candidacy also received the support of Irving Brown, at this stage the main conduit of OPC funds to the Congress. Gradually, however, it became apparent that the CCF's emergent *apparat* did not share Koestler's vision of the organisation's future. Fischer was dumped at a November 1950 meeting of the Congress's International Committee in Brussels. According to Brown, one of the reasons for this move was a prejudice on the part of some participants against ex-communists.[100] Instead, Josselson turned to his friend Nicolas Nabokov, who shared his preference for a cultural strategy in the battle for hearts and minds (Nabokov was also the preferred candidate in Washington, where during the war years he had been a member of George Kennan's Georgetown set). Plans for a mass rally in Paris in the summer of 1951 were abandoned. When an increasingly disgruntled Koestler learned that the Congress was considering instead the possibility of staging a cultural event to which it would invite such notorious Cold War neutralists as Jean-Paul Sartre, he angrily threatened to resign from the Executive Committee.[101] He eventually severed his ties with the Congress in July 1951, by which time Nabokov, now installed in the organisation's Parisian head-quarters, was firming up plans for an arts festival to be held in Paris the following year.[102] Given his temperamental unsuitability for administrative work, Koestler's withdrawal from the CCF might well have been a blessing in disguise. However, it was not done voluntarily. As he told a friend, 'I was made to withdraw in a gentle and effective way'.[103]

Instrumental in Nabokov's appointment had been another member of the Berlin Congress's unofficial steering committee, James Burnham.[104] Although he had agreed to retire discreetly from public view in the wake of the founding conference, Burnham continued to exercise a powerful, behind-the-scenes influence on the CCF in his role as an OPC consultant on émigré and cultural affairs, particularly with regard to appointments to the Paris secretariat. He used this position to try and shape the embryonic organisation into a political force which reflected not only his faith in Comintern-like tactics but also his growing political conservatism, that is an 'anti-communist front' embracing the 'non-Socialist Right as well as [the] traditional Left'.[105] In this he was to prove unsuccessful. Key personnel in Paris, including even his own nominees, such as Director of Publications, François Bondy, preferred to concentrate on appealing solely to the centre-left. Louis Gibarti, another of Burnham's contacts in Paris, echoed Brown by reporting a prejudice against ex-communists who had travelled to the political right within Congress circles.[106] Burnham interpreted this emphasis on the non-communist left as evidence of factional meddling in the CCF's affairs by Brown and the Lovestoneites. Hence, when the Gaullist Daniel Apert's position as head of the Paris office was usurped in January 1951 by unionist Jean Enoch, he wrote to CIA officer Gerald Miller claiming that Josselson had fallen into 'a political trap' and predicting that the Congress would be reduced 'to [a] province of [the] Lovestone empire'.[107] Like earlier attempts to secure Apert's position by introducing him to Joseph Bryan,[108] these entreaties failed. Apert was not reinstated, and Burnham was apparently persuaded by explanations of his removal that

106

centred on alleged personality defects.[109] By the summer of 1951 the CCF had, after a period of political uncertainty, definitely emerged as an organisation of the non-communist left. How much this had to do with Lovestoneite influence, though, is open to question. The FTUC was by this point pulling out of the CCF, partly as a result of its deteriorating relations with the CIA, and partly as a result of growing disillusionment with the efficacy of cultural operations (although Brown, despite personal reservations, did stay on the Congress's Executive Committee). In any case, the result was to leave Josselson and the IOD more firmly in operational control of the CCF.

Of the three prominent ex-communists who had helped create the CCF in the first place, it was Sidney Hook who remained most closely involved with the organisation. In addition to acting as the American representative on its Executive Committee, he was also the key figure in its American affiliate, the American Committee for Cultural Freedom (ACCF), which he helped launch in January 1951. The organisational roots of the ACCF lay in earlier communal activities of the New York intellectuals. Indeed, its name deliberately echoed that of the Committee for Cultural Freedom, the anti-Stalinist action group created by Hook in 1939 in response to the Nazi-Soviet Pact.[110] However, the ACCF was not simply another New York intellectual organisation. From the CIA's point of view, its principal purpose was to support the international programme of the Congress for Cultural Freedom by creating, as Tom Braden later put it, 'the impression of some American participation in the European operation'.[111] Moreover, during a crucial phase of the CCF's early existence, between the FTUC's withdrawal from the scene and the point when the Farfield Foundation was set up, the American Committee functioned as its parent organisation's main source of funding.

It is possible to infer something of the scale and nature of this 'backstopping' operation from documents amongst the Burnham papers. These reveal the ACCF's New York-based Executive Secretary Pearl Kluger engaged in a number of secret transactions on the CCF's behalf: transmitting the sum of $2,000 to the organisers of a conference in New Delhi intended to secured a foothold for the Congress on the Indian sub-continent;[112] sending $3,500 to Japan in an effort to kick-start a national affiliate there;[113] and underwriting a variety of CCF activities in Europe itself, for example, a series of Youth Meetings in Berlin, for which the sum of $15,000 was transferred from New York to Paris.[114] The documents in question also hint at some of the operational problems

107

involved in this complex and devious exercise. Kluger, confronted with the challenge of managing the international Congress's finances, while at the same time providing cover for the ACCF by organising committees and public meetings in New York, felt increasingly over-burdened and under-resourced. 'When I complained to our friend that Santa Claus did not come down the chimney this month', she told Burnham in March 1951, 'he said he had not understood that this was a six-month Christmas'.[115] With such large sums of money going out to so many different parts of the globe, it was not always possible to keep a close eye on expenditure. A banker's draft of $1,000 sent to organisers of a Congress affiliate in India simply disappeared: Burnham suspected an Indian magazine editor of purloining it for his publication.[116] This tendency on the part of foreign intellectuals to appropriate CCF subsidies for their own purposes, which was to become a chronic irritant to the US's Cultural Cold War effort, helps explains why the ACCF's 'donor' requested a monthly accounting of the organisation's spendings, in a move reminiscent of earlier attempts to monitor the FTUC's expenditure. 'Unless the donor is completely informed of the American Committee's activities', Pearl Kluger was told, 'he is not in a position to approve further grants of money for the development of the Committee's projects'.[117]

Then there were the security risks which arose from the operation, a major concern for the CIA given the location of the ACCF's offices in Manhattan, long a stronghold of the American communist movement. Kluger was extremely alert on this score, on one occasion suggesting to Burnham that a 'Vogue Travel Service' based in the same building as the ACCF 'be investigated' after a colleague had recognised a Stalinist veteran of the Abraham Lincoln Brigade entering its offices, and on another reporting that she had 'played dumb' when 'asked numerous questions concerning the financing of the Committee' by an 'over-eager' visitor claiming to be from the 'State Department'.[118] It was possibly reports such as these that persuaded the Agency of the need for extra security measures when the Committee began handling the large sums of money required to mount Nicolas Nabokov's 1952 Paris arts festival.

A 'separate bank account and room' were arranged to ensure that festival business was not 'mixed up in the other activities of the organi-sation',[119] and a 'Mr Albert Donnelly' was hired as 'Mr Fleischmann's assistant' – the IOD had just created the Farfield Foundation specifically for the purpose of funding Nabokov's initiative – to undertake 'all necessary negotiations for the Festival'. ACCF staff were instructed

108

not to make or receive any 'phone calls from persons in Washington, including Mr B. and Mr. F.': 'Mr Donnelly has certain telephone facilities at his disposal which make any further indiscretions of this nature unnecessary.'[120] Clearly these measures worked: the Farfield was considered such a successful innovation that it was retained as the principal 'pass-through' for all future Congress operations.[121] As far as the CIA was concerned, the ACCF had now served its main purpose.[122]

Unfortunately for the Agency, this view was not shared by the Committee itself. By 1952, the organisation had grown into a distinguished body of several hundred members engaged in a busy programme of public activities.[123] The extent to which this membership knew of the CIA's behind-the-scenes role is still a matter of dispute, but what is clear is that most if not all of the Committee's officers were 'witting'.[124] Still, this does not appear to have prevented them from treating the organisation as if it really were a *bona fide* intellectual body, indeed, as if it were *their own*. The most obvious sign of this lack of appreciation of the ACCF's intended tactical function as cover and back-stop for the international Congress was the organisation's support for two strategic options, advocated by Koestler and Brown in 1950 yet rejected by the CCF's leadership: the adoption of an overtly political position and the inclusion of conservative elements in a united front against communism. The first of these policies, which reflected the New York intellectuals' intense anti-Stalinism and confident belief that they knew best how to combat the ideological threat of communism, even led the American Committee to criticise the tactics of its parent body. Sometimes the ACCF's criticism was implicit, as when it took steps to protest Soviet violations of human rights or rebut anti-American communist propaganda to which the CCF had not responded.[125] At other times the Committee explicitly questioned the relevance of the Congress's cultural activities to the Cold War: Nabokov's Paris festival was a particular target for criticism by the New York intellectuals, who clearly thought that the neutralist atmosphere of the French capital was rubbing off on the CCF's officers.[126] The Congress itself was understandably annoyed by these attacks from within its own camp, and took an increasingly stern line with its American affiliate during the early 1950s. Sidney Hook found himself in the position of mediator between the two organisations, trying to explain the CCF's cultural strategy to his comrades in New York, while at the same time defending the ACCF's hardline political pronouncements to other members of the Congress's Executive Committee in Paris.[127]

The other main tactical bias of the ACCF, towards a broad, inclusive membership policy – a late victory for Burnham, who had advised Hook to advertise the new Committee 'outside of the old radical and avant-garde circles' among 'more conventional "American" types'[128] – resulted in a body which resembled, in the apt phrase of historian William L. O' Neill, 'a Popular Front of anti-Stalinists, something like the League of American Writers in reverse'.[129] At first the Committee's leftist and conservative members rubbed along together, perhaps in part because potentially disruptive individuals on the left wing of the New York intellectual community were either not invited or refused to join (the launch of the journal *Dissent* in 1954 gave this non-conformist element an alternative base around which to rally).[130] By 1952, however, the issue of domestic communism and, in particular, the anti-subversive campaigns of Joe McCarthy were causing major ructions within the Committee. The internal controversy which engulfed the organisation following a defence of the Wisconsin Senator at a public meeting in March 1952 by Max Eastman has been described in detail elsewhere, so will not be gone over again here.[131] One thing worth noting, though, is the fairly clear doctrinal lines along which the schism occurred. On one side of the divide, if not positively defending McCarthy then at least downplaying the threat he posed to American cultural freedom, were ex-communists such as Burnham, Karl Wittfogel and Eugene Lyons. On the other, urging the ACCF to make criticism of McCarthyism its main priority, were socialists and liberals of the Union for Democratic Action/ADA variety, such as Arthur Schlesinger Jr. and Norman Thomas, plus the dissident New York intellectuals who had attempted to launch Europe–America Groups in 1948, Dwight Macdonald and Mary McCarthy. In other words, the division within the ACCF was not unlike the communist/socialist split which underlay disagreements between AFL and CIO foreign policy operatives in the same period. The distinction was not hard and fast: the anti-McCarthy side included some ex-communists, such as James Weschler, while lumped in with the hardline camp were two magazine editors, Elliot Cohen of *Commentary* and Sol Levitas of *The New Leader*, neither of whom had ever been Bolsheviks. Nonetheless, the factional undercurrents at play were evident enough to the disputants. 'By and large', remarked Chicagoan novelist James T. Farrell, 'the New York ex-radical intellectuals are not likely to be strongly anti-McCarthy'.[132] Schlesinger, who the previous year had been hissed when giving a 'mild, Anglo-Saxon address' to an ACCF gathering of 'ex-Coms', agreed.[133] 'There is some deep sickness in certain sectors of the New York intellectuals', he told Dwight Macdonald, 'particularly in the *Commentary* crowd'.[134]

Schlesinger had reported his humiliating experience in 1951 to Nicolas Nabokov, an old Georgetown friend, who reassured him that the international Congress was taking a different approach from the American Committee. When Nabokov learned from Schlesinger of the public fracas over McCarthyism, however, he was less sanguine. 'The presence of some dozen McCarthyites on the Committee not only compromises his work in Europe', explained his wife Patricia Nabokov, 'but compromises him personally'.[135] The reaction within the CIA to the ACCF's difficulties was similar. Schlesinger (who, it is worth pointing out, was heavily involved in the jockeying for political position which had occurred in the early months of the Congress for Cultural Freedom's existence, suggesting to Irving Brown that ADA Vice-Chairman Reinhold Niebuhr be considered for the post of Secretary-General),[136] was in frequent social contact with Frank Wisner, whom he had met at Joe Alsop's house, and had taken to briefing him about developments within the American Committee.[137] When Wisner learned about the row over McCarthyism – an extremely sensitive subject within the Agency due both to its capacity for arousing anti-Americanism abroad and the threat to liberal elements it posed at home – he was furious. 'I can understand how ... a group of American private citizens interested in cultural freedom would feel that it would have to take a position on McCarthyism', he told a CIA colleague. 'However, that is not the nature of the American Committee for Cultural Freedom which ... was inspired if not put together by this Agency for the purpose of providing cover and back-stopping for the European effort.' Steps had to be taken immediately to repair the damage. Ideally, Wisner would have preferred 'that the entire debate on this subject, from the beginning, be expunged from the record'. If this was not possible, then at the very least, 'an appeal to unity and concord ... might be successful'.[138]

In the event, the CIA chose a third course of action, that is, secretly intervening in the ACCF via such moderates as Schlesinger (who regularly sent copies of the Executive Committee's minutes to Cord Meyer, Tom Braden's successor as head of IOD)[139] and Daniel Bell (who during a year spent working in Paris developed a close relationship with Michael Josselson)[140] in an effort to check the excesses of the hardliners. The latter persisted in their ways, however. An attempt to settle the McCarthy issue once and for all by publishing a scholarly monograph on the subject in 1954 led instead to the noisy resignations of Burnham and Eastman. By September of that year, Michael Josselson had decided that the ACCF was a liability and terminated all financial assistance from the international Congress, the Committee's main source of financial support after the Farfield Foundation had turned off the tap the previous year.[141] Sidney Hook, however, on this occasion siding with New York rather than Paris, approached Allen Dulles directly and secured a grant of $10,000 from the Farfield.[142] Cord Meyer explained the reasoning for Dulles's decision to Schlesinger, who by this point was debating quitting the ACCF to spend more time on the ADA,[143] in the following words: 'Our hope is that the breathing space provided by this assistance can be used by ... yourself and the other sensible ones to reconstitute the Executive Committee and draft an intelligent programme that might gain real support from the Foundations.'[144]

Meyer's hope was in vain. Despite attempts by Schlesinger and Bell to rein them in, 'hot-heads' such as German-born journalist Norbert Muhlen and union official Arnold Beichman kept up their calls for a policy of stiffer resistance to the Soviet threat. In his memoirs, Sidney Hook tells how on one occasion the ACCF even debated petitioning the international Congress to intervene in Indonesia against the communist-backed President Ahmed Sukarno (Hook succeeded in dissuading his colleagues from this 'open foray into politics' and struck any reference to it from the minutes).[145] Similarly, despite Burnham's departure in 1954, factional warfare carried on between New York intellectuals obsessed with the communist threat and liberal/socialist types more concerned with the stultifying cultural effects of excessive anti-communism. The pressure of attempting to unify these warring camps eventually got to the Committee's Chairman from 1954, James Farrell, who resigned dramatically in 1957 after an apparently drunken outburst against US Cold War foreign policy.[146] Coming soon after a particularly acrimonious public altercation between the ACCF and one of the CCF's Honorary Chairmen, Bertrand Russell,[147] this incident sounded the death knell of the US affiliate (a cable from Farrell to Paris suggests that he might have been put up to his resignation by Josselson, who had not given up hope of the 'unnecessary' New York outfit dying through lack of funds: 'Have broken up American Committee. Your advantage. Have kept my word.')[148] The ACCF went into suspended animation in late 1957. However, even after that point it remained the focus of New York literary infighting. Reactivated as a tax shelter for the *Partisan Review* in 1958, its Chair Diana Trilling became embroiled in a nasty feud with *Partisan Review* editor William Phillips, leading to her resignation in

1960.[149] The same year saw Sidney Hook participating in his last meeting of the International Congress's Executive Committee. 'My inactivity by this time was not unwelcomed', he later wrote, 'since I was regarded by the Parisian directorate as a representative of the obnoxious American Committee for Cultural Freedom'.[150]

The messy and protracted demise of the American Committee for Cultural Freedom goes to show that the CIA did not always exercise complete control over the leftist organisations it secretly sponsored. It might well have been the case that intelligence professionals viewed such bodies as mere instruments of their will – Frank Wisner used to boast to colleagues that he could play any tune he wanted on his 'Mighty Wurlitzer' of front operations.[151] It might also have been true that the CIA did often succeed in reducing the influence of individuals it felt were too independent-minded or otherwise undependable. However, the organisations themselves never became entirely compliant. Rather their public, 'authentic' identities – as, in the case of the FTUC, the foreign policy arm of the AFL and, the ACCF, a community forum for the New York intellectuals – survived official attempts at repression, constantly returning to undermine their covert purpose. While the American Committee might have contained some liberal intellectuals who shared the same social background and, to a certain extent, politics as the CIA operatives responsible for running the non-communist left, it was mainly made up of ex-communists who, like the Lovestoneites of the FTUC, believed that their experience of New York communist politics equipped them to fight the Cold War more effectively than Ivy League-educated government officials. Hence, while Arthur Koestler and James Burnham might have been marginalised by the Congress for Cultural Freedom, the Cold War tactics they advocated lived on in the policies and actions of the organisation's American affiliate. It has already been suggested that labour-management relations might be a more appropriate metaphor for the partnership between the FTUC and OPC than the puppet-on-a-string image favoured by earlier authors. Perhaps it would be similarly helpful to reconceptualise the collaboration between the CIA and NCL American intellectuals, which has previously been portrayed in musical imagery involving wurlitzers or pipers, as more akin to the relationship between cultural patron and artist. Many Agency officers, after all, were well suited by virtue of their patrician personal origins to the role of patron, much as the typical New York intellectual was a struggling magazine editor on the lookout for a wealthy 'angel'. Like earlier patrons of the

113

arts, the CIA was to discover that although it paid the bills, it could not always dictate the behaviour of the artist or, for that matter, the contents of the art-work.

NOTES

1. See, for example, Philip Taft, *Defending Freedom: American Labor and Foreign Affairs* (Los Angeles: Nash, 1973).
2. See Ronald Radosh, *American Labor and United States Foreign Policy* (New York: Random House, 1969). The classic 'revisionist' critique of American non-communist left intellectuals' behaviour in the Cold War is Christopher Lasch, *The Agony of the American Left* (New York: Vintage, 1968), chap. 4.
3. Quoted in Evan Thomas, *The Very Best Men. Four Who Dared: The Early Years of the CIA* (New York: Simon and Schuster, 1995), p. 23.
4. Walter L. Hixson, *Parting the Curtain: Propaganda, Culture and the Cold War, 1945–61* (New York: St Martin's Press, 1997), p. 5.
5. Sallie Pisani, *The CIA and the Marshall Plan* (Edinburgh University Press, 1991), p. 55.
6. According to Pisani, the label was coined by Richard M. Bissell Jr. in 1983. Ibid., p. 3.
7. Ibid., chap. 2.
8. See Scott Lucas, *Freedom's War: The US Crusade Against the Soviet Union, 1945–56* (Manchester University Press, 1999), chap. 5; Peter Grose, *Operation Rollback: America's Secret War Behind the Iron Curtain* (Boston: Houghton Mifflin, 2000), pp. 1–8, 93–9.
9. Quoted in C. Thomas Thorne Jr. and David S. Patterson (eds), *Foreign Relations of the United States, 1945–50: Emergence of the Intelligence Establishment* (Washington DC: US Government Printing Office, 1996), p. 617.
10. See Lucas, *Freedom's War*, p. 48.
11. Quoted in Thorne and Patterson (eds), *Foreign Relations*, pp. 668–72.
12. See ibid., pp. 618–21.
13. Quoted in ibid., p. 713.
14. Grose, *Operation Rollback*, pp. 107–8. Intriguingly, George Kennan's list of nominees for chief of OPC included Irving Brown, 'a very able and active citizen', according to Kennan. Quoted in Thorne and Patterson (eds), *Foreign Relations*, p. 716.
15. Quoted in Thomas, *Very Best Men*, p. 16.
16. Frank Wisner to Roscoe Hillenkoetter, 29 October 1948, quoted in Thorne and Patterson (eds), *Foreign Relations*, pp. 730–1.
17. See Pisani, *CIA and Marshall Plan*, pp. 72–8.
18. See Thomas, *Very Best Men*, p. 40.

19. Quoted in Thorne and Patterson (eds), *Foreign Relations*, p. 670.
20. Lucas, *Freedom's War*, p. 2; Gerald Miller, 'Office of Policy Coordination, 1948–52', CIA Historical Study (February 1973), p. 12.
21. Frank Wisner, quoted in Thomas, *Very Best Men*, p. 25.
22. Quoted in Thorne and Patterson (eds), *Foreign Relations*, p. 670.
23. Grose, *Operation Rollback*, p. 126; Lucas, *Freedom's War*, p. 67.
24. Quoted in Grose, *Operation Rollback*, p. 127.
25. See Lucas, *Freedom's War*, pp. 100–4.
26. Ibid., pp. 109–10.
27. Quoted in Thorne and Patterson (eds), *Foreign Relations*, p. 670.
28. John Hickerson, quoted in Anthony Carew, *Labour under the Marshall Plan: The Politics of Productivity and the Marketing of Management Science* (Manchester University Press, 1987), p. 45.
29. Joseph W. Alsop, *I've Seen the Best of It: Memoirs* (New York: Norton, 1989), p. 271.
30. Arthur M. Schlesinger Jr., interview with author, 15 July 1998, New York.
31. Quoted in Frances Stonor Saunders, *Who Paid the Piper? The CIA and the Cultural Cold War* (London: Granta, 1999), p. 63.
32. Quoted in Thomas, *Very Best Men*, p. 62.
33. Quoted in Iain Hamilton, *Koestler: A Biography* (London: Secker and Warburg, 1982), p. 138.
34. Ibid., p. 143.
35. Joseph Bryan to James Burnham, no date, James Burnham Papers, Hoover Institution, Stanford University. On Bryan and OPC's Psychological Warfare Workshop, see Thomas, *Very Best Men*, p. 33.
36. Joseph Bryan to James Burnham, 30 June 1949, Burnham Papers.
37. Frederick W. Williams to James Burnham, 21 July 1949, Burnham Papers.
38. Quoted in Saunders, *Who Paid the Piper?*, p. 87. In 1953 Burnham consulted with Kermit Roosevelt while he was planning his successful coup in Iran. Miles Copeland, an Agency officer with responsibility for 'handling' President Nasser of Egypt, later recalled there being 'some fuss about the Burnham flirtation with the "extreme Left"' which ceased when it was pointed out that the philosopher had never been actually been a Communist, only 'a mere Trotskyist', and that his past radicalism put him in 'good company in the CIA's stable of on-call consultants'. Copeland personally was glad of Burnham's theoretical input as it enabled him to 'hold [his] own with the intelligentsia' on the CIA's covert operations staff. Miles Copeland, 'James Burnham', *National Review* 11 September 1987.
39. James Burnham to Sidney Hook, 30 January 1949, Sidney Hook Papers, Hoover Institution, Stanford University. Burnham briefly entertained the suspicion that *Kultura* was 'MVD'. See James Burnham to Sidney Hook, 31 January 1949, Hook Papers.
40. James Burnham to Sidney Hook, 19 August 1946, Hook Papers.

41. James Burnham to Sidney Hook, 3 December 1948, Hook Papers.
42. James Burnham to Sidney Hook, 22 December 1948, Hook Papers; James Burnham to Arthur Koestler, 14 September 1950, Burnham Papers.
43. James Burnham 'The strategy of the Politburo, and the problem of American counter-strategy', no date [presumably 1950], Burnham Papers.
44. Walter Bedell Smith to Edward Barrett, 28 July 1950, Hook Papers.
45. See Saunders, *Who Paid the Piper?*, p. 158; Sidney Hook to Raymond Allen, 26 November 1951, Hook Papers.
46. James Burnham to Sidney Hook, 11 January 49, Hook Papers. In April 1950, Burnham wrote to Hook from Washington informing him that he had 'been discussing several of your admirable ideas with persons here'. This suggests that Hook had still not been directly approached by the OPC. James Burnham to Sidney Hook, 5 April 1950, Burnham Papers.
47. J. Edgar Hoover to 'SAC, New York', 5 January 1943, Sidney Hook FBI file. The resulting file, no. 100-176573, was placed in a 'closed status' after a Special Agent submitted a singularly unsensational report on Hook's Trotskyist activities in October 1944. Hoover requested the file be reviewed in March 1949 so that a 'recommendation' could be made. This suggests that OPC might have been investigating Hook as a possible security risk after Burnham had recommended him for consultancy work. J. Edgar Hoover to 'SAC, New York', 18 March 1949, Hook FBI file.
48. Sidney Hook to Harold M. Janis, 2 April 1948, Hook Papers.
49. Sidney Hook to James Burnham, 15 September 1948, Hook Papers.
50. Quoted in Kevin J. Smant, *How Great the Triumph: James Burnham, Anti-communism and the Conservative Movement* (Lanham, NY: University Press of America, 1992), p. 34. James Burnham, 'The strategy of the Politburo and the problem of American counter-strategy', no date [presumably 1950], Burnham Papers.
51. Ted Morgan, *A Covert Life. Jay Lovestone: Communist, Anti-Communist and Spymaster* (New York: Random House, 1999), p. 197.
52. Anthony Carew, 'The American labor movement in Fizzland: The Free Trade Union Committee and the CIA', *Labor History* 39 (1998), 26. This article is a pioneering exploration of the relationship between the FTUC and CIA to which the current account is indebted.
53. Ben Rathbun, *The Point Man: Irving Brown and the Deadly Post-1945 Struggle for Europe and Africa* (London: Minerva, 1996), pp. 91–6.
54. See, for example, Jay Lovestone to Irving Brown, 15 January 1951, Irving Brown Papers, George Meany Memorial Archives, Silver Spring, Maryland; Jay Lovestone to Lillie Brown, 27 March 1951, Brown Papers; Jay Lovestone to Irving Brown, 13 March 1951, Brown Papers.
55. See Morgan, *Covert Life*, pp. 202–6.
56. See Carew, 'American labor in Fizzland', 26.
57. Ibid., 27.
58. Ibid., 25.

59. See Morgan, *Covert Life*, p. 194.
60. Jay Lovestone to Irving Brown, 4 January 1951, Jay Lovestone Papers, Hoover Institution, Stanford University.
61. See Morgan, *Covert Life*, p. 205.
62. Irving Brown to Jay Lovestone, 1 April 1951, Lovestone Papers; Irving Brown to Jay Lovestone, 9 January 1951, Lovestone Papers; Jay Lovestone to Lillie Brown, 27 March 1951, Brown Papers.
63. See Carew, 'American labor in Fizzland', 41, 28.
64. Jay Lovestone to Irving Brown, 2 April 1951, Lovestone Papers; Jay Lovestone to Irving Brown, 4 April 1951, Brown Papers.
65. Jay Lovestone to Samuel Berger, 4 April 1951, Lovestone Papers.
66. Jay Lovestone to Carmel Offie, 1 May 1950, Lovestone Papers.
67. Irving Brown to Jay Lovestone, 21 May 1951, Brown Papers.
68. See Carew, 'American labor in Fizzland', 28–9.
69. See Morgan, *Covert Life*, pp. 219–20.
70. Jay Lovestone to Lillie Brown, 27 March 1951, Brown Papers.
71. See Carew, 'American labor in Fizzland', 29.
72. Ibid., 31.
73. Jay Lovestone to Irving Brown, 30 April 1951, Brown Papers.
74. Jay Lovestone to Samuel Berger, 18 May 1951, Lovestone Papers.
75. See Thomas W. Braden, 'I'm glad the CIA is "immoral"', *Saturday Evening Post* 20 May 1967.
76. For more on this reorganisation, see John Ranelagh, *The Agency: The Rise and Decline of the CIA* (Sevenoaks: Sceptre, 1988), pp. 198–202; Miller, 'Office of Policy Coordination', pp. 22–6; David F. Rudgers, 'The origins of covert action', *Journal of Contemporary History* 35 (2000), 257–9.
77. See Carew, 'American labor in Fizzland', 33–4.
78. Ibid., 35.
79. Quoted in ibid.
80. In 1951, the right-wing journalist Westbrook Pegler began writing hostile articles about Lovestone and Brown. The Lovestoneites suspected that he had been primed by anti-labour elements in the CIA. In January 1953, Carmel Offie told Brown that Pegler's 'informants are in Fizzland who are giving him this stuff to discredit primarily labor, then Dubinsky, you and Jay and to show in a sinister underlying rhythm that all these people who "run" things are Jews'. Carew, 'American labor in Fizzland', 38; Carmel Offie to Irving Brown, 23 January 1953, Brown Papers.
81. Jay Lovestone to Irving Brown, 26 March 1951, Brown Papers.
82. Anonymous, 'Notes on conversation with Joseph Czapski', 4 June 1951, Burnham Papers.
83. See Morgan, *Covert Life*, p. 22.
84. Jay Lovestone to Irving Brown, 24 May 1952, Brown Papers.
85. See Carew, 'American labor in Fizzland', 40.
86. See Morgan, *Covert Life*, chap. 13.

87. See, especially, Peter Coleman, *The Liberal Conspiracy: The Congress for Cultural Freedom and the Struggle for the Mind of Postwar Europe* (New York: Free Press, 1989), chaps. 1–2; Pierre Grémion, *Intelligence De L'Anti-communisme: Le Congrès pour la liberté de la culture à Paris (1950–75)* (Paris: Fayard, 1995), chap. 1; Saunders, *Who Paid the Piper?*, chaps. 1–5.

88. Quoted in Michael Warner, 'Origins of the Congress for Cultural Freedom, 1949–50', *Studies in Intelligence* 38 (1995), 92. This is an immensely useful article written by a member of the CIA's History Staff on the basis of still classified Agency documents.

89. See Coleman, *Liberal Conspiracy*, p. 27.

90. Arthur Koestler, 'Berlin Diary', 25 June 1950, Arthur Koestler Papers, Edinburgh University Library; quoted in Saunders, *Who Paid the Piper?*, p. 82.

91. Quoted in Warner, 'Origins of Congress for Cultural Freedom', 97.

92. The phrase 'Cultural Cold War' was coined by Christopher Lasch. See Lasch, *Agony of American Left*, chap. 4.

93. Quoted in Warner, 'Origins of Congress for Cultural Freedom', 92.

94. Quoted in ibid., 97.

95. Quoted in ibid., 94.

96. Melvin J. Lasky, interview with author, 13 August 1997, Rusper, Sussex.

97. Anonymous, 'Report on Congress for Cultural Freedom', no date, Lovestone Papers. According to this report, 'Koestler spoke four or five times and there was generally a marked tendency to build him up as a kind of *praeceptor mundi*. He seems to have enjoyed himself in the role of a task-master censoring and lecturing the delegates.'

98. See Coleman, *Liberal Conspiracy*, p. 34.

99. Arthur Koestler to Bertrand Russell, 22 September 1950, Koestler Papers.

100. Irving Brown to Arthur Koestler, 2 November 1950, Brown Papers.

101. Arthur Koestler to Denis de Rougemont, 29 January 1951, Burnham Papers.

102. Nabokov told his old Georgetown friend, Arthur Schlesinger Jr., that he was planning 'a huge international affair which I believe will have much more *retentissement* than a hundred speeches by Arthur Koestler, Sidney Hook and James Burnham, about the neurosis of our century'. Nicolas Nabokov to Arthur Schlesinger Jr., 19 July 1951, Nicolas Nabokov Papers, Harry Ransom Humanities Research Center, University of Texas at Austin.

103. Quoted in David Cesarani, *Arthur Koestler: The Homeless Mind* (London: William Heineman, 1998), pp. 382–3. Having withdrawn from the CCF, Koestler now devoted some of his considerable energies to a new venture, the Fund for Intellectual Freedom, a scheme which involved his donating a percentage of his royalties – and encouraging other authors to do the same – to émigré writers. By the mid-1950s, he had abandoned politics altogether.

104. See, for example, Nicolas Nabokov to James Burnham, 21 January 1951, Burnham Papers.
105. James Burnham to François Bondy, 6 February 1951, Burnham Papers.
106. The ex-communist Gibarti's recommendations for Congress activities sounded even more Leninist than Koestler's. 'The organisational strategy must always consist of efforts to provide broad cadres by means which profoundly touch the masses', he told Burnham, for example. 'Copy of letter from Louis Gibarti', 8 September 1950, Burnham Papers. It was Gibarti who first alerted Burnham to Bondy's defection, after he had glimpsed a telegram to David C. Williams in London stating that, 'We are, of course, swinging away from a political line. Broadly speaking, we are swinging away from Burnham.' Louis Gibarti to James Burnham, 2 November 1950, Burnham Papers.
107. James Burnham, 'For: Gerald Miller', 22 January 1951, Burnham Papers.
108. James Burnham to Daniel Apert, 10 January 1951, Burnham Papers.
109. See James Burnham to Denis de Rougemont, 28 February 1951, Burnham Papers.
110. See James Gilbert, *Writers and Partisans: A History of Literary Radicalism in America* (New York: Wiley, 1968), pp. 165, 202–3.
111. Quoted in Saunders, *Who Paid the Piper?*, p. 203.
112. Anonymous, 'Cable received from Josselson', 14 February 1951, Burnham Papers.
113. James Burnham to Herbert Passin, 9 July 1951, Burnham Papers.
114. Anonymous, 'Conversation with Pearl Kluger', 19 July 1951, Burnham Papers.
115. Pearl Kluger to James Burnham, 9 March 1951, Burnham Papers.
116. Anonymous, 'Telephone conversation with Pearl Kluger', 6 July 1951, Burnham Papers. This incident possibly explains why soon afterwards Burnham instructed one of the CCF's Asian experts, Herbert Passin, to monitor the fate of the Committee's Japanese grant. James Burnham to Herbert Passin, 9 July 1951, Burnham Papers.
117. Anonymous, 'Requested of Pearl Kluger', no date, Burnham papers.
118. Pearl Kluger to James Burnham, 27 February 1951, Burnham Papers; anonymous, 'Conversation with Pearl Kluger', 19 July 1951, Burnham Papers.
119. James Burnham to Sidney Hook, 17 August 1951, Burnham Papers.
120. Anonymous, 'Requested of Pearl Kluger', no date, Burnham papers.
121. See Saunders, *Who Paid the Piper?*, p. 116.
122. This was demonstrated by the fact that the evidently very efficient and enterprising Pearl Kluger was seconded to Paris to assist Nabokov with the staging of the festival and did not return as ACCF Executive Secretary. ACCF Executive Committee minutes, 16 April 1952, ACCF Papers, Tamiment Institute Library, New York University.
123. On the ACCF, see Coleman, *Liberal Conspiracy*, chap. 9; Sidney

Hook, *Out of Step: An Unquiet Life in the Twentieth Century* (New York: Harper and Row, 1987), chap. 26; Guenter Lewy, *The Cause That Failed: Communism in American Political Life* (Oxford University Press, 1990), pp. 108–14.

124. Sidney Hook's papers include a bad-tempered exchange of letters between Diana Trilling and Arnold Beichman dating from 1985, in which the former claims that knowledge of secret funding was universal in the ACCF, and the latter denies having been 'witting'. Diana Trilling to Arnold Beichman, 4 January 1985, Hook Papers; Arnold Beichman to Diana Trilling, 13 January 1985, Hook Papers.

125. See Coleman, *Liberal Conspiracy*, pp. 163–4.

126. See, for example, Elliot Cohen, letter to Sidney Hook, 5 October 1951, Burnham Papers. For a list of the ACCF's objections to the structure and policies of the CCF, see 'Draft statement for the Congress for Cultural Freedom', 6 January 1955, ACCF Papers.

127. See CCF Executive Committee minutes, 24–5 January 1955, CCF Papers, Joseph Regenstein Library, University of Chicago; ACCF Executive Committee minutes, 15 February 1955, ACCF Papers. 'Life would be easier for me if the Committee didn't survive', Hook once told Arthur Schlesinger Jr. Sidney Hook to Arthur Schlesinger Jr., no date, Arthur M. Schlesinger Jr. Papers, John F. Kennedy Memorial Library, Boston.

128. James Burnham to Sidney Hook, 20 October 1950, Burnham Papers.

129. William L. O' Neill, *A Better World. The Great Schism: Stalinism and the American Intellectuals* (New York: Simon and Schuster, 1982), p. 298.

130. Radical literary critic Irving Howe was one of those deliberately excluded. Art historian Meyer Schapiro turned down an invitation to join explaining that 'my experience has made me wary of organisations which conceal their purpose behind an appeal to other (and less obviously political) ends'. Meyer Schapiro to Irving Kristol, 22 October 1952, ACCF Papers.

131. See Saunders, *Who Paid the Piper?*, pp. 198–208.

132. James Farrell to Arthur Schlesinger Jr., 6 March 1952, Schlesinger Papers.

133. Arthur Schlesinger Jr. to Nicolas Nabokov, 18 June 1951, Nabokov Papers.

134. Arthur Schlesinger Jr. to Dwight Macdonald, 29 April 1952, Dwight Macdonald Papers, Sterling Memorial Library, Yale University.

135. Patricia Nabokov to Arthur Schlesinger Jr., 9 October, no year [presumably 1952], Schlesinger Papers. Typically, Hook attempted to reassure Nabokov that the split in the ACCF was not as serious as it had been made to appear, telling him that 'the differences were of emphasis rather than of principle'. Sidney Hook to Nicolas Nabokov, 24 April 1952, ACCF Papers.

136. Arthur Schlesinger Jr. to Irving Brown, 18 July 1950, Brown Papers.

137. See Saunders, *Who Paid the Piper?*, p. 201.

138. Quoted in ibid., pp. 201–2.

139. Cord Meyer to Arthur Schlesinger Jr., 16 February 1954, Schlesinger Papers.

140. Michael Josselson to Daniel Bell, 27 April 1956, CCF Papers.
141. Michael Josselson to Sol Stein, 22 September 1954, ACCF Papers.
142. ACCF to Michael Josselson, 9 May 1955, ACCF Papers. The Farfield's Directors stipulated that the money be spent on 'activities which relate to the international program of the Congress for Cultural Freedom'.
143. Arthur Schlesinger Jr. to Nicolas Nabokov, 27 February 1955, CCF Papers.
144. Cord Meyer to Arthur Schlesinger Jr., 16 May 1955, Schlesinger Papers.
145. See Hook, *Out of Step*, p. 424.
146. See Saunders, *Who Paid the Piper?*, pp. 232–3.
147. See chap. 6.
148. Quoted in Coleman, *Liberal Conspiracy*, p. 169.
149. ACCF Board of Directors minutes, 13 December 1960, Bertram D. Wolfe Papers, Hoover Institution, Stanford University.
150. See Hook, *Out of Step*, p. 449.
151. Quoted in Thomas, *Very Best Men*, p. 61.

4

A Case Study: *The New Leader* and the Cultural Cold War

Among the several journals associated with the New York intellectuals, the one least written about by academic historians is *The New Leader*. This scholarly neglect has served as a source of bewilderment to several of the intellectuals themselves. For example, in his 1987 memoirs, *Out of Step*, Sidney Hook felt moved to call into question the centrality accorded the *Partisan Review* in histories of the American non-communist left, suggesting instead that 'the real center of political anti-communist thought and activity was *The New Leader*, whose editor, Sol Levitas was, until his death, the central figure'[1] – a claim backed up in the *New York Times Book Review* by Daniel Bell.[2] The probable explanation for the dearth of scholarship on the *NL* is its failure to capture the political imagination of young intellectual historians searching for a usable radical past. Compared with *PR*'s eye-catching blend of independent Marxism and literary Modernism, the political weekly's characteristic editorial stance of hardline anti-communism combined with liberal reformism appears to offer little in the way of theoretical or practical inspiration to the left of today.[3] If this is the case, then the recent revelation by Frances Stonor Saunders that the publication received covert funding from the CIA in the Cultural Cold War will hardly have enhanced its historical reputation.[4] Nor will the implication contained in the title of her book, *Who Paid the Piper?*, that the Agency effectively called the tune of those benefiting from its clandestine patronage.

The main aim of this chapter is not to discover some hitherto un-detected leftist potential in *The New Leader* (although, incidentally, such a project should not be written off out of hand, given the publication's consistent support for industrial unionism, anti-fascism and anti-anti-Semitism, as well as its advocacy of the Civil Rights movement). Rather, it is to follow Sidney Hook's lead by investigating the paper's function as a centre of leftist anti-communism during the period when its influence was generally agreed to have been at its height, the late 1940s and early 1950s, and in doing so contest the suggestion that its role in the Cold War was merely that of a mouthpiece for the American national security establishment, a 'piper' for the CIA. Such an interpretation, it will be argued, overlooks three important factors. First, it fails to take account of the *NL*'s pre-Cold War history as a vocal opponent of communism dating as far back as the 1920s. Second, as is revealed by an analysis of its contents during the early postwar period, the paper did not merely reflect official attitudes towards communism in the Cold War; if anything, it helped to shape them. Finally, to dismiss *The New Leader* as a mere functionary of the CIA is to ignore archival evidence of tension and conflict between the magazine and its secretive patron.

The other main purpose of the chapter is to discuss *The New Leader*'s relationship with the British non-communist left and thereby provide a bridge to the examination of the impact of joint CIA/NCL covert operations on Britain which follows. Several commentators have already noted evidence that the *NL* was well known in Labour Party circles, especially among the Gaitskellites, who read it, wrote for it and even entertained Sol Levitas when he visited Britain.[5] Not surprisingly, considering the rumours of intelligence connections which hung around the publication long before Saunders's confirmation of CIA funding, the *NL*'s involvement in Labour politics has been viewed as intrusive and sinister, another prong in the Cold War American campaign to declaw British socialism. A careful reading of the publication's British coverage in this period, however, suggests a rather more complicated relationship.

BEFORE THE COLD WAR

Although Bell and Hook stressed the differences between *The New Leader* and the *Partisan Review*, the early histories of the two publications were strikingly similar. Both began life as official organs of left-wing organisations, then grew frustrated with the constraints of party patronage, before eventually breaking away and striking out on their own. That said, there was one crucial difference between them: in the case of *The New Leader*, the organisation concerned was the Socialist rather than the Communist Party. Indeed, unlike *PR*, the *NL* was anti-communist from the moment of its birth. Launched in New York in January 1924 under the editorship of the staunch midwestern socialist, James Oneal, it routinely denounced the Soviet Union for having betrayed the ideals of true socialism and warned the Socialist Party against forming a 'united front' with communists. This line received strong backing from anti-communist New York labour leaders like David Dubinsky, who regarded the paper as a valuable tool of worker education. It was less popular with the 'Militants', that is younger, pro-Soviet socialists who favoured a united front strategy and who, after the onset of Depression, began challenging the anti-communist 'Old Guard' for leadership of the SPA.[6] During the early 1930s *The New Leader* was protected from the Militants by the solidly anti-communist New York Party organisation. In May 1936, however, after having been refused seats at the SPA's national convention, the New York Old Guard bolted the Party and formed a new organisation, the Social Democratic Federation (SDF).[7] *The New Leader* followed suit shortly afterwards, becoming the SDF's official organ. Although relations with this new sponsor were initially good, tensions soon began to arise over claims by the SDF that the paper's preoccupation with anti-communism was eroding its positive commitment to democratic socialism. These intensified after Oneal acrimoniously resigned his editorship in 1940,[8] and the remaining editorial staff forged a new alliance with the Union for Democratic Action.[9] Eventually, *The New Leader* severed its ties with the SDF, converting from newspaper to tabloid format at the same time.

The New Leader's movement rightwards in this period was largely due to the influence over its editorial policy of its business manager (later, executive editor), Samuel M. (Sol) Levitas. A Russian-born social democrat or Menshevik, who had fled the Soviet Union in 1923 disguised in a Red Army colonel's uniform, Levitas nursed a visceral hatred of communism and an ambition to turn the *NL* from the mouthpiece of an obscure socialist sect into the leading political organ of the American non-communist left.[10] To this end, he courted contributions from a wide variety of anti-communist intellectuals. These included fellow Mensheviks like Raphael Abramovitch, Boris Nicolaevsky and David Dallin, who had arrived in New York as members of the 'Foreign Delegation' in 1940, and whom Levitas provided with food, shelter and a place to publish their expert commentaries on communism and the Soviet Union.[11] Levitas also threw the *NL*'s pages open to prominent American anti-communists from outside the socialist movement, such 'names' as Max Eastman, Eugene Lyons and, of course, Sidney Hook, whose past links with communism might have led one to expect a closer association with the *Partisan Review*, yet who found that magazine too 'cultural' for his largely political tastes. Finally, Levitas made a point of nurturing 'talent', up-and-coming young writers with their roots in the socialist and Trotskyist movements, future New York intellectuals like Irving Kristol, Melvin Lasky and Daniel Bell, all of whom worked in the *NL*'s offices during the 1940s and displayed an intense personal loyalty to their Menshevik boss.[12]

For these various intellectuals, *The New Leader* was not only an important publishing outlet; it also served as campaign headquarters in their crusade against communism. Among the numerous anti-communist activities with which Levitas and his paper were identified during the 1930s and early 1940s were the creation in 1939 of the anti-Stalinist front organisation, the Committee for Cultural Freedom; the campaign to publicise the mysterious disappearance of Henryk Erlich and Victor Alter, two Polish Bund leaders who had sought refuge from Nazism in the Soviet Union; and the whipping-up of protest at the apologetic portrayal of Stalinism contained in the 1943 Warner Brothers production, *Mission to Moscow*, a film adaptation of the book of the same title by the former US ambassador to the USSR, Joseph E. Davies, a notorious 'fellow-traveller'.[13] In other words, Sol Levitas's *New Leader* was a (to quote Hook's phrase again) 'center of political anti-Communist thought and activity' long before the start of the Cold War or, for that matter, the creation of the CIA.

COMMUNISM ABROAD

A second argument that can be made in, as it were, the *NL*'s defence is prompted by two recent developments in historical scholarship about the Cold War. One of these is the attention historians are increasingly paying to the part played by non-governmental forces in the anti-communist politics of the Truman–Eisenhower era, both at home (witness, for example, the importance attributed by Ellen Schrecker to private anti-communist networks in the genesis of McCarthyism) and abroad (where, according to such diplomatic historians as Scott Lucas, citizen groups were active across a wide range of US foreign policy initiatives, especially covert operations).[14] The other is the growing interest shown by Cold War scholars in the role of ideology and, in particular, ideology's discursive embodiment as *rhetoric*, in shaping American attitudes towards communism during the early stages of the conflict, again on both its domestic and foreign fronts.[15] As private citizens who specialised in the creation of anti-communist ideas and language, the intellectuals associated with *The New Leader* might be viewed in the light of these new concerns as having made a more important contribution to the growth of what might be called 'Cold War consciousness' in America than has previously been supposed. At the very least, an examination of the *NL*'s international coverage during the late 1940s and 1950s reveals the publication as engaged in a massive intellectual effort to construct communism as a threat to American national survival.

A good starting point for such an analysis is intellectual historian Abbot Gleason's suggestion that *The New Leader* was instrumental in introducing the term 'totalitarian' into American discourse about the Soviet Union.[16] It is possible to detect three rhetorical techniques at work here. The first and most obvious was the paper's constant privileging of the 'expert' commentary on Soviet affairs of its Menshevik contributors, all of whom subscribed to the view that communist Russia was totalitarian.[17] One leading Menshevik, Solomon Schwarz, deployed detailed statistic evidence to build up a grimly convincing picture of the Soviet 'command' economy. Another, Boris Nicolaevsky, working from the assumption that in a totalitarian society the only potential for political change existed at the leadership level, provided minute analyses of power struggles in the politburo, in the process pioneering the new discipline of 'Kremlinology'. Finally, 'the ultimate Menshevik pundit',[18] David Dallin, throughout this period an associate editor of and weekly columnist in the paper, provided his American readers with their first terrifying glimpse inside the Gulag in such pieces as his 1947 'World Events' pamphlet, 'Concentration Camps in Soviet Russia'.[19]

In exposing the scandal of forced labour in the Soviet Union, Dallin furnished the US government with a useful propaganda weapon in the Cold War and, no less importantly, helped establish the Gulag as the dominant symbol of communist totalitarianism in the American imagination. 'The forced labour camp', explained the Lovestoneite Sovietologist Bertram Wolfe in the *NL*, 'is an enormous concave mirror reflecting and magnifying ... the totalitarian society of which it is the product'.[20] The actual or metaphorical captivity of communist subjects – which was often contrasted, both implicitly and explicitly, with the voluntary associationalism of American citizens – was a constant theme in the Cold War *New Leader*. The terrible testimony of incarcerated dissidents who had managed to escape to the free west; the rhetorical trope of slavery, with its peculiarly powerful reverberations in an

American context (one of which was to associate the US cause in the Cold War with that of the Union in the American Civil War); even allusions to such famous fictional portrayals of political imprisonment as *1984* and *Darkness at Noon* (a free copy of which was given to every new subscriber) all featured frequently.[21]

Third, the *NL* performed important work in promulgating the axiomatic Cold War idea that communism was essentially identical with fascism. This had long been a firm conviction of the editors, who were proud of their record of predicting the Nazi–Soviet pact in early 1939. However, the notion of 'Red Fascism' assumed even greater prominence in the late 1940s and early 1950s, as *The New Leader* struggled to negate the positive perceptions of the Soviet Union current in wartime.[22] Sometimes the concept was expounded at length, as in the *NL* pamphlet, 'The Brothers Communazi'. At others it was merely a passing rhetorical flourish, for instance a throw-away reference to 'Generalissimo Stalin'.[23] Whatever form it took, the *NL*'s insistent use of the fascist–communist equation – which must have had an especially poignant resonance for the paper's large Jewish readership[24] – served as a powerful device in the construction of the Soviet Union as totalitarian.

Of course, in addition to emphasising the internally oppressive character of the Soviet regime, the concept of Red Fascism also carried strong overtones of external aggressiveness. *The New Leader* had always maintained that Stalin nursed imperialistic ambitions, citing Marxist–Leninist doctrine as proof of communist Russia's inherent expansionism. The Soviet annexation of eastern Europe during the late 1940s, then, came as no surprise to the publication, which nevertheless described the process in highly emotive, often strikingly gendered language, as in this passage from a 1948 column by David Dallin:

> The abhorrent spectacle of rape is evolving before our eyes. With her clothes torn, her body lacerated and bleeding, Czechoslovakia's resistance is fast failing. And the peoples of the world, like a bunch of demoralized soldiers, stand aside and watch the crime – with horrified interest but no action.[25]

As this excerpt clearly implies, it was less Soviet rapaciousness *per se* than the tacit complicity of other countries that enraged the *NL* writers. European democracies such as France were denounced for their reluctance to engage in the defence of the continent. The irresolution of the United Nations was another cause of complaint.[26]

It was the United States, though, that came in for the harshest criticism from *The New Leader*. Here the Nazi–Soviet equation came into play again. The US, it was constantly stated, was guilty of the same sort of appeasement that had permitted Hitler a free hand in Europe during the 1930s and led directly to the Second World War. William Henry Chamberlin, whose weekly column 'Where the News Ends' set the overall tone of the *NL*'s international coverage as much as Dallin's contributions, was especially vociferous on this point. The outcome of the Yalta conference was a source of particular vexation for Chamberlin. The date of the Yalta Agreement should, he proposed, be commemorated 'as a day of national shame and mourning'.[27] In order to avoid repeating the mistakes of the thirties – 'Munich-applied-to-Moscow' – and avert a third world war, the US must adopt a 'bold, clear, and firm' policy of resistance to Soviet expansion.[28] Signs that the Truman administration was doing just that in 1947 were greeted by the *NL* as welcome but long overdue. 'The Right Note At Last', was Chamberlin's verdict on the Truman Doctrine.[29] However, reservations about official determination to combat communism remained – 'Appeasement Is a Lively Corpse', announced Melvin Lasky in August 1947 – and opinion in *The New Leader* about the Cold War continued to move ahead of that in government circles, with the paper urging an escalation of the US's psychological warfare effort, and the abandonment of containment in favour of liberation, long before either of these policies received any official backing, at least in public.[30]

Another pivotal Cold War idea to which *The New Leader* gave currency was the notion of communism as a monolithic, Soviet-led world movement. This conviction, which like the view of Stalinist Russia as totalitarian and expansionist predated the Cold War, blinded the *NL* writers to divisions and conflicts within the communist bloc. Titoist Yugoslavia, for example, was perceived as a 'Soviet satellite' and Tito himself as 'the Stalin of the Balkans'.[31] Similarly, David Dallin constantly described the Chinese Communist Party as a puppet of Moscow, and criticised both State Department officials and prominent columnists Joseph and Stewart Alsop for suggesting otherwise.[32] 'It is hard for Americans to understand the true relations of the master-planet and its satellites', explained Dallin.

> It is hard because only those who have seen it first-hand can appreciate the tremendous pressure exerted by a great industrial and military power upon its weak neighbor. And there is a constant

128

radiation of power from the Asian borders of Russia – a radiation of plans, a radiation of orders, a radiation of will. Day after day, these rays penetrate deeper and farther, engulf new provinces, embrace new groups of people and consolidate the 'monolithic bloc'.[33]

Given this remorseless logic, it was not surprising that *The New Leader* should have taken a very hard line on the Korean War. 'If the Soviet Union is allowed to disturb the peace in Korea', proclaimed an editorial in July 1950, extending the appeasement metaphor to the Far East, 'it will proceed with impunity to initiate new aggressive moves – as Hitler did in similar circumstances'.[34] Soon Dallin was urging that North as well as South Korea be liberated from communism, a move that might lead to a democratic revolt in China.[35] The increasingly conservative William Henry Chamberlin even suggested 'outfitting Chiang Kai-Shek's troops for a resumption of the struggle on the mainland and systematic, all-out bombing of every military industrial installation in China'.[36] As this last comment suggests, *The New Leader* was none too choosy about its allies in the Cold War: the homogenisation of all communist movements into a single, undifferentiated entity was accompanied by a similar typing of all anti-communists, regardless of their other political beliefs, as defenders of 'the free world'. Hence the publication's championing of the nationalist Chiang Kai-Shek in Asia and its near sanctification of the partisan Draza Mihailovich in Yugoslavia.[37] In time, even Tito himself was grudgingly recognised as a potential ally against the Soviet Union.[38]

This is not to say that *The New Leader*'s international coverage in the early Cold War period utterly lacked complexity or nuance. Contributors did occasionally remark on causes of communist insurgency other than Soviet influence; both Stalin's death and the 'de-Stalinization crisis' caused the publication's Soviet experts to acknowledge the possibility of internal change in communist Russia; and the residual traces of fascism in Franco's Spain and Peron's Argentina were denounced no less loudly than communism (true to their convictions about the monolithic character of totalitarianism, the editors even speculated that Stalin would forge a new axis with Franco and Peron).[39] It should also be pointed out that *The New Leader* often linked its anti-communist stance abroad with its advocacy of liberal causes at home, using the Cold War as a lever for advancing its domestic reform agenda. In 1946, for example, Liston M. Oak argued that anti-labour legislation would aid the Soviet cause by sowing class division in American society. In a similar vein, William

Gordon welcomed the Supreme Court's 1954 *Brown* decision declaring racial segregation unconstititutional as 'a most damaging blow against Communism'.[40] The publication itself, then, was not entirely univocal or 'monolithic' on the Cold War: such contents existed alongside its more extreme anti-communist pronouncements, exposing them to a kind of ongoing internal critique. That said, its editorial voice, heard in features such as the regular columns by Dallin and Chamberlin, was remarkably consistent, even monotonous. Soviet society was totalitarian; Stalin was an imperialist; and communism everywhere was controlled by the Kremlin. For all the 'inside knowledge' of its contributors and geographical range of its coverage, the basic tendency of *The New Leader*'s foreign reportage in the late 1940s and early 1950s was towards simplification. Its peculiar achievement, perhaps, was to provide an apparently authoritative, 'expert' *Cold War* reading of the postwar international order.

COMMUNISM AT HOME

The New Leader's reputation for Cold War expertise was not confined to the international sphere. Like the private network of anti-communist activists portrayed by Schrecker, writers on the paper had been battling communist influence in American life for years before the start of the Cold War. During the late 1930s and early 1940s, for example, New York journalist Victor Reisel had used his 'Heard on the Left' column to attack suspected communists in the US labour movement, such as west-coast longshoreman leader Harry Bridges and Mike Quill of the Transport Workers Union. Come the postwar period another regular department, 'Alert!',[41] carried on the crusade in the unions, for instance exhorting the Congress of Industrial Organizations leadership to purge communists in the organisation's ranks,[42] but carried the fight to many other areas of society as well, such as the African–American community, the literary intelligentsia and the media.[43] To cite just one example, it waged a relentless campaign of exposure against Johannes Steel, a New York radio broadcaster suspected of having communist sympathies, until he was forced off the air by station WHN in December 1946.[44]

Such individuals, the *NL* claimed, not only contaminated the institutions they had infiltrated with their hateful ideology; in the context of the rapidly escalating Cold War, they constituted a domestic 'fifth column' in the service of a hostile foreign power. Nor did it matter that there were apparently so few of them: as German-born journalist Norbert Muhlen explained in a special *New Leader* 'World Events' pamphlet about the US communist movement, Lenin himself had decreed that revolution was to be accomplished by small cadres of 'professional revolutionaries'.[45] Muhlen's assumption that the intentions of American communists could be inferred directly from Marxist–Leninist texts was mirrored elsewhere in the *NL*'s pages by extensive references to such revolutionary 'blueprints' as J. Peters's notorious *Manual on Organization*, published in 1935 (and later used in the Smith Act trials of US communist leaders).[46] Hence, in addition to the important business of exposing individual communists, *The New Leader* also contributed to the intellectual construction of what Schrecker has called a 'demonized image' of the American communist movement as a whole.[47]

Another reason why *The New Leader* saw no cause for complacency in the relatively small size of the American Communist Party was the existence around it of a vast penumbra – what Muhlen, again quoting Lenin, referred to as a 'solar system'[48] – of sympathetic individuals and organisations. The fellow traveller or 'Commibut' ('I'm not a Communist, but...') was perhaps the most despised figure of all in the *NL*'s Cold War demonology. Joseph Davies, author of *Mission to Moscow* (or 'Submission to Moscow', as Muhlen joked) remained a favourite polemical target.[49] Others included political weeklies 'enamored of the false utopia portrayed by Communists', *The Nation*, *New Republic* and *PM* (short for 'Pravda Minor', according to Chamberlin).[50] Above all, though, it was Henry Wallace, America's most distinguished advocate of peaceful coexistence with the Soviet Union, who excited the *NL*'s wrath. During the run-up to the presidential election of 1948, the paper's office became a leading centre of anti-Wallace activism, publicising the pronouncements of the ADA, denouncing Wallace when he was on a speaking tour of Britain in a cable to Ernest Bevin and, just before voters went to the polls, printing a statement by the doyen of American liberalism, John Dewey, alleging that the Progressive Party had 'its deepest roots in the sub-soil of Soviet totalitarianism'.[51] As this last quotation suggests, the campaign against Wallace was highly vituperative, with *The New Leader* deploying every rhetorical weapon in its Cold War arsenal to ensure his defeat. Conjuring the Munich analogy, it charged him with 'appeasement'; his personal behaviour was described, in the newly fashionable psychological parlance of the day, as 'irrational', while his supporters were dismissed, in less clinical language, 'as so many crackpots and screwballs'; finally, the common Cold War metaphor of puppetry was invoked to portray the Progressive Party as a 'Stalinite fifth column' in which sinister communists pulled the strings of liberal 'marionettes'.[52]

In the event, of course, Wallace received only about a million votes and America was spared having a Commibut in the White House. However, this did not remove the danger of communism in federal government. *The New Leader* had commentated on the unmasking of the Canadian spy ring in 1946 with grim humour ('Here was Stalin caught with his NKVD down'), and the following year printed defector Igor Gouzenko's shocking testimony in the case as a series of articles.[53] Throughout the late 1940s it urged greater vigilance on the US government, welcoming the draconian Federal Employee Loyalty Program of 1947 with the same sort of 'better late than never' attitude with which it had greeted the Truman Doctrine.[54] In 1949 it even carried an essay by no less an authority on espionage than Allen Dulles claiming that America was 'the subject of a systematic program of penetration by skilled artisans of world revolution' and calling for the creation of a new internal security commission.[55] A particular preoccupation of the paper, consistent with its hard line on China, was the political allegiance of such State Department advisers on Asian matters as Owen Lattimore and John Stewart Service. Its pronouncements on this issue, especially those delivered by Ferdinand Lundberg, Ralph de Toledano and Eugene Lyons, verged on the hysterical.[56] Indeed, Lyons was probably only half-joking when, in an *NL* article entitled 'In Defense of Red-Baiting', he proposed the formation of a new organisation to be called 'Red-Baiters, Inc.'.[57]

Considering this sort of comment, it is not surprising that some historians, including most recently Abbot Gleason, have assumed that *The New Leader* was a supporter of Joe McCarthy.[58] Such a judgement, though, is too harsh. It overlooks criticism by the publication of what it viewed as over-zealous anti-communist measures, such as the McCarran Internal Security Act of 1950 ('an appalling monument to panic and ignorance') or the firing of a legless war veteran from a US government job because of his past membership of a Trotskyist organisation ('Justice Department travesty').[59] It also fails to take into account the fact that, as McCarthyism took hold in the early 1950s, the *NL* devoted less and less space to the exposure of domestic communism. Indeed, a common feature of the paper in this period was explicit criticism of McCarthy himself. Granville Hicks, the paper's literary editor during this period, was particularly forthright in this respect, for example proclaiming in

132

May 1950 that, 'The discrediting of McCarthy ... is something to be as devoutly desired as the discovery of a cure for the common cold'.[60] Other members of the editorial board shared this view, locating the Wisconsin senator in a dishonourable American tradition of 'rabble-rousing demagogues' which included such liberal hate-figures as Theodore G. Bilbo and Gerald L. K. Smith.[61] This is not to say, however, that they rejected the premises of the Cold War Red Scare: guilt by association, American communists' culpability for foreign policy setbacks and so on. Moreover, they tended to oppose McCarthy on the grounds that he was damaging the American Cold War effort – witness their complaints that his attack on the Voice of America had harmed the US's psychological warfare capability[62] – rather than out of any tenderness for the civil liberties of his victims. Indeed, Hicks's full-frontal opposition to McCarthyism sometimes drew criticism from other *NL* writers, such as Eugene Lyons, who believed that domestic communism was a greater threat to the freedom of American citizens than excessive anti-communism.[63] In sum, it would probably be fairest to say that, as private 'Red-Baiter' Alfred Kohlberg suggested in an angry letter to the editors, *The New Leader* was *confused* about McCarthyism.[64] In this regard, it perhaps merely reflected the attitude of the American non-communist left as a whole.

PIPER FOR THE CIA?

Despite the contradictions in its stance on the McCarthy question, *The New Leader* enjoyed a growing reputation for anti-communist expertise in this period, not only on the non-communist left but also amongst élite US government officials in Washington, especially those responsible for planning and implementing Cold War covert operations. George Kennan, for example, considered Boris Nicolaevsky 'an expert on Soviet Russia and consulted him in important matters related thereto'. [65] William Henry Chamberlin was similarly valued for his knowledge of Soviet history (if not his strategic advice). 'The Russian revolution and civil war have had no finer historian in this country than yourself', Kennan once told him.[66] Another influential admirer of *The New Leader* was *Time-Life* Vice-President and, from 1953 to 1954, President Eisenhower's principal adviser on psychological warfare, C. D. Jackson, who reckoned it to be 'virtually the only ... pro-American, high-quality, left-wing literature that exists on either side of the Atlantic'.[67] In 1953, Jackson arranged an annual *Time* grant of $5,000 to the magazine in return for 'Research Data' on the international communist movement; he also recommended that Sol Levitas serve as one of the small number of civilian witnesses called to testify before the President's Committee on International Information Activities (better known as the Jackson Committee), whose report furnished the basis of the Eisenhower administration's subsequent Cold War propaganda effort.[68] Allen Dulles, too, Eisenhower's Director of Central Intelligence (and, as already noted, *New Leader* contributor in 1949), consulted with Levitas and Chamberlin on a number of occasions. 'I know the publication well and think highly of it', he told former CIA officer Franklin A. Lindsay in 1956.[69] Other prominent American citizens friendly towards the publication, or at least prepared to donate money to its publisher, the American Labor Conference on International Affairs, included W. Averell Harriman, William Donovan and Frank Altschul.[70]

The New Leader's value to these individuals did not lie merely in its function as a source of expert, 'inside' intelligence about the international communist movement. The publication also offered a potential means of influencing a body of opinion that was deemed to be of crucial strategic significance in the Cold War. When compared with the readership of commercial news magazines such as *Time*, the *NL*'s paying audience was tiny: roughly 28,000 subscriptions in 1955, of which 19,000 were individual, and 9,000 bulk purchases by US unions (this is, incidentally, about three times *Partisan Review*'s circulation in the same period).[71] However, this audience consisted of precisely those groups on the non-communist left the CIA was most concerned to win over in its Cold War struggle for 'hearts and minds' with the Soviet Union, that is literary intellectuals, trade unionists and socialist politicians. As C. D. Jackson explained to Allen Dulles, it was not circulation figures that mattered: 'The particular tone of voice with which Levitas speaks to a particular group of people here and abroad is unique and uniquely important'.[72]

It was this combination of perceived usefulness in the Cultural Cold War and relatively low sales figures that put *The New Leader* in line for covert financial assistance from the CIA. The evidence concerning this funding is patchy but conclusive. During the early 1950s Irving Brown generated extra revenue and readers for the magazine by the simple expedient of arranging for thousands of new European subscriptions to be taken out free of charge.[73] On at least three separate occasions during the same period, Tom Braden resorted to the more direct method of personally handing sums of about $10,000 to Sol Levitas.[74] Finally, the National Committee for a Free Europe paid the *NL* an annual grant of $25,000.[75] Although this subsidy was cancelled in 1955, additional covert funding was secured thanks to a 'Save *The New Leader*' drive launched by Franklin Lindsay, which by the end of 1956 had netted the magazine donations totalling $45,000.[76] These various ploys were intended, as C. D. Jackson put it, 'for all of us to have our Levitas and let him eat, too'.[77]

The New Leader, then, was 'on the take'. However, it does not necessarily follow from this, as many writers about the Cultural Cold War have assumed, that the CIA therefore exercised complete control over its client – or 'called the tune', to use Saunders's musical metaphor. To begin with, the funding was irregular, and, at least in the view of *NL* insiders, inadequate to the demands of weekly publication. Moreover, rather than being foisted on the paper, it was actively solicited. Braden recalls Levitas 'sitting across the table, pleading for money'.[78] Irving Brown was similarly urged to 'continue the pressure' and 'see that those subscriptions are renewed'.[79] However, Levitas's most insistent begging was reserved for Michael Josselson of the Congress for Cultural Freedom. Indeed, the tone of Levitas's frequent petitions to Josselson grew distinctly querulous, as he accused the CCF of neglecting his paper in favour of other, far less deserving causes (including the organisation's own English-language organ, *Encounter*, which the Menshevik viewed as ineffectual in the Cold War).[80] For his part, Josselson became increasingly irritated by Levitas's recriminations, remarking darkly on 'the alarming degree of irresponsibility shown recently by some of our "friends" in New York'.[81] One gets little impression from these exchanges of a puppet-master CIA pulling the strings of a marionette *New Leader*. Again, the relationship is more reminiscent of that between a cultural patron and a somewhat temperamental artist.

Another source of irritation for Josselson was the fact that the *NL* was clearly identified with the hardline anti-communist tendency of the CCF's tactically inept American affiliate, the American Committee for Cultural Freedom. After briefing the CCF's General Secretary, Nicolas Nabokov, about the extremist anti-communism of the ACCF's leadership, Arthur Schlesinger Jr. concluded bitterly that '*The New Leader* variety of ex-Communist is really too much for me'.[82] (As this comment suggests, relations between the Harvard historian and the *NL* were distinctly frosty: Schlesinger was unhappy that Levitas had added his name to the telegram sent to the British government about Henry Wallace without first consulting him; suspected William Henry Chamberlin of harbouring

135

6 Allen Dulles, Director of Central Intelligence from 1953, and ardent advocate of covert operations. (Richard J. Aldrich)

fascist sympathies; and in 1953 collaborated with other leading non-communist left intellectuals in an abortive attempt to launch a new magazine, *The Critic*, partly in response to what he perceived as the dullness and conformism of publications like the *NL*.)[83] Schlesinger's linkage of *The New Leader* and the ACCF was understandable: the magazine and organisation shared the same politics, personnel, and even, briefly, offices.[84] It should come as no surprise to learn, therefore, that the *NL* was heavily implicated in the ACCF's several rows with Bertrand Russell, which culminated in 1957 with the British philosopher's resignation from his honorary chair of the CCF, an event deemed a major propaganda victory for the Soviets by a furious Michael Josselson.[85] In other words, *The New Leader*, at least tactically speaking, stood to the *right* of the main architect of the CIA's Cultural Cold War effort.

A third major problem in the relationship between the CIA and the circle around the *NL* was the factionalism of the latter. Left-wing politics in New York had always been afflicted by ugly factional feuds, as was demonstrated by the turbulent history of the ACCF, but in the case of the *NL* this tendency was made even worse by the presence around it of so many Russian émigrés. Although the Mensheviks had by the late 1940s reached agreement on the divisive question of whether the Soviet Union would eventually evolve into a truly socialist society (it would not), the Foreign Delegation was now split (fatally, so it would prove) over another issue, the postwar immigration of anti-communist refugees and defectors from the eastern bloc countries. As André Liebich shows in his history of Russian social democracy, *From The Other Shore*, the New York Mensheviks, as 'Great Russians' and self-perceived socialists, tended to view these new arrivals, many of whom hailed from 'minority nationality' or satellite state backgrounds, and were rabidly anti-Marxist, with a mixture of suspicion and condescension (it is not impossible, by the way, that factors such as these were at play in the strained personal relations between the Russian Levitas and Estonian-born Michael Josselson).[86] Liebich goes on to document, using newly available FBI files, the confusion of Bureau agents assigned to monitor these various groups, 'not really sure to the end' with whom they were dealing.[87] The CIA, which of course had its own share of internal ideological divisions, faced similar problems understanding the complexities of émigré politics.

The best evidence of this is to be found in the papers of James Burnham, the CIA's chief intellectual consultant on émigré affairs. A series of memoranda, anonymously written but clearly intended for

7 C. D. Jackson, *Time-Life* executive and President Eisenhower's chief adviser on psychological warfare. (Dwight D. Eisenhower Library, Abilene, Kansas)

the attention of senior Agency personnel, reports on the factional manoeuvering of Levitas and other Russian-born Mensheviks as they sought to consolidate their position in America at the expense of the more recent arrivals. According to one, Raphael Abramovitch was spreading rumours to the effect that Burnham, who favoured a united front of émigré groups in a campaign of liberation, was anti-Semitic.[88] Another speculated that Boris Nicolaevsky was using Agency money intended for anti-communist research by his partner, Anna Bourgina, 'to finance his present intrigues'.[89] A third, and the most detailed, alleged 'that the Russian Menshevik émigrés (Abramovitch, Nicolaevsky, Levitas, et al) are developing a deliberate and well-organized campaign' designed to 'defend and enlarge the position which they have won in the anti-Stalinist front, and particularly in the American section of that front'. Among the targets of this campaign were:

A. The non-Menshevik anti-Stalin Russians, particularly those who are openly anti-Marxist....
B. The lesser Soviet nationalities (Ukrainians, Georgians, etc.).
C. Americans who are, or seem to be, supporting any of the persons or groups in A or B.

Various pieces of evidence were cited in support of this claim, including Levitas's denunciation of rival anti-communist C. N. Boldyreff, and a *New Leader* book review by David Shub which described Burnham as 'a monarchist reactionary'. Most egregious, though, were the Mensheviks' attempts to sabotage the founding Berlin conference of the Congress for Cultural Freedom in June 1950 through 'their protégé' Melvin Lasky.

They fought to keep the non-Menshevik Russians ... off the official list of Congress participants. They ... succeeded in hiding and obscuring the official greetings of Ukrainian organizations which were addressed to the Congress. They changed Nicolaevsky's Russian broadcast speech at the last moment.[90]

In brief, Burnham's papers reveal the *New Leader* Mensheviks trying to exploit the CIA's patronage for their own selfish, factional purposes, and in the process undermining the US's major covert operation in the Cultural Cold War.

BRITISH LABOUR

Throughout the late 1940s and early 1950s *The New Leader* devoted a considerable amount of space to discussion of the British Labour movement. In part this reflected the American left's traditional admiration for Labour: like the Union for Democratic Action and its London representative, David Williams, the intellectuals around the *NL* were interested in learning positive lessons about the prospects for social and economic reform in America from the example of the Attlee government. In March 1946 Frederick Scheu, the first '*New Leader* London correspondent' of the period, hailed the 'Nationalization of Coal and Social Insurance' as 'Two Steps Ahead' towards the realisation 'of British Socialism'.[91] In May of the same year the first 'Eight Months of Socialist Government' were described by Robert J. Alexander, who had preceded Scheu in London during his US army service, as a 'Truly Noble Experiment'.[92] This initial enthusiasm was dampened somewhat by the harsh winter of 1947 and Labour's accompanying political setbacks. Irving Kristol, who replaced Scheu in November 1946 after crossing to England to study with his wife, historian Gertrude Himmelfarb, at Cambridge, employed an altogether more sober tone when reporting on British affairs than had his predecessors.[93] Nonetheless, the fraternal spirit remained, as did a confident belief that the Attlee government would eventually overcome its difficulties.[94] This tendency was reinforced by David Williams's decision in 1949 to add the role of *NL* London correspondent to his duties as UDA representative. The magazine's reportage of Labour's domestic affairs from then until the General Election defeat of 1951 and Williams's return home was consistently sympathetic and occasionally flattering (see, for example, Williams's overly optimistic claim in 1950 that British labour was in the process of adopting an American model of non-political trade unionism).[95] It is also possible to detect an Anglophile note in other sections of the *NL* during this period, especially the regular column on 'The Home Front' by veteran socialist William Bohn, who was an ardent advocate of transatlantic unity.[96]

Such faith in the Anglo–American relationship was not felt universally, however. *The New Leader*'s generally enthusiastic support for the Attlee government's domestic programme was in contrast to its often critical attitude towards Labour's record on foreign affairs. Again like Williams and other UDA-ers, the *NL* intellectuals' instinctive suspicion of British 'imperialism' was exacerbated by Bevin's stance on Palestine. 'Unfortunate, tactless and inept', was how one contributor characterised the Foreign Secretary's comments on the issue at the 1946 Labour Party conference.[97] It was the threat of communist expansion which most concerned the magazine, however, and on this question Bevin's anti-Soviet and pro-American position was more to its liking. Hence when the Labour left staged its foreign policy rebellion in the autumn of 1946, the *NL* quickly weighed in to express its support for the Party's official line.[98] When the *Keep Left* group moderated its criticism of government policies during the late 1940s, *The New Leader*'s hostility towards it diminished correspondingly. After 1950, however, the rise of Bevanism (a development discussed in greater detail in the next chapter) caused a further hardening of the magazine's standpoint vis-à-vis Labour Britain. Aneurin Bevan himself came to serve as a powerful symbol of European anti-Americanism and neutralism; negative references to the rebel leader littered the *NL*'s pages during the early 1950s.[99] At the same time there was a marked increase in criticism of official Labour policy, especially with regard to the matter of European unity and the anti-communist struggle in Asia.[100] William Henry Chamberlin was predictably out-spoken in this last respect. 'Is British Labour's Conscience Dead?', he demanded to know in 1953, after the Party's annual conference had voted in favour of admitting China to the UN.[101]

For the most part, though, *The New Leader* still differentiated between the 'responsible' behaviour of Labour's centre-right leadership and the 'irresponsibility' of its left wing. Indeed, the magazine made a particular point of praising certain leaders it considered 'dependable' on the Cold War and deliberately courted contact with them. For their part, the individuals concerned appeared to welcome the *NL*'s attentions and reciprocated the praise. A long-standing British friend of the publication was Herbert Morrison who, in 1954, was invited to speak at its thirtieth anniversary dinner. The deputy leader of the Labour Party (and former Foreign Secretary) identified *The New Leader* as expressing 'the general view of progressives and of the labour movement' in the US and, while confessing he did 'not always agree with its views', acknowledged that it was 'sincere', 'alive' and showed 'every sign of continuing its vigorous services to the American liberal spirit'.[102] Hugh Gaitskell, unofficial leader of Labour opposition to the Bevanites and from 1955 official leader of the Party, was a particular British favourite of the magazine's. A report on his performance at the 1955 Margate conference by Irving Kristol (back in England to edit another organ of the non-communist left, *Encounter*), was lyrical in its approbation, describing his 'intangible aura of certainty, self-confidence, almost inevitability'.[103] Although Gaitskell declined an invitation by Sol Levitas to respond to Kristol's comments, he did subsequently strike up a friendship with the *NL*'s executive editor, meeting with him several times in both Britain and America.[104] Indeed, it was only two weeks after lunching with him in London in December 1960 (an occasion also attended by Kristol's successor as American editor of *Encounter* and another product of *The New Leader*'s journalistic academy, Melvin Lasky), that Gaitskell learned of Levitas's death. 'We always knew over here that in him we had a friend who could be relied on on all occasions', the Labour leader wrote to *NL*'s grieving staff. 'We shall miss him very much.'[105] A similar message expressing 'sorrow over loss of great editor and good friend' was sent by Denis Healey, now a Labour MP, and perhaps Levitas's closest ally on the British left.[106] Healey had taken over the role of *NL* London correspondent in 1955, receiving fees of $30 for his frequent contributions. He later recalled of Levitas, 'many of America's best journalists were proud to write for him, and he assembled round him the cream of New York's Jewish intelligentsia'.[107]

Considering the magazine's covert connections in this period, it is perhaps not surprising that links between *The New Leader* and Atlanticist, revisionist elements within the Labour Party should have given rise to talk of the CIA taking the teeth out of British socialism. By consistently attacking Bevanism and giving support, both moral and (in Healey's case) material, to the Gaitskellites, the *NL* did arguably lend some impetus to the Labour Party's rightwards movement during the 1950s. In particular, it helped speed up the process whereby, under the pressure of the Cold War, internationalist and Third Force impulses in the British labour movement gradually narrowed to Atlanticism and the notion of a transatlantic non-communist left. As is discussed below, this was a tendency reinforced during the 1950s by another intellectual publication funded by the CIA, *Encounter*.

This was not, however, a simple relationship of control. Viewed from the British perspective, *The New Leader* served the purposes of the Labour leadership as much as vice versa. For example, as Party Secretary Morgan Phillips discovered, it was willing to publish official Labour statements on such matters as European federalism and party unity, even when they conflicted with the viewpoint of the editors. Granted Morrison's description of the *NL* as the principal mouthpiece of the American labour movement, Phillips must have been delighted by this easy opportunity to propagate the party line abroad.[108] Conference speeches were another form of Labour publicity to which the magazine was ready to give free air-time: both Morrison in 1952 and Gaitskell in

1960 (when he promised to 'fight, fight and fight again') benefited from this service.[109] Denis Healey's London Letters might be read in a similar light, that is less as exhibiting a political consciousness colonised by the CIA than as putting a carefully prepared case to an important foreign audience. Certainly, the former Secretary of the International Department rarely missed an opportunity to criticise the Conservative government or to talk up Labour's unity and therefore electability.[110] Finally, it is worth remarking that not all the British leftists admitted to the pages of *The New Leader* expressed undiluted admiration of the US or its foreign policies. Indeed, one of Healey's predecessors as London correspondent, the literary critic T. R. Fyvel (other British writers who held this position during the early Cold War period included Donald Bruce, Graham Miller and G. L. Arnold) was surprisingly quick to convey British concerns about American actions to the magazine's readership. When the former literary editor of *Tribune* (and occasional contract worker for the Information Research Department) sent in a piece entitled 'How London Views the World', which *inter alia* explicitly protested at recent *NL* attacks on British foreign policy, the magazine responded with an editorial defending its views and rebutting those of its London correspondent.[111] After this very public falling out, Fyvel contributed only one more London Letter.

The imprudence of leaping to the conclusion that *The New Leader* was pulling the strings of British Labour is best illustrated by an incident involving Sol Levitas, Hugh Gaitskell and the Soviet premier Nikita Khrushchev. In the spring of 1956, Levitas decided to take advantage of the new mood of political uncertainty in the Soviet Union created by the death of Stalin to raise the fate of those social democrats and trade unionists imprisoned in communist bloc countries during the Stalinist era. If the new Soviet leadership responded by releasing those prisoners still alive, or rehabilitating the reputations of those already dead, then the appeal would have worked; if Khrushchev failed to act, he would be revealed to be as tyrannical as his predecessor and the west would score a propaganda victory. On 18 April a letter drafted by Levitas and signed by an '*Ad Hoc* Labor Committee' which included James Carey, A. Philip Randolph and Norman Thomas was sent to the Soviet Embassy in Britain, where Khrushschev and the Russian prime minister, Nicolai Bulganin, were undertaking an official visit; it was accompanied by a list of 245 political prisoners.[112] To ensure that his appeal was not buried by Soviet bureaucracy, Levitas also sent copies of his letter and list to leaders of the British labour movement, including Gaitskell, who were urged to give them the widest possible distribution.[113] Gaitskell's response must have delighted Levitas: 'You can be sure that we will make representations to Mr Bulganin and Mr Khrushchev on behalf of the Labour and Social Democratic comrades still suffering under Communist dictatorships', he cabled New York on April 19.[114]

A few days later Gaitskell fulfilled this promise in the most spectacular manner imaginable. On the evening of Monday 23 April, the National Executive Committee (NEC) of the Labour Party held a dinner in honour of the Soviet delegation in the House of Commons. The evening passed uneventfully until Khrushchev rose at the end of the meal to deliver an impromptu speech which turned into an hour-long harangue of the west ('an exhibition of crude Stalinism', according to Denis Healey's *New Leader* report of the event), interrupted only by alcohol-fuelled barracking from the notoriously outspoken shadow cabinet member, George Brown.[115] Hugh Gaitskell began his response in a conciliatory enough vein, telling Khrushchev that 'it would be discourteous to pursue any kind of argument with him', but then raised the question of imprisoned 'social democrats in countries of Eastern and Central Europe who are our comrades'. The Labour Party, he explained, had a list of such social democrats which it believed was 'reasonably up-to-date' and it now proposed to hand its Soviet guests this document in the hope they might intercede on the prisoners' behalf. Khrushchev's reaction to Gaitskell's mild remarks astonished his audience. 'We are not in a position to accept the list', he told his hosts, nor was he prepared to 'tolerate any interference in the internal affairs of our country'. Gaitskell politely repeated Labour's appeal on behalf of its social democratic comrades: 'All that we ask is that he should use his influence as Secretary of the Russian Communist Party ... [to] secure their release.' 'We cannot take that obligation upon ourselves', replied Khrushchev. 'You must look for other agents to protect the enemies of the working class.' At this point Gaitskell's friend Sam Watson of the Durham miners and his old sparring partner Aneurin Bevan joined in the argument, the latter advancing on Khrushchev and demanding to know if he would take any action. By now, the evening had degenerated into a shouting match. Eventually, the NEC's chairman Edwin Gooch attempted to bring proceedings to a cordial conclusion by declaring, 'Here's to our next meeting!' 'But without me', Khrushchev was heard to mutter as he stalked out of the dining room.[116]

The reason for Khrushchev's violent response to the Labour Party's appeal became evident shortly after his return to Moscow. In early May,

Pravda carried an article headlined, 'To Someone Else's Whistle', with a subhead, 'Who Incited Gaitskell's Provocational Scheme?' According to this story (which, ironically enough, drew heavily from a report in the New York *Herald Tribune*), the Labour Party's appeal on behalf of the imprisoned social democrats had been inspired by Sol Levitas of *The New Leader*, a 'weekly sheet ... notorious for carrying out the dirtiest assignments of Wall Street, busying itself with concocting the most absurd anti-Soviet slander'. The idea of confronting the Soviet delegation with a list of political prisoners had, allegedly, been hatched at a meeting between Levitas and several American labour leaders a week before the Labour Party dinner. 'Thus, the script for this vile-smelling operation was prepared in New York.' The behaviour of Gaitskell and his 'Labourite' colleagues, *Pravda* reflected, was reminiscent of a passage in Gogol describing 'compliant people who are able to "dance best of all to someone else's whistle"'.[117]

Judging by the *Pravda* story (which was also broadcast on Radio Moscow), Khrushchev thought that the list in Gaitskell's possession was the same document he had been sent via the Soviet London Embassy by Levitas and the '*Ad Hoc* Labor Committee'. This would explain his comment about 'other agents' protecting 'the enemies of the working class', a reference to the New York labour leaders harbouring the Menshevik Foreign Delegation. He was not alone in making this assumption. Various American observers accepted the *Pravda* version of events at face value. Walter Reuther, for example, believed that the row between Gaitskell and Khrushchev had been caused by a list sent to the former by 'Socialists in New York' (Reuther, incidentally, suspected the hand of Jay Lovestone in the affair).[118] Similarly, Franklin Lindsay, the former CIA officer who took it upon himself to fund-raise for *The New Leader*, viewed the incident as a stunning vindication 'of the one-man psychological warfare job conducted by Levitas'. As he told Bill Furth of *Time*, 'That needling job on B[ulganin] and K[hrushchev] on the Social Democrats in Russia was worth a million bucks of anybody's propaganda budget'.[119] Understandably enough, given the promotional value of the story, *The New Leader*'s own reportage of the incident tacitly endorsed that of *Pravda*. According to Lindsay, 'Levitas's cheerful comment' on his new-found infamy in Moscow was: 'Now at least all my friends in Russia know that I am still alive.'[120]

In truth, however, the list referred to by Gaitskell was not the one compiled by Levitas. As Peter Ericsson, Denis Healey's successor as Secretary of Labour's International Department, explained to Richard Crossman shortly after the disastrous meeting with the Soviet delegation,

8 Hugh Gaitskell (*centre*), pictured shortly before becoming Labour Party leader in 1955, flanked by two powerful supporters in the British labour movement, Sam Watson of the Durham miners (*left*) and Trades Union Congress official, Vic Feather. (By Permission of People's History Museum)

the Labour Party had its own list 'concerned with Socialists for the most part arrested after 1947' that was 'totally different' from the list of 'old Mensheviks and 1918 cases' compiled by *The New Leader*. According to Crossman, Ericsson was angry about the way in which the confusion had arisen, feeling 'the whole thing had been mismanaged'.[121] Indeed, he was sufficiently disturbed to write to Sol Levitas in order to 'point out that we used our own list which has been checked over a period of time from various sources, and not the one sent over by you'.[122] Rather than publicly correcting the misunderstanding in the pages of *The New Leader*, Levitas's reaction was to cable Hugh Gaitskell asking to be shown the Labour Party list so that he could bring his own up to date.[123] Ericsson's response was a terse note stating that the Labour list would not be made available.[124] To sum up, then, the Labour leadership's confrontation with Khrushchev and Bulganin was not, as both the Soviets and Americans believed, a 'put-up job' by *The New Leader*; rather, it was the independent action of a group of determinedly anti-communist social democrats.

Sidney Hook and Daniel Bell were right to claim that *The New Leader*'s political significance has been underestimated by historians. During the late 1940s and 1950s, the intellectuals associated with the publication played an important part in the American Cold War effort. In part, their contribution was ideological and rhetorical. By consistently portraying communism as totalitarian, innately aggressive and monolithic, they helped create a discursive environment in which both the Soviet Union and the American communist movement came to be perceived as deadly enemies of US national security. At another level, the *NL* intellectuals were more directly involved in the formulation and execution of Cold War foreign policy, both as expert advisers to élite officials and participants in one of the era's most sophisticated covert operations. All this, of course, was far removed from their obscure origins on the American or, in the case of the Menshevik émigrés, Russian left. To adopt the terminology of the Italian Marxist Antonio Gramsci, they had been transformed from 'organic intellectuals', spokespersons of the oppositional social class from which they had originally emerged, into the deputies of the ruling group, or 'traditional intellectuals'. In a word, their function in the American Cold War effort was *hegemonic*.[125]

This should not be taken as meaning, however, that *The New Leader* was a mere puppet of the US Cold War spy establishment. To perceive it as such would be to repeat the same error it made when it represented

147

the American communist movement as solely motivated by obedience to Moscow. A hegemony, after all, in the Gramscian sense of the term, is not a simple state of dominance by one group over others; it is rather an historical bloc, or alliance – and, like any alliance, involving elements of negotiation and even contestation. Certainly the latter was true of the *NL*'s relationship with the CIA, which was characterised as much by conflict as cooperation. There is, perhaps, a wider lesson to be learned here about the dynamics of the state–private networks which under-pinned much of the American Cold War effort.

In any event, it is worth bearing in mind that, as socialists and social democrats, the intellectuals around *The New Leader* had been fighting communism long before the liberal anti-communists of the CIA came on the scene. If anything, anti-communism belonged more to them as an ideology than it did the postwar liberal élites who made US foreign policy. Viewed from this angle, it is possible to see the Cultural Cold War as, to some extent at least, an internal struggle on the American left suddenly projected onto an international backdrop. Indeed, considering the prominence of Russian social democrats around the *NL*, it is tempting to trace the doctrinal roots of the conflict even further back, to the Menshevik/Bolshevik split that affected the Russian left prior to the revolution of 1917.

That said, it would equally be a mistake to *overestimate The New Leader*'s influence on the course of the Cultural Cold War. As the incident involving Khrushchev and Bulganin reveals, observers during the 1950s and since have been too ready to assume that the paper and its shadowy friends in the US government succeeded in pulling the strings – or to use the metaphor more commonly applied in this particular instance, calling the tune – of the Gaitskellites. In fact, British responses to covert American pressure in the Cold War were rarely so straight-foward.

NOTES

1. Sidney Hook, *Out of Step: An Unquiet Life in the Twentieth Century* (New York: Harper and Row, 1987), p. 509. This followed an earlier letter making the same claim by Hook and Arnold Beichman to the editor, *New York Times Book Review* 25 March 1984. *Partisan Review*'s founding editor, William Phillips, always jealous of his magazine's reputation, privately described Hook's comments as 'silly, inaccurate, and ... mean-spirited'.

William Phillips to Sidney Hook, 10 April 1984, Sidney Hook Papers, Hoover Institution, Stanford University.

2. Daniel Bell to the editor, *New York Times Book Review* 3 May 1987. The previous month Hook had told Bell that, '"*The New Leader* Under Sol Levitas" should be an article in a serious, scholarly publication'. Sidney Hook to Daniel Bell, 7 April 1987, Hook Papers.

3. Typical of this perception is Alan Wald's dismissal of *The New Leader* as 'a halfway house for right-wing social-democratic anti-communists from which virtually no one returned'. Alan M. Wald, *The New York Intellectuals: The Rise and Decline of the Anti-Stalinist Left* (Chapel Hill: University of North Carolina Press, 1987), p. 5. Wald's comment echoes earlier hostile references to *The New Leader* by left-wing members of the New York intellectual community, such as Dwight Macdonald, who described the publication as an 'extreme right-wing labor paper, of a low intellectual level'. Dwight Macdonald to Victor Serge, 27 February 1945, Dwight Macdonald Papers, Sterling Memorial Library, Yale University.

4. See Frances Stonor Saunders, *Who Paid the Piper? The CIA and the Cultural Cold War* (London: Granta, 1999), especially pp. 162–4. Two other recent publications that refer to *The New Leader* in passing are Abbot Gleason's treatise on the discursive career of totalitarianism, *Totalitarianism: The Inner History of the Cold War* (Oxford University Press, 1995), pp. 62–3, and André Liebich's history of Menshevism, *From the Other Shore: Russian Social Democracy after 1921* (Harvard University Press, 1997), pp. 299–309. The only extended study of the publication of which I am aware is a 1949 Columbia University dissertation by Paul Kessler, 'History of *The New Leader*', held by the Tamiment Institute Library, New York University. I am grateful to Gail Malmgreen for alerting me to the existence of this dissertation.

5. See Richard Fletcher, 'How CIA money took the teeth out of British socialism', in Philip Agee and Louis Wolf (eds), *Dirty Work: The CIA in Western Europe* (London: Zed Press, 1978), pp. 190–4; Kees van der Pijl, *The Making of an Atlantic Ruling Class* (London: Verso, 1984), pp. 153–4, 219; Robin Ramsay, 'The clandestine caucus: Anti-socialist campaigns and operations in the British labour movement since the War', *Lobster* special issue, 13.

6. For more detail on the Old Guard-Militant split, see Guenter Lewy, *The Cause That Failed: Communism in American Political Life* (Oxford University Press, 1990), pp. 18–24. A useful if partisan account of the split as it affected *The New Leader* is James Oneal, 'Some pages of party history', no date [probably 1934], American Socialist Party (Daniel Bell) Papers, Tamiment Institute Library, New York University.

7. The New York Old Guard's bolt from the SPA is extensively documented in the Bell Papers.

8. Oneal quit *The New Leader* claiming that a faction of the publication's staff

led by Sol Levitas was seeking to transform it from the organ of the SDF into a mouthpiece for 'the liberal intelligentsia'. James Oneal, statement to City Central Committee of Local New York, SDF, 5 June 1940, SDF Papers, Tamiment Institute Library, New York University.

9. The SDF officially censured the *NL*'s relationship with the UDA in a 'Report of the Sub-Committee on Relations of the SDF and *The New Leader*', no date [probably September 1942], SDF Papers.

10. For more biographical detail, see Daniel Bell, 'S. M. Levitas, 1894–1961', *The New Leader*, 9 January 1961, 2–3.

11. Mitchel Levitas, interview with author, New York, 16 July 1998.

12. Bell, who worked for the paper between 1940 and 1944 as a staff writer and managing editor, recalls contributing four or five items an issue under a variety of pseudonyms, including Andrew Marvell and John Donne. Daniel Bell, interview with author, Cambridge, MA, 13 November 1995. Bell's loyalty to Levitas had an almost filial quality. See Howard Brick, *Daniel Bell and the Decline of Intellectual Radicalism: Social Theory and Political Reconciliation in the 1940s* (Madison: University of Wisconsin Press, 1986), p. 149.

13. Sidney Hook to William Phillips, 16 April 1984, Hook Papers; Bell, letter to *New York Times*. For details of the campaign against *Mission to Moscow*, see William L. O'Neill, *A Better World. The Great Schism: Stalinism and the American Intellectuals* (New York: Simon and Schuster, 1982), pp. 74–7.

14. See Ellen Schrecker, *Many Are the Crimes: McCarthyism in America* (Princeton University Press, 1998), chap. 2. For private groups' participation in the US's overseas Cold War effort, see Scott Lucas, *Freedom's War: The US Crusade Against the Soviet Union, 1945–56* (Manchester University Press, 1999), chap. 8.

15. See, for example, Lynn Boyd Hinds and Theodore Otto Windt Jr., *The Cold War as Rhetoric: The Beginnings, 1945–50* (New York: Praeger, 1991); Martin J. Medhurst, Robert L. Ivie, Philip Wander and Robert L. Scott, *Cold War Rhetoric: Strategy, Metaphor and Ideology* (East Lansing: Michigan State University Press, 1997); Martin J. Medhurst and H. W. Brands (eds), *Critical Reflections on the Cold War: Linking Rhetoric and History* (College Station: Texas A&M University Press, 2000).

16. See Gleason, *Totalitarianism*, pp. 62–3.

17. According to André Liebich, the Mensheviks had already contributed to the theoretical development of 'totalitarianism' by 'inciting the leading German Marxist theoretician, Rudolf Hilferding, to apply the concept ... to Soviet Russia in 1940, well before such application had become popular'. André Liebich, 'Mensheviks wage the Cold War', *Journal of Contemporary History* 30 (1995), 258–9. Also see his *Other Shore*, pp. 299–309, for more detail on the Mensheviks' *New Leader* articles.

18. See Liebich, *Other Shore*, p. 302.

19. See, for example, Solomon Schwarz, 'Plain facts on the Russian "utopia"',

The New Leader, 2 August 1947, 9; Boris Nicolaevsky, 'Palace revolution in the Kremlin', ibid., 19 March 1949, 8–9; David Dallin, 'Concentration camps in Soviet Russia', *New Leader* 'World Events' pamphlet, 29 March 1947.

20. Bertram Wolfe, 'The man who returned from the dead', *The New Leader*, 15 May 1948, 10.

21. See, for example, Wolfe, 'Man who returned'; Eugene Lyons, 'The new slavery and a proposal', ibid., 8 November 1947, 1. For details of the Mensheviks' involvement in the famous 'Kravchenko case', see Liebich, *Other Shore*, p. 298. I am grateful to Susan Carruthers for drawing my attention to the prevalence of captivity narratives in early Cold War America.

22. See Thomas G. Paterson, *Meeting the Communist Threat: Truman to Reagan* (Oxford University Press, 1988), chap. 1, for more on 'Red Fascism'.

23. The notion of 'Red Fascism' could even acquire visual form. See, for example, cartoon, *The New Leader*, 5 June 1948, 4.

24. The *NL* made particular efforts to refute what it regarded as the myth of Soviet philo-Semitism. See, for example, Jacob Pat, 'The fate of the Jews in the Soviet Union', ibid., 3 May 1947, 9.

25. David Dallin, 'The rape of Czechoslovakia', ibid., 28 February 1948, 1–2.

26. See, for example, David Dallin, 'France – The West's weakest link', ibid., 18 December 1950, 11; Matthew Woll, 'Abolish the veto power in the UN', ibid., 26 January 1946, 9.

27. William Henry Chamberlin, 'The bankruptcy of Yalta', ibid., 23 February 1946, 16.

28. Kenneth G. Crawford, 'Era of appeasement ending', ibid., 2 February 1946, 1; editorial, 'Must we fight Russia?', ibid., 28 September 1946, 1.

29. William Henry Chamberlin, 'The right note at last', ibid., 22 March 1947, 16.

30. Melvin Lasky, 'Appeasement is a lively corpse', ibid., 2 August 1947, 6; Anatole Shub, 'How to make the T-Bomb', ibid., 22 July 1950, 10–12; David Dallin, 'Liberation or containment?', ibid., 29 September 1952, 2–4.

31. Liston Oak, 'Fact and fiction in *The New Republic*', ibid., 14 September 1946, 2; David Dallin, 'Tito: "Stalin of the Balkans"', ibid., 3 July 1948, 2.

32. David Dallin, 'Mao no Tito; US must act', ibid., 7 May 1949, 1-2; David Dallin, 'Myth of Chinese "Titoism" revived', ibid., 27 August 1951, 13.

33. David Dallin, 'Notes on Geneva', ibid., 26 April 1954, 4.

34. Editorial, 'We must defend Korea', ibid., 1 July 1950, 30–1. The communist insurgency in Vietnam was similarly perceived as the first step towards 'the Sovietization of Indo-China'. The Menshevik patriarch Raphael Abramovitch labelled the Geneva conference 'a second Munich' and wondered: 'Will the Communist victory set off a vital chain reaction, as did Hitler's unopposed remilitarization of the Rhineland in 1936?' David Dallin, 'Notes on Geneva', ibid., 26 April 1954, 4; Raphael Abramovitch, 'After Geneva', ibid., 2

August 1954, 3. The consequences of the Munich syndrome for US policy in Indo-China during the 1960s are analysed in Yuen Foong Khong, *Analogies at War: Korea, Munich, Dien Bien Phu and the Vietnam Decision of 1965* (Princeton University Press, 1992).

35. David Dallin, 'Unite the two Koreas', *The New Leader*, 8 July 1950, 2–4.
36. William Henry Chamberlin, 'High notes of irresponsibility', ibid., 14 July 1952, 15.
37. See, for example, editorial, 'Death at Belgrade', ibid., 20 July 1946, 9.
38. David Dallin, 'Problem of Tito: Should we accept undemocratic allies?', ibid., 11 August 1952, 11.
39. For David Dallin's thoughts on Stalin's death, see his 'New Deal in Moscow?', ibid., 27 April 1953, 6–7. For a statement of the *NL*'s long-standing opposition to Franco, see editorial, '*The New Leader*', 6 May 1950, 30–1. See also Robert J. Alexander's several articles about Peronism, for example, 'Peron and Argentine labor', ibid., 11 January 1947, 9.
40. Liston Oak, 'Trends', ibid., 26 January 1946, 2; William Gordon, 'Southern negroes and the Court decision', ibid., 2 August 1954, 22–3. 'We cannot fight intolerance and bigotry on an international scale', explained the same 1950 editorial which had denounced Franco, 'without opposing them with the same passion at home'. Editorial, '*The New Leader*', 31.
41. This department's full title was, 'Alert! Dedicated to an exposé of all totalitarian enemies of democracy'. Although most of its coverage was given over to communism, it did also devote attention to racist and anti-labour groups and individuals.
42. Wilbur H. Baldinger, 'Time to act, Mr Murray', *The New Leader*, 14 September 1946, 3; Julien Steinberg, 'The CIO starts to clean house', ibid., 15 February 1947, 4; editorial, 'Unity against the totalitarians', ibid., 8 May 1948, 1.
43. See, for example, George S. Schuyler, 'Reds outwit NAACP in drive to capture negro leadership', ibid., 10 August 1946, 5; Raymond Howard, 'American writers refuse to don AAA uniform', ibid., 21 September 1946, 5; Norbert Muhlen, 'Fellow-traveler by air: Johannes Steel', ibid., 9 February 1946, 5.
44. Norbert Muhlen, 'Exit Johannes Steel', ibid., 28 December 1946, 4. The similarity of their names invites speculation that the fictional character of Iron Rinn, the black-listed radio actor in Philip Roth's novel *I Married a Communist* (New York: Random House, 1998), is at least partly based on Steel.
45. As Muhlen put it, skilfully weaving the Nazi–Soviet equation into his analysis, 'Lenin's basic blueprint for revolution ... has remained the Soviet *Mein Kampf* for the conquest of the minds and the control of the masses'. Norbert Muhlen, 'Submission to Moscow: A fellow-travelogue in the empire of the mind', *The New Leader* 'World Events' pamphlet, 12 October 1946, 4.
46. Richard B. Cantor, 'Inside the Communist Party, USA', *The New Leader*, 4

September 1948, 4. See also Jan Valtin, 'A blueprint for treason', ibid., 16 October 1948, 9, a condensation of *The Struggle Against Imperialist War and the Tasks of the Communists*, published in 1934.

47. See Schrecker, *Crimes*, p. 120.
48. See Muhlen, 'Submission to Moscow', 4.
49. See, for example, editorial, *The New Leader*, 23 February 1946, 4.
50. Editorial, ibid., 2 February 1946, 8; Chamberlin, 'Right note'. Tension between the NL and Freda Kirchwey's *Nation* led to a libel suit involving art critic Clement Greenberg and foreign editor J. Alvarez del Vayo. See O'Neill, *Better World*, pp. 291–4.
51. Leon Henderson (National Chairman, Americans for Democratic Action), 'Liberalism in the 1948 campaign', *The New Leader*, 10 July 1948, 1, 12; editorial, '70 Americans send a cable to Bevin', ibid., 25 January 1947, 1; John Dewey, 'Wallace vs. a new party', ibid., 30 October 1948, 1.
52. William Henry Chamberlin, 'Wallace's appeasement fantasy', ibid., 28 September 1946, 16; William Henry Chamberlin, 'Henry Wallace: Political irrationalist', ibid., 28 June 1947, 16; William Henry Chamberlin, 'The Wallace Communist front', ibid., 2 October 1948, 16; Lewis Corey, 'What is Henry Wallace?', ibid., 2 October 1948, 8–9, 15.
53. Anonymous, 'The Soviet spy rings – Canada and USA', ibid., 23 February 1946, 5; Melvin Lasky (ed.), 'The Gouzenko Story', ibid., 18 January 1947, 10 (and following issues). The story of a another defector, Oksana Kosenkina, who famously leapt to freedom from the third-floor window of a Soviet consulate, also featured in the NL. William Henry Chamberlin, 'The testimony of Kosenkina', ibid., 21 August 1948, 16.
54. Editorial, 'The anti-totalitarian broom', ibid., 29 March 1947, 1.
55. Allen Dulles, 'Security without witch hunts', ibid., 14 May 1949, 7.
56. See, for example, Ferdinand Lundberg, 'Background of the spy disorders', ibid., 21 August 1948, 1, 12; Ralph de Toledano, 'The Bentley–Chambers story', ibid., 14 August 1948, 1, 15.
57. Eugene Lyons, 'In defense of red-baiting', ibid., 7 December 1946, 8.
58. See Gleason, *Totalitarianism*, p. 62.
59. Editorial, *The New Leader*, 30 September 1950, 30; David Dallin, 'Justice Department travesty', ibid., 25 June 1949, 2.
60. Granville Hicks, 'Owen Lattimore and Louis Budenz', ibid., 6 May 1950, 15.
61. Editorial, 'How to beat McCarthy', ibid., 22 September 1952, 30.
62. See editorial, 'Our lost voice', ibid., 4 May 1953, 22–3.
63. See the exchange between Hicks and Lyons in the letters column, ibid., 27 April 1953, 27–9.
64. Alfred Kohlberg to the editors, ibid., 15 October 1951, 27–8.
65. FBI file on Nicolaevsky, quoted in Liebich, *Other Shore*, p. 312.
66. George Kennan to William Henry Chamberlin, 17 September 1956, George F. Kennan Papers, Seeley G. Mudd Manuscript Library, Princeton University.

67. C. D. Jackson to Abbot Washburn, 6 February 1953, US President's Committee on International Information Activities (Jackson Committee) Records, 1950–53, Dwight D. Eisenhower Library, Abilene, Kansas.
68. Bernard Barnes to Allen Grover and C. D. Jackson, 22 May 1959, C. D. Jackson Papers, Dwight D. Eisenhower Library, Abilene, Kansas; C. D. Jackson to Abbot Washburn, 10 March 1953, Jackson Committee Records. 'I think very highly of Levitas's ability and intelligence', Jackson told Washburn, 'and he's well worth listening to'.
69. Allen Dulles to Franklin Lindsay, 20 December 1956, Allen W. Dulles Papers, Seeley G. Mudd Manuscript Library, Princeton University.
70. Shepard Stone to Central Files, 8 August 1956, RO 503 Grant No. 56–299, Ford Foundation Papers, New York.
71. Bill Furth to Henry Luce and C. D. Jackson, 24 July 1956, Jackson Papers.
72. C. D. Jackson to Allen Dulles, 21 February 1956, Jackson Papers.
73. Sidney Hook to Irving Brown, 31 October 1951, Irving Brown Papers, George Meany Memorial Archives, Silver Spring, Maryland; Irving Brown to Sidney Hook, 3 November 1951, Brown Papers.
74. See Saunders, *Who Paid the Piper?*, p. 163.
75. Bill Furth to Henry Luce and C. D. Jackson, 24 July 1956, Jackson Papers.
76. Franklin Lindsay to C. D. Jackson, 13 December 1956, Jackson Papers.
77. C. D. Jackson to Allen Dulles, 21 February 1956, Jackson Papers.
78. See Saunders, *Who Paid the Piper?*, p. 163.
79. Sol Levitas to Irving Brown, 24 June 1953, Brown Papers; Sol Levitas to Irving Brown, 12 May 1953, Brown Papers.
80. See, for example, Sol Levitas to Michael Josselson, 26 January 1954, CCF Papers, Joseph Regenstein Library, University of Chicago; Sol Levitas to Irving Brown, 30 November 1954, Brown Papers.
81. Michael Josselson to Sol Levitas, 3 March 1955, CCF Papers.
82. Arthur Schlesinger Jr. to Nicolas Nabokov, 18 June 1951, CCF Papers.
83. Sol Levitas to Arthur Schlesinger Jr., 23 January 1947, Arthur M. Schlesinger Jr. Papers, John F. Kennedy Memorial Library, Boston; Sol Levitas to Arthur Schlesinger Jr., 27 May 1947, Schlesinger Papers; Arthur Schlesinger Jr. to Sol Levitas, 28 May 1947, Schlesinger Papers. 'There are many excellent things in *The New Leader*', wrote Schlesinger in this last letter to Levitas, 'but I cannot but feel occasionally that anti-Soviet sentiment by itself is considered a sufficient credential for your writers'. Schlesinger's collaborators on *The Critic* included veteran left-wing foes of the *NL*, Dwight Macdonald and Mary McCarthy.
84. See Hook, *Out of Step*, p. 420. The ACCF shared the *NL*'s offices at the Rand School for a brief period after it had been established in 1951. Later, when the organisation was formally dissolved, the publication was bequeathed half its remaining funds, the other half going to the *Partisan Review*. Ibid., p. 426.
85. For more on the CCF's problematic relationship with Bertrand Russell, see chap. 6.

86. See Liebich, *Other Shore*, pp. 292–6.

87. Ibid., p. 317. As noted in chapter 3, there were right-wing elements in the CIA strongly opposed to the tactic of employing the non-communist left in covert operations. This, presumably, is why an Agency report in 1952 described the Mensheviks as a 'medium for Bolshevik propaganda ... and for Soviet intelligence activity' in the US. Evidently such comments were reported to Sol Levitas, who complained to Irving Brown the following year that 'some evil forces in Washington are concentrating their best efforts in an attempt to reduce help to the labor and socialist movement of Europe, to discharge people who are not Sons of the American Revolution, etc.'. Ibid., p. 311; Sol Levitas to Irving Brown, 12 May 1953, Brown Papers.

88. Anonymous, memorandum, 13 October 1950, James Burnham Papers, Hoover Institution, Stanford University.

89. Anonymous, 'Conversation with Pearl Kluger', 17 July 1951, Burnham Papers.

90. Anonymous, 'For the record. Subject: A campaign by the Russian Menshevik émigrés', no date, Burnham Papers. The Shub review appeared in *The New Leader*, 23 September 1950, 20–2. See also Liebich, *Other Shore*, pp. 292–5, and Lucas, *Freedom's War*, p. 200, on the problems of the American Committee for the Liberation of the Peoples of Russia, the main émigré organisation with which the Mensheviks were involved.

91. Frederick Scheu, 'The spearhead of British socialism', *The New Leader*, 30 March 1946, 7.

92. Robert Alexander, 'Eight months of socialist government', ibid., 11 May 1946, 6.

93. See, for example, Irving Kristol, 'British Labour today', ibid., 15 February 1947.

94. See, for example, Reinhold Niebuhr, 'Overseas report: Day by day life in Britain', ibid., 8 March 1947, 6.

95. David Williams, 'Is British Labour unity cracking?', ibid., 23 September 1950, 7. See also Williams's 'end-of-term report' on the Labour government's domestic record, 'British Labour after six years', ibid., 17 September 1951, 11–14.

96. See, for example, William Bohn, 'America mourns with Britain', ibid., 18 February 1952, 5. Bohn shared David Williams's slightly implausible belief that British workers were undergoing conversion to the American 'productivity gospel'. See, for example, his 'British Labour and Britain's job', ibid., 2 September 1950, 5–7.

97. Joseph Dunner, 'If you were a Jew, Mr Bevin: Open letter to the British Foreign Minister', ibid., 22 June 1946, 11.

98. The same cable to Bevin which denounced Henry Wallace also assured the Foreign Secretary that 'Americans want no part of a new appeasement program'. 'A cable to Bevin', ibid., 25 January 1947, 1, 19. See chap. 1 for David Williams's negative reaction to this initiative.

99. See, for example, Salvador de Madariaga, 'An open letter to Aneurin Bevan', ibid., 14 April 1952, 12–13; Peter Meyer, 'The illusions of Aneurin Bevan', ibid., 29 June 1953, 11–14, and 6 July 1953, 12–14; and editorial, 'When romantics roar', ibid., 7 May 1951, 30.

100. On Europe see, for example, Albert Guerard, 'Britain and united Europe', ibid., 12 August 1950, 15. For a list of the *NL*'s grievances about Labour foreign policy, see editorial, 'Our British friends', ibid., 23 February 1953, 30–1.

101. William Henry Chamberlin, 'Is British Labour's conscience dead?', ibid., 30 November 1953, 18.

102. Transcript of speech by Herbert Morrison, 8 October 1954, Jay Lovestone Papers, George Meany Memorial Archives, Silver Spring, Maryland.

103. Irving Kristol, 'Notes on Margate', *The New Leader*, 24 October 1955, 15.

104. Sol Levitas to Hugh Gaitskell, 28 October 1955, Hugh Gaitskell Papers, University College London; Hugh Gaitskell to Sol Levitas, 2 November 1955, Gaitskell Papers.

105. Hugh Gaitskell to Myron Kolatch, 9 January 1961, Gaitskell Papers.

106. Denis Healey, 'Message of condolence', *The New Leader*, 16 January 1961, 6.

107. Denis Healey, *The Time of My Life* (London: Michael Joseph, 1989), p. 200.

108. See, for example, 'A statement by Morgan Phillips', *The New Leader*, 1 July 1950, 6; and Morgan Phillips, 'British Labour stands united', ibid., 21 May 1951, 11.

109. Gaitskell received a communication from Levitas congratulating him on his 'wonderful fighting speech' and assuring him 'that all of us are with you in this struggle inside and outside the Labour Party'. Sol Levitas to Hugh Gaitskell, 25 October 1960, Gaitskell Papers. Gaitskell's speech was reproduced in the *NL*, 14 November 1960, 9–11. See also Herbert Morrison, 'British Labour must face facts', ibid., 10 November 1952, 4–7.

110. See, for example, Denis Healey, 'After the Mideast War', ibid., 3 December 1956, 14–15; and Denis Healey, 'The state of British parties', ibid., 4 November 1957, 10–11.

111. T. R. Fyvel, 'How London views the world', ibid., 23 February 1953, 8–10; editorial, 'Our British friends'. Also worth noting in this connection is the 'Trans-Atlantic dialogue' which took place between Sidney Hook and several 'English friends' in the pages of the *NL* during the winter of 1952–53. See Sidney Hook, 'Letter to an English friend', ibid., 13 October 1952, 16–18; also 'A Trans-Atlantic dialogue', ibid., 8 December 1952, 15–20.

112. James Carey et al. to Nikita Khrushchev and Nicolai Bulganin, 18 April 1956, Gaitskell Papers.

113. Sol Levitas to Hugh Gaitskell, 19 April 1956, Gaitskell Papers.

114. Hugh Gaitskell to Sol Levitas, 19 April 1956, Gaitskell Papers. Gaitskell

also received a letter from Adolph Held of the Jewish Labor Committee urging him to raise the fate of Soviet Jews with the visiting leaders. The fact that he explicitly referred to Jews in his comments at the infamous dinner with Khrushchev and Bulganin was perhaps interpreted in New York as a victory for the JLC. Adolph Held to Hugh Gaitskell, 17 April 1956, Gaitskell Papers.

115. Denis Healey, 'Labour unmasks Khrushchev', ibid., 7 May 1956, 3.

116. This description of the evening is based on notes in a file entitled 'Papers relating to the visit of Mr Khrushchev and Mr Bulganin, April 1956', in the Gaitskell Papers. Several published, first-hand accounts of the row exist, including Janet Morgan (ed.), *The Backbench Diaries of Richard Crossman* (London: Hamish Hamilton, 1981), pp. 486–7; George Brown, *In My Way* (London: Gollancz, 1971), pp. 71–4; and Philip M. Williams (ed.), *The Diary of Hugh Gaitskell, 1945–56* (London: Jonathan Cape, 1983), pp. 506–9.

117. Quoted in 'Between issues', *The New Leader*, 14 May 1956, 2.

118. Jay Lovestone to Allen Dulles, 21 May 1956, Jay Lovestone Papers, Hoover Institution, Stanford University.

119. Quoted in Bill Furth to Henry Luce and C. D. Jackson, 24 July 1956, Jackson Papers.

120. Quoted in Bill Furth to Henry Luce, 11 July 1956, Jackson Papers.

121. See Morgan, *Crossman Diaries*, p. 488.

122. Peter Ericsson to Sol Levitas, 25 April 1956, International Department, Labour Party Papers, National Museum of Labour History, Manchester.

123. Sol Levitas to Hugh Gaitskell, 27 April 1956, Labour Party Papers.

124. Peter Ericsson to Sol Levitas, 1 May 1956, Labour Party Papers.

125. Antonio Gramsci, *Selections from the Prison Notebooks* (London: Lawrence and Wishart, 1971).

5

Labor Diplomacy

As the Second World War drew to a close, United States government officials began to realise that, with the European right largely driven from power by a resurgent labour movement, they would have to practise a new kind of diplomacy. As it evolved in the late 1940s, US 'labor diplomacy' moved beyond the mere monitoring and reporting of overseas labour developments. The rapidly intensifying Cold War demanded an aggressive response to attempts by the Soviets to capture the political allegiance of European workers. In this, its interventionist aspect, American labour diplomacy was characterised by two main impulses, one negative and the other positive. The negative was the task of waging political warfare on communism, which tended to mean in practice covertly supporting indigenous anti-communist groups on the European left. The positive was to spread the so-called 'productivity gospel', that is the values of non-political trade unionism, labour-management cooperation and modern working practices, with the twin aims of protecting European economies against communist destabilisation and bringing them within the American economic orbit. In other words, what was envisioned was the exporting to Europe of the anti-communist, productivist consensus which had recently achieved hegemonic dominance over American labour. And, as with the construction of any hegemony, this was to be achieved by a mixture of public and private efforts, a combined front of government agencies and the two leading American labour organisations, the American Federation of Labor and the Congress of Industrial Organizations.

US labour diplomacy was at its most intense in those areas of continental Europe perceived to be under greatest threat from communist takeover, in particular France and Italy. It is not surprising, therefore, that most scholarship on the subject has tended to concentrate on these two countries.[1] However, American labour diplomats were active all over Europe, including Britain, which, while not regarded as 'high-risk', was nonetheless considered strategically 'sensitive'. There were several reasons for this: the fact that many US officials viewed labour as the new British 'ruling class'; the strategic importance in the Cold War of the Anglo–American alliance; and American concerns about the Cold War allegiance of the left wing of the British labour movement. Indeed, Britain was enough of a priority for it to be included in the labour operations of several different US government agencies. These included, through its Labor Attaché and information programmes, the Department of State; the Marshall Plan administration, the Economic Cooperation Agency; and, finally, the newly formed intelligence service, the CIA. Moreover, among those labour diplomats assigned to Britain were three of the ablest individuals ever to operate in the field: Samuel Berger, William Gausmann and Joseph Godson. As is revealed below, these men not only proved to be first-rate analysts of labour affairs in Cold War Britain; they were also remarkably successful at discharging the interventionist mission of US labour diplomacy, penetrating the highest echelons of the British labour movement, fomenting anti-communist activities and publicising American labour values.

This helps explain why it is that, in the small amount of scholarship on the subject undertaken so far, there has been a tendency to portray these individuals as distinctly sinister figures, manipulating labour leaders from behind the scenes, secretly sabotaging the left and generally subjecting Britain to a campaign of insidious ideological subjugation.[2] While this view might have the comforting effect of pinning the blame for unwonted developments in postwar British socialism on a baleful external agency, it does not fully capture what was in fact an extremely complex historical situation. For one thing, it oversimplifies the British response to the American campaign, which, far from being one of dumb sub-ordination, involved a variety of reactions, including active cooperation, creative appropriation and outright resistance. For another – and this is main point developed below – it exaggerates the concertedness and effectiveness of the US intervention. The American labour diplomatic effort was badly divided along a number of internal fault-lines. The public–private alliance of government officials and American trade unionists was plagued by tension and conflict; the negative, anti-communist and positive, productivist messages frequently jarred against each other; and the domestic rivalry between the AFL and CIO constantly spilled over into the foreign sphere. Even the *language* of the US campaign proved problematic, with different discourses of American labour competing for dominance. The project of translating the American hegemony to Britain was fraught with contradictions.

THE UNIONS

Before examining US labour diplomacy in Cold War Britain, it is first necessary to give a brief account of relations between the main labour organisations involved, if only because they were to prove such an important influence on the official diplomatic effort. The early years of the Cold War found the historic fraternal relationship between the American Federation of Labor and Trades Union Congress still very much alive, with leaders of the two national centres exchanging brotherly greetings and anti-communist intelligence across the Atlantic.[3] However, there were also clear strains between the two sides, which worsened as the Cold War escalated. The hesitancy with which the TUC leadership quit the World Federation of Trade Unions – the result of its desire not to move too far ahead of rank-and-file internationalism – exasperated the hardline anti-communists of the AFL, particularly the Lovestoneites who manned its Free Trade Union Committee. The Americans regarded the British as excessively cautious and bureaucratic in their approach to international affairs, frequently complaining about the TUC's lack of 'drive', 'dynamism' and 'urgency'.[4] There was also some thinly veiled proletarian contempt for the British honours system, with Jay Lovestone evincing the class consciousness of his earlier radical days by sneeringly referring even to TUC leaders who had yet to receive knighthoods as 'Sir'. For their part, British unionists regarded their counterparts in the AFL as lacking experience in international relations, brashly insensitive to European feelings and obsessed with 'negative' anti-communism.[5] The AFL's primary foreign policy goal in the postwar period was indeed the defeat of communism; other objectives, such as spreading the productivity gospel, were secondary. For the TUC, however, whose approach to the issue of domestic communism had always been more pragmatic than the AFL's, the anti-communist cause could best be served by more positive means.

In this regard, the TUC had more in common with the AFL's domestic rival, the Congress of Industrial Organizations. True, by 1949 the latter had demonstrated its abandonment of the internationalist principles which had guided its foreign policy in the immediate postwar years by withdrawing from the WFTU. Still, even at the height of the Cold War, the Congress tended to emphasise the positive strand of American labour diplomacy over the anti-communist. Walter Reuther, the organisation's leader from 1952, was particularly skilful at combining the message of American productivism with the language of European social democracy. Hence the rapturous reception he received in 1957 when he addressed the annual congress of the TUC in Blackpool, speaking of the need for technological progress and 'positive' anti-communism. The Lovestoneites were dismayed by performances such as these, as well as by other evidence that the Reuther brothers were determined to project their influence abroad, such as Victor's arrival in Paris (previously Irving Brown's exclusive domain) in 1951 to set up a CIO European office, and increasingly suspected that the TUC was aligning itself with the CIO against the AFL. Sometimes the 'YPSLs' were perceived as having the upper hand in this alliance; at others, it was the British who were viewed as the dominant partners, as when Brown informed Lovestone that 'the CIO ... are just being used, although they don't know it, by the TUC'. [6] Either way, the result was the same: social democrats were dividing the forces of free trade unionism and thereby aiding the communist cause. Significantly, during the early 1950s the Lovestoneites began merging the derogatory epithets they used for their American and British opponents: the YPSLs became 'Sir Walter' and 'Sir Victor'. [7]

Considering this tangle of personal and ideological conflicts involving key AFL, CIO and TUC personnel, it is hardly surprising the new anti-communist labour international launched in 1950, the International Confederation of Free Trade Unions, barely succeeded in getting off the ground. As has been comprehensively demonstrated by historian Anthony Carew, the Confederation was paralysed during the 1950s by a series of factional disputes, for example concerning the election as president in 1951 of TUC General Secretary Vincent Tewson (the 'pompous clerk', as the Lovestoneites called him); the running of factional candidates in 1955 for the new post of Director of Organisation; and, especially during the late 1950s, the TUC's refusal to give up its interest in the labour movements of Commonwealth countries. This reluctance to cease independent activities was mirrored on the American side by the AFL's unwillingness to do away with its Lovestoneite foreign policy apparatus. Not even the merger of the Federation and CIO put a stop to the FTUC's covert operations, with Lovestone successfully resisting the attempts of Walter Reuther to bring him to account by continuing to run his global network of agents and informants. [8]

Although there was no FTUC agent as such based in Britain at this time, Lovestone did have a number of British contacts capable of informing him about developments within the Labour Party and the TUC. These included several prominent journalists and industrial correspondents, among them Hugh Chevins of the *Daily Telegraph*, Eric Wigham of *The Times* and Richard Lowenthal of the *Observer*.[9] Lovestone's most important link to British labour, however, was his Irish friend, the former Wobbly (member of the Industrial Workers of the World) and communist Jack Carney who, as well as distributing FTUC literature in London and liaising with visiting AFL leaders, sent Lovestone weekly bulletins crammed with information about the activities of the Labour leadership, the internal politics of the major unions and British foreign policy debates.[10] In return for these reports, classed by Lovestone as 'splendid' and 'full of dynamite', Carney would receive food parcels and lengthy missives from his old comrade.[11] Lovestone's letters to Carney reveal the AFL's foreign policy operative to have been a knowledgeable if extremely prejudiced, not to say scurrilous, commentator on British politics. While generally dismissive of the Labour leadership as lacking vigour and aggression in the fight against communism, he reserved his worst spleen for the irresponsible intellectuals on the Party's left wing. Here he is, for example, on the *New Statesman*, its editor, Kingsley Martin and Richard Crossman:

> Yes, *The New Statesman and Nation* is a source of poison. That paper is dishonest and its source of support is dishonest. I cannot prove it in a court of law but my nose leads me to that conclusion. It has done so for a number of years – particularly after a very personal discussion with Kingsley Martin. Crossman is a cheap opportunist.[12]

Even more objectionable in Lovestone's eyes was Aneurin Bevan. Not only had the ex-miner become leader of the Labour left, he was also friendly with Walter Reuther, a relationship about which the head of the FTUC was evidently well informed:

> Of course, I have known about the thickness and thievery of the friendship between Walter Reuther and Nye Bevan. I know when the ICFTU Congress took place in London, Jennie [Lee] and her spouting spouse arranged a special shindig in Parliament for Walter. We know exactly what happened at that shindig.[13]

9 Jay Lovestone, the CIA's chief agent in the labour field, second from left in front row, visiting London with an American trade union delegation in 1955. (Jay Lovestone Papers, Hoover Institution, Stanford University)

Jay Lovestone, then, had the Cold War British left under a state of constant surveillance. The official US labour diplomatic effort in Britain was conducted against a complex background of inter-union tension and privately conducted covert operations.

SAMUEL BERGER AND THE LABOR ATTACHÉ PROGRAMME

This intrusion of the private into the public was very much evident in the US government's first official venture into the field of labour diplomacy, the Labor Attaché programme. Launched in 1942 – the initial inspiration came, ironically, from the success of British Labour Attaché Archie Gordon's wartime posting in Washington DC – this new service had two main purposes: the reporting of overseas labour developments with possible implications for US security interests, such as manpower problems and industrial disputes; and the cultivation of personal contacts with foreign labour leaders, so as to 'influence their thinking and decisions in directions compatible with American goals'.[14] As the strategic importance of labour increased during the late 1940s, so the programme expanded, with the result that by 1953 there were as many as 33 full-time US Labor Attachés posted around the world.[15] This growth was all the more remarkable as it was achieved in the face of considerable obstacles: the opposition of Foreign Service traditionalists hostile to the very concept of 'labor diplomacy', the unwelcome attentions of McCarthyite anti-communists in the federal internal security bureaucracy and a series of territorial disputes between the Departments of State and Labor.[16] Most disruptive, however, to the day-to-day operation of the service, was competition between the AFL and CIO over the appointment and control of Attachés. Both sides looked upon the new programme as a means of spreading the influence of their particular brand of unionism abroad.[17] Lovestone, in particular, tended to regard the Attachés as potential agents in his private diplomatic effort. In the face of this kind of interference from the private sphere, government officials needed all the diplomatic skills they could muster to assert official ownership of the service.

If Archie Gordon's performance in Washington had provided the inspiration for the American Labor Attaché programme, the individual who did most to shape the post itself was Samuel Berger, the first US Labor Attaché in London. Berger, a former assistant of the renowned labour scholar, Selig Perlman, at the University of Wisconsin and, briefly

164

during the late 1930s, a student at the London School of Economics, returned to Britain in 1942 as the labour specialist in W. Averell Harriman's Lend-Lease mission. As such, he was the only officer in Ambassador John Gilbert Winant's Embassy, with the exception of Winant himself, to possess any knowledge of British labour – according to Berger's later testimony, 'The others didn't even know who Bevin was'.[18] In addition to his Lend-Lease work, the tireless Berger spent his days in wartime Britain writing reports to his patrons in government and the unions back home, and travelling the country cultivating friendships with sympathetic labour leaders such as Sam Watson, hence anticipating the two main duties of the Labor Attaché before the post had been created. It was not until December 1945 that Berger himself was officially appointed London Labor Attaché, by which time he had earned himself and the whole notion of labour diplomacy considerable prestige by being the only member of Winant's staff, the Ambassador included, to predict correctly the result in the General Election of that year.[19]

Thanks to his wartime endeavours, the new Labor Attaché now enjoyed, in the words of Philip M. Kaiser (Assistant Secretary of Labor for International Affairs from 1949), 'extraordinary access to many members of the Cabinet, including the Prime Minister', making him 'the key member of the Embassy'.[20] Never one to rest on his laurels, Berger carried on his mission of establishing new personal contacts throughout the late 1940s, hosting cocktail parties, working the House of Commons Lobby and generally keeping 'a flow of ideas circulating between the US Embassy and the British labor movement'.[21] Indeed, he now tended to prioritise such work over his other main duty, reporting, which he usually delegated to his able young Assistant Attaché, Herbert Weiner. That said, he did still send dispatches to the State Department when circumstances demanded. These show him to have been an extremely perceptive and surprisingly unbiased observer of the British labour scene. For example, a February 1948 dispatch on 'Communism in the British Trade Union Movement' criticised Eric Wigham of *The Times* for his tendency to 'exaggerate the real influence of the Communists' in Britain and 'understate the forces which hold the Communists in check'.[22] As will be seen, such judiciousness and restraint were not always characteristic of Labor. Attaché reports from London.

Nor was Berger always so impartial in his private communications with US union leaders. These reveal him to have been a partisan of the AFL camp of American labour diplomacy, irritated by the tendency of both the CIO and TUC to 'wobble about' in their approach to international affairs. One letter to AFL boss George Meany ended with a declaration which might easily have been uttered by Jay Lovestone:

> I am more and more convinced, as I study the European labor scene, that they have neither the ideas, power, courage, energy or leaders to lead this fight in the trade union world. Unless we furnish the drive, I don't know how it will end.[23]

This is not to say that Berger was a 'Lovestoneite'. His academic and politically moderate background was very different from that of the former commissar. Indeed, the two men did not meet until May 1948, when they seem instantly to have conceived a strong mutual dislike. Lovestone henceforth referred to Berger with heavy irony as 'the prophet', while the latter formed the impression of 'a man who could be utterly unscrupulous, so that one had to be cautious and guarded in working with him even when pursuing the same ends'.[24]

However, as this last comment implies, Berger and Lovestone were prepared to set aside their personal feelings in the anti-communist cause. After their first meeting, they began trading Cold War intelligence; when Berger returned to Washington DC in 1950 as a special assistant to his former boss, Averell Harriman, now Director of Mutual Security, he became an important point of government contact for Lovestone (as is discussed below); and Berger's assistant, Herb Weiner, was a loyal Lovestoneite.[25] Moreover, there was an excellent working relationship between Berger and Lovestone's lieutenant Irving Brown. During the late 1940s the two men – described by the latter's biographer as 'kindred spirits: alley-wise and hard-nosed, 100 percent politicos'[26] – engaged in a variety of joint covert operations, for example foiling a communist plot to raid funds in a London bank account intended for free trade unionists in Czechoslovakia, travelling together in 1947 to Cold War hot-spot Greece in order to break the communist grip on the Greek labour movement and conspiring to undermine the WFTU.[27] If not a card-carrying Lovestoneite, the London Labor Attaché was nonetheless a keen practitioner of 'Lovestone diplomacy'.

Considering this, it was perhaps only to be expected that observers on the left wing of the British labour movement should have viewed Berger as a machiavellian figure, 'a diplomatic Svengali' who 'guides and directs centre and right-wing union leaders in Britain'. Willie Gallacher, Chairman of the British Communist Party and MP for West Fife, even claimed, 'Nothing happens in Britain without consultation with Samuel

Berger'.[28] However, there are a number of factors that this characterisation of Berger's role in Labour politics ignores. To start with, the very fact that such a charge was made against him (and repeated, incidentally, in the House of Commons)[29] testifies to the difficulties – the suspicion, resentment and outright resistance – that any American official operating in postwar British labour circles encountered on an almost daily basis. Conversely, Gallacher's complaint ignored the spontaneous personal and political sympathy which existed between Berger and his contacts on the right wing of the Labour Party and TUC. Denis Healey, for example, then Labour's International Secretary, later fondly recalled the Attaché as a man who 'had a warm heart and was deeply committed to working people'.[30] Following on from this, it should be born in mind that Britain's labour leaders were involved in their own Cold War crusade during the late 1940s, both at home, where the TUC launched an anti-communist campaign in 1948, and abroad, where Labour politicians like Healey helped disseminate the output of the Information Research Department. For that matter, there was even British involvement in American anti-communist warfare, including the joint operations of Berger and Brown, whose trip to Greece in 1947 was originally suggested by none other than Ernest Bevin and carried out with help from the British Labour Attaché in Rome, W. H. Braine, as well as Vincent Tewson.[31] Finally, it would not do to underestimate the British capacity for making use of American labour diplomats in ways presumably unintended by Washington. Such acts of appropriation could be quite subtle. Hugh Chevins, for example, regularly consulted Irving Brown, whose knowledge about European labour affairs was immense, as a source for his *Daily Telegraph* column, yet deliberately kept Brown's fanatical master, Lovestone, at arm's length.[32] They could also be more literal, for instance Sam Watson using Berger's Embassy apartment as a *pied-à-terre* in London or asking the Labor Attaché to obtain FA Cup tickets on his behalf.[33] In any event, the British response to the American diplomatic effort was clearly more complex and *creative* than Gallacher and most subsequent commentators would have us suppose.

WILLIAM GAUSMANN AND THE MARSHALL PLAN

When the Marshall Plan was announced in 1947, American labour diplomacy acquired a new mission. The European Recovery Program (ERP) was intended not only to provide short-term economic aid to war-torn Europe; it also aimed at nothing less than a long-term transformation of the continent's economies based on the principles of productivity, efficiency and technology.[34] In order to achieve this extraordinarily ambitious goal, the Economic Cooperation Agency (ECA), the body charged with the administration of the ERP, embarked on a massive information campaign designed to convert Europe's industrial workers to the productivity gospel. Millions of dollars from the counterpart funds set aside for administering the Marshall Plan were spent on this effort. A Labor Information Division staffed predominantly by American unionists was established in the Paris-based headquarters of the ECA, the Office of the Special Representative (OSR), and Labor Information Officers (LIOs) assigned to ECA missions in Marshall Plan countries.[35] According to Edward Lilly, official historian of the US's pyschological warfare effort in the first stages of the Cold War, ECA LIOs tended to be 'uninhibited and energetic operators' who had the latitude to '"free wheel" informationally'.[36]

William Gausmann arrived in London to take up the post of ECA LIO in 1949. Like most LIOs, he came from a labour and socialist, as opposed to government or academic, background. Born in Washington DC and educated at George Washington University, he had sat on the National Executive Committee of the Socialist Party of America and carried out local work for the CIO during the 1930s. In the early 1940s he was briefly employed by the Office of War Information, before being fired from his post for allegedly passing official materials to friends in the socialist movement. While serving in the US army, he spent nearly a year in England, returning there for three months at the end of the war to study at Oxford. After going back to America, he worked for a short time on the *Socialist Call* and then in 1948 became editor of the Labor Press Associates, a news service for union papers. He came to London having only just resigned from the Socialist Party NEC and looking forward to seeing at first hand Labour Britain's experiment with democratic socialism.[37]

Gausmann lost no time in getting to work on his information duties. Among the many activities listed in his monthly reports to ECA headquarters were collaborating with the BBC on broadcasts about the Marshall Plan, providing the research department of the TUC with information about the latest technical developments in the American textile industry and speaking at a Scottish union banquet on the recent history of the US labour movement.[38] Gausmann proved highly effective at reactivating his wartime British labour contacts and using them to spread the productivity gospel. His relationship with the group of social democratic intellectuals associated with the journal *Socialist Commentary* was particularly notable in this respect. In an arrangement reminiscent of David Williams's role at *Tribune*, Gausmann was, for all intents and purposes, the 'American editor' of this important publication, which during the 1950s served as the theoretical organ of the modernising Labour revisionists.[39] He was also founder member of the think-tank organisation Socialist Union, launched in 1951 as an offshoot of *Socialist Commentary*, and convenor of its working party on Labour Party democracy.[40]

However, Gausmann's work as ECA LIO was not confined to the productivity dimension of American labour diplomacy. After the outbreak of the Korean War in June 1950 and the US government's declaration of a 'psychological offensive' against communism, the Marshall Plan information campaign acquired an aggressive edge which it had previously lacked. In Britain Gausmann monitored the preparations for the communist-influenced Sheffield Peace Congress; visited South Wales in order to debate with Communist Party secretary Idris Cox about the Marshall Plan, and while there helped launch a new labour weekly, *The Democrat*, to counter what he described (perhaps unfairly) as 'the almost open field for Communist propaganda' in that region; and 'conducted numerous discussions' with leading Labour Party and TUC officials about the development of a 'counter-offensive' against the communist peace campaign.[41] In this side of his work Gausmann even assisted the British government's own secret propaganda war – whether knowingly or not is unclear – by helping the Labour Party promote Denis Healey's anti-communist collection *The Curtain Falls*, which had been published with the covert support of IRD.[42] By 1953 Gausmann had grown so knowledgeable about the British communist movement that he sent a proposal for a book on the subject to the Rand Corporation.[43] He was, in short, one of the most energetic and experienced exponents of anti-communist political warfare in Cold War Britain.

This does not mean, however, that he was a labour diplomat cast in the AFL, Lovestoneite mould. Rather, his loyalties lay with the social democratic, industrial wing of the American labour movement. There were several indications of this. Throughout his tour-of-duty in London (which was interrupted in 1951 when he was transferred to Paris, but resumed in 1953 when he returned as a United States Information Agency LIO), Gausmann performed a role for the CIO leadership similar to that which Jack Carney played for Lovestone, regularly sending his friend Victor Reuther news about internal Labour Party affairs and advising him how to handle TUC leaders.[44] Gausmann's CIO allegiances were also reflected in his informational activities. For example, he tended to steer British unionists visiting the US on government exchange programmes away from the Lovestoneite citadel, New York, and towards the Reuthers' hometown, Detroit, where he believed they would receive a proper American education in modern production and bargaining techniques.[45] Third, Gausmann played a crucial part in Walter Reuther's triumphant tour of Britain in 1957, helping arrange his itinerary, organise sympathetic press coverage and even write his famous Blackpool speech. Letters concerning the latter included advice that the CIO boss stress the positive achievements of American unions, avoid the use of Americanisms ('"Agreements" should always be used instead of "contracts"; "branches" instead of "locals"; a union has a "conference" and not a "convention"') and, above all, keep it short: 'The Angel Gabriel couldn't hold TUC real attention for over 30 minutes.'[46] Finally, and most significantly, Gausmann served secretly as a personal link between the CIO and TUC leaderships in their factional manouevrings against the AFL. In 1955, for example, Victor Reuther asked him 'to feel out the British TUC key people' about CIO plans to bring 'an end to the separate Lovestone-type activities'. In response, Gausmann reported that Vincent Tewson fully shared the CIO's desire for the 'complete termination of the influence of certain persons'.[47]

Indeed, Gausmann positively detested Lovestoneism. Proof of this can be found in the form of an 'historical survey' of the subject he co-authored with fellow ECA LIO, Maurice Goldbloom, and sent to Victor Reuther in the hope that a friendly journalist might be able to use it as the basis of an exposé of the FTUC's secret operations.[48] This revealing document, which contained a brief biography of Lovestone and country-by-country summaries of his overseas activities, lodged three main allegations. The first of these was that, despite Lovestone's repudiation of communism, he and his agents were continuing to use communist methods – 'deceit, intrigue, bribery and strong-armed tactics' – in pursuit of anti-communist ends. Not only that, their hatred of Communism was so fanatical that they were prepared to make alliances quite indiscriminately with any and all anti-communists, including several former fascists. Echoing the first charge of 'Communism-in-reverse', Gausmann and Goldbloom described this tactic as a 'form of decadent "Popular Frontism"'. The final accusation was that the Lovestoneites had done irreparable damage to the reputation of organised labour in

America by appearing to foreign unionists to be 'mere apologists for and special agents of' the US government. Instead of this 'negative, military-oriented, dead-end anti-Communism', Gausmann and Goldbloom concluded, American labour must rededicate itself to the task of fostering 'democratic, humanitarian trade unionism'.[49]

Lovestone repaid Gausmann's animosity with interest.[50] In his correspondence with Jack Carney, who in addition to his other surveillance activities kept a close watch on US government personnel in Britain, Lovestone returned to the subject of the ECA LIO repeatedly. Again, the language used is indicative. Sometimes Gausmann was described in terms reminiscent of earlier tirades against the Reuther brothers as 'a boy scout Socialist – a YPSL pure and simple'. At others, he was folded into the category of British enemy and ennobled as 'Sir Gausmann'. Finally, Lovestone betrayed his contempt for the positive mission of American labour diplomacy as well as for government officials in general by dismissing all 'ECA niks' as 'overstuffed and overpaid bureaucrats' who lacked the stomach for the real anti-communist fight.[51] Gausmann personified all that Lovestone thought was most self-defeating in the official US Cold War effort.

One last point worth making about Gausmann is that, as his allegiance to socialism and the CIO might lead one to expect, he harboured a genuine sympathy for the cause of British labour. Indeed, he sometimes sounded more British than American, as when he remonstrated with his division chief in Paris that 'there are all too many people in the OSR prepared to believe the worst about the British and at the same time completely insensitive to the resentment that the constant pressure of American advice causes'.[52] This identification with the British position even extended to support for 'responsible' strikes by the country's industrial workers. Whereas most American labour diplomats feared any sign of industrial unrest in Britain as a potential threat to the economic stability of America's most important western ally, Gausmann was all in favour, as he told Victor Reuther, of 'the sort of intelligent industrial militancy that we want to see developed'.[53] In other words, for all his anti-communist political warfare activities, Gausmann appears to have viewed his own role as less that of a US government agent promoting official American interests than a fellow democratic socialist gently nudging his British brethren in the right productivist direction. This might explain why in 1953 he was subjected to a loyalty investigation which nearly resulted in his second firing from a government post (Sam Berger, incidentally, suffered a similar setback around the same time,

171

being exiled to New Zealand after he had aroused the hostility of one Richard Nixon).[54] This is also presumably why, while by no means liked universally, Gausmann was the most popular of the US labour diplomats operating in Cold War Britain. When he left London in 1961, a *Daily Telegraph* article entitled 'Insight with Tact' observed that 'unlike some of his compatriots', he had 'tactfully contrived to give no impression of unwarrantable intrusion into our affairs'.[55]

USIE AND USIA

During the late 1940s, with Sam Berger hard at work, William Gausmann just arrived and the Labour left apparently behaving 'responsibly' in the Cold War, the British section of the International Information and Educational Exchange Program (USIE), the State Department's information service, was left to operate 'on a basis of bare minimum needs'.[56] This state of affairs changed in 1950, when the outbreak of war in Korea caused an upsurge of neutralism and anti-Americanism on the British left. Responding to Washington's declaration of an anti-communist offensive, London Embassy Public Affairs Officer Mallory Browne identified labour as the 'highest priority target for USIE activities in the UK'.[57] Elaborating on this statement in his 1950 'Country Paper' for Britain, Browne explained that 'the labour operation of USIE in the United Kingdom is not, as on the Continent, a direct and open fight against Communists'. Rather, its aims should be:

> to combat the prejudices of British Labour toward its own misconceptions of capitalist America; to replace these misconceptions with an up-to-date picture of the modern American democratic system of free enterprise and individual initiative, with all the advantages this system awards to the workers; to counteract deliberate misrepresentations by Communist propaganda of the status of labor in the United States.[58]

As a result of Browne's representations, a new post was created in the London Embassy for a USIE Labor Information Officer, whose duties were to correct 'vague stereotypes about American social realities', elucidate 'American policies and Anglo–American mutual interests' and assist the 'leadership of the labor movement ... [in] its own largely successful struggle against destructive elements in its ranks'.[59] The first person to fill this post was a former Consular Attaché in Scotland by the name of Patrick O'Sheel, who moved from Glasgow to London in January 1951. As already noted, O'Sheel was succeeded two years later by William Gausmann, at the same time that the State Department's international information activities were absorbed by the United States Information Agency (USIA).

Three aspects of the new LIO's work are particularly noteworthy. One was 'labor press and publishing', the main venture in this area being *Labor News from the US*, a bi-weekly newsletter about the American union scene that was distributed free of charge to over 1,000 members of the British labour movement, 'including Labour MPs, socialist and trade union newspapers and periodicals, workers' education officers and industrial correspondents'.[60] This publication studiously avoided the appearance of Cold War partisanship: it contained no editorial comment and no anti-Soviet content, consisting as it did entirely of articles culled from such sources as the Labor Press Associates, the AFL and CIO's weekly papers, and ECA press releases. As Patrick O'Sheel remarked, any other approach was ruled out by 'the hypersensitivity of nearly all British editors to foreign "influence"'.[61] That said, the LIO's editorial policy was far from neutral: an official 1953 reader survey noted that 'high priority has been given to items that coincide with US policy objectives (e.g. support of the foreign policy of American labor, positive achievement in productivity, etc.)'.[62] Also, *Labor News* was strategically distributed so that it could be employed by friendly labour elements engaged in anti-communist factional warfare. According to a 1959 USIA assessment report, the newsletter was particularly well received in areas of traditional communist strength such as Sheffield and North London, 'where the anti-Communist militants are eager to come by any material they can use in their struggle'.[63] This perhaps explains why some respondents to the 1953 reader survey complained that *Labor News* was 'anti-Communist propaganda'. This viewpoint, however, appears to have been a minority one, and did not deter O'Sheel from distributing other American publications to sympathetic British labour editors, including State Department pamphlets on 'Our Foreign Policy' and 'An Outline of American History'.[64]

A second method of improving British labourites' first-hand knowledge of America was that vital tool of cultural diplomacy, the exchange programme. Although the leader-specialist grants established under the Smith–Mundt Act of 1948 were meant to be distributed evenly across the political spectrum, in practice priority tended to be given to politicians and unionists on the right wing of the labour movement. The criteria used for selecting such grantees were implicit in the language used by Patrick O'Sheel in July 1951 to describe some recently successful candidates. One, John Lang, chairman of the Scottish TUC, was a 'powerful anti-Communist'; another, George Morgan Thomson, editor of the Glasgow labour weekly *Forward*, had 'taken a growing anti-Communist stand in the past two years, partly owing to our services and ECA's'; a third, T. R. Fyvel, was 'planning a new quarterly magazine devoted to British–American interest in the "Atlantic community"' (a venture about which more below).[65] In other words, Smith–Mundt awards were deployed to foster and reward the growth of pro-American and anti-communist sentiment.

On the whole the programme seems to have accomplished this aim. Such exchange visitors as Douglas Jay and Patrick Gordon-Walker reported on their trips in glowing terms, the latter having taken advantage of his presence in the US to hold meetings with several Assistant Secretaries of State, Allen Dulles and the Reuther brothers.[66] Roy Jenkins later recalled his two-month tour of America in 1953 on a Smith–Mundt grant as 'a brilliant piece of unforced propaganda' and 'a fairly sound investment of not much more than $3,000'.[67] An official 1956 report on the exchange programme concluded that grantees had 'profited by their visits to the US',

> whether by becoming assured of the peaceful aims of American foreign policy, by relief from doubts as to the cultural, religious or educational standards of the US or by increased insight into American labor relations and information activities.[68]

The programme was not without its problems, however. One Scottish labour leader, Frank Donachy, was prevented from taking up his award when communists on his union's general executive voted to turn down his application for leave.[69] Also, there was no guarantee that exchange visitors would leave America with positive impressions of the place. Shortly after returning home, Labour MP Woodrow Wyatt, despite his 'reputation within the Labour Party for being "pro-American"', published two articles in the *Daily Herald* critical of the US (one about McCarthyism and the other American policy in Korea) which were seized on as anti-American propaganda by the *Daily Worker*.[70] He was, reportedly, 'resentful and scornful' about the 'patronising' attitudes he had encountered towards Britain and other nations receiving American economic aid.[71] Finally, Smith–Mundt suffered from the effects of the same sort of reactionary anti-communism which had impeded the development of the Labor Attaché programme. Two outstanding candidates for awards, Denis Healey (described as 'an important anti-Communist' and 'valuable source of information to the Embassy') and *Tribune* editor Evelyn Anderson ('a useful pro-American influence on that periodical') were denied visas to enter the US due to their past membership of the Communist Party and had to be withdrawn from the competition, despite repeated testimony from London-based officials (including Gausmann) as to their anti-communist *bona fides* and warnings that such a course of action 'would place the Embassy in an extremely embarrassing position'.[72] In addition to these operational glitches, there were frequent (and perhaps inevitable) complaints from the London LIO about financial under-resourcing.

This last problem was mitigated to an extent by the fact that labour research scholars and industrial correspondents were eligible for awards under the academic side of the Smith–Mundt scheme and that the Fulbright exchange programme, set up in 1946, facilitated travel by American labour specialists in the other direction.[73] Also of some help was a 'Workers' Travel Grants Scheme' launched in late 1954 by the Current Affairs Unit of the English-Speaking Union (ESU), with the aim of sending British unionists on month-long tours of the US.[74] This leads the discussion onto a third area of work for the USIE/USIA LIO, that is liaison with already-existing, local pro-American organisations. Foremost of these in Britain was that indefatigable promoter of the Anglo–American alliance, the ESU. In his 1951 'Progress Report', O'Sheel described a plan hatched jointly with the ESU and the British–American Associates to establish a new bureau which would 'take the offensive in dealing with anti-American sentiment' and function as '"cover" for distribution of ... propaganda'.[75] In January 1953 the ESU, with funding from an American source described as a private donor, established a Current Affairs Unit under the direction of intelligence expert General Leslie Hollis and the chairmanship of Francis Williams, former press adviser to Clement Attlee, who announced his determination 'to eradicate anti-American prejudices among the trade unions and the "ordinary folk"'.[76] TUC officer Vic Feather was also on hand to advise the Unit's full-time administrative staff about 'specific irritants which may become apparent in Trades Union circles from time to time'.[77] Other Atlanticist organisations with labour links included Friends of Atlantic Union, 'a small "all-party" organisation launched in 1952', and the

British Atlantic Committee, set up the following year.[78] In short, American labour diplomats could draw on a large reservoir of good will and even financial support amongst supporters of the Atlantic alliance within both British labour and intelligence circles.

However, not all of the British labour movement was so amenable to the American information effort. The flurry of Atlanticist organisational activity which occurred in 1952 and 1953 was partly a response to the growth of a new concern for the 'anti-anti-Americans', namely Bevanism. Although Aneurin Bevan and his followers frequently denied that they were anti-American, their repeated questioning of the Atlantic alliance struck many observers as posing a serious threat to American strategic interests. Throughout the early 1950s anxious officers in the London Embassy 'continuously furnished' the State Department with 'detailed reports' about this 'increasingly disturbing factor'.[79] Certain aspects of the phenomenon were perceived as especially ominous. One was Bevan's undoubted personal charisma, which made other Labour leaders look 'pale and tepid' in comparison; [80] another was his talents as a 'demagogue', which enabled him to exploit the patriotic impulses of the Labour rank-and-file.[81] Compounding these factors were the lack of 'firm and imaginative leadership' from the moderate majority of the Labour Party and the communists' ingenuity at exploiting Bevanism for their own purposes.[82] As the 1950s wore on, circumstances appeared to be conspiring to strengthen the Bevanites' position and weaken that of the moderates. First, there was Korea and the divisive controversy concerning the question of German rearmament; then came the defeat of Labour in the General Election of 1951, which Embassy officials feared would lead to a new phase of 'irresponsible' behaviour in Labour circles; finally, the victory of the Republican candidate in the 1952 US presidential election stimulated left-wing British fears of a new phase of capitalist reaction in America.[83] By 1953 the danger of Labour anti-Americanism struck one American Embassy official as so grave that he recommended Britain be placed on the new USIA's list of 'high priorities'.[84] Evidently circumstances demanded more aggressive measures than the subtle strategy advocated by Patrick O'Sheel in 1951.

JOSEPH GODSON

It was during the Bevanite crisis that the third member of the triumvirate of US labour diplomats arrived on the Cold War British scene in the

176

shape of the new Labor Attaché, Joseph Godson. Transferred from Ottawa in December 1952, Godson descended on London at a time when the post of Labor Attaché there appeared to be experiencing a crisis of its own. Despite Sam Berger's extraordinary record of achievement, subsequent Attachés had found it difficult to break into the inner circles of the British labour movement. According to Juan de Zengotita, Assistant Labor Attaché after Herbert Weiner departed London for Australia in 1949, American labour diplomats might initially receive 'a pleasant reception' in Britain, but they soon discovered that 'British union leaders are not really very hospitable', indeed were often 'personally remote'.[85] This perhaps explains why Glenn R. Atkinson, Joseph Godson's immediate predecessor, left London (in the words of Jack Carney) 'very much disgruntled', not even leaving 'a memo for Joe as to who to meet and what to do'.[86] Finally, within a few months of his arrival Godson was deprived of his Assistant Attaché, after the post was dropped in the reorganisation and reduction in force of 1953.[87] All this at a time when Bevanism struck many seasoned observers as about to wreck the American labour diplomacy effort in Britain.

Godson, however, appears to have been entirely undaunted by the challenge facing him. As Jack Carney, who acted as an unofficial, Lovestoneite welcoming committee for him, soon realised, 'Joe can take it'.[88] Approaching his task with a 'combination of enthusiasm and doggedness', Godson rapidly breathed new life into the post of London Attaché.[89] Within a year of his arrival he had thrown a large party for an AFL delegation en route to an ICFTU congress in Stockholm, to which was invited almost the entire Labour leadership; arranged a meeting between such right-wing unionists as Lincoln Evans and the *grande dame* of American liberalism, Eleanor Roosevelt, when she passed through London; and ensured that anti-communist stalwarts Arthur Deakin and Alfred Robens received the red-carpet treatment from both the AFL and CIO when they visited the US.[90] As well as engaging in such overt acts of labour diplomacy, Godson was busy behind the scenes cultivating the confidence of key Labour personalities, such as Sam Watson (whose daughter later married one of Godson's sons) and Hugh Gaitskell. As several historians have noted, the published edition of the latter's diaries reveal that the Attaché was present at meetings of the Labour leadership in March 1955 when the possibility of expelling Nye Bevan from the Party was discussed – perhaps the most dramatic recorded incident of US labour diplomacy intruding into internal British politics.[91]

10 Aneurin Bevan, Hugh Gaitskell and Sam Watson board a flight to Germany in 1959. 'Bevanism' had proved a source of considerable concern in Cold War Washington. (By Permission of People's History Museum)

By joining in the Gaitskellite plot against Bevan, Godson was not only demonstrating the threat Bevanism was perceived as posing to US interests, he was also pointing up his membership of the AFL as opposed to CIO camp of American labour diplomacy. Godson was a Lovestoneite through and through. A Polish immigrant product of Lovestone's *alma mater* City College, he belonged to the Communist Party Opposition during the 1930s; his first experience of the international field was earned in the Lovestoneite role of public relations director for David Dubinsky's Jewish Labor Committee; and he owed his appointment as Labor Attaché in Canada to Lovestone's influence.[92] It was to be expected, therefore, that Godson would adopt an AFL-like, hardline position during this tour-of-duty in London, much as the personal background of his contemporary, USIA LIO William Gausmann, predisposed the latter to represent the interests of the CIO (a fact which bred an enduring tension between the two labour diplomats).

Godson's Lovestoneism was also evident in his reporting to Washington. His many dispatches to the State Department reveal him as, like his predecessor Berger, an astonishingly well-informed observer of British labour affairs. This is perhaps unsurprising when one learns that his sources included lengthy conversations with Arthur Deakin and confidential TUC and Labour Party papers furnished by Sam Watson.[93] However, it is possible to detect traces of bias in Godson's dispatches which were generally absent from Berger's. One example should suffice. In his report on the General and Municipal Workers' conference of 1954, Godson noted 'a growing tendency among important segments of right-wing British labor groups to soft-pedal somewhat the anti-communist ideological struggle in order to move to a closer working relationship with the Soviets and Communist China'. Despite this development, 'right-wing union chiefs have given very little leadership', as have 'most of the right-wing Labour Party leaders, who instead of leading seem increasingly to be led by the sentiments and emotions of their followers'.[94] In contrast 'the Bevanites appear to be militantly on the offensive'. All the classic Lovestoneite complaints about British trade unionism are here: the lack of firm, dynamic leadership, the emotionalism of the rank-and-file and the threat of Bevanite demagogy. Such reporting can only have reinforced the worst prejudices of the Lovestoneites and fuelled the more repressive aspects of Cold War US labour diplomacy.

However, Godson's official reporting was a model of moderation compared with his private correspondence with Jay Lovestone. Following Jack Carney's unexpected death in early 1956, Godson inherited the function of Lovestone's London informant, sending his old political master regular 'Reports from England'. These revealed the Labor Attaché in his true Lovestoneite light. In early 1956, for example, dropping the sober tone of his dispatches to State and falling into the tough-guy, hard-boiled idiom favoured by Lovestone, Godson condemned 'the signs of increasing Commie strength in the union movement' and the fact that 'Saint V.'s headquarters [Vincent Tewson's TUC] is dead but pretends not to know it'. [95] Later that same year Hugh Gaitskell was praised as 'splendid' and 'ahead of all the others' for having confronted Nikita Khrushchev over the question of the imprisoned social democrats.[96] Finally, in an instructive contrast with his official dispatch on the same subject, Godson described the historic 1957 Blackpool 'Reuther Congress' as 'the dullest meeting in years. The top abdicated completely.... This was just the right atmosphere for Sir Walter. He played up to the gallery and made impressions on the crowd.'[97] Yet another public US official is revealed by his language as a combatant in the private factional wars of the American labour movement.

Godson's Lovestoneism ensured that he never won the same degree of personal popularity during his six years' tour in Britain (he was posted to Belgrade in 1959) as Gausmann or Berger. True, his contacts with the British labour movement's centre-right leadership were impressive. According to Geoffrey Goodman of the *Daily Mirror*, his Kensington flat doubled as 'a salon for Gaitskellites'.[98] However, his Lovestoneite style – obsessively anti-communist, hectoring, conspiratorial – in time alienated even his closest allies. For example, Arthur Deakin, that most hardline of labour anti-communists, entertained misgivings about his involvement in TUC affairs, while Gaitskell himself had similar concerns about his role in the Labour Party.[99] Likewise, although Godson earned a reputation among Britain's industrial correspondents for being 'impossible to ignore', this was due to his knowledge of international labour affairs rather than any ideological affinity. Geoffrey Goodman consulted him as a journalistic source frequently but remained staunchly Bevanite in terms of his personal political allegiances.[100] Indeed, the left wing of the British labour movement was deeply suspicious of Godson, even more so than of his predecessor Berger. Tony Benn was disquieted by his knowledge of confidential Labour Party business; the Bevanites simply regarded him as a spy from the American Embassy.[101] In sum, while Godson might have done a good job discharging the negative mission of American labour diplomacy – although with the likes of Deakin around, it is questionable how much help the labour leadership needed seeing off the communist threat – his presence in London during the 1950s might have done as much to stoke British anti-Americanism as dampen it.

For reasons that hardly need stating, it is very hard to tell whether or not the CIA intervened directly against the Bevanites during the early years of the Cold War, as opposed to engaging in arm's-length operations designed to strengthen the Gaitskellites. On the one hand, there is documentary evidence indicating that Bevanism was a source of considerable concern in American intelligence circles. Officials on the Psychological Strategy Board (PSB) – the body created by the Truman administration in April 1951 to coordinate US psychological warfare activities – were much exercised by the subject in the early years of the decade. In 1952, for example, Waldemar A. Nielsen identified 'Bevanism and those who urge social welfare above defense' as constituting 'a very serious problem' for US security interests in western Europe.[102] When in January 1953 the PSB considered a draft report on the 'Psychological Impact in the UK of US Foreign Economic Policies and Programs' which consistently downplayed the threat to western unity of British anti-Americanism – claiming, for instance, that 'in no case do the resentments even of the Bevanites constitute a challenge to the alliance itself' – an anonymous reviewer repeatedly objected that the 'CIA has reservations as to this statement and has requested reconsideration at the next revision of this paper'.[103] Certainly, the CIA's principal agent in the field of covert labour operations, Jay Lovestone, rarely missed an opportunity to talk up the Bevanite threat, especially after the death of Arthur Deakin in 1955.[104]

Whether these concerns were ever translated into concrete action, though, is less clear. Unwritten agreements between the British and American secret services dating back to the Second World War prohibited both sides from carrying out unauthorised operations on the other's soil.[105] It would appear that this statute of limitations was honoured even when Cold War tensions were at their height. In 1953, for example, the head of the American section of the English-Speaking Union asked 'psy-war' supremo C. D. Jackson to sound out Allen Dulles and Walter Bedell Smith about the possibility of the CIA funding ESU activities in Britain (presumably the Current Affairs Unit and Workers'

Travel Grants Scheme referred to above). 'The people mentioned think well of the work but have virtually declared a moratorium on money from that source being used in that particular country', Jackson responded. 'There is a sort of gentlemen's agreement on that matter.'[106] Unilateral intervention by the CIA against Bevanism, then, seems not to have been countenanced. This, though, is not to rule out the possibility of the American and British intelligence services collaborating on *joint* operations to discredit members of the Labour left, much as they co-operated on ventures designed to support Labour's centre-right, such as *Encounter*.[107] Joint campaigns mounted against the Wilson government in the 1960s are already well documented.[108] Rumours of similar operations against leading Bevanites were current on the British left during the 1950s.[109]

Another rumour that circulated during the 1950s – and has cropped up several times since[110] – suggested that one or other of the Labor Attachés at the London Embassy was a CIA officer operating under cover. Again, the evidence here is inconclusive. Certainly, it was not unknown for the Agency to use labour postings as cover. Irving Brown's case officer, Paul Sakwa, ostensibly in Brussels as Assistant Labor Attaché, was a case in point.[111] Moreover, there were documented links between the CIA and both Sam Berger and Joe Godson in this period. After he returned to Washington as a member of Averell Harriman's staff, the former consulted regularly with both the Psychological Strategy Board and Allen Dulles on international labour affairs.[112] He also provided, as already noted, liaison between the CIA and Jay Lovestone. Similarly, correspondence between Godson and Lovestone contains examples of the slightly absurd code-language used by Lovestoneites when referring to official covert business, with references to 'the Parisian W.', 'the Brussels business' and even 'the "feather"'.[113] None of this, though, proves that either Attaché was a CIA officer at the time of his presence in London. What it does show, rather, is that the boundaries between the realms of overt labour diplomacy and private covert operations were frequently blurred.

There was, however, one definite link with the CIA. By the mid-1950s, Lovestone's role in the CIA had shifted from covert operations to intelligence-gathering, as he routinely passed the reports he received from his global network of informants to his controller, head of counter-intelligence James Jesus Angleton, who then disguised their source and placed them in his 'JX files' for use by his intelligence 'customers'.[114] These reports included the Carney correspondence – and in all probability Godson's 'Reports from England', as well. This arrangement generally worked well, but there was one occasion, described to Lovestone's biographer Ted Morgan by an anonymous former CIA officer stationed in London during the 1950s, when it nearly resulted in a serious diplomatic breach between the American and British intelligence services. As part of their ongoing exchange of information, the CIA regularly sent copies of Angleton's JX files to MI6. Included in one batch was a lengthy report by Carney on a TUC congress. However, as the source of the report had been disguised, MI6 mistakenly concluded that the CIA must have placed an agent in the British labour movement. '"The Brits were aghast"', Morgan quotes his CIA contact as saying, '"and my station chief said, 'God, this looks like we've got an agent in the TUC'. The Brits wanted to know who the agent was, but Jim kept mum."'[115] Here, then, in this muddle of Anglo–American intelligence cooperation and public/private covert operations, is further evidence of the complicated and even confused nature of the US labour diplomacy effort in Britain.

In 1960, looking back over a decade and a half of intense diplomatic activity, US government officials might have been forgiven for feeling a little complacent about their record of achievement in Cold War Britain. Three individuals in particular, Samuel Berger, William Gausmann and Joseph Godson, had succeeded in infiltrating the innermost circles of the British labour movement, conducting extensive anti-communist political warfare and gathering some excellent intelligence. British labour had ended the 1950s with its communist elements effectively contained and its right wing decisively to the fore. At the same time, British industry had been firmly anchored within the orbit of American capitalism.

How much these developments had to do with American labour diplomacy, though, is very much open to question. Centre-right labour leaders had, arguably, always had the communists under control; certainly they were no less ready than the Americans to resort to covert anti-communist political warfare when circumstances appeared to demand it, as is shown by their links with such semi-secret bodies as Common Cause and the Industrial Research and Information Services.[116] It is also arguable that the leadership's occasional anti-communist campaigns in this period were mere skirmishes in what historian Nina Fishman has called a 'phoney war' between the left and right wings of the British labour movement: the underlying reality was one of a pragmatic *modus vivendi* which not even such temporary alarms as the rise of Bevanism seriously threatened.[117] Similarly, while it is true that the more positive productivist message of American labour diplomacy found a receptive audience amongst British labour leaders, this was largely because it dovetailed with already existing assumptions about Britain's need for scientific management and increased production.[118] However, as later decades of labour-management conflict would attest, neither industrial workers nor, for that matter, managers necessarily shared these beliefs.[119] To the extent that British industry did buy into the American model, it was probably as much the consequence of growing economic dependence on Marshall aid and private American investment as any conversion to the productivity gospel.

The main impression one carries away from an examination of the American labour diplomacy effort in Cold War Britain is one of conflict. Government officers competed with private unionists for control of various diplomatic initiatives; CIO personnel with a background in the Socialist Party and the mass-production industries of cities such as Detroit struggled with AFL types whose origins lay instead in New York's communist movement and craft-unions; negative anti-communist objectives fought with positive social democratic impulses. In this struggle certain aspects of the official diplomatic effort tilted in one direction or the other: the ECA and regular information services were more the territory of CIO-ers like Gausmann, while the Labor Attaché programme became something of a Lovestoneite preserve. Overall, it was probably the AFL, with its more repressive brand of anti-communism, which got the upper hand. That said, the CIO's alluring combination of social democracy and productivist know-how remained Britain's preferred image of American labour. Hence, if the US ever did succeed in establishing an ideological hegemony over British labour during the early Cold War period, it was at best a highly contested, unstable one.

NOTES

1. See particularly Ronald L. Fillippelli, *American Labor and Postwar Italy, 1943–53* (Stanford University Press, 1989) and Federico Romero, *The United States and the European Trade Union Movement, 1944–51* (Chapel Hill: University of North Carolina Press, 1992).
2. See, for example, Robin Ramsay, 'The clandestine caucus: Anti-socialist campaigns and operations in the British labour movement since the War', *Lobster* special issue, 4.

3. See, for example, Vincent Tewson to David Dubinsky, 16 September 1949, Jay Lovestone Papers, Hoover Institution, Stanford University; Matthew Woll to Sam Watson et al., 22 October 1952, Lovestone Papers, Stanford.

4. See, for example, Jay Lovestone to Jack Carney, 22 October 1951, Lovestone Papers, Stanford; Irving Brown to Jay Lovestone, 30 July 1949, Lovestone Papers, Stanford.

5. These temperamental differences were eloquently summarised by British industrial correspondent Hugh Chevins in a letter to Jay Lovestone: 'We have, in the trade union movement on this side of the Atlantic, a number of leaders who are stuffy, dull, pompous and at the same time sincere, and with whom you ebullient Americans must find it sometimes irksome to deal.... On the other hand, while your people are big and dynamic, they do on occasions rub our people the wrong way by, if I may say so, a lack of tact.' Hugh Chevins to Jay Lovestone, 3 March 1958, Hugh Chevins Papers, British Library of Political and Economic Science, London.

6. Irving Brown to Jay Lovestone, 2 December 1951, Lovestone Papers, Stanford.

7. See, for example, 'Letter from JG' [Joseph Godson], 5 September 1957, Jay Lovestone Papers, George Meany Memorial Archives, Silver Spring, Maryland.

8. Anthony Carew, 'Conflict within the ICFTU: Anti-Communism and anti-colonialism in the 1950s', *International Review of Social History* 41 (1996), 147–81. See also Ted Morgan, *A Covert Life. Jay Lovestone: Communist, Anti-Communist and Spymaster* (New York: Random House, 1999), chap. 16.

9. In 1951, Brown and Lovestone attempted unsuccessfully to obtain a visa for Richard Lowenthal to visit the US by taking up his case with Carmel Offie. Lowenthal was eventually permitted to enter America in 1956. Jay Lovestone to Irving Brown, 13 March 1951, Irving Brown Papers, George Meany Memorial Archives, Silver Spring, Maryland; Richard Lowenthal to Irving Brown, 27 August 1956, Brown Papers. A list of British contacts found in Irving Brown's papers contains the names of, amongst others, Isaac Deutscher, Malcolm Muggeridge and Woodrow Wyatt.

10. See Morgan, *Covert Life*, p. 135. For an example of a Carney report, see Jack Carney to Jay Lovestone, 31 December 1950, Lovestone Papers, Stanford.

11. Jay Lovestone to Jack Carney, 14 September 1954, Lovestone Papers, Maryland; Jay Lovestone to Jack Carney, 3 April 1950, Lovestone Papers, Stanford.

12. Jay Lovestone to Jack Carney, 7 September 1950, Lovestone Papers, Stanford.

13. Jay Lovestone to Jack Carney, 22 October 1951, Lovestone Papers, Stanford.

14. Don Kienzle and Thomas Bowie (eds), *Historical Lessons of Labor Diplomacy: A Seminar Report in Washington DC, April 27, 1995* (Washington DC: Friedrich-Ebert-Stiftung, 1995), p. 4; Philip M. Kaiser,

Journeying Far and Wide: A Political and Diplomatic Memoir (New York: Charles Scribner's Sons, 1992), p. 118.

15. See Kaiser, *Far and Wide*, p. 117.
16. Ibid., p. 105; memorandum on 'Selection and assignment of Labor Attachés', 2 September 1954, Records of the Department of Labor, Record Group (RG) 174, National Archives, Washington DC.
17. See Kaiser, *Far and Wide*, p. 119.
18. Samuel Berger, interview by Terry Anderson, 18 April 1978, Indiana University Oral History Research Project.
19. Herbert Weiner, interview by Roger Schrader, 18 June 1991, Labor Diplomacy Oral History Project.
20. See Kaiser, *Far and Wide*, p. 120. Among Berger's confidantes in the Labour Government were Bevin ('a very good Secretary of State', the American later recalled), Hector McNeil, Hugh Gaitskell and Evan Durbin ('three of the best leaders they had, the sharpest, toughest minds'). Quoted in Graenum Berger, *A Not So Silent Envoy: A Biography of Ambassador Samuel David Berger* (New Rochelle, NY: John Washburn Bleeker Hampton Publishing Co., 1992), p. 48.
21. Jack Carney to Jay Lovestone, 7 December 1950, Lovestone Papers, Stanford.
22. Samuel Berger, 'Communism in the British trade union movement', 17 February 1948, Records of Foreign Service Posts of the Department of State, RG 84, National Archives.
23. Samuel Berger to George Meany, 23 December 1948, Lovestone Papers, Stanford.
24. Quoted in Morgan, *Covert Life*, p. 174. My thanks to Tony Carew for informing me about Berger's Lovestoneite nickname.
25. Ibid., pp. 173–4.
26. Ben Rathbun, *The Point Man: Irving Brown and the Deadly Post-1945 Struggle for Europe and Africa* (London: Minerva, 1996), p. 187.
27. See Graenum Berger, *Not So Silent Envoy*, pp. 84–6.
28. *New York Times*, 22 February 1948, quoted in ibid., p. 41.
29. Ibid., pp. 54–5.
30. Denis Healey, *The Time of My Life* (London: Michael Joseph, 1989), p. 113.
31. Graenum Berger, *Not So Silent Envoy*, p. 43. However, there were also some British misgivings, official as well as unofficial, about Brown and Berger's activities in Greece. See H. G. Gee, note, 10 May 1947, 'AFL General File', LAB13/656, Public Record Office (PRO), London. W. H. Braine, who later succeeded Archie Gordon as Labour Attaché in the Washington British Embassy, remained highly critical of Brown. See W. H. Braine to G. C. Wilson, 4 May 1956, LAB13/603, PRO. Similarly, the bizarre antics of Richard Deverall, Lovestone's agent in Japan, were an ongoing source of irritation for the British authorities in Hong Kong. See file on 'Activities in Hong Kong of R. F. Deverall', LAB13/766, PRO.

32. See Hugh Chevins to Irving Brown, 2 January 1950, Chevins Papers; Hugh Chevins to Jay Lovestone, 3 March 1950, Chevins Papers.
33. Sam Watson to Samuel Berger, 29 March 1950, Sam Watson Papers, Durham County Record Office, Durham; Sam Watson to Joseph Godson, 5 April 1955, Watson Papers.
34. For two influential interpretations of the Marshall Plan and the productivity gospel, see Charles S. Maier, 'The politics of productivity: Foundations of American international economic policy after World War II', and Michael J. Hogan, 'The Marshall Plan', both in Charles S. Maier (ed.), *The Cold War in Europe: Era of a Divided Continent* (Princeton, NJ: Markus Wiener Publishers, 1996), pp. 169–201 and 203–40, respectively.
35. For more detail on the ECA's labour information campaign, see Anthony Carew, *Labour under the Marshall Plan: The Politics of Productivity and the Marketing of Management Science* (Manchester University Press, 1987), chap. 6.
36. Edward P. Lilly, 'Psychological Operations, 1946–51', 21 December 1951, White House Office, National Security Staff Papers, 1948–51, Operations Coordinating Board Secretariat Series, Dwight D. Eisenhower Library, Abilene, Kansas.
37. Anonymous, finding aid, William C. Gausmann Papers, Archives of Labor and Urban Affairs, Wayne State University, Detroit; anonymous, 'Gausmann takes job in England', news report, no date, Gausmann Papers.
38. William Gausmann, 'UK activities reports' to Joseph S. Evans and Harry Martin, 15 September 1950 and 15 March 1950, Records of US Foreign Assistance Agencies, RG 469, National Archives; Pete Maas to Pat Frayne, 'Trip to United Kingdom', 14 November 1950, RG 469, National Archives.
39. William Gausmann to Labor Information Division, OSR, 'Reply to LI questions', 23 January 1950, Gausmann Papers.
40. Minutes of 'Foundation Meeting of Socialist Union', 31 March 1951, Socialist Vanguard Group Papers, Modern Records Centre, Warwick University; Rita Hinden to 'Friend', 2 November 1954, Socialist Vanguard Papers.
41. William Gausmann, 'UK activities reports' to Joseph S. Evans and Harry Martin, 17 November 1950 and 1 February 1951, RG 469, National Archives; anonymous, 'Gausmann blasts CP's anti-recovery stand', news report, no date, Gausmann Papers. For further detail on Gausmann's anti-communist activities, see Carew, *Marshall Plan*, pp. 127–30.
42. William Gausmann, 'UK activities report' to Joseph S. Evans and Harry Martin, 2 April 1951, RG 469, National Archives.
43. William Gausmann to Hans Speier (Rand Corporation), 1 June 1953, Gausmann Papers.
44. See Box 95, UAW International Affairs Department – Reuther and Carliner Files, 1955–63, Archives of Labor and Urban Affairs, Wayne State University, Detroit.

45. William Gausmann to Victor Reuther, 24 March 1955, CIO Washington DC Office Papers, Archives of Labor and Urban Affairs, Wayne State University, Detroit.

46. William Gausmann to Victor Reuther, 6 August 1957, UAW President's Office: Walter P. Reuther Papers, Archives of Labor and Urban Affairs, Wayne State University, Detroit.

47. Victor Reuther to William Gausmann, 7 March 1955, Washington Office Papers; William Gausmann to Victor Reuther, 18 March 1955, Washington Office Papers.

48. Gausmann to Reuther, 18 March 1955.

49. William Gausmann and Maurice Goldbloom, 'Jay Lovestone and the strategy of the American labor movements abroad', no date, Victor G. Reuther Papers, Archives of Labor and Urban Affairs, Wayne State University, Detroit.

50. There was also considerable friction between Gausmann and Irving Brown. See, for example, Irving Brown to Jay Lovestone, 16 November 1950, Lovestone Papers, Stanford.

51. Jay Lovestone to Jack Carney, 8 October 1951, Lovestone Papers, Stanford. Carney shared Lovestone's disdain for the 'bright boys' at the American Embassy who work 'in the shadow of fear that if they associate with an ex-member of the CP ... they will endanger their own jobs'. Jack Carney to Jay Lovestone, 7 December 1950, Lovestone Papers, Stanford.

52. William Gausmann to Harry Martin, 3 January 1950, RG 469, National Archives.

53. William Gausmann to Victor Reuther, no date, UAW International Papers.

54. William Gausmann to John N. Hutchison, 31 August 1953, Gausmann Papers; Graenum Berger, *Not So Silent Envoy*, chap. 7.

55. Anonymous [probably Hugh Chevins], 'Insight with tact', *Daily Telegraph*, 5 January 1961, Gausmann Papers. See also anonymous, 'New tone?', *Daily Herald*, 19 January 1961, Gausmann Papers. Gausmann appears to have been particularly well regarded by British industrial correspondents. His friends included Chevins of the *Daily Telegraph* and Geoffrey Goodman of the *Daily Mirror*.

56. Giora Goodman, '"Who is anti-American?": The British left and the United States, 1945–56', Ph.D. thesis, University College London (1996), p. 168.

57. Mallory Browne to State, 31 October 1950, Records of the Department of State (Central Files), RG 59, National Archives.

58. Mallory Browne, 'Country paper – USIE in Great Britain', 3 November 1950, RG 59, National Archives.

59. Jack C. McDermott, 'Functions of a Labor Information Officer, USIE-London', 5 March 1951, RG 59, National Archives.

60. Patrick O' Sheel, 'Progress report on labor information activities, Britain', 25 July 1951, RG 59, National Archives.

61. Ibid.

62. USIS London, 'Survey on Mission publication', *Labor News*, 6 November 1953, Records of the USIA, RG 306, National Archives.

63. Bowen Evans, 'USIS/United Kingdom annual assessment report – October 1 1957 through September 30, 1958', 19 January 1959, RG 306, National Archives. The same report recorded that the circulation of *Labor News* had climbed to just over 8,200.

64. See O'Sheel, 'Progress report'.

65. Ibid. For an account of the occasion in 1956 when the Gaitskellite organ *Forward* received an indirect subsidy from the Jewish Labor Committee in the form of an inflated expenses cheque made out to Hugh Gaitskell, see Carew, *Marshall Plan*, pp. 129–30.

66. Memorandum of 'Exit interview' with Patrick Gordon-Walker, 13 February 1959, RG 59, National Archives.

67. Roy Jenkins, *A Life at the Centre* (London: Macmillan, 1991), p. 101.

68. 'Semi-annual report on the International Educational Exchange Program', 29 March 1956, RG 59, National Archives. It was not only labour leaders whose attitudes were changed as a consequence of Smith–Mundt grants. Morlais Summers, a Cardiff funeral director, returned from the US 'with certain concepts of undertaking', including the building of 'a funeral home and chapel in American style', with the result that he soon acquired a reputation as 'the most progressive undertaker' in South Wales. Neil M. Ruge to State, 'Cultural exchange: American mortician's Cardiff film show', 9 May 1956, RG 59, National Archives.

69. Richard P. Taylor to State, 'Leader Specialist Frank Donachy', 13 August 1952, RG 59, National Archives.

70. David Linebaugh to State, 'Woodrow Wyatt's views on the United States', 25 November 1952, RG 59, National Archives.

71. Quoted in Goodman, 'Who is anti-American?', p. 302.

72. O'Sheel, 'Progress report'; Richard P. Taylor to State, 'Leader Specialist Program – Mrs Evelyn Anderson and Denis Healey', 19 June 1951, RG 59, National Archives.

73. O'Sheel, 'Progress report'. For information about the Anglo–American Council on Productivity, which enabled a number of British unionists to experience US industrial practices at first hand, see Carew, *Marshall Plan*, chap. 9.

74. 'Commonwealth–American Current Affairs Newsletter', January–February 1955, Trades Union Congress Papers, 973/42, Modern Records Centre, Warwick University.

75. See O'Sheel, 'Progress report'.

76. Quoted in Goodman, 'Who is anti-American?', p. 300.

77. Peter Storrs to General Leslie Hollis, 2 July 1953, TUC Papers, 973/41.

78. See Goodman, 'Who is anti-American?', p. 288.

79. 'USIE Country Plan, United Kingdom, Priority V', January 1952, RG 59, National Archives.

80. David Linebaugh, memorandum of conversation with Maurice Edelman, 13 February 1952, RG 59, National Archives.
81. Juan de Zengotita to Glenn Atkinson, no date [probably July 1951], RG 59, National Archives.
82. 'Gifford' to State, 4 October 1952, RG 59, National Archives; Juan de Zengotita, 'Recent British Communist developments', 28 February 1951, RG 84, National Archives.
83. See 'Semi-Annual Evaluation Report, December 1–May 31, 1951', 27 July 1951, RG 59, National Archives; 'Semi-Annual Evaluation Report, June 1-November 30, 1952', 18 February 1953, RG 59, National Archives.
84. Ibid.
85. Juan de Zengotita, 'The post of the Labor Attaché in London', no date, RG 174, National Archives.
86. Jack Carney to Irving Brown, 7 January 1953, Brown Papers.
87. 'Inspection report on London Embassy', 28 September 1955, RG 174, National Archives.
88. Jack Carney to Irving Brown, 7 January 1953, Brown Papers.
89. Anonymous, obituary, Joseph Godson, *The Times* 6 September 1986.
90. Joseph Godson to Arnold L. Steinbach, 3 July 1953, 29 July 1953 and 13 November 1953, RG 84, National Archives.
91. Philip M. Williams (ed.), *The Diary of Hugh Gaitskell, 1945–56* (London: Jonathan Cape, 1983), pp. 384, 395, 398.
92. Godson obituary; Morgan, *Covert Life*, p. 144.
93. For a reference to Deakin, see Joseph Godson, 'The Communist angle in the recent dock strike', 23 November 1953, RG 59, National Archives. Other dispatches included lengthy excerpts from TUC reports. See, for example, Joseph Godson, 'Wages and prices council established', 13 August 1957, RG 59, National Archives. Geoffrey Goodman recalls stumbling into a hotel room during a meeting of the Socialist International and discovering Watson handing documents to Godson. Geoffrey Goodman, interview with author, 1 September 2000, London.
94. Joseph Godson, report on NUGMW Conference, 25 June 1954, RG 174, National Archives.
95. Joseph Godson, 'Report from England', 9 January 1956, Lovestone Papers, Maryland; Joseph Godson, 'Report from England', 15 April 1956, Lovestone Papers, Maryland.
96. Joseph Godson to Ann Stolt, 30 April 1956, Lovestone Papers, Maryland; Joseph Godson, 'Letter from JG', 26 May 1956, Lovestone Papers, Maryland.
97. Joseph Godson, 'Letter from JG', 5 September 1957, Lovestone Papers, Maryland.
98. Goodman interview.
99. Ibid.; Williams, *Diary of Hugh Gaitskell*, p. 384.
100. Goodman interview.

190

101. Ruth Winstone (ed.), *Tony Benn, Years of Hope: Diaries, Letters and Papers, 1940–62* (London: Hutchinson, 1995), pp. 267, 271–2; Goodman interview.

102. Waldemar A. Nielsen, 'Significant psychological activities of the Office of the Special Representative in Europe and of the European Information Division of the Mutual Security Agency from late spring to early fall, 1952', 17 October 1952, Psychological Strategy Board Files, 1951–53, Harry S. Truman Library, Independence, Missouri.

103. Psychological Strategy Board, 'An evaluation of the psychological impact in the United Kingdom of United States foreign economic policies and programs', 28 January 1953, Records of the Department of State (Lot Files), RG 59, National Archives.

104 See for example, Jay Lovestone to Allen Dulles, 22 July 1955, Lovestone Papers, Stanford, in which Lovestone referred to British unionists' continuing readiness to send delegations to visit communist-bloc countries, a practice which appalled the anti-communists of the AFL. 'When Deakin was alive', Lovestone wrote, 'the Transport Workers organization ... was vigorously anti-Communist and resolutely opposed to sending delegations to Iron Curtain countries. The other day, as you know, this great organization adopted a resolution to send delegations to ALL countries.... I can tell you the most fascinating and frightening stories about the value of such delegations to Moscow.'

105. See Stephen Dorril, *MI6: Fifty Years of Special Operations* (London: Fourth Estate, 2000), p. 55.

106. C. D. Jackson to William V. Griffin, 11 May 1953, C. D. Jackson Papers, Dwight D. Eisenhower Library, Abilene, Kansas. Funding for the ESU exchange scheme was subsequently obtained from the Ford Foundation.

107. See chap. 8.

108. See Stephen Dorril and Robin Ramsay, *Smear! Wilson and the Secret State* (London: Fourth Estate, 1991).

109. According to Geoffrey Goodman, it was widely suspected that both the American and British intelligence services were behind a story in the *Spectator* alleging that Aneurin Bevan and Richard Crossman were drunk during a visit to Belgrade. Goodman interview.

110. See Ramsay, 'Clandestine caucus', 4.

111. Paul Sakwa, interview with author, 21 June 1997, Washington DC.

112. See Graenum Berger, *Not So Silent Envoy*, pp. 89–90.

113. Joseph Godson, 'Letter from JG', 10 June 1957, Lovestone Papers, Maryland; Joseph Godson, 'Letter from JG', 19 September 1957, Lovestone Papers, Maryland.

114. See Morgan, *Covert Life*, p. 246.

115. Ibid., pp. 246–7. Angleton's Lovestone operation carried on until it was shut down by DCI William Colby in the mid-1970s. See Tom Mangold, *Cold Warrior: James Jesus Angleton, the CIA's Master Spy Hunter* (New York: Simon and Schuster, 1991), pp. 291–2.

116. See chap. 2.
117. See Nina Fishman, 'The phoney Cold War in British trade unions', *Contemporary British History* 15.3 (2001), 83–104.
118. See Rhiannon Vickers, *Manipulating Hegemony: State Power, Labour and the Marshall Plan in Britain* (Basingstoke: Macmillan, 2000), pp. 126–31.
119. See Nick Tiratsoo, '"What you need is a Harvard": The American influence on British management education', in Terry Gourvish and Nick Tiratsoo (eds), *Missionaries and Managers: American Influences on European Management Education, 1945–60* (Manchester University Press, 1998), pp. 140–56.

6

Unwitting Assets?
British Intellectuals and the
Congress for Cultural Freedom

At first sight, the CIA's campaign in the Cultural Cold War – the superpower contest for the support of intellectuals – appears to have gone extremely well in Britain, certainly far better than the US labour diplomacy effort. True, British intellectuals were not a priority target of the Agency: there were other European countries where the communist threat to 'cultural freedom' was greater and, in any case, by the end of the 1950s, Asia and Africa were replacing Europe as the principal theatres of the Cultural Cold War. Nonetheless, there was enough concern in American intelligence circles about the persistence of neutralist sentiment in Britain, as well as sufficient appreciation of the potential value of British intellectuals as spokespersons for cultural freedom in the 'third world', for the Congress for Cultural Freedom to undertake a range of activities there. These included – as is documented in the first half of this chapter – the founding of a national affiliate, the fostering of contacts with intellectuals in the Labour Party and the forging of links with British academe. Although the initial response to these overtures was indifferent, if not downright hostile, by 1960 the CCF had succeeded in establishing a significant presence in British literary, political and academic circles which was quite separate from the success of the Congress's main venture in Britain, the magazine *Encounter*.

Considering this, and given the source of the CCF's funding, it is perhaps no wonder that several commentators have interpreted the organisation's reception in Britain as evidence that the US had covertly reduced British intellectuals to a state of mental subservience in the Cold War, accomplishing in the realm of ideas what American foreign policy had already brought about in the economic and military spheres. As with all influential historical interpretations, there is an element of truth to this scenario: the CCF did succeed in binding left-wing British intellectuals more tightly to a transatlantic, non-communist left community of intellectual discourse. The effect of this development – which, as discussed further below, was even more pronounced in the case of *Encounter* – was to strengthen Atlanticist and social democratic, as opposed to Third Force and socialist, impulses within the British left. However, this was not the whole story. As the second half of this chapter shows, the CCF also encountered a number of problems in Britain, some arising from the persistent influence over the CIA's cultural operations of American ex-communists, others from the often unpredictable behaviour of the British themselves. The question mark in the chapter title is not meant to insinuate that, despite the Agency's characterisation of them as 'unwitting assets', British intellectuals in fact knew about the CCF's link with the CIA – although in many cases this might have indeed been the case. Rather, it is to suggest that intelligence officers were mistaken in assuming that the intellectuals in receipt of their patronage necessarily served them as assets.

BERLIN AND AFTER

The relationship between the Congress for Cultural Freedom and British intellectuals could not have got off to a more inauspicious start. Only a handful of Britons attended the organisation's founding Berlin conference in June 1950. Particularly conspicuous by their absence were intellectuals belonging to the governing Labour Party. This was perhaps no bad thing given that Arthur Koestler, the event's most visible mover, used one of his several speeches as an occasion to deliver an attack on Labour's contribution to the Cold War, citing in particular its resistance to European unification. The émigré novelist's role in the Congress did not go unchallenged, however. When it became the turn of historian Hugh Trevor-Roper to speak, he moved away from his original text to defend the ideal of intellectual tolerance and criticise the 'dogmatism' exhibited by Koestler. Subsequently he and his Oxford colleague, the philosopher A. J. Ayer, became a focus of opposition amongst the Congress's participants to the militantly anti-communist stance of its organisers. During the final debate Koestler was forced to eliminate a clause from his 'Freedom Manifesto' that Trevor-Roper had interpreted as calling for a legal ban on western communist parties.[1] This incident did not go unnoticed by the Congress's secretive official sponsors. Shortly after returning to Britain, Trevor-Roper (who along with Ayer had worked for the Special

Operations Executive during the War and remained well-connected officially afterwards) learned that a friend in the Foreign Office had been asked by a US State Department official, 'Why did your man spoil our Congress?'[2]

Trevor-Roper's reasons for speaking out against Koestler became apparent in a critical report on the Congress published in the *Manchester Guardian* soon after his return home, 'Ex-Communist v. Communist'.[3] Two aspects of the event in particular had disturbed him. One was the nationalistic mood of the Berlin audience, evinced in the 'hysterical German applause' which had greeted an anti-Soviet outburst by Franz Borkenau, which struck the author of *The Last Days of Hitler* as alarmingly reminiscent of Nazism. The other was the domination of proceedings by an alliance of 'rootless European ex-Communists' led by Koestler and American intellectuals who shared Koestler's obsessive hatred of communism, such as James Burnham. Leaving to one side the fairness of these charges (which caused Melvin Lasky to wonder whether Trevor-Roper 'really knew what the "last days of Hitler" were like, or the first days, or any day'),[4] the *Guardian* report clearly struck a responsive chord amongst British intellectuals wary of foreign ideological excesses. Bertrand Russell, one of the Congress's Honorary Chairmen, promptly resigned his post on reading it – although he was later lured back after personal appeals from Koestler, Arthur Schlesinger Jr. and Sidney Hook.[5] Other attempts at damage limitation, however, failed to dispel the impression that the Congress was a sinister cabal of fanatical ex-Nazi and communist ideologues.[6]

It was in part because of this negative reaction to the Berlin rally that, as the Congress was established on a permanent basis in the months that followed, its officers made a particular point of courting the support of British intellectuals. In October, Burnham wrote to his friend the Conservative MP Julian Amery, one of the British participants in the June conference, suggesting he organise a meeting to 'conciliate Ayer and Trevor-Roper, or counteract the negative effect of their post-Congress comments', and form 'a potential nucleus for the Congress in England'.[7] By early November, the CCF had 'successfully contacted' the journalists T. R. Fyvel and Malcolm Muggeridge, who had in turn put the organisation in touch with, amongst others, the poet Stephen Spender, publisher Victor Gollancz and editor John Lehmann.[8] This new receptivity to the Congress's overtures was possibly the consequence of the organisation's shift to a cultural, 'non-communist left' strategy, and the concomitant marginalisation of Koestler and Burnham. According to David Williams,

195

who played an important role in securing the Congress British support before his return to Americans for Democratic Action headquarters in Washington, the same period also witnessed a distinct hardening of Cold War resolve amongst Britain's anti-communist intellectuals.[9] In any case, the CCF's tactic of pitching its appeal to literary intellectuals on the non-communist left evidently worked, for when during the following year Secretary-General Nicolas Nabokov undertook a good-will tour of England, he soon formed the impression (as reported to Burnham) that, whereas before the Congress had been perceived 'as some kind of semi-clandestine American organisation controlled by you, Koestler and ... Borkenau', British 'misgivings' about it now seemed to have 'dissipated to some degree'.[10] The scene was set for the creation of an official British national affiliate of the CIA-controlled CCF.

THE BRITISH SOCIETY FOR CULTURAL FREEDOM

The founding meeting of the British Society for Cultural Freedom was held on 11 January 1951 at the Authors' Club, Whitehall, an appropriate choice of venue given the organisation's literary complexion. Among those present were David Williams, Julian Amery, journalist (and Lovestoneite contact) Richard Lowenthal and Stephen Spender, who took the chair. A list of desirable collaborators was drawn up, which included the names of Ayer, Trevor-Roper, Michael Foot, Herbert Read and Harman Grisewood (Controller of the BBC Third Programme). Michael Goodwin and John Lowe were appointed Joint Honorary Secretaries.[11] The international secretariat observed these developments with interest, proposing that Lowe receive a regular Congress salary and 'keep of course in frequent personal contact with Paris'.[12] Meanwhile, T. R. Fyvel pledged to keep 'a watching brief on arrangements in London' on behalf of his friend, Irving Brown.[13] Through the efforts of Spender, Fyvel and the others, the nascent British organisation gradually built up friendly contacts in the British news media.[14] Nicolas Nabokov undertook his good-will tour in June, meeting 'important personalities like T. S. Eliot, Isaiah Berlin, Lord David Cecil, the heads of the British Council, the Third Programme of the BBC, the Secretary General of the Labour Party, Richard Crossman, and many others'.[15] By July the British affiliate was able to boast 'a membership superior to that enjoyed by any other like organisation in this country, both as regards the breadth of its representation and the influence of its members', including as it did the likes of Max Beloff, Crossman, Gollancz, Michael Oakeshott, Michael Redgrave and Hugh Seton-Watson.[16] The remainder of the year was passed in such activities as sponsoring speaking tours by visiting anti-communist intellectuals, publicising the work of sympathetic writers and helping the international Congress set up other national affiliates.[17]

Early in 1952, following meetings in Paris between Spender and members of the Congress secretariat,[18] the British Society was substantially reorganised. A new Executive Committee was elected, which in turn elected a new Chairman (Grisewood), Vice-Chair (Muggeridge, who later took over the chair when Grisewood stepped down, and who appears from that point to have been the dominant personality in the Society), Treasurer (Fredric Warburg) and Secretary (Goodwin, Lowe having slipped from the picture by this point).[19] At the same time, John Clews, a former National Union of Students (NUS) President who had sat on the Executive of the International Union of Students (IUS), was appointed to a new post, that of full-time National Organiser (later General Secretary).[20] Under this reformed régime, the British Society entered what was probably the most active phase of its existence. It provided useful support to the CCF's 'Masterpieces of the Twentieth Century' festival, for example, obtaining the participation of such British literary celebrities as Louis MacNiece, Herbert Read and Cyril Connolly; distributed thousands of copies of two pamphlets written by Clews, one exposing communist infiltration of the IUS and the other rebutting Soviet propaganda about the alleged American use of 'germ warfare' in Korea; organised lecture tours by Czeslaw Milosz and Raymond Aron as well as talks by various members of the Executive Committee; built up a small reference library for use by various organisations and individuals; and consolidated its contacts with a range of institutions and groups, including the Labour and Conservative Parties, the NUS, the BBC and the Arts Council.[21]

In addition to these overt anti-communist measures, the British Society for Cultural Freedom also appears, judging by remarks scattered throughout the papers of the CCF, to have engaged in covert, political warfare against communism, including the surveillance of communist or suspected communist-front organisations. One of Michael Goodwin's achievements as the Society's Secretary, for example, was the setting up of a special sub-committee 'to keep a watching brief' on the Authors' World Peace Appeal, the literary front in the Cominform's peace offensive.[22] Goodwin's successor Clews was even more active in this regard, carrying on the campaign against the Authors' Peace Appeal and, as already noted, working to counteract communist germ warfare propaganda. According to a 1953 report by him on the previous year's activities, 'Meetings of Communist front and "suspect" organisations have been attended by me or on my behalf and much useful information has been obtained in this way for the files'.[23] To what extent this side of the Society's work overlapped with the Cold War operations of such state agencies as the Information Research Department is unclear. Evidently though there was some private/public cooperation. The minutes of an Executive Committee meeting in July 1951 noted Julian Amery's intention of keeping 'in touch informally' with the Foreign Office; both Goodwin and Clews also had links to IRD, the former as a contract writer and the latter as a channel of publicity material to the student movement; and Muggeridge, a wartime Secret Intelligence Service officer, regularly used IRD materials in his *Daily Telegraph* columns, as well as performing consultancy work for his old colleagues in SIS.[24]

LABOUR INTELLECTUALS

Having linked up with Britain's literary intellectuals, the CCF now began to turn its attention to the politically most important segment of the country's non-communist left – the young intellectuals on the right wing of the Labour Party known as the Gaitskellites. As it turned out, the Congress's most active collaborator within this group proved to be also (by general agreement) its most brilliant member, Anthony Crosland. It was Hugh Gaitskell who first put the CCF in contact with Crosland, recommending him and Roy Jenkins to Nicolas Nabokov in July 1954 as 'easily our two brightest young people in the House on the economic side'.[25] The future Labour Foreign Secretary subsequently performed a number of tasks on behalf of the CIA-financed organisation. In November 1955, for instance, after attending a Congress conference at Gothenberg, he undertook a tour of the Scandinavian sections of the organisation, reporting his impressions, which were generally unfavourable, in sur-prisingly frank terms to the secretariat, and offering 'to provide a fairly wide-ranging list of names of people who, if the Swedish Committee is really to be influential, should certainly be on it'.[26] Later, he was to play a pivotal role in the CCF seminar series on 'Tradition and Change'.

Of no less strategic significance were the CCF's links with Rita Hinden, editor of the journal *Socialist Commentary*, the principal theoretical organ of the Labour revisionists.[27] The Congress undertook subscription drives on behalf of the magazine in Asia and Africa in order to show that (as Irving Kristol put it) 'there's another kind of socialism possible, aside from the *New Statesman*'s'.[28] In 1957 Paris paid for Hinden to travel to a Congress seminar in Tokyo via Burma, India, Singapore and Malaya, so that she could lecture audiences there and research 'a study of the factors which divide Asia from the West'.[29] On her return to London in May 1957, Hinden reported to the CCF secretariat on the enthusiastic reception given her by Asian intellectuals eager for information 'about socialist "new thinking"', something the Labour Party had so far failed to provide. 'Even in spite of the sneer "American money"', she told John Hunt, an under-cover CIA officer recently seconded to Paris to assist Michael Josselson in his duties, 'good people – and in good numbers – turned up to all the meetings of the Congress I attended, and never did anyone suggest to me that I was an American capitalist stooge – though I was once called a British imperialist agent!'.[30] The following year Hinden contributed further to the cause of east–west dialogue by helping to bring the Indian leader Jayaprakash Narayan, preferred by western governments to the neutralist Nehru, on a CCF-sponsored visit to London. The thinking that lay behind this trip – Hinden wanted to let 'people know that Nehru's is not the only voice in India'[31] – was reminiscent of that which had prompted the Congress's support for *Socialist Commentary* in Asia and Africa.

Perhaps the most spectacular proof of the CCF's success in cultivating Labour intellectuals was the 'Future of Freedom' conference held in Milan in 1955. Taking place over a week in late September, this event brought together 140 intellectuals from countries all over the world to discuss such issues as the causes of totalitarianism, the performance of the Soviet economy and the consequences of colonialism.[32] In contrast with the Berlin rally of 1950, the Milan conference was attended by a sizeable contingent of Labour MPs, including Hugh Gaitskell, Denis Healey, Roy Jenkins and Tony Crosland (who at Gaitskell's suggestion had served on the event's planning committee).[33] The Gaitskellites performed a prominent part in proceedings, delivering papers, chairing panels and dominating discussion periods. In one session, for example, Healey engaged in a 'short but fierce debate' with Richard Crossman about democratic control of foreign policy, prompting the American chairman of the panel immediately following to open with the words, 'This afternoon we are likely to have a peaceful time. There are no members of the British Labour Party on the platform.'[34] Indeed, so conspicuous

11 British-based chemist and philosopher Michael Polanyi, French sociologist Raymond Aron and Hugh Gaitskell during the opening session of the Congress for Cultural Freedom's conference on the Future of Freedom, Milan, 1955. (Congress for Cultural Freedom Papers, Joseph Regenstein Library, University of Chicago)

was the British delegation at Milan that it was generally perceived as having set the ideological tone of the meeting. According to French historian Pierre Grémion, it was 'the driving force of the conference and the pivot of European participation'.[35] Another contrast with the founding Berlin conference worth mentioning is the British press reaction. The *Guardian*, for example, which had published Hugh Trevor-Roper's critical comments in 1950, reported the Milan gathering in extremely favourable terms.[36] Similarly, Max Beloff, in his report on the event in the *Spectator*, while echoing some of Trevor-Roper's earlier observations about German fanaticism and excessive anti-communism – 'anti-Communism by itself is an inadequate bond between people and a still more inadequate foundation for social inquiry or social action' – nevertheless concluded that the debates in Milan had 'in some important respects altered the shape of our mental world'.[37] One British intellectual for whom this was probably true was Tony Crosland, whose seminal revisionist tract, *The Future of Socialism*, published the following year, was clearly influenced by the ideas of American intellectuals who had also been in Milan, such as Daniel Bell.

THE UNIVERSITIES

As the CCF stabilised its operations during the 1950s it became in-creasingly active on a third intellectual front: the universities. In part this arose from a straightforward desire to broaden, and normalise, its influence in international intellectual life. However, it also reflected a more specific concern about scientists, a group whose expert knowledge had come to acquire massive military significance in the age of the atom, yet who on the whole appeared – at least to the officers of the CCF – to lack the kind of ideological common sense that literary and political intellectuals had acquired through either personal experience or reflection. Anxieties on this score seem to have been particularly intense in Britain, where in 1951 the British Society for Cultural Freedom considered plans for a conference to investigate 'Communist influence among scientists in this country, ... the intellectual centre of Communism in this field'.[38] Although a CCF conference on science was eventually held in Hamburg in 1953, and not as originally proposed at Oxford the previous year, the job of organising a permanent post-conference Committee on 'Science and Freedom' was entrusted to a British-based intellectual, the émigré chemist and polymath Michael Polanyi (who also, incidentally, helped organise the Milan Future of Freedom meeting). Assisted by his son George, a fellow academic at Manchester University, and supported by a group of honorary sponsors which included Karl Jaspers, Salvador de Madariaga, Robert Oppenheimer and Bertrand Russell,[39] Polanyi engaged in a wide range of activities on behalf of the Congress, publishing a regular *Bulletin* exposing violations of academic freedom around the world, addressing public meetings on the subject of apartheid and organising protests to the Soviet Embassy in London following the 1956 Hungarian uprising.[40] Under Polanyi's energetic stewardship, the Committee on Science and Freedom provided the CCF with, in the words of Michael Josselson, 'a direct link to the academic world'.[41]

Polanyi also played an important part in the 'Tradition and Change' seminars, launched in 1957 with a grant to the CCF by the Ford Foundation of $500,000. The aim of this venture, Polanyi explained from the chair to a December 1957 Planning Committee meeting attended by Tony Crosland, Arthur Koestler, Michael Josselson and Melvin Lasky, was to build on the international contacts established at earlier international conferences and to strengthen the CCF's ties with the university world.[42] Over the course of the next few years, Polanyi and the Planning Committee, regularly attended by Crosland, organised seminars in locations as diverse as Rhodes, Vienna, Khartoum, Tunis and Karachi, where the subject matter ranged widely over such topics as 'representative government in the newly independent states, workers' participation in management, tradition and change in the arts, education in the new states, and Islam in the modern world'.[43]

The most important Congress meeting to take place at a British university was the 'Changes in Soviet Society' seminar hosted by St Antony's College, Oxford, in June 1957. Funded partly, like the 'Tradition and Change' series, from Ford Foundation money, and planned over a year and a half with the help of expert consultants on both sides of the Atlantic (including Isaiah Berlin, Hugh Seton-Watson and Charles Bohlen), this week-long meeting was designed to provide a multi-disciplinary assessment of recent upheavals in Soviet society for the benefit of 'policy makers and the educated public'.[44] Among the nine papers prepared for the conference were contributions by two members of St Antony's College, Max Hayward and Geoffrey Hudson, concerned respectively with intellectual dissidence in the Soviet Union and relations between the USSR and the west. Other speakers and topics included Bertram Wolfe, who talked about the prospects for internal political liberalisation, and Daniel Bell, who analysed 'ten different theories of

Soviet behaviour'.[45] Among the British discussants at the sessions where these papers were delivered were Max Beloff, Isaiah Berlin, Richard Lowenthal and Robert Carew-Hunt. Americans participants included Joseph Alsop and Charles Thayer, making the event something of a reunion of the Georgetown set which had invented the concept of the NCL ten years earlier.[46] The conference, which was judged a great success by participants and sponsors alike,[47] might be viewed as marking the final transformation of the study of Soviet Russia from the obscure preserve of a few supposedly 'rootless' ex-communists into the respectable academic discipline of 'Sovietology'.[48]

UNWITTING ASSETS?

The 1957 St Antony's seminar might also be regarded as marking the final 'arrival' in Britain of the Congress for Cultural Freedom. Seven years earlier in Berlin two Oxford dons had led those questioning the CCF's purpose and inspiration. Now the organisation was using the country's most ancient university as a venue for its programme of seminars. The process whereby this dramatic improvement in the CCF's reputation had been accomplished began with the wooing of the country's literary intellectuals (the use of the imagery of courtship here, by the way, is deliberate: Congress officials often employed a sexualised language of flirtation and seduction when describing their attempts to earn the trust of foreign intellectuals). Next the CCF had secured the cooperation of the Gaitskellites, thereby giving it the opportunity to influence the ideological development of the Labour Party's future leadership and at the same time providing it with an entrée to socialist intellectuals in the developing world. Finally, it had managed both to extend and institutionalise its presence in British intellectual life by establishing bases of support in the country's university system, most notably at Manchester and Oxford. This is not to mention the stunning success of the CCF's highest-profile venture in Britain, the journal *Encounter*. Considering all this, it is easy to see why, when the organisation's secret relationship with the CIA was revealed in the late 1960s, some observers concluded that the US had colonised the consciousness of Britain's Cold War intelligentsia.

However, there are several other factors which also need to be taken into account before one can arrive at a full and balanced assessment of the Congress for Cultural Freedom's influence on Cold War Britain. To begin with, despite some of the claims made by New Left commentators in the late 1960s, the CCF cannot be blamed for – or credited with – having originally interested British intellectuals in the defence of cultural freedom against communism. The anti-communist literary intellectuals who joined the British Society for Cultural Freedom in the early 1950s had long championed this cause, as had such campaigners for a 'self-governing scientific community' as Michael Polanyi.[49] In this connection, it is worth remembering that the Information Research Department, whose existence of course predated that of the Office of Policy Coordination, was the creation, at least in part, of young Labour politicians of the sort who only became involved with the CCF much later. While on the subject of IRD, it might also be mentioned that the CIA was not alone in giving covert encouragement to the development of Sovietology; the Foreign Office too had links with such experts on Soviet matters as Robert Carew-Hunt and Robert Conquest.[50] The involvement of St Anthony's in the CCF's seminar programme appears as less surprising when one bears in mind that the college had long functioned as an interface between British academe and the secret services. Similarly, the suggestion that the Congress manufactured the revisionist ideas of Gaitskellites like Crosland – which later became Labour Party orthodoxy and, eventually, government policy – is obviously erroneous. Labour intellectuals had been engaged in the revisionist project of which *The Future of Socialism* was the culmination ever since the 1930s, and had also been in personal contact with social democratic American intellectuals long before the CCF came on the scene.[51] The Congress for Cultural Freedom did not make non-communist left British intellectuals into Cold Warriors, revisionists or Atlanticists. They already were these things.

The notion that Britain's Cold War intellectuals were so many puppets of the CIA is problematic for other reasons, as well. First, it supposes that those involved in such ventures as the British Society for Cultural Freedom were invariably passive and dependable agents of American ideological influence. Yet this was not in fact the case. From the outset there were disagreements between the CCF and its British affiliate over what tactics the latter should employ in the battle for cultural freedom. Granted, all parties accepted that the relative weakness of communism in Britain and a British propensity for anti-Americanism ruled out a crudely propagandistic approach.[52] Moreover, the Congress's adoption of a cultural, non-communist left strategy in the months after Berlin demonstrated its understanding of the need for tact and diplomacy in the contest for hearts and minds. Still, the *literati* of the British Society for Cultural Freedom appear to have favoured an even more oblique method of waging Cultural Cold War than the CCF. 'If anything significant and far-reaching is to be achieved', explained a 'Plan of Work' for the organisation in 1951, 'infiltration must be the order of the day, the "wheels within wheels" mentality must be constantly respected and the approach must for the most part be overt'.[53] What was needed in particular was 'positive' material celebrating the cultural accomplishments of the free west. 'We should not merely be "anti"', Honorary Secretary John Lowe told a meeting of the CCF's Executive Committee in Paris in February 1951, 'we must also be "for".' Such utterances did not meet with universal approval in the Congress's international councils, however. Executive Committee members Salvador de Madariaga, Raymond Aron and David Rousset all took issue with Lowe's comments, claiming that he had underestimated the influence of communism in Britain and remarking on the need for anti-communist political education there. According to Rousset, it was of crucial importance to the international efforts of the Congress that the British be induced to take a more active role in the defence of cultural freedom, both at home and abroad.[54]

These differences soon crystallised around a specific issue. In addition to being the British Society's joint Honorary Secretary with Lowe, Michael Goodwin was also an editor of the venerable journal of opinion, *The Nineteenth Century and After*. Under Goodwin's influence, this publication had spoken out in defence of the Congress for Cultural Freedom after Hugh Trevor-Roper's attack on it. It had also agreed to house the British Society for Cultural Freedom in its offices when the organisation was formed in January 1951 (an arrangement reminiscent of the help provided the American Committee for Cultural Freedom in the early days of its existence by *The New Leader*). As Goodwin pointed out in a 'Manifesto and Statements of Aims' sent to Irving Brown, *The Twentieth Century* (as the magazine had been renamed in an attempt to cast off its somewhat fusty image) shared the CCF's determination to combat the contagion of neutralist and fellow-travelling ideas among left-wing intellectuals. It was also firmly committed to the principle of Atlantic unity and therefore capable of functioning as a point of contact or 'clearing house' between 'progressive liberal forces in America and their counterparts in Europe'.[55] Finally, it was ready and willing to publish or 'leak' Congress materials, a service it had previously performed for 'the Foreign Office more than once in every year of its existence' (Goodwin was editor of the Bellman Books series, which was published by Ampersand, IRD's front publishing operation).[56] Goodwin had pressed all the right buttons. In August 1951 the Congress for Cultural Freedom offered to pay off *The Twentieth Century*'s deficit of £2,000, cover its next printing bill of £700 and subsidise it to the tune of £150 a month.[57] Now confident of the magazine's financial future, Goodwin set about building up its reputation as an organ of the trans-atlantic 'non-Communist left' (the actual phrase he had employed in his 'Manifesto'), approaching Arthur Schlesinger Jr., James Farrell and Irving Kristol for help setting up a special American advisory board.[58]

Already, however, doubts were being expressed about the CCF's decision to support *The Twentieth Century*. For British literary intellectuals still mourning the death of Cyril Connolly's *Horizon* in 1949, the magazine did not pay enough attention to the arts and, despite its name change, remained rather 'dull'. Meanwhile, in the CCF's Paris headquarters, another objection was forming: *The Twentieth Century* was not doing enough to tackle the threat of neutralism in Britain head-on and, in particular, was failing 'to take up any issues which are constantly being hammered away at by *The New Statesman and Nation*'.[59] It was against this background of mounting discontent on both sides of the English Channel that the Congress began listening favourably to suggestions from British intellectuals that it launch a brand new magazine of its own. In May 1951, for example, Nicolas Nabokov told the former *Horizon* assistant editor Stephen Spender that the CCF was 'extremely interested' in a proposal for a new 'trans-Atlantic quarterly' that had originally been advanced by Richard Crossman.[60] Irving Brown responded in similar fashion when he was informed in August that T. R. Fyvel had been discussing the 'idea for an Anglo–American Left-of-Centre publication' with, amongst others, Crossman, Denis Healey and David Williams.[61] Dissatisfaction with *The Twentieth Century* culminated in December 1951 when Spender was instructed by the CCF's Executive Committee (of which he was now the British member) to advise the magazine's staff that unless 'radical changes' were made, its subsidy would be terminated.[62] As Spender subsequently told the journal's Editorial Board (evidently with some pleasure – he appears to have harboured a strong personal dislike for Michael Goodwin), the CCF objected to a recent issue's cover, 'the editorial, the editorial notes and a good many of the contents'. The poet, who only six months earlier had supported *The Twentieth Century*'s bid for Congress support,[63] went on to point out, somewhat ominously:

206

> There are almost no good magazines in England today, and there is a tremendous opportunity, either in *The Twentieth Century*, or in some new magazine, of getting both the best writers and the most interested public.[64]

When Goodwin protested to the CCF at what he saw not only as an attempt to wriggle out of its financial commitment to *The Twentieth Century* but also as a challenge to his editorial independence, Nicolas Nabokov denied any intention of dictating terms to the magazine but then advised Goodwin, in what can only be interpreted as a thinly veiled threat, 'that these criticisms be seriously considered by yourself and your Editorial Board, if you and your Board are interested in a continuance of the backing of our organisation'.[65]

Shortly after this bruising encounter, the animosity between Spender and Goodwin erupted in outright factional warfare. Early in January 1952, Spender travelled to Paris in order to discuss with the international secretariat plans for expanding the British organisation's operations and appointing a paid, full-time director.[66] A meeting held on 7 January and attended by Michael Josselson and Irving Brown resolved to separate out the affairs of the Society and *The Twentieth Century*, and search for an organiser 'who can arrange the relationship with Paris on a proper footing'.[67] While Spender was out of the country, Goodwin initiated a postal ballot of the Society's members for elections to its Executive Committee, claiming that the present committee had shrunk to unfeasibly small proportions and was in any case improperly constituted.[68] On his return Spender tried to cancel the ballot, convened an emergency meeting of the Executive Committee which voted to sack Goodwin, and wrote to Paris demanding that the Society's funds be suspended until a new Secretary had been appointed.[69] At this point the warring factions began consulting solicitors.[70] Meanwhile another row within the organisation, this one arising from the co-option of Labour MP Woodrow Wyatt onto the Executive Committee (an idea originally proposed by T. R. Fyvel to Irving Brown),[71] resulted in the noisy resignation of another member, Peter Calvocoressi.[72] It would seem that, in addition to literary feuds, the British Society for Cultural Freedom was also troubled by party political conflict.

Dismayed by this turmoil, Nicolas Nabokov wrote to the Society's Executive Committee urging an end to hostilities, the withdrawal of solicitors and the holding of peace talks. 'We are convinced that any factional strife at this time will only give aid and comfort to our enemies', he told Spender, using language similar to that he would employ only months later when attempting to smooth over arguments within the American Committee for Cultural Freedom about McCarthyism.[73] Under pressure from Paris, Spender eventually consented to the ballot, and a new Committee was duly elected in late February (the defeat of T. R. Fyvel in this election caused Spender to resign from the Society, although he rejoined not long after when Fyvel was co-opted back onto the Committee).[74] Meeting for the first time in March, the Committee confirmed the choice of Malcolm Muggeridge as Vice-Chairman, Fredric Warburg as Treasurer and John Clews as National Organiser. Yet, despite this change of régime, the Society's problems had still not disappeared. Resignations from the Executive Committee continued: Chairman Grisewood, Secretary Goodwin (presumably thoroughly disgruntled by the CCF's treatment of him and his magazine) and eventually even Muggeridge, supposedly the 'sparkplug' of the new leadership, all left in the course of the following year. Those who remained behind appeared incapable of reaching even the most basic agreement on the aims of the Society. The question of a constitution was raised on a number of occasions, and Michael Oakeshott submitted a draft at the request of the Committee. This was discussed in May, but was later deferred indefinitely.[75] In June 1952, Warburg visited Paris and reported to François Bondy that the Society 'has no Chairman, no organisation and, as far as he is aware, no policy'. John Clews had proved a disappointment as National Organiser, preoccupied as he was with student politics. Moreover, the new Executive Committee was excessively right-wing and therefore unable to challenge effectively 'the pro-Communist line of the *New Statesman* and Bevanism'.[76] Warburg would later echo these complaints in his memoirs. 'Sterile discussions dragged on for months', he recalled of the British Society, 'and Muggeridge, an impatient man, pressed for our dissolution. "There's altogether too much cultural freedom already", he is reported as saying, "any man who hasn't got a platform to sound off from must be a fool."' He and the organisation's other officers were, Warburg claimed, 'bored to tears'.[77]

Not even the political warfare side of the operation ran smoothly. In September 1953 Warburg approached his friend Jasper Ridley, an ex-communist who would later achieve distinction as a historical biographer, and asked him if he would like to take over the running of the British Society from Clews, who was 'too student-orientated, and could not adequately deal with leading intellectuals'. Ridley accepted this invitation and, as instructed by Warburg, sent Paris a resumé of his career deliberately omitting mention of his communist past. This proved a mistake. Irving Brown was tipped off (probably by Jack Carney) and told Michael Josselson. In December Ridley was summoned to Paris, where he endured two days of cross-examination about his political associations from Josselson and Nabokov. The former, he recalled, 'could have been an actor playing the part of a domineering, bullying Soviet *apparatchik*'. Why Josselson was so suspicious of Ridley is not entirely clear: there were, after all, numerous former communists on the CCF's books. It may have been that the young Briton was a comparatively recent convert from communism – he had been expelled from the Party in 1949 for publicly supporting Tito – or that he was perceived as a factional candidate of the British. 'I think the British Committee regarded Clews as Paris's man and the international committee regarded me as London's man', he later wrote. In any case, the extraordinary situation soon developed that, while Ridley was permitted to replace Clews (although his appointment was never made permanent), the latter would regularly visit the Society's offices and report on his successor's activities to CCF headquarters. Stranger still, Ridley, although aware that he was under surveillance, positively welcomed Clews's presence, since he regarded him as a personal friend with better political contacts than himself. Indeed, the two men would often joke together about Congress affairs and speculate about the organisation's source of funding, which Clews surmised must be the US State Department. 'Our chief activity', Ridley remembers, 'was inviting eminent intellectuals to have lunch with us in expensive Soho restaurants at the expense of the Society for Cultural Freedom.'[78]

As this last comment suggests, the British literary intellectuals associated with the CCF appear to have adopted a rather relaxed approach towards its monies. Their expenditure, suggested an officer of rival anti-communist organisation, Common Cause, to Irving Brown, 'has not always been marked by that strict economy which would have yielded the greatest advantage in the fight against Communism'.[79] This was not merely a matter of fiddling with expenses, although that did go on.[80] Rather, it amounted to a more serious and fundamental problem for the CCF, bound as it was to give at least the appearance of respecting the intellectual independence of its national affiliates and by the secrecy of its relationship with the CIA. Patronage for the arts was a scarce commodity in postwar Britain – witness the recent folding of *Horizon* and several other literary magazines – and there was no shortage of, as Isaiah Berlin put it, 'English intellectuals with outstretched hands making eyes at affluent American widows'.[81] Although never stated explicitly, it is likely that one of the factors underlying the row over *The Twentieth Century* was Stephen Spender's desire to edit his own English-language magazine along the lines of the defunct *Horizon* using Congress money. Certainly he was eager to be associated with the proposal for a new Anglo–American publication to replace *The Twentieth Century* that eventually became *Encounter*. In any event, by January 1952 the CIA-funded CCF was firmly of the view that Britain was not pulling its financial weight in the Cultural Cold War, telling Spender that, 'The present situation of the British Society of being exclusively supported from the American side is only temporary and cannot continue without money raising or search for funds on the British side'.[82] This admonition was heeded by Malcolm Muggeridge, who used his intelligence connections to obtain a covert subsidy for the Society from the Secret Intelligence Service.[83] It is doubtful, though, that he was acting out of obedience to Paris. He later suggested that he had obtained secret British money in order to win himself and his friends some independence from American influence.[84]

THE RUSSELL AFFAIR(S)

The most dramatic example of the contradictions inherent in the relationship between British intellectuals and the Congress for Cultural Freedom was provided by the mathematician and philosopher Bertrand Russell. On the one hand, Russell was just the sort of eminent intellectual that the CCF, with its commitment to a front strategy in the Cultural Cold War, wanted to capture for its cause. He was fiercely anti-communist, had a reputation for speaking out loudly in defence of cultural freedom and knew America well, having visited it on numerous occasions and even briefly resided there. In all these respects he was an obvious choice for one of the Congress's Honorary Chairs, which he was persuaded to fill shortly before the Berlin rally. This represented a significant coup for the new organisation, as the philosopher's name commanded immense prestige around the world, not least in Asia, an area of growing Cold War strategic significance. However, using Russell could lead to problems. He was highly susceptible to flattery but also extremely sensitive to criticism; he had pacifist leanings and was increasingly alarmed by the threat of nuclear war, which made his name susceptible to appropriation by the Soviet peace offensive; and he was inclined to bouts of anti-Americanism, the legacy perhaps of some nasty run-ins with the US

210

authorities during the 1940s. This last characteristic meant that, unlike many other intellectuals belonging to the CCF, he was equally as likely to protest violations of cultural freedom in America as in the communist countries, something for which there was increasing scope in the McCarthyite atmosphere of the early 1950s.[85] Indeed, during this period he became convinced that the US was growing into a repressive police state not unlike the Soviet Union. According to his fellow philosopher and old friend Sidney Hook, who tried throughout the 1950s to persuade him that intellectual repression in America was not as severe as he had been led to believe, Russell even 'bet Malcolm Muggeridge five pounds that Joe McCarthy would become President of the United States'.[86]

Russell's views on McCarthyism need not necessarily have led to conflict with the Congress for Cultural Freedom. Under the tactically astute stewardship of Michael Josselson, the organisation was careful to distance itself from the vagaries of domestic American politics. It had also proved itself adept at 'handling' Russell in the wake of the Trevor-Roper *Guardian* report on the Berlin rally and his subsequent resignation from his Honorary Chair, when it not only succeeded in luring him back into the fold but also persuaded him to take on the Presidency of the British Society for Cultural Freedom. However, not everyone associated with the CCF shared Josselson's tactical adroitness where McCarthyism was concerned nor his sensitivity to the personal feelings of famous European intellectuals. A hint of the trouble that was to come from the New York section of the non-communist left was provided in January 1951 when William Henry Chamberlin of *The New Leader* wrote an angry letter to the *Guardian* protesting an article by Russell, 'Democracy and the Teachers in the United States', which had portrayed American academic freedom as under serious threat from extremist anti-communism.[87] Another row broke out a year later when the *NL* printed an editorial denouncing two pieces by Russell which had appeared simultaneously in the *New York Times Magazine* and the *Herald Tribune*, one attacking McCarthyism and the other urging a search for international peace. Russell's reply was published in a March 1952 issue of the *NL* under the title, 'Is America in the Grip of Hysteria?' An accompanying editorial comment claimed that 'anti-Americanism in England and Europe, and the xenophobic isolationism such sentiment provokes in America, serve not the cause of freedom and peace but the cause of the Kremlin'.[88]

This was the opening salvo in a war Russell would wage with the New York intellectuals throughout the 1950s. However, it was not *The New Leader* that would prove the focal point of this conflict but rather the organisation with which it shared offices for a brief period, the American Committee for Cultural Freedom. In April 1953 Katherine B. Faulkner, officer of a Popular Front-style, anti-McCarthy organisation called the Emergency Civil Liberties Committee (ECLC), which the ACCF had branded (probably with some justification) as communist-influenced, wrote to Russell accusing the CCF's American affiliate of employing 'the best McCarthy tactics of smear and guilt-by-association' and expressing surprise at seeing his name listed as one of its sponsors: 'We ... cannot believe that you would knowingly support an organization which ... is helping to bring to pass in this country the very totalitarianism it fears.'[89] Russell, 'very much in sympathy' with the predicament of the ECLC and 'shocked' by this information about the ACCF, immediately wrote withdrawing his name from the organisation.[90] In response, two of Sol Levitas's less hot-headed protégés, Irving Kristol (who had just stepped down from the Executive Directorship of the ACCF to take up the American editorship of *Encounter*) and Daniel Bell attempted to refute the suggestion that the American Committee was McCarthyite and pointed out that, even if it was, Russell's position as Honorary Chairman of the CCF did not imply any responsibility for the actions of its national affiliates.[91] On this occasion the philosopher allowed himself to be talked round. 'You may take my previous letter as not having been written', he graciously informed Bell.[92]

This was not an end to the matter, however. In March of the following year Russell was persuaded by the ECLC to send a message of greeting to a conference on academic freedom it had organised at Princeton University in honour of Albert Einstein's seventy-fifth birthday (another instance of a front organisation trying to harness the prestige of a world-famous intellectual reputation). Russell's name was already associated with Einstein's in the fight against McCarthyism: in June 1953 he had written to the *New York Times* in support of the physicist's controversial advice to intellectuals not to cooperate with congressional committees investigating alleged communist subversion.[93] This is why the ACCF was perhaps ill-advised to intervene in the situation as it did, urging Russell to 'withdraw support from this undertaking which does no honor to Einstein's great name'.[94] The philosopher was furious. 'I do not see any reason why I should withdraw the message', he wrote to the ACCF, 'since it only expressed admiration for Einstein, which I would express to the devil himself if asked to do so.'[95] The ECLC, which had distributed photostats of Faulkner's correspondence with Russell from the previous year at the Princeton meeting, heaped fuel on the fire. 'They are so intent

212

upon pointing out the beam in Russia's eye', one of its officers told Russell, referring to the leadership of the ACCF, 'that they appear unwilling to admit the possibility of a mote in America's'.

> Moreover, they strive to destroy any other organization which disagrees with them. The source of their funds is a mystery but there appears very good reason to believe that a part of them come from the State Department.[96]

Like Kristol and Bell the year before – although using a markedly less conciliatory tone – the American Committee's new Executive Director, Sol Stein, tried to convince Russell that the ECLC's accusations of McCarthyism were unfounded.[97] 'I hope this will pacify Lord Russell', Stein wrote to Michael Josselson,

> and I hope that sometime somebody can reciprocate and pacify us here about Lord Russell's maliciously deceitful articles in the American press....[W]hat the hell does Russell want us to do: assassinate McCarthy the way Huey Long was assassinated?[98]

The relationship between the CCF and Russell reached crisis point in 1956, and again the Congress's American affiliate was at the root of it. On 26 March 1956, the *Guardian* (ever a thorn in the CCF's side, despite its pro-American stance on the Cold War) published a letter from Russell protesting the imprisonment of Morton Sobell for suspected involvement in the Rosenberg spy ring as a miscarriage of justice. According to Russell, the methods used to apprehend Sobell were illegal, the atmosphere of 'political hysteria' in which his trial was conducted prejudicial and the evidence used to convict him unsafe. The most objectionable aspect of the case, in Russell's view, was the behaviour of the FBI, whose actions he likened to 'atrocities' of a sort 'familiar in other police states such as Nazi Germany and Stalin's Russia'.[99] The letter was reported in both the communist press and major American newspapers. When it came to the attention of the ACCF, the Board of Directors instructed Chairman James Farrell to send Russell a public response challenging his account of the Sobell case as 'totally mistaken' and questioning the propriety of 'an officer of the Congress for Cultural Freedom' making 'false and irresponsible statements about the process of justice' in the US. 'Your remarks', Farrell told Russell, 'constitute a major disservice to the cause of freedom and democracy in our troubled world, and a major service to the enemies we had supposed you engaged to combat.'[100] The philosopher's reaction to his public censure was predictable. On 10 April 1956, he wrote to Stephen Spender, British representative on the CCF's International Executive Committee, stating his intention of resigning from his honorary position with the Congress.

> Some years ago I decided to resign because the American Committee appeared to me to be merely anti-Communist, but on that occasion I was over-persuaded. On this occasion, as I am the subject of criticism, there can be no question of my remaining connected with your body.[101]

There followed several months of bitter recriminations between the Paris secretariat and New York. As far as the CCF was concerned, the American Committee should have consulted it before embarking on a course of action likely to have serious international repercussions, was unfair in placing Russell under suspicion of 'ulterior motive' and was mistaken in its characterisation of Russell as an 'officer' of the CCF, because his post was purely honorary, making the public response to his *Guardian* comments entirely inappropriate. Such, anyway, was the burden of an official statement reprimanding the ACCF drafted by Michael Polanyi (who found the American Committee's letter to Russell 'intolerable' and 'deplorable') and issued by the CCF on 24 April 1956.[102] In its response, formulated by Farrell's successor Diana Trilling, the American Committee insisted on its right to respond publicly to Russell, rejected the CCF's insinuation that it had imputed the philosopher with communist sympathies, claiming it had only suggested his remarks might furnish political succour to the communists, and demanded to know 'how untruthful about America may a man be and still be useful to an organization which is pledged to truth and which numbers among its affiliates an American branch'?[103] These official communications were accompanied by a heated private correspondence between individual representatives of the CCF and ACCF. Speaking on behalf of the former, Michael Josselson pointed out the prestige which accrued to the Congress from its association with Russell, 'especially in Asia', and expressed his dismay at the tactical ineptitude of the American Committee, which 'seems to recognise only one weapon in the fight against Communism: denunciation'.

> Don't take this for a moment as a general defense of Russell. We all know that he's 84 years old, anti-American, and ripe for posthumous

12 Bertrand Russell, an honorary chairman of the Congress for Cultural Freedom until 1957 when he resigned after rowing with the American Committee for Cultural Freedom. (Photograph by Ida Kar, National Portrait Gallery, London)

215

Communist claims. This latter is exactly what we have been struggling to prevent, and one of the ways is to keep him as an Honorary Chairman of the Congress.[104]

Defending the ACCF against Josselson's charges, Sidney Hook suggested that Russell's melodramatic view of political conditions in America was derived from communist propaganda, a fact which revealed 'that he is, for reasons I can't develop here, prepared to go along with the communists for the sake of "peace"'.[105]

This last remark of Hook's is telling, as it shows how Russell's pacifist inclinations and fear of nuclear war made him, at least in the eyes of the CCF's American supporters, vulnerable to co-optation by the Cominform's peace campaign. The difficulties of maintaining a position which was independent of both sides in the Cold War, of belonging to a third camp in an increasingly bipolar world order, were very well explained by Russell himself in a letter to his old philosophical sparring partner, Hook.

> Mankind is divided into two classes: those who object to infringements to civil liberties in Russia, but not in the US; and those who object to them in the US, but not in Russia. There seems to be hardly anybody who just objects to infringements of civil liberties (period)....The fundamental fallacy which is committed by almost everyone is this: 'A and B hate each other, therefore one is good and the other is bad.' From the evidence of history, it seems much more likely that both are bad, but everybody vehemently rejects this hypothesis.[106]

Hook, of course, was horrified by this neutralist talk of moral equivalence between the superpowers and demanded to know how anyone could compare the 'independent judiciary of the US' with 'the Soviet courts which are ruled by the secret police', the Rosenberg case with the Moscow Show Trials and Eisenhower with Khrushchev. Russell was, Hook suggested, 'being used – and effectively used – as a weapon in the Communists' political war against the United States'.[107] Despite vehement rejections of this charge from Russell, who reminded his American friend that, 'When I first met you in 1924, I was anti-Soviet and you were pro', Hook continued to believe that the Briton's combination of anti-Americanism, third camp-ism and pacifism effectively made him, despite his anti-communism, an ally of the Soviet Union.[108]

Whatever the rights and wrongs of Russell's 1956 clash with the American Committee for Cultural Freedom, its main practical consequence was clear enough. As in the earlier incidents, there were desperate attempts on the part of the international Congress to win back the support of its Honorary Chair. Michael Josselson, for example, tried to persuade the 'reasonable' members of the ACCF, such as Daniel Bell and Arthur Schlesinger Jr., to issue a letter of apology, while the famously charming Nicolas Nabokov was dispatched to Russell's Richmond home.[109] All to no avail, though: as Russell told Nabokov, 'I do not want to have anything to do with people who behave like your friends of the American Committee.'[110] In November 1956, Russell seized on a public statement about the Hungarian uprising by Denis de Rougemont, Chair of the CCF's Executive Committee, to force the issue of his resignation, demanding to know what the Congress proposed doing about its American affiliate.[111] Despite some further attempts to mollify him – and the fact that, as was pointed out to him several times, the ACCF had by this point become so incapacitated by factional infighting that it had more or less ceased to function – Russell finally reaffirmed his decision to resign from the Honorary Chair on 25 February 1957, stating his unwillingness to continue representing an organisation which appeared readier to protest violations of cultural freedom in some parts of the world than others.[112] As Michael Josselson put it, the Congress had lost one of its 'biggest attractions'.[113]

In sum, the British intellectuals connected with the Congress for Cultural Freedom obstructed and hampered the American Cultural Cold War effort in a number of ways. First, there was their annoying habit of arguing amongst themselves; then there was their tendency to appropriate CCF funds for purely cultural purposes – something which the CIA had great difficulty in preventing, because of the condition of secrecy under which it was forced to operate; and, finally, there was the fact that certain British intellectuals favoured a definition of cultural freedom that was more expansive than and, therefore, sometimes in conflict with that of the American section of the non-communist left. In view of these various problems, it is not perhaps surprising that American frustration with the British should have occasionally boiled over, as when George Kennan, one of the architects of Cold War US covert operations, denounced the 'self-destructive streak in the British liberal intellectuals which causes them to act as though their own sets of values were in no way affected by Soviet phenomena'.[114] (Reverting briefly to the point raised above, about the sexualised imagery in which much Cultural Cold War discourse was couched, US irritation with British neutralism was sometimes equated rhetorically with the heterosexual American male's suspicion of effeminacy and bisexuality – both traits associated with some of the Bloomsbury *literati* in CCF circles.) When the CIA's role in financing the CCF and *Encounter* was revealed in the late 1960s, much attention focused on the question of whether or not the intellectuals involved were 'witting' about the arrangement (most of the British intellectuals concerned have since admitted that they did know of or at least suspected secret US government funding, with the exception of Stephen Spender, who appears to have tried very hard not to know).[115] What is being suggested here is that the CIA's characterisation of these intellectuals as 'assets' is equally questionable.

This is not to say that the CIA's Cultural Cold War effort in Britain was entirely ineffectual. While the CCF's adoption of a 'soft-sell', cultural strategy might have misfired in the British context, saddling the CIA with the patronage of Bloomsbury intellectuals whose main interest was not so much fighting communism – a battle they felt had already been won in Britain – as launching new literary magazines, the Congress's other main tactical preference, that is appealing to the non-communist left, proved more successful. Once it had overcome initial suspicions of excessive American or continental anti-communism, and identified itself with the more positive intellectual project of fostering links between progressive elements in the US and Europe, the CCF became an important institutional point of reference for the young revisionist intellectuals of the Labour Party. Although such events as the Milan Future of Freedom conference did not transform the Gaitskellites into Atlanticist social democrats overnight, they did reinforce such impulses, thereby expediting the integration of Labour into postwar transatlantic élites. The same tendency was even more evident in the CCF's London organ, *Encounter*, and another transatlantic organisation with covert connections launched in the 1950s, the Bilderberg Group.

NOTES

1. See Peter Coleman, *The Liberal Conspiracy: The Congress for Cultural Freedom and the Struggle for the Mind of Postwar Europe* (New York: Free Press, 1989), pp. 27–32.

2. Quoted in Frances Stonor Saunders, *Who Paid the Piper? The CIA and the Cultural Cold War* (London: Granta, 1999), p. 84.
3. Hugh Trevor-Roper, 'Ex-Communist v. Communist', *Guardian* 10 July 1950.
4. Melvin Lasky to editor, *Guardian*, 24 July 1950, Sidney Hook Papers, Hoover Institution, Stanford University.
5. See Coleman, *Liberal Conspiracy*, p. 36.
6. Hence, in early 1951 Koestler and Burnham were constantly lumped together in a bad-tempered correspondence between Richard Crossman and Sidney Hook about the question of whether or not war with the Soviet Union was 'inevitable'. Richard Crossman to Sidney Hook, 28 February 1951, Hook Papers; Sidney Hook to Richard Crossman, 16 March 1951, Hook Papers; Richard Crossman to Sidney Hook, 30 March 1951, Hook Papers; Sidney Hook to Richard Crossman, 18 April 1951, Hook Papers.
7. James Burnham to Julian Amery, 27 October 1950, James Burnham Papers, Hoover Institution, Stanford University.
8. François Bondy to Julian Amery, 9 November 1950, Congress for Cultural Freedom Papers, Joseph Regenstein Library, University of Chicago.
9. David Williams, 'Britain's cultural committee', *The New Leader*, 26 March 1951, 17–18.
10. Nicolas Nabokov to James Burnham, 6 June 1951, Burnham Papers.
11. John Lowe to François Bondy, 16 January 1951, CCF Papers.
12. François Bondy to Stephen Spender, 22 January 1951, CCF Papers; François Bondy to John Lowe, 23 January 1951, CCF Papers.
13. T. R. Fyvel to Irving Brown, 3 February 1951, Irving Brown Papers, George Meany Memorial Archives, Silver Spring, Maryland.
14. CCF Executive Committee minutes, 15 May 1951, CCF Papers.
15. Nicolas Nabokov to James Burnham, 6 June 1951, Burnham Papers.
16. Michael Goodwin, 'The British Society for Cultural Freedom: Plan of work, 1951–52', no date, Brown Papers; International Movement for Cultural Freedom (British Section), Executive Committee minutes, 11 July 1951, CCF Papers.
17. 'Dr Rainer Hildebrandt's visit to London, September 29 – October 4 [1951], as the guest of the British Society for Cultural Freedom: Extracts from press cuttings', Brown Papers; Goodwin, 'British Society for Cultural Freedom'.
18. Stephen Spender to Nicolas Nabokov, 17 January 1952, CCF Papers.
19. Stephen Spender to Nicolas Nabokov, 27 February, no year [probably 1952], CCF Papers; T. R. Fyvel to Nicolas Nabokov, 11 March 1952, CCF Papers; CCF Executive Committee minutes, no date [probably early 1952], CCF Papers.
20. British Society for Cultural Freedom, Executive Committee minutes, 5 March 1952, CCF Papers.
21. John Clews, 'British Society for Cultural Freedom: Report of retiring General Secretary', 20 February 1953, CCF Papers.

22. See Goodwin, 'British Society for Cultural Freedom'.
23. See Clews, 'British Society for Cultural Freedom'.
24. International Movement for Cultural Freedom minutes; Saunders, *Who Paid the Piper?*, pp. 110–12; Richard J. Aldrich, *The Hidden Hand: Britain, America and Cold War Secret Intelligence* (London: John Murray, 2001), pp. 132–3. Clews had become an IRD asset in late 1950 after overcoming initial suspicions that he was over-eager to assist the Department in its work. See the IRD file on Clews, FO 1110/322, Public Record Office, London.
25. Hugh Gaitskell to Nicolas Nabokov, 5 July 1954, Hugh Gaitskell Papers, University College London.
26. Anthony Crosland, 'Report on the conference held by the Congress for Cultural Freedom at Gothenburg, November 1955', no date, CCF Papers.
27. See Lawrence Black, 'Social democracy as a way of life: Fellowship and the Socialist Union, 1951–59', *Twentieth Century British History* 10 (1999), 499–539.
28. Irving Kristol to Michael Josselson, 19 July 1955, CCF Papers.
29. Rita Hinden to Michael Josselson, 26 August 1956, CCF Papers.
30. Rita Hinden to John Hunt, 14 May 1957, CCF Papers.
31. Ibid. Despite the warmth of the relationship between Hinden and the CCF, a proposal by her and her Socialist Union comrade Allan Flanders for a new international quarterly of socialist thought embracing east and west (with an executive committee comprising, amongst others, Denis Healey and Kenneth Younger) failed to win the organisation's approval, possibly because it too closely resembled *Encounter*. Rita Hinden to Herbert Passin, 12 December 1957, CCF Papers; Michael Josselson to Rita Hinden, 22 August 1958, CCF Papers.
32. Programme for 'The Future of Freedom' conference, CCF Papers.
33. Hugh Gaitskell to Nicolas Nabokov, 19 July 1954, Gaitskell Papers; Nicolas Nabokov to Anthony Crosland, 22 July 1954, Gaitskell Papers.
34. Special correspondent, 'Food for thought at Milan Congress', *Guardian* 20 September 1955.
35. Pierre Grémion, *Intelligence De L'Anti-communisme: Le Congrès pour la liberté de la culture à Paris (1950–75)* (Paris: Fayard, 1995), p. 157.
36. 'If anyone is leaving the congress no wiser than when he came', wrote a special correspondent, 'either he is a Solomon or he has been lulled to sleep by the excellence of Milan's menus'. Special correspondent, 'Food for thought'.
37. Max Beloff, 'L'Avenire della liberta', *Spectator* 30 September 1955.
38. Bertrand Russell, President of 'International Movement for Cultural Freedom, British Section', 28 August 1951, CCF Papers.
39. George Polanyi to Salvador de Madariaga, 11 November 1955, CCF Papers.
40. CCF Executive Committee minutes, 12-13 January 1957, CCF Papers; Michael Polanyi to editor, *South Africa*, 24 February 1958, CCF Papers.
41. Michael Josselson, 'Application for grant to cover program of international

activities', July 1957, RO 2174 Grant No. 570-0395, Ford Foundation Papers, New York.

42. Planning Committee on 'Tradition and Social Change (Problems of Progress)' minutes, 3 December 1957, CCF Papers. For more on the Ford Foundation's role in the Cultural Cold War, see Volker R. Berghahn, *America and the Intellectual Cold Wars in Europe: Shepard Stone Between Philanthropy, Academy and Diplomacy* (Princeton University Press, 2001).

43. Planning Committee on 'Tradition and Social Change (Problems of Progress)' minutes, 17 June 1958, CCF Papers; anonymous, 'A report on nine years of activity', no date, CCF Papers.

44. Anonymous, 'Application for a grant for the holding of a seminar on changes in Soviet society', no date, CCF Papers.

45. 'Changes in Soviet Society' press release, June 1957, CCF Papers.

46. 'Changes in Soviet Society' programme, St Antony's College, Oxford, 24–29 June 1957, CCF Papers.

47. Anonymous, 'The conference on changes in Soviet society, Oxford, June 24–29, 1957. A report to the Ford Foundation', September 1957, RO 0526 Grant No. 570-0099, Ford Foundation Papers.

48. See Melvin Lasky, '"The Sovietologists"', *Encounter* 9.3 (September 1957), 64-8.

49. See Coleman, *Liberal Conspiracy*, pp. 105–6.

50. See Richard Fletcher, 'British propaganda since World War II: A case study', *Media, Culture and Society* 4 (1982), 97–109.

51. See Stephen Brooke, 'Atlantic crossing? American views of capitalism and British socialist thought, 1932–62', *Twentieth Century British History* 2 (1991), 107–36.

52. See, for example, David Williams, 'Britain's cultural committee', 18.

53. See Goodwin, 'British Society for Cultural Freedom'.

54. CCF Executive Committee minutes, 9 February 1951, CCF Papers.

55. Michael Goodwin, '*The Twentieth Century*: Manifesto and statement of aims', no date, Brown Papers.

56. Goodwin, 'British Society for Cultural Freedom'; Paul Lashmar and James Oliver, *Britain's Secret Propaganda War, 1948–77* (Stroud: Sutton, 1998), p. 100.

57. Michael Goodwin to Nicolas Nabokov, 13 August 1951, Brown Papers. In May 1951, Irving Brown had made a one-off emergency grant to Goodwin that he had used to pay off rent owed on *The Twentieth Century*'s offices. Michael Goodwin to Nicolas Nabokov, 31 July 1951, Brown Papers.

58. See Goodwin, 'British Society for Cultural Freedom'.

59. Nicolas Nabokov to Michael Goodwin, 11 January 1952, CCF Papers.

60. Nicolas Nabokov to Stephen Spender, 30 May 1951, CCF Papers.

61. T. R. Fyvel to Irving Brown, 4 August 1951, Brown Papers.

62. Nicolas Nabokov to Michael Goodwin, 19 December 1951, CCF Papers.

63. Stephen Spender to Michael Goodwin, 2 January 1952, CCF Papers.

64. Stephen Spender, 'Statement to editorial board of *Twentieth Century*', 20 December 1951, CCF Papers.
65. Michael Goodwin to Nicolas Nabokov, 31 December 1951, CCF Papers; Nicolas Nabokov to Michael Goodwin, 11 January 1952, CCF Papers.
66. Stephen Spender to Nicolas Nabokov, 17 January 1952, CCF Papers.
67. Resolutions of meeting in Paris, 7 January 1952, CCF Papers.
68. Michael Goodwin to members of British Society for Cultural Freedom, no date, CCF Papers.
69. Stephen Spender, 'Statement' (dictated by telephone from London, 10 January 1952), CCF Papers; Stephen Spender to Michael Goodwin, 11 January 1952, CCF Papers; Stephen Spender to Nicolas Nabokov, 13 January 1952, CCF Papers.
70. Stephen Spender to Nicolas Nabokov, 17 January 1952, CCF Papers.
71. T. R. Fyvel to Irving Brown, 3 February 1951, Brown Papers.
72. Michael Goodwin to Nicolas Nabokov, 15 January 1952, CCF Papers.
73. Nicolas Nabokov to Stephen Spender, 26 January 1952, CCF Papers.
74. Stephen Spender to Nicolas Nabokov, 27 February no year [presumably 1952], CCF Papers; T. R. Fyvel to Nicolas Nabokov, 11 March 1952, CCF Papers; CCF Executive Committee minutes, no date [probably early 1952], CCF Papers.
75. See Clews, 'British Society for Cultural Freedom'.
76. François Bondy, 'Visit of Mr Warburg', 9 June 1952, CCF Papers.
77. Fredric Warburg, *All Authors Are Equal: The Publishing Life of Fredric Warburg, 1936–71* (London: Hutchinson, 1973), p. 155.
78. Jasper Ridley, unpublished memoir entitled 'My experiences with the British Society for Cultural Freedom from September 1952 to June 1953', 7 September 1997. My thanks to Frances Stonor Saunders for showing me this document and Jasper Ridley for allowing me to quote from it.
79. Anonymous, 'British Society for Cultural Freedom', no date, Brown Papers. The same document hints at territorial tensions between the British Society and Common Cause. 'For some unknown reason', its anonymous author – probably C. A. Smith – reports, 'Clews has adopted an attitude of marked hostility to Common Cause, from which he resigned'. That said, the two bodies did cooperate during Ridley's spell as Secretary, as when they jointly hosted a lecture series by Margarete Buber-Neumann, widow of the German communist leader Heinz Neumann and vocal opponent of totalitarianism.
80. Ridley later remembered Fredric Warburg instructing him to write him a cheque on the British Society's account for £100 after a trip to Paris. 'I think that Warburg either pocketed the £100 or spent it in buying jewellery for his attractive wife, Pamela de Bayou', he recalled. Quoted in Saunders, *Who Paid the Piper?*, p. 175.
81. Isaiah Berlin to Arthur Schlesinger Jr., 6 June 1952, Arthur M. Schlesinger Jr. Papers, John F. Kennedy Memorial Library, Boston.
82. Resolutions of meeting in Paris, 7 January 1952, CCF Papers.

83. This money ultimately went to fund the British editorship of *Encounter*. Goronwy Rees, 'Conversation with Fred Warburg', 12 May 1967, *Encounter* Papers, Boston University. For further details, see Saunders, *Who Paid the Piper?*, pp. 174–5.
84. See Malcolm Muggeridge, 'When I hear the word "Gun" I reach for my culture', *New Statesman* 19 May 1967.
85. My thanks to Ray Monk for discussing Russell's personality and Cold War politics with me.
86. Sidney Hook, *Out of Step: An Unquiet Life in the Twentieth Century* (New York: Harper and Row, 1987), p. 367.
87. Barry Feinberg and Ronald Kasrils (eds), *Bertrand Russell's America. Volume 2: 1945–70* (London: Allen and Unwin, 1983), pp. 38–41.
88. Quoted in Feinberg and Kasrils (eds), *Russell's America*, p. 38.
89. Katherine Faulkner to Bertrand Russell, 24 April 1953, American Committee for Cultural Freedom Papers, Tamiment Institute Library, New York University.
90. Bertrand Russell to Katherine Faulkner, 16 May 1953, ACCF Papers.
91. See Feinberg and Kasrils (eds), *Russell's America*, pp. 59–60.
92. Bertrand Russell to Daniel Bell, 14 June 1953, ACCF Papers. See also Bertrand Russell to Irving Kristol, 14 June 1953, ACCF Papers.
93. See Feinberg and Kasrils (eds), *Russell's America*, pp. 60–1.
94. Quoted in ibid., p. 64.
95. Bertrand Russell to ACCF, 10 March 1954, ACCF Papers.
96. Quoted in Feinberg and Kasrils (eds), *Russell's America*, p. 65.
97. Sol Stein to Bertrand Russell, 24 March 1954, ACCF Papers.
98. Sol Stein to Michael Josselson, 8 June 1954, CCF Papers.
99. Bertrand Russell to editor, *Guardian*, 26 March 1956, CCF Papers.
100. James Farrell to Bertrand Russell, 5 April 1956, CCF Papers.
101. Quoted in Feinberg and Kasrils (eds), *Russell's America*, p. 79.
102. CCF statement, 24 April 1956, CCF Papers; Michael Polanyi to Sol Levitas, 29 June 1956, Hook Papers. Polanyi still found much to admire in the pages of *The New Leader*, he told Levitas, but believed that McCarthyism had not been 'effectively faced and combated in your columns'.
103. Diana Trilling to Nicolas Nabokov, 18 May 1956 [sent June 1], Hook Papers.
104. Michael Josselson to Sidney Hook, 13 April 1956, CCF Papers; Michael Josselson to Sidney Hook, 20 April 1956, CCF Papers.
105. Sidney Hook to Michael Josselson, 16 April 1956, CCF Papers.
106. Bertrand Russell to Sidney Hook, 8 June 1956, Hook Papers.
107. Sidney Hook to Bertrand Russell, 18 June 1956, Hook Papers.
108. Bertrand Russell to Sidney Hook, 26 June 1956, Hook Papers. Conflict between Hook and Russell over the latter's increasingly 'irresponsible' position on the Cold War, accompanied by philosophical differences over pragmatism and the legacy of Hook's mentor, John Dewey, continued

during the late 1950s, surfacing again in 1960 in the pages of *The New Leader*. See Feinberg and Kasrils (eds), *Russell's America*, pp. 118–23.

109. See Michael Josselson to Daniel Bell, 27 April 1956, CCF Papers. In a letter to Josselson describing a meeting of the ACCF's Executive Committee held in the wake of the CCF's censure, Bell described himself, Sidney Hook and Norman Thomas as attempting 'to provide some understanding of the consequences of the action' and 'the majority' of those present as 'hostile'. Daniel Bell to Michael Josselson, 1 May 1956, CCF Papers.

110. Minutes of Nicolas Nabokov's visit to Bertrand Russell, no date, CCF Papers. Russell's mood was probably not improved by further criticism of him – or, more precisely, of a foreword he had contributed to the British edition of a book by Columbia University professor and (at least in the eyes of the New York intellectuals) notorious fellow traveller Corliss Lamont, *Freedom Is As Freedom Does* – that appeared in *The New Leader* in early 1957. See Feinberg and Kasrils (eds), *Russell's America*, chap. 8.

111. See Coleman, *Liberal Conspiracy*, pp. 167–8.

112. Russell wrote to Nabokov in January 1957, 'I am reluctantly confirmed in the view that you object to interferences with the liberty of culture much more vehemently when they are committed by Communist nations than when they are committed by those which are anti-Communists'. Bertrand Russell to Nicolas Nabokov, 28 January 1957, CCF Papers.

113. Michael Josselson to Sidney Hook, 20 April 1956, CCF Papers.

114. George Kennan to Arthur Schlesinger Jr., 10 May 1951, Schlesinger Papers.

115. See chap. 8.

7

The CIA, the European Movement and Bilderberg

In 1962, two years after making his famous promise to 'fight, fight and fight again', Labour leader Hugh Gaitskell appeared before his Party's annual conference in Brighton to speak about British entry into the European Economic Community (EEC). Previously, Gaitskell had avoided taking a clear position on Europe. Several of the young, revisionist intellectuals grouped around him were keen advocates of European integration; most of the Labour left and rank-and-file, however, were opposed to the Common Market. Whereas Gaitskell had been prepared to take his Party on over unilateralism, an issue about which he had strong political convictions, he was personally ambivalent over Europe, torn between his ties to continental social democracy on the one hand and a mixture of Atlanticism and Little Englandism on the other. In the event, it was the latter impulse which won out. Not only would British membership of the EEC spell 'the end of Britain as an independent European state', Gaitskell told Conference, it would also mean 'the end of a thousand years of history'.[1] In a telling contrast with 1960, when Michael Foot had been moved by Gaitskell's attack on unilateralism to mutter dark thoughts to a neighbour, on this occasion it was a young Gaitskellite, the ardent European William Rodgers, who turned to the Party's press officer, John Harris, and said, 'I'm through with that man, John'.[2]

As well as disappointing several of his own followers, Gaitskell's 1962 speech signified the defeat of a key CIA objective in the early Cold War. It is only recently, thanks largely to pioneering research in the field by intelligence historian Richard J. Aldrich, that the role of the Agency in supporting the cause of European union has begun to be revealed.[3] Newly available documentation shows that a CIA front organisation similar to the Free Europe Committee, the American Committee on United Europe (ACUE), was responsible for channelling millions of dollars to pro-unity groups in Europe, foremost of which was the European Movement (EM), in what was one of the Agency's most concerted and determined attempts to influence western European politics. Among the recipients of this covert American largesse were a number of British campaigners for European union, including prominent Conservative politicians, the prestigious current affairs magazine *The Economist*, and, most pertinently from the point of view of this study, several Labour MPs.

However, as with other US covert operations involving the British left, the story of the ACUE's dealings with Britain in general and the Labour Party in particular is far from a straightforward one of covert manipulation. Despite later attempts to present itself as the British party of Europe, Labour in the early Cold War period was distinctly hostile to the proposals for European federation then being advanced by many continentals and Americans. Granted, there were individuals on the Party's right wing, such as Bill Rodgers and, most conspicuously, Roy Jenkins, who favoured greater British involvement in Europe; but, as Gaitskell's 1962 speech showed, their arguments failed to persuade the leadership, at either an emotional or tactical level. Consequently, although the CIA engaged in what was perhaps its most direct intervention in internal Party affairs on this issue, Labour proved one of the most obdurate obstacles in the path of the Agency's desired goal of a federal Europe.

Far more successful at corralling Labour leaders was another international organisation created in this period, with secretive tendencies and an interest in European union (although its interest in Atlantic union was even greater), the Bilderberg Group. Indeed, whereas Gaitskell kept the European Movement at arm's length, he, along with the Party's chief international strategist, Denis Healey, was a leading member of Bilderberg, helping organise the Group's first meeting at the eponymous Dutch hotel in 1954 and subsequently joining enthusiastically in clandestine arrangements to make it a regular event. In this regard, he was establishing a precedent for future centre-right leaders of the Labour Party, most notably Tony Blair, who attended a meeting of Bilderberg in the early 1990s. Was this, then, as many have interpreted it, a victory for the CIA? Indeed, what exactly is Bilderberg, this mysterious annual conclave of Atlantic élites, which in recent years has attracted the attention of conspiracy theorists convinced it is the seat of a secret global government, the 'New World Order'?[4] Again, new documents, including Gaitskell's own papers, suggest a reality that was at once less dramatic and more complex than the conspiracy theories would suggest.

THE ACUE AND THE EUROPEAN MOVEMENT

There were several reasons why Americans supported European union. First, proposals for the federation of Europe offered the flattering prospect of a continent made over in the image of the United States. What more dramatic vindication of the American experiment with federalism? Then there were practical and strategic considerations. Federation would, it was believed, make for 'a more rational and efficient Europe', thereby reducing the need for continuing American assistance in the long term and, at the same time, contain the two major security risks in the area, German militarism and Soviet expansionism.[5] Third, as if the possibility of such 'double containment' was not incentive enough, there was a powerful idealistic impulse behind American support for measures intended to prevent future wars in Europe, exemplified by such young veterans of the Second World War as Cord Meyer, leading spokesman for 'world federalism', and his predecessor as head of the CIA's International Organizations Division, Tom Braden.[6]

The immediate stimulus for American backing of the pro-unity campaign, however, was the prompting of Europeans themselves, such as the émigré Austrian aristocrat, Count Richard Coudenhove-Kalergi. A prominent 'pan-Europeanist' since the First World War, Kalergi had fled to the US in 1940, finding refuge at New York University, from where he set about spreading the gospel of European union in the New World.[7] This missionary work proved remarkably successful. Among Kalergi's American converts to pan-Europeanism were such influential citizens as Office of Strategic Services chief William Donovan and Senator J. William Fulbright, who in 1947 introduced a resolution in Congress calling for the creation of a United States of Europe. Hence, when in the same year the count launched an organisation called the European Parliamentary Union (EPU) in Gstad, with the aim of coordinating the efforts of federalist parliamentarians throughout Europe, he felt confident of securing American backing. This confidence appeared vindicated when in April 1948 Donovan's old deputy, Allen Dulles, helped him set up the American Committee for a Free and United Europe, with Senator Fulbright in the chair.[8]

However, Kalergi was not the only European pro-unity campaigner with a talent for cultivating the company of powerful politicians and intelligence chiefs. At the same time that the count was setting up shop in New York, a member of the Polish government-in-exile in London by the name of Joseph Retinger was forging links with leading officers of

227

the British secret services, including the executive director of the Special Operations Executive, Sir Colin Gubbins. Indeed, in 1943 the frail Polish scholar would parachute behind German lines as an SOE agent, sustaining crippling injuries but accomplishing his mission of making contact with the Polish Home Army. After the war, still supported by Gubbins and other SOE veterans such as Edward Beddington-Behrens, Retinger travelled Europe mobilising élite support for continental union, for example helping the future Belgian Foreign Minister, Paul van Zeeland, establish the influential Independent (later European) League for Economic Cooperation (ELEC). Meanwhile, pro-unity elements in Britain discovered a forceful new advocate in the shape of Winston Churchill – at the time probably the most distinguished statesman in the west – who founded the United Europe Movement (UEM), with his son-in-law, Duncan Sandys, as its Honorary Secretary. In 1947 the UEM and ELEC combined with several other organisations to form the Joint International Committee of the Movement for European Unity (JICMEU). This was the body responsible for arranging the extraordinarily success-ful conference of European federalists held at the Hague in May 1948, with finances provided, at Retinger's request, from the same Economic Cooperation Agency counterpart funds which subsidised the Office of Policy Coordination. Later in the same year, the JICMEU was formally established as the European Movement, with Sandys as its President and Retinger its Secretary-General. In July 1948, the officers of the EM travelled to the US to try and win American backing for their campaign.[9]

It was the success of the Hague conference which persuaded Allen Dulles to dump Kalergi and throw his weight behind Retinger.[10] The American Committee for a Free and United Europe was disbanded with-out ever actually having met, the Austrian count protesting bitterly all the while, and replaced by a new body designed to provide American backing for the EM.[11] The American Committee on United Europe (ACUE) was officially incorporated in February 1949 (as with the NCFE, Dulles looked after the legal paperwork) and launched at a luncheon held in honour of Churchill the following month.[12] After efforts to persuade Dwight Eisenhower to fill the chair had failed, Donovan stepped into the breach; Dulles became Vice-Chairman. To manage the day-to-day business of the Committee, Donovan brought in Tom Braden, then in charge of the Museum of Modern Art in New York, telling him this was his opportunity to atone for the 'bad book' about the OSS he had written with Stewart Alsop, *Sub Rosa*.[13] Braden helped assemble a Board of Directors which looked like a 'who's who' of the Cold War state–

private network, including as it did the likes of Walter Bedell Smith, Jay Lovestone and Marshall Plan Administrator Paul G. Hoffman. In addition to its main purpose – lending 'all support including financial to those groups within Europe seeking to accomplish unity'[14] – the ACUE also conducted a domestic publicity campaign intended to galvanise American support for European union, publishing a newsletter, lobbying Congress and financing research projects at US universities.[15] These activities enabled the Committee to maintain a public existence with offices on Fifth Avenue.

However, as the numerous intelligence connections of its officers strongly suggest, ACUE was in fact an OPC/CIA front operation much like the NCFE.[16] Agency money began flowing to the Committee in 1951, after it had become evident that private donations alone were not sufficient to keep the European Movement afloat. According to Braden's later recollection, the first payment arrived in the form of a bag containing $75,000 dumped on his desk by CIA officer Pinky Thompson with the words, 'This is for you'.[17] Later, after Braden had himself joined the Agency and the Committee had established a Paris office to administer its European programme, the covert funding was arranged on a more business-like footing, as is revealed by an extraordinarily frank memorandum filed amongst the papers of Paul Hoffman (who effectively took over the duties of ACUE Chairman in the mid-1950s after Bill Donovan fell ill) at the Truman Presidential Library in Missouri. According to this document, which was penned by ACUE official John D. Blumgart on 15 April 1957, 'initial recommendations' as to which European groups should receive funding were made by the Paris office, all of whose staff were 'witting to [the] company connection' (the 'company', of course, being the CIA). These were reported 'to a company representative in Paris', who then passed them to 'the company's office in Washington', where decisions were taken 'in consultation with the New York office'. The scale of the funding arranged in this fashion was massive. According to Blumgart, 'the company's budget' for European projects in the fiscal year 1957 came to about $900,000. In contrast, ACUE raised a mere $30,000 annually 'from private sources'. Only 'about one-third of total disbursements' were recorded on the ACUE's books, however, and these were disguised as gifts from 'fictitious donors' or 'company-sponsored foundations and trusts'. The remaining two-thirds were 'transacted covertly'.[18] In short, Blumgart's memo suggests that the CIA was passing nearly a million dollars a year via the ACUE to the European unity campaign in the mid-1950s. This is considerably more than previous estimates of the Committee's budget, which have been based only on recorded transactions.[19]

Were the Europeans who received ACUE grants aware of their true source? Given his excellent links with British intelligence, it would seem reasonable to assume that the EM's founder, Joseph Retinger, had a pretty good idea. After learning that Warren Fugitt, a member of the ACUE Paris office with whom he had developed a good working relationship, was about to be recalled to New York, Retinger wrote to Shepard Stone of the Ford Foundation, a psychological warfare expert with close ties to the CIA, asking him to impress on his 'friends in Washington' the 'desirability of leaving Fugitt in Paris'.[20] There is also evidence of rumours about the American Committee's covert connections circulating amongst continental federalists during the 1950s. When Paul Hoffman visited Europe in 1957 to undertake a review of ACUE operations there, he had a 'disturbing' encounter with Jean Monnet, head of the influential Action Committee for a United States of Europe and the man commonly regarded as having 'founded' European federalism, who voiced his suspicion, apparently shared by others, that the Committee 'received government support' and was 'a cover for governmental operation'. Despite attempts by Hoffman to convince him otherwise, at a second meeting 'Monnet reaffirmed his opinion that ACUE was some kind of cloak-and-dagger operation and expressed concern about the source of ACUE funds'.[21] Small wonder, then, that Committee officers should have been keen to stress to the leaders of the EM the need to be 'very discreet regarding our grants' or that the Europeans themselves readily agreed 'to treat ACUE grants as confidential information'.[22]

PROBLEMS WITH THE BRITISH

The enthusiasm of US officials for European federation was in stark contrast to the attitudes of the British Labour government. Granted, Ernest Bevin had once advocated the idea of 'Western Union', even employing the leftist notion of the Third Force to describe his plan for a British-led, Euro–African bloc mediating between the Americans and Soviets. However, as events during 1948 and 1949 combined to undermine the Third Force, so the Foreign Secretary's interest in European union waned. Other strategic commitments assumed greater importance: the Sterling area, the Commonwealth, above all (ironically, considering US support for European federalism) the Anglo–American alliance.

There were also powerful psychological factors at play, including Britain's traditional insularity, its continuing self-image as an imperial power and the simple fact that, in contrast to many continental countries, British nationalism had not been dented or discredited as a result of military defeat or occupation during the Second World War. Increasingly, the Labour government favoured what became known as the 'functional' approach to European union – that is, engaging in inter-governmental cooperation on specific issues of mutual interest – as opposed to the 'federalist' concept of a supra-national authority with sovereign powers over member states.[23]

Labour opposition to European federalism manifested itself in a number of ways. As early as January 1947 the Party leadership, convinced that Churchill's United Europe Movement was a vehicle for Conservative Party revanchism, instructed Labour supporters to concentrate instead on supporting the United Nations. (This injunction left British Labourites committed to European union, such as UEM's Vice-Chairman, Victor Gollancz, 'in a horrible state of uncertainty'.)[24] Similar efforts were made to prevent any Labour attendance at the Hague Congress of 1948, General Secretary Morgan Phillips writing to MPs who had expressed an interest in going to inform them that the event was a Conservative front.[25] When the European Movement was formed in the same year, it was treated by the Labour leadership as if it were a proscribed organisation.[26] Second, Bevin blocked continental moves to endow the new Council of Europe – the main practical accomplishment of the Hague conference and institutional legacy of the European Movement – with supra-national powers, thereby 'emasculating' it as a form of federal government.[27] Labour delegations to meetings of the Council's Consultative Assembly in Strasbourg, backed by representatives of the Scandinavian countries, stuck to a rigidly functionalist interpretation of European union.[28] This view was elaborated by Denis Healey in several Party pamphlets of the period, most notably *European Unity*, published in June 1950, which explicitly rejected any notion of the Labour government pursuing a Third Force foreign policy, 'stressing instead the need for unity throughout the free world in which the USA must play a full part'.[29]

Considering all this, it is not surprising that the American Committee on United Europe, with its declared interest in rapid federation, should have grown increasingly irritated with the Labour government. Several of the organisation's officers, among them Donovan and Braden, were present at the 1949 meeting of the Council of Europe and witnessed for themselves the effects of British obstructionism.[30] Later that year,

Donovan attempted to force Labour's hand on the issue by addressing a letter to European leaders in which he demanded to know their attitudes towards unity and integration, and pointing out, in a thinly veiled threat, that Congress was shortly due to start debating the renewal of Marshall aid.[31] (This was, incidentally, a relatively restrained statement when compared with some of the opinions on the subject voiced privately by American officials.)[32] At a press conference held in New York in February 1950, Donovan, flanked by Retinger and Braden, revealed that, of the 32 replies he had received, 'only the British Labour Government, the traditionally neutral Swiss and the Russian-occupied Austrians held back', and 'took occasion to attack Ernest Bevin and the British Labourites for being unenthusiastic about European Union'.[33] The publication shortly afterwards of the Party pamphlet on *European Unity* was greeted by another ACUE-convened press conference, this time held in the law office of Allen Dulles, during which the organisation's Vice-Chairman accused Labour of taking an 'insular position' and failing 'to meet the hard test of these times'.[34]

By this stage, the Americans were also growing frustrated with the Conservative leadership of the European Movement. During the bitter disputes which had accompanied ACUE's transfer of support from Kalergi to Retinger, the Austrian count had repeatedly warned his erstwhile American patrons that the British-led EM would resist European federation.[35] It was not long before this prophecy was fulfilled. When pressed in Parliament by Labour MPs to clarify his position on Europe, Churchill revealed that he would oppose the surrender of any British sovereignty to a European government. Meanwhile, Sandys, who naturally shared his father-in-law's functionalist inclinations, attracted growing criticism from continental federalists for allegedly sabotaging proposals to extend the powers of the Council of Europe. A rift was also opening between the EM's President and its Secretary-General, Retinger. The latter objected to what he regarded as Sandys's arbitrary and high-handed running of the international secretariat's office in London, which had led to the resignations or sackings of a number of talented young administrators, including the highly regarded Dunston Curtis.[36] Another cause of contention was money: Retinger blamed lax financial management by Sandys for a funding crisis which beset the EM in 1949 and necessitated an emergency grant from ACUE. He also found 'very strange and alarming' the fact that, when the American money arrived, it was siphoned off to settle EM's debts to Churchill's United Europe Movement.[37] By March 1950 Retinger was advising Sandys to resign from the

232

EM presidency, 'for the sake of the idea of the Unity of Europe, of the European Movement, as well as for your own benefit'.[38]

Sandys was also on the receiving end of similarly frank advice from the Americans, who were by now thoroughly disillusioned with the European Movement's British leadership. During a meeting 'inadvertently' attended by Braden, Donovan was so 'derogatory' about Britain in general and Sandys personally that, much to the Americans' disgust, the EM's President 'began to cry'.[39] In May, ACUE stopped its payments to Sandys and, in June, dispatched Donovan and Braden to Europe to investigate alternative leadership options. Braden returned convinced that the countries of western Europe were 'on the brink of federation' and that, if support from the US was not forthcoming, 'leadership on the continent will go to British Labour'.[40] To avoid this disastrous eventuality, Braden proposed that ACUE transfer its allegiance to the Belgian President of the Council of Europe, Paul-Henri Spaak, a convinced federalist of high political standing. This was a move widely supported in 'the top echelons' of the State Department and ECA, which promised secret financial assistance for a continentally-led federalist movement.[41] Although Sandys initially indicated his willingness to step aside for Spaak, he was still in post when the Consultative Assembly met in Strasbourg in August 1950.[42] The scene was set for several weeks of vigorous lobbying by ACUE officers – according to one observer, Donovan had meetings with 'Spaak, Churchill, Reynaud, Bidault, Macmillan, Dalton, etc.' – at the end of which Sandys was finally prevailed upon to resign.[43] The task of overseeing the transfer of the EM's secretariat from London to Brussels was entrusted to Retinger and his Deputy Secretary-General, the former French resistance leader, Georges Rebattet, who was personally handed the requisite funds.[44] Dunston Curtis, one of the several victims of Sandys's dictatorial management style in London, was reinstated as 'propaganda chief' of the new Belgian office.[45] With that single exception, British influence, both Labour and Conservative, was now eliminated from the leadership of the European Movement.

THE MACKAY PLAN

As the Sandys affair demonstrates, the ACUE was quite prepared to intervene directly in the affairs of the EM when it felt the need to do so. This reflected its leaders' belief that, as Allen Dulles put it at a preliminary

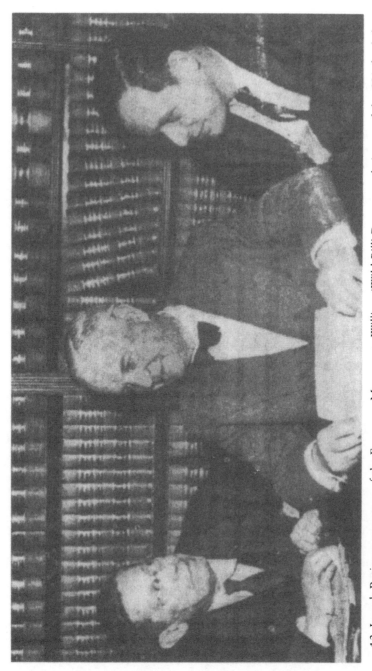

13 Joseph Retinger, secretary of the European Movement, William 'Wild Bill' Donovan, chairman of the CIA-funded American Committee on United Europe, and Tom Braden, ACUE's executive director, pictured at the 1950 press conference in New York during which Donovan reproved the Labour Party for obstructing European union.
(*New York Times*/American Committee on United Europe Papers, Lauinger Memorial Library, Georgetown University)

meeting of the organisation in January 1949, the nations of Europe would not unite 'without some discreet pushing from us'.[46] The application of such pressure to the British Labour Party took several forms, some more subtle than others. In 1950, the Committee granted the young French federalist André Voisin $10,000 to research ways 'to shock the British into compromise'. When Voisin came up with a plan for a 'lateral Assembly' to meet in close proximity to the Council of Europe in Strasbourg, the Americans pledged a further $70,000. The 'Council of Vigilance' staged a public rally directly across the street from the Consultative Assembly in November 1950, calling for immediate European federation. Labour delegates were reportedly 'worried' by this apparently spontaneous display of popular federalism and put 'in a mood for compromise'.[47] Around the same time, ACUE granted a further $1,000 to the leading French socialist André Philip to write a response to the Labour Party's pamphlet on *European Unity*. The resulting publication, 'Socialism and European Unity – Answer to the Executive of the Labour Party', explicitly encouraged British socialists to oppose the official Labour line on European federation.[48]

The most significant attempt by ACUE to sow federalist dissent in the ranks of the Labour Party involved R. W. G. Mackay, Labour MP for Hull North-West (1945–1950) and Reading North (1950–1951). The Australian-born Mackay, an academic and solicitor before he took up politics, became a follower of the pan-Europeanist Kalergi during the Second World War. In December 1947, he established a Labour 'Europe Group' in an attempt to persuade the Party leadership to adopt the cause of European union, then a few weeks later helped launch an All-Party Group of the Austrian count's European Parliamentary Union (EPU) in collaboration with such prominent Conservatives as Robert Boothby. A 'Memorandum on United Europe' produced by this Group revealed Mackay's talent for tactical compromise, combining as it did federalist proposals by himself with passages which reflected Boothby's preference for a functional approach. This pragmatic tendency would lead the following year to a falling out with the famously idealistic Kalergi, which in February 1949 resulted in Mackay leading the All-Party Group out of the EPU and into the rival European Movement. Despite his abandonment of pan-Europeanism, the Labour MP remained a committed federalist, promoting the European cause with a degree of energy and ingenuity that was rare amongst the EM's British leaders.[49]

These qualities soon brought Mackay to the attention of the American Committee on United Europe, which invited him to a meeting of its

Executive Committee at the Wall Street Club in January 1950. Addressing an audience which included Dulles, Braden and Jay Lovestone, Mackay described the All-Party Group and summarised its discussions concerning two economic measures widely considered crucial for European integration, the abolition of customs barriers and the creation of a common currency. He then went on to outline plans for the formation of a European committee, with headquarters in either Paris or London, to draft treaties on economic relations for debate at the next meeting of the Consultative Assembly of the Council of Europe. The same body would also consider ways in which the Consultative Assembly's General Affairs Committee – of which Mackay was a member – might work to increase the Council's political power in Europe. Mackay offered to raise half the sum of £10,000 he believed was necessary to finance this undertaking; he asked ACUE to provide the remainder.[50]

After running a series of background checks on Mackay (the experience of dealing with Sandys had clearly made the ACUE wary of British collaborators), the Americans eventually decided to advance him a pilot grant of £1,000.[51] This proved an extremely good investment. In July 1950, Braden returned from his trouble-shooting mission to Europe reporting that, 'We are, all of us, impressed with Mackay', and proposing that additional cash be made available to him (although with the proviso that 'one of us on the ground working within the European Movement be detailed to "watch dog" the funds').[52] After the August session of the Consultative Assembly, Mackay began elaborating his proposals for economic union into a more ambitious programme for a 'European political authority with limited functions but real powers'.[53] The result was the 'Mackay Plan', a clever synthesis of federalism and functionalism, which provided for the transformation of the Council of Europe into a European parliament by a gradualist process of inter-governmental cooperation.[54] In its November session the Assembly, pressurised (or, in Braden's phrase, 'solidified') by the demonstration mounted across the street by the Council of Vigilance, adopted the Mackay Plan and created a special committee to draw up a protocol for consideration by the member governments before its next meeting.[55] ACUE's officers were delighted by these developments, variously describing Mackay as 'most energetic', 'effective' and 'exceptional', and immediately increased their payments to him so that he could devote more time to perfecting his plan and mobilising European support.[56] In this latter respect, for example, Mackay received 'encouragement' from General Donovan 'to set up a small committee of Labour MPs to propagandise for European Union on a trade union level'.[57] In total, ACUE granted Mackay $5,500 in 1950 and $6,000 in 1951.[58]

Whether or not the Labour leadership had any inkling of the financial assistance Mackay was receiving from the Americans is unclear. What is clear, though, is that his activities on behalf of European federation earned him considerable resentment and suspicion within the higher reaches of the Party hierarchy. In 1949, Hugh Dalton, leader of the Labour delegation to the first meeting of the Consultative Assembly in Strasbourg, complained to Clement Attlee that Mackay, 'a fanatical federalist', was 'inclined to talk a bit too much', especially to 'British Tories and other unsympathetic types'. 'He was the nearest approach to a lone wolf in our Labour pack', Dalton continued, 'and we shall have to keep an eye on him'.[59] After the events of 1950 – the meeting of the Council of Vigilance and the adoption of the Mackay Plan – Dalton toyed with the idea of leaving the MP for Reading North out of the Labour delegation to Strasbourg in 1951 altogether (he had already been deselected from the Assembly's powerful General Affairs Committee), before deciding that such a step would be 'a great tactical error', as it 'would give an appearance of victimisation' and might even lead to an invitation from the Conservatives to join their group. 'It is much better to take him', Dalton concluded, 'but to make sure that he is isolated within our Delegation'.[60]

In the event, this tactic appears to have worked. Mackay enjoyed some moments of success at the May 1951 session of the Consultative Assembly, for example his restoration to the General Affairs Committee in the powerful position of *Rapporteur*.[61] However, when he presented his draft protocol to the Committee, its British and Scandinavian members 'flatly refused to commit themselves to any part of it'. As a consequence, the Mackay Plan was not reported out of the Committee to the General Assembly.[62] Although a much modified version of the Statute was eventually adopted at the Assembly's November session, Mackay, who by this point was no longer a representative in Strasbourg, having lost his parliamentary seat in the October General Election, had evidently failed to convert the Labour Party to his enthusiasm for European federation.

OTHER ACUE ACTIVITIES IN BRITAIN

Combined with mounting evidence that Winston Churchill's new Conservative government was no more interested in European federation

14 R.W.G. Mackay, Labour MP, European federalist and recipient of ACUE funding. (By Permission of People's History Museum)

than its Labour predecessor, the failure of the Mackay Plan in the summer of 1951 added further impetus to a new trend in the federalist campaign, already apparent in Paul-Henri Spaak's leadership of the European Movement, away from the cultivation of élite support and towards the agitation of mass opinion. This shift of emphasis was reflected in the domestic campaigns of the American Committee on United Europe, which shifted up several gears in 1951. Its clearest manifestation was the creation of the European Youth Campaign (EYC), a unity drive amongst western European youth devised by Retinger, Spaak and André Philip, with the encouragement of such Americans as Shepard Stone, in response to youth activities organised by the Comintern in the eastern bloc. So important was this struggle for popular and, in particular, youth support considered that, after 1951, the majority of ACUE funds earmarked for Europe were spent on the EYC, which used them to conduct 'a massive propaganda campaign of conferences and exhibitions, cinema shows, radio broadcasts and a large array of publications'.[63]

The launch of this youth campaign in Britain was greeted with some suspicion. 'In the early days, the EYC was subject to attack and ill-feeling by various youth and student organisations', Barney Hayhoe, President of the organisation's British Committee, told a visiting ACUE officer in 1957.[64] This might have been a veiled reference to the decision of the Labour League of Youth (LLY), the youth section of the Labour Party, to disaffiliate from the EYC in 1952 due to suspicions about the source of its funding.[65] Later, however, according to Hayhoe, the EYC was 'accepted' and its programme ceased to be 'a matter of controversy'. Indeed, from the mid-1950s the Campaign mounted an impressive range of activities in Britain, including, for example, the organisation and financing of 'an extensive young adult debate competition on European issues' and the mounting of conferences 'for young business executives' on various aspects of European economic union.[66] This improvement in the EYC's fortunes was due in part to the hard work of its British Secretary, the future Labour MP and minister Maurice Foley, who was generally recognised as 'an able man … doing an excellent job'.[67] Another important Labour supporter of the EYC was the MP Geoffrey de Freitas, an ardent federalist who sat on the Campaign's International Commission.

The vitality of the British section of the EYC contrasted sharply with the continuing inertia of the European Movement in Britain. The UK Council of the EM, dominated as it was by such functionalist

Conservatives as Robert Boothby, was the target of frequent attack by federalist observers (and even some of its own officers), who perceived it as deliberately obstructing European integration.[68] There were, however, other organisations in Britain with an interest in Europe. The most active of these was Federal Union, the British section of the Paris-based European Union of Federalists, which enjoyed close links with the EYC and ACUE. Indeed, in December 1956 officers of the Federal Union helped ACUE set up the 'Britain and Europe Fund', in effect a fence for American monies destined for projects whose purpose was 'to furnish factual information for use by elements in Britain favoring closer British ties with the Continent'. One such venture was a survey of opinions held by members of parliament in Commonwealth countries about the 'Free Trade Area', the British government proposal for a loose form of economic union with the European continent. As John Blumgart explained, opponents of the Free Trade Area liked to argue that a strengthening of Britain's continental ties would 'weaken her ties with the Commonwealth and Empire'. The aim of the poll was to show that, in fact, a majority of Commonwealth parliamentarians were either indifferent to or in favour of British participation.[69] The survey, which eventually produced the anticipated results, was based on a questionnaire drawn up by a market research company run by Martin Maddan, a Conservative MP and officer of Federal Union. Maddan was also responsible for the bank account into which was paid the £2,800 donation from ACUE set aside for the poll.[70]

The most important project funded by the Britain and Europe Fund involved the Economist Intelligence Unit (EIU), the prestigious research team attached to the eponymous weekly news magazine. *The Economist* had long been identified with the federalist cause, constantly urging Britain's political and business leaders not to squander the economic opportunities offered by European union. Moreover, the magazine had a direct link to ACUE in the person of its former editor Lord Layton, who in 1950 had undertaken a lecture tour of the US under the Committee's auspices. In January 1957, the American organisation authorised a payment of $10,000 to the Britain and Europe Fund to finance an EIU study of the potential impact of membership in the Free Trade Area on British industry. The result was (in the words of John Blumgart) 'a reasoned and compelling policy document' which contrasted 'the considerable net gains for Britain of joining ... against the considerable net losses of remaining outside'.[71] Serialised in the London *Observer*, then published in book form in December 1957, *Britain and Europe* attracted widespread and generally favourable media attention.[72] It was the model for a further ACUE-funded, EIU study, *Britain, the Commonwealth and European Free Trade*, which appeared in August 1958 and enjoyed a similar reception. By this point the Britain and Europe Fund, its coffers swollen by ACUE grants and matching donations from pro-European British industrialists, had accumulated a sufficient surplus to launch a new organisation, 'Britain in Europe', with the aim of further stimulating British support for European integration. ACUE, which was delighted by the fruits of its patronage of the EIU, gladly turned over its share of the surplus, amounting to $4,000, to this body.[73] The Committee remained reticent, however, about advertising its sponsorship. Its role, it instructed the EIU, was to be 'given minimal publicity'.[74]

The impact of these CIA-funded initiatives is extremely hard to measure. For example, it is arguable that the funding of pro-European projects by the EIU did exert some influence on British business attitudes, thereby helping prepare the way for Britain's application to join the EEC in 1961; but such a hypothesis is difficult to prove. Similarly, while ACUE-sponsored youth activities of the sort arranged by Maurice Foley might have shaped the views of future politicians responsible for making government policy on Europe, such influence is impossible to quantify. Reviewing the whole course of ACUE operations – the organisation's officers suspended its activities in 1960, reasoning that with the postwar revival of Europe's economies, European integrationists were now capable of funding their own campaigns – it is hard to escape the suspicion that they only served to convince further those who already believed in the pro-unity cause. As with so many of its covert programmes, the CIA's strategy for European union was to sponsor those federalist groups which naturally shared its objectives. Indeed, ACUE funds were often actively solicited by Europeans, such as during the late 1940s when the EM's British officers approached the Committee urging it to support them rather than Kalergi's EPU.[75] In Richard J. Aldrich's apt summary, 'The history of ACUE shows us prominent European politicians in search of discreet American assistance, rather than the CIA in search of proxies'.[76]

Where support for European federalism did not already exist in significant measure, as in the leadership of the Labour Party, it proved very hard to manufacture. Hence, while there is evidence that ACUE-funded activities in 1950 such as the Council of Vigilance did have some pressurising effect on Labour opinion,[77] it was insufficient to prevent the British delegation at Strasbourg killing the Mackay Plan in 1951. Not even Hugh Gaitskell, an outspoken supporter of American policy in so many other policy areas (and, incidentally, one of the British politicians visited by Paul Hoffman on his ACUE-sponsored tour of Europe in 1957) was ready to challenge the majority opinion of his Party on this issue.[78] 'The Durham miners won't wear it', Herbert Morrison is reputed to have said of European integration.[79] Try though it might, the CIA could not alter that fact.

THE ORIGINS OF BILDERBERG

As with the European Movement, the original inspiration for the Bilderberg Group came not from the US but rather from Europe. Indeed, several of the same Europeans who had helped launch the EM were also present at the creation of Bilderberg, including that '*eminence grise* of Europe' or 'Talleyrand without portfolio', Joseph Retinger.[80] By the beginning of 1952, the focus of Retinger's attention had shifted from European union to the Atlantic alliance, which he believed was being undermined by the rise of anti-Americanism in Europe and a corresponding resurgence of isolationism in the US. In May 1952, following conversations with his long-time collaborator Paul Rykens, the Dutch Chairman of Unilever, Retinger presented a plan to Bernhard, Prince-Consort of the Netherlands, and a fellow campaigner for European union who was well-known and respected in the US. Bernhard was to help Retinger assemble a team of leading Europeans to exchange views about and prepare a report on the causes of European anti-Americanism. This report would be transmitted to a counterpart American group, which would have the opportunity to respond to the criticisms raised in it at a private, high-level meeting. The ensuing transatlantic dialogue, it was hoped, would result in a new appreciation of the fundamental values shared by Europeans and Americans.[81] As well as revealing Retinger's almost mystical faith in Atlanticism, this plan demonstrated the extreme importance he still attached to the mobilisation of élite, as opposed to mass, opinion.

Having secured Bernhard's support, Retinger set about recruiting his team of European experts. In Britain, for example, his old friend the SOE veteran Colin Gubbins wrote on his behalf to Hugh Gaitskell inviting him to lunch 'to discuss a matter which we think is of international importance', assuring him that, 'No publicity of any kind is attached'.[82] The meeting was clearly a success: shortly afterwards Gaitskell submitted a report on 'American–European relations' to Retinger. Other European leaders followed suit, among them the Italian Prime Minister Alcide de Gasperi, the Belgian Foreign Minister Paul van Zeeland and the French Prime Minister Antoine Pinay (Gubbins and Lord Portal of Hungerford, Chairman of Barclays Bank and Marshal of the RAF, also reported from Britain). Retinger then synthesised their observations into a single document summarising the main European criticisms of American policy.[83] This was discussed at a meeting of the reporters held at the apartment of the Baron François de Nervo in Paris in September 1952 – the private venue reflecting Retinger's desire to conduct his business as far as possible in secret – then dispatched by Prince Bernhard to his friend, Walter Bedell Smith.[84]

The American response to this European initiative was surprisingly slow in coming. Retinger's report was considered so controversial that American politicians were reluctant to handle it until after the 1952 presidential election had run its course. Then Smith's appointment as Under-Secretary of State in the new Eisenhower administration intervened. Eventually, in July 1953, a somewhat aggrieved Bernhard wrote to 'Beedle' asking what had become of his proposal.[85] At this point, Smith decided to turn the matter over to another of the Prince's old acquaintances, C. D. Jackson, who at first was equally unsure how to proceed with it.[86] While he was 'stewing about how to get out of the trap', word reached Jackson that a new Committee for a National Trade Policy was about to form under the chairmanship of Detroit industrialist John S. Coleman. Here, it seemed, was an opportunity for yet more buck-passing. Jackson asked if the Committee would respond to the Retinger report and, 'to [his] amazement, Coleman agreed to take on the project'.[87] It was not, however, until November that the 'counter-report' was completed and passed to Retinger.[88] Over a year had passed since the Americans had first been invited to join in the Bilderberg planning process.

Events at last began to gather some momentum. Colin Gubbins, convinced that 'the need for appropriate action' was now 'more urgent' than ever, prepared a joint summary of the European and American reports. This identified four main areas of transatlantic 'misunderstanding': 'International policies, with particular reference to Communism; the colonial problem; economic questions; [and] questions of "method".' Gubbins also proposed various types of 'remedial measure', giving as an example 'of what could be done' the organisation of 'a semi-private conference at the highest level'. This possibility was explored further at a second meeting of Retinger's European team – now referred to simply as 'the Group' – which took place in Paris in January 1954.[89] The following month the Group met again, this time with several Americans in attendance, namely Coleman, the President of his Committee Senator Charles Taft and its Secretary George Ball. Here it was agreed that a larger meeting would be held in May somewhere in the Netherlands so that a group of leading US and European citizens could thrash out the problems identified in the earlier discussions.[90] In March, Coleman sent letters to about 40 Americans inquiring if they would be willing to attend such a conference as 'guests of the Dutch Government' and in April Bernhard issued formal invitations.[91]

The conference took place over three days at the end of May 1954 in a small hotel near Arnhem called the Bilderberg. There were 75 participants in total, all men: Bilderberg during the 1950s was an exclusively male environment. The 20-strong American contingent included, besides Jackson, Irving Brown, Paul Nitze (George Kennan's successor as head of the Policy Planning Staff and author of the highly influential defence paper, NSC–68) and David Rockefeller of the Chase National Bank. The Chair was occupied by Bernhard; as leaders of the American and European groups respectively, John Coleman and Paul van Zeeland served as Vice-Chairmen. Retinger was designated Secretary-General (he had resigned from the same post in the European Movement the previous year). The meeting itself was, as Bernhard's biographer Alden Hatch describes it, 'perhaps the most unusual international conference ever held until then'.

> There was absolutely no publicity. The hotel was ringed by security guards, so that not a single journalist got within a mile of the place. The participants were pledged not to repeat publicly what was said in the discussions. Every person present – Prime Ministers, Foreign Ministers, leaders of political parties, heads of great banks and industrial companies, and representatives of such international organisations as the European Coal and Steel Community, as well as academicians – was magically stripped of his office as he entered the door, and became a simple citizen of his country for the duration of the conference.[92]

Retinger's efforts to create an environment in which European and American leaders felt able to express themselves freely, without fear of international repercussion, paid off. The discussion was frank and sometimes heated (especially, as is noted below, when it turned to the subject of McCarthyism) but, thanks to Bernhard's deft chairmanship, cordial throughout. The conference broke up on 31 May in, as C. D. Jackson recalled later, 'a rosy glow of Americano–European friendship and cooperation'.[93]

Nonetheless, contrary to the impression given in Hatch's account, the Bilderberg's future as a regular forum for the 'Atlantic community' was far from certain. In the months that followed, Retinger travelled between Paris, London and Washington, attempting to raise support for a follow-up meeting to be held in the US the following year.[94] The American response was, as before, lukewarm. The reason for this appears to have been that the scheming Retinger was suspected of being, in the phrase of C. D. Jackson, 'a British secret agent'.[95] As Jackson pointed out in a letter to Ann C. Whitman, President Eisenhower's private secretary, the Polish émigré, ('who acted as one-man brain trust, whipper-in, and *rapporteur* for Bernhard'), was already well-known in American intelligence circles due to his 'connection with various Central and Eastern European activities'. Indeed, 'no matter where the rug was placed, whether New York, London, Paris, Munich, Rome, or what have you, Retinger always managed to crawl out from under it at the most awkward moment'. Moreover, in his current campaigning on behalf of Bilderberg, he appeared 'to have complete *carte blanche* from Bernhard, and considerable freedom of movement from invisible sources of income'. Jackson's conviction that Retinger was a British agent was, he told Whitman, 'pretty well shared by some other people who are in a position to know better than I', a reference, presumably, to the CIA.[96]

These suspicions about Retinger and British Intelligence's interest in Bilderberg intensified when the Pole started a whispering campaign against the leader of the American group, John Coleman, alleging the businessman lacked the intellect and personality necessary for this crucial role. When in November 1954 Bernhard wrote to Eisenhower requesting his assistance in sidelining Coleman, and a clearly irritated President demanded an explanation from his adviser on psychological warfare, Jackson decided to take drastic action.[97] At his request, Eisenhower dictated a 'brutal' reply to Bernhard (while, incidentally, having his hair cut) stating that, although he was aware Coleman 'may not possess every single one of the qualifications needed to make him an ideal leader of the American group', he would not be prepared, 'under any circumstances, to reward his hard and disinterested work in the field, and to damage his usefulness in other American fields, by just coldly

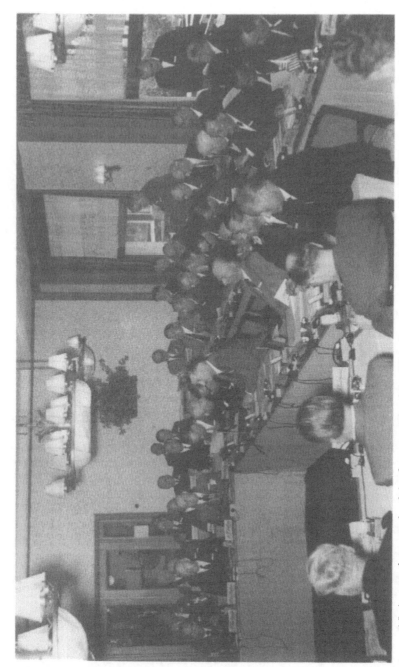

15 A rare photograph of the first meeting of the Bilderberg group in 1954. Hugh Gaitskell is seated to the left of the rear window. (Hugh Gaitskell Papers, University College London)

giving him the sack'.[98] The Prince's response to this put-down – which shows Eisenhower's personal diplomatic style in a revealing light – was profusely apologetic.[99]

This exchange seems to have cleared the air. American reservations about Retinger remained: when in late 1955 a US foundation official attempted to bring a discrepancy of $500 in the Bilderberg accounts to his attention, the Pole angrily pointed out that he had 'already had to complain of the fact that some members of the American group expressed doubts about my general activities in postwar Europe, suggesting that I had turned into a "professional promoter" of organisations in Europe profitable to me personally', then demanded that 'all innuendoes about me and my so-called personal gains be dropped once and for all on your side'.[100] However, as Jackson appreciated, none of the suspicions which had attached themselves to Retinger meant 'that his energy and ingenuity and enthusiasm and experience should not be welcomed by us, and used to the fullest in those endeavors where our causes are joint'.[101] Jackson accordingly proposed, via the President, a compromise measure: instead of removing Coleman, the Americans would appoint one or two co-chairmen 'who would supply the element he apparently lacks'. In return, the Europeans were to arrange the agenda of the next meeting so that it included 'really functional or action items', such as, Jackson suggested, 'a World Economic Plan for the USA'.[102]

This suggestion was reported by Bernhard and Retinger to a meeting of the European group held in Paris in December 1954, where it was warmly received.[103] In January of the following year, Jackson approached Walter Bedell Smith asking if he would take on the leadership of the American group (after the flap involving Retinger, Coleman had suffered a heart attack and resigned his chair). By this point the President's adviser was of the firm belief that Bilderberg was 'a good and highly useful endeavor, definitely to be cooperated with'.[104] In the event, Smith's other duties only permitted him to accept the co-chairmanship of the Group: the chair went instead to Dean Rusk, President of the Rockefeller Foundation.[105] Shortly afterwards, another American foundation entered the scene: the Ford agreed to subsidise the second meeting, now scheduled to take place in March 1955 in Barbizon, a village near Paris, with the Carnegie Endowment for International Peace actually handling the finances.[106] With unequivocal American support now secured, Bilderberg's survival, so long in the balance, was at last assured.

LABOUR PARTICIPATION

In contrast with the Americans, leaders of British Labour joined in Bilderberg with an enthusiasm which had been conspicuously lacking in their approach to the European Movement. Hugh Gaitskell, a founder member of both 'the Group' and the Steering Committee formed after the 1954 meeting, performed a number of activities on behalf of Bernhard and Retinger (who, incidentally, had good Labour connections, having married the daughter of journalist politician E. D. Morel during his exile in London).[107] For example, he helped prepare the report on economic problems which formed the basis for much of the discussion at Barbizon.[108] He was also Retinger's principal source of advice about and point of contact with other British Labourites, sounding out Denis Healey and Sam Watson about attending the Bilderberg meeting before Bernhard issued formal invitations. (Watson, by the way, declined, telling Gaitskell, ' I trust you understand my motive, which is mainly instinctive, but I feel it is the right move to make'. His place was taken instead by Tom Williamson.)[109] Among the Labour MPs and leading trade unionists who did attend Bilderberg conferences during the 1950s on Gaitskell's recommendation were Alfred Robens, Douglas Jay and George Brown. (It is interesting to note that in 1958, when the meeting took place in Buxton, England, Aneurin Bevan – who had declared his opposition to unilateralism the previous year – was considered as a possible participant. Evidently his recent rapprochement with Gaitskell had prepared the way for acceptance into the Atlantic fold. In the event, however, he was unable to attend.)[110] In the run-up to the Buxton conference, Gaitskell even volunteered to help its organisers raise funds from British industry, writing a letter they could discreetly show to leading businessmen in which he stated his belief that such events helped 'to remove causes of friction and misunderstanding'.[111] No wonder, then, that when the Labour leader stood down from the Steering Committee in 1958, Retinger should have thanked him effusively 'for the help, cooperation and advice' he had given Bilderberg over the years.[112] The baton now passed to Denis Healey, a co-opted member of the Steering Committee since 1956, who was to prove no less energetic in the role of Bilderberg's Labour point-man.[113]

Gaitskell also immersed himself fully in the clandestine culture that surrounded Bilderberg, for example advising Healey in 1954 to 'treat the whole matter as absolutely confidential, and say nothing about it to anybody'.[114] Indeed, when the question of publicity for the 1954 conference came up, Gaitskell was amongst those pushing for complete secrecy. 'I have always assumed that it would never be anything else but private', he told Retinger, 'and I feel pretty certain that the other members would strongly concur.'[115] There was even a hint of cloak-and-dagger intrigue about the arrangements made by Paul Rykens, who had raised the European funds for the Bilderberg meeting, to reimburse the Labour politician his 'incidental expenses' for his trip to the Netherlands, which involved the driver of the car that greeted him at the airport handing him an envelope containing 100 Dutch guilders.[116]

Once ensconced at the Bilderberg, Gaitskell found himself rubbing shoulders with conservative politicians, military top-brass and wealthy capitalists. Retinger's determination to bring together representatives of all the interests and groups which had a stake in the Atlantic alliance made for some strange encounters. Shortly after the first meeting, Gaitskell sent a copy of the new edition of Evan Durbin's *Politics of Democratic Socialism* to David Rockefeller. The Wall Street banker (a close friend of Allen Dulles and Tom Braden) thanked the Labour MP for the gift warmly and observed in language similar to that Gaitskell would use later when appealing for funds to British businessmen, 'I believe that conferences such as the one we attended can be helpful in bringing out and explaining the reasons for our differences which, in turn, tend to reduce feelings of resentment and mistrust'.[117]

Considering all this, it was perhaps only to be expected that Bilderberg should have been denounced on the left as, in the words of Denis Healey, 'a capitalist plot to undermine socialism'.[118] Once again, the hoary tropes of betrayal and hoodwinking were invoked: Gaitskell and his cronies were either being duped by Wall Street bankers bent on declawing the European left, or were deliberately selling out their followers by consorting with enemies of the working class. This leftist conspiracy theory – the mirror image of what was believed in America, where Bilderberg was regarded, to quote Healey again, 'as a left-wing plot to subvert the United States' – led inevitably to the allegation that the Group was funded by the CIA.[119] Indeed, rumours of CIA funding of the first meeting have now acquired the status of historical 'fact', repeated in all of the few scholarly accounts of the subject.

However, nowhere in the newly available documentation is there any evidence to support this claim. The CIA did have knowledge of the venture: C. D. Jackson showed Gubbins's synthetic report on European anti-Americanism to Allen Dulles.[120] There is also the possibility that the travel costs of the US delegation at the 1954 meeting were paid for by the Agency. After all, precedent for such an arrangement existed in the form of the secret grants given to American intellectuals attending the founding conference of the Congress for Cultural Freedom in 1950. In contrast with this earlier event, however, most of the US citizens travelling to the Netherlands in 1954 were wealthy businessmen or professionals capable of paying their own passage. Moreover, whereas documents relating to other CIA-front activities in this period contain various clues to Agency involvement, such as references to 'the company', 'our friends in the South' or the 'Fizz-kids', papers in the Jackson collection relating to the Bilderberg do not. Instead, accounts of the Group's income and expenditure in the 1950s filed amongst the Ford Foundation papers in New York indicate that funding for the meetings, including the first 1954 event, came from private European sources such as Paul Rykens's Unilever or bona fide private American foundations.[121] What hints there are of a covert dimension point towards the hand of British rather than American intelligence, for example Jackson's description of Retinger as a 'British secret agent' and the important role played in proceedings by Gubbins, who maintained his links with the Secret Intelligence Service long after the disbanding of the Special Operations Executive.[122]

In any event, what the documents do demonstrate is that this was very much a European initiative, with the Americans coming on board only late in the day and, even then, with some misgivings. Moreover, the fragmentary record of what actually took place at Bilderberg meetings – the published reports circulated confidentially to participants after each conference do not identify speakers by name, so to find out what specific individuals said one has to rely on other sources, such as notes scribbled by C. D. Jackson – suggests that Labour participants played a far from passive role in discussions. After the first conference, for example, Jackson reported to Eisenhower that 'the American side' had been the target of 'some very skillful attacks from a large number of Europeans, chiefly British Labourites'.[123] The note of grudging admiration detectable in this remark was echoed in Jackson's diary log of the event. 'Outstanding performance turned in by British Labourites Gaitskell, Healey, Oliver Franks', it noted. With the leader of the American delegation, John Coleman, apparently content to sit on the sidelines, Jackson decided to carry the counter-attack 'in face of brilliantly executed British hostility to every American point of view'.

Tried to use British technique of a combination of humor, sarcasm, interlarded with unpleasant facts, which seemed to be very successful. As conference developed each item, it became standard for European position to be made, then for me to present American position.... Then after each British rebuttal, I would sur-rebut. It got to be a real contest.[124]

On the final day Jackson asked Bernhard if he could open a discussion about McCarthyism, a subject on which the Europeans had been 'needling' the Americans throughout the meeting.[125] He spoke for fifteen minutes, 'then answered questions for another hour. Must have been okay, because Oliver Franks whispered "Jolly good show", which I considered praise indeed.'[126]

The 'sparks' that flew between the Labourites and Jackson at the Bilderberg appear to have had a beneficial effect, dissipating 'the really bad misunderstandings between Europeans and Americans' and clearing the atmosphere 'like lightning'.[127] Labour opposition to the American line was not always received in such good heart, however. Another occasion when electricity was discharged was the first Bilderberg meeting held in the US, the St Simon's Island, Georgia, conference of 1957. The discussion began acrimoniously as 'the French, British and Americans almost came to blows over Suez' following a provocative speech on the subject by Raymond Aron.[128] Lord Kilmuir, the British Lord Chancellor, who had deliberately been sent to the meeting by Harold Macmillan 'to help heal the bruises' caused by Suez, gave (according to notes by American participant Michael A. Heilperin) 'a reasoned and dispassionate presentation of the British case'.[129] Denis Healey, spotting the opportunity to score a partisan point against the Conservative government, retorted that, 'We lit ourselves the forest fire we set out to extinguish in the Middle East'.

Healey's most controversial statements at St Simon's, however, touched more directly on American strategic interests. While presenting his report on 'Nationalism and Neutralism in the Western Community', the Labour MP turned away from his text to argue that the recent emergence of the 'Bandung group' of Asian and African countries was in part a defensive response to the formation of NATO.[130] Later he continued his 'interesting, if doubtfully valid, critique of NATO' by outlining what C. D. Jackson soon nick-named the 'Healey Doctrine', a plan for reunifying and neutralising Germany based on the removal of the Red Army from East German soil and a corresponding withdrawal of NATO forces so that they would in future act only as 'trip-wire' in the event of a communist invasion of western Europe. Current NATO strategy was,

Healey suggested, based on two assumptions that no longer held true: 'the existence of an absolute Soviet will to aggression against the West' and 'an absolute ability of the West to defend effectively western Europe'.[131] Not surprisingly, these remarks aroused a heated discussion: Jackson engaged Healey in a pyrotechnical argument (a *feu d'artifice*, according to Heilperin) and Air Chief Marshall William Elliot delivered a 'brilliant debating speech' before Lord Kilmuir attempted to draw a line under the 'Healey doctrine' by concluding that the west should not 'press for an immediate answer to the problem of German reunification'.[132] Clearly, though, NATO supporters were rattled by what they had heard. 'Healey's paper and speech most important and dangerous to NATO', scribbled Jackson as he sat listening. 'So plausible and tempting, so right in many respects.'[133] What particularly worried the *Time-Life* executive was the similarity of the Healey doctrine to recent pronouncements by the German Social Democratic Party, some of whose leaders were present at St Simon's. As he reported to Henry Luce after his return home, 'The German Socialists hung on Healey's every word, and it was obvious that they were expecting not only support but considerable brain trusting from British Labour in their eagerness to Munichize NATO'.[134]

The furore Healey provoked at St Simon's in 1957 did not deter him from striking a similar stance the following year, when the venue was the Derbyshire resort town of Buxton. 'Perhaps the biggest single mistake made by the West in recent years', the Labour MP suggested in a paper entitled 'Living with Khrushchev', 'has been the tendency to treat the Communist bloc as the monolithic structure it is claimed to be by Soviet propaganda, rather than the disintegrating empire it is in practice'. Western leaders must seize the opportunity presented by the recent relaxation of Cold War tensions, Healey advised, to establish 'separate diplomatic contact with the various Communist states'. Above all, the 'absurd anomaly' of China's exclusion from the UN 'should be ended as soon as possible'.[135] These pronouncements – which flew in the face of official British and American policy – suggest that, far from having been duped by Bilderberg, Healey turned the meetings to his own advantage, using them as a platform for presenting alternative Cold War strategies to a powerful international audience, something otherwise unavailable to him due to Labour's exclusion from power. Hugh Gaitskell, too, appears to have looked upon his membership of 'the Group' partly as a device for putting across the Labour viewpoint to influential Americans: his report on European anti-Americanism to the first Bilderberg conference contained a number of criticisms of US trade policy and a reminder that, contrary to American perceptions, 'Socialist parties ... are in fact bitterly opposed to Communism'.[136] It is even possible that Healey, while he was attending a Bilderberg meeting at Fiuggi in Italy in 1957, sought out Shepard Stone to petition him for Ford Foundation support for his new think-tank on Cold War nuclear strategy, the Institute of Strategic Studies (ISS), which had recently run out of money.[137]

If allegations of hoodwinking ignore evidence that Healey and Gaitskell brought their own agenda to Bilderberg, so talk of betrayal disregards the substantial correspondences that existed between the political culture of the Group and the Gaitskellites. As the British historian Lawrence Black has persuasively argued, the clandestine nature and élitism of the Bilderberg conferences had powerful antecedents in revisionist organisations like the XYZ Club – the secretive discussion group of Labour intellectuals and City financiers attended by Gaitskell since the 1930s – as well as in already-existing revisionist discourses about the dangers of mass participation in foreign policy-making, such as Denis Healey had articulated in 1955 at the Congress for Cultural Freedom meeting in Milan. This helps explain why Gaitskell felt so comfortable in the vaguely conspiratorial atmosphere of Bilderberg (also perhaps why Sam Watson, who was more in touch with the labourist culture of the movement's grass-roots, with its historic mistrust of intellectuals and cabals, instinctively rejected his invitation to the first conference). Then there were doctrinal homologies between revisionism and the kind of corporate liberalism typically espoused by the American industrialists, foreign-policy experts and foundation personnel who attended Bilderberg. The revisionist project of modernising socialism and humanising capitalism could not have been accomplished, the Gaitskellites might have argued, without the kind of corporatist dialogue that Bilderberg made possible. Finally, there was the lure of the high standards of hospitality on offer at these meetings, a less trivial consideration than it might at first appear due to the prominence amongst the revisionists of such celebrated *bon viveurs* as Tony Crosland, who had almost made a political principle out of enjoying the good life.[138] Bilderberg, then, might not have appealed to the most high-minded or democratic elements of Gaitskellism, but it does not follow from this that it constituted a Labour *trahison des clercs*.

Arguing that Labour participants were not the victims of a capitalist plot to undermine socialism is not to endorse the equivalent American conspiracy theory that Bilderberg was an anti-US stratagem concocted by wily European socialists. Again, the conspiracy theory fails to capture the complex reality of the Group's early history. As events in the immediate aftermath of the first meeting showed, the Americans were careful to dictate the terms of their subsequent involvement in, and support of, the venture, Jackson for example demanding the insertion in the agenda of the next conference the item about the US world economic plan. Indeed, Eisenhower's 'brutal' slapping down of Bernhard could be interpreted as the symbolic moment when control of the promising initiative passed from European to American hands. For that matter, Jackson was quite successful at manipulating discussion even at the first meeting in Holland, as his deliberate raising of McCarthyism on the final day demonstrates. (The fact that he correctly predicted McCarthy's downfall only months before the demagogue was formally censured by the US Senate greatly impressed the European Bilderbergers – as well as furnishing conspiracy theorists with supposed evidence that the Group secretly controlled world events.)[139]

So, then, if Bilderberg was neither a CIA plot nor a socialist conspiracy, what was it? Here it might prove helpful to invoke recent writings by the so-called Amsterdam School of International Relations, in particular those of Kees van der Pijl, which stress the need to move beyond the traditional, nation state-centred analysis of world politics to an approach emphasising the development of a transnational society.[140] One thing that the new documentary evidence does show clearly is that it is extremely difficult to locate Bilderberg's origins in terms of national history. The Group was neither an entirely European nor American invention, but rather the result of a highly complex process of Atlantic interaction. For that matter, it is equally difficult to tell whether Bilderberg was the creation of state agencies, specifically the western intelligence services, or non-government actors. In the curious person of its principal founder, the wandering scholar Retinger, the distinction between the private and official realms, civil society and the state, seem to collapse altogether, as indeed does the very concept of nationality.

The statelessness of Retinger, reminiscent of the *deraciné* character of other private players in the covert Cold War such as Arthur Koestler, is perhaps the most powerful proof of van der Pijl's contention that Bilderberg was basically a transnational phenomenon. One does not have to accept all of the Marxist assumptions inherent in the Dutch scholar's analysis to agree that there were striking correspondences between the Group and earlier attempts to construct a bourgeois transnational network or 'imagined community' through such élitist, secretive, male-only organisations as the Freemasons or the Rhodes/Milner 'Round

Table'. That said, there is considerable explanatory force in his argument that the early Cold War witnessed the emergence of a new 'Atlantic ruling class' whose power was based on the liberal corporate order of New Deal America but which also incorporated fractions of European élites who shared its modernising, internationalist outlook.[141] These, it might be argued, included the revisionist intellectuals of the British Labour Party, a group already committed to a New Deal-style agenda of labour–capital corporatism, welfarism and Keynesian planning. This spontaneous identity of interest explains why, despite the occasional flare-up over issues such as McCarthyism, the debates at Bilderberg were basically so consensual: regardless of their nationality, the participants were all members of the same imagined community. It also helps account for the extraordinary amount of hostile comment the Group has recently attracted from European conservatives jealous of their national sovereignty and American extremists unsettled by the onwards march of globalisation. In this regard, it is perhaps the New World Order, out of all the conspiracy theories spawned by Bilderberg, that, despite its obvious idiocies, comes closest to the truth.

NOTES

1. Quoted in Hugo Young, *This Blessed Plot: Britain and Europe from Churchill to Blair* (Basingstoke: Macmillan, 1998), p. 163.
2. Quoted in Richard Fletcher, 'Who were *they* travelling with?', in Fred Hirsch and Richard Fletcher (eds), *The CIA and the Labour Movement* (Nottingham: Spokesman Books, 1977), p. 63.
3. See, particularly, Richard J. Aldrich, 'OSS, CIA and European Unity: The American Committee on United Europe', *Diplomacy and Statecraft* 8 (1997), 184–227; and Richard J. Aldrich, *The Hidden Hand: Britain, America and Cold War Secret Intelligence* (London: John Murray, 2001), chap. 16.
4. For a highly entertaining exploration of the conspiracy theories surrounding Bilderberg, see Jon Ronson, *Them: Adventures with Extremists* (Basingstoke and Oxford: Picador, 2001), chap. 6.
5. Geir Lundestad, *'Empire' by Integration: The United States and European Integration, 1945–97* (Oxford University Press, 1998), p. 13.
6. See Cord Meyer, *Facing Reality: From World Federalism to the CIA* (New York: Harper and Row, 1980); Thomas W. Braden, interview with author, 18 June 2001, Woodbridge, VA.
7. See Arnold J. Zurcher, *The Struggle to Unite Europe, 1940–58* (Westport, CT: Greenwood Press, 1975), chaps. 1–2.

8. Richard Coudenhove-Kalergi to Allen Dulles, 12 April 1948, Allen W. Dulles Papers, Seeley G. Mudd Manuscript Library, Princeton University.
9. For a more detailed account of these events, see Stephen Dorril, *MI6: Fifty Years of Special Operations* (London: Fourth Estate, 2000), pp. 455–64. See also the extremely informative doctoral dissertation by F. X. Rebattet, son of EM officer George Rebattet, 'The European Movement, 1945–53: A study in national and international non-governmental organisations working for European unity', Ph.D. thesis, Oxford (1962).
10. Allen Dulles to Charles R. Hook, 12 July 48, Dulles Papers.
11. ACUE Executive Committee minutes, 1 July 1949, ACUE Papers, Lauinger Library, Georgetown University.
12. ACUE Board of Directors minutes, 17 March 1949, Dulles Papers; ACUE, programme for luncheon in honour of Winston Churchill, 29 March 1949, Dulles Papers.
13. Braden interview.
14. Tom Braden to Allen Dulles, 14 November 1949, Dulles Papers.
15. See Aldrich, 'OSS, CIA and European Unity', 203–5.
16. Indeed, there was some overlap between the western European operations of the ACUE and the eastern bloc activities of the NCFE. See Aldrich, *Hidden Hand*, p. 364.
17. Braden interview.
18. John Blumgart, 'ACUE: Notes on organization and finances', 15 April 1957, Paul G. Hoffman Papers, Harry S. Truman Library, Independence, Missouri.
19. Aldrich suggests that ACUE's total budget for its entire existence was about £4 million. Of course, not all American funding for the European unity campaign came from the CIA. Private donors and other US government agencies such as the ECA also contributed. See Aldrich, 'OSS, CIA and European Unity', 212–13.
20. Joseph Retinger to Shepard Stone, 11 December 1956, Joseph Retinger Papers, Polish Library, London.
21. John Blumgart, 'Meeting with Mr Hoffman', 8 October 1957, Hoffman Papers.
22. Allan Hovey Jr., 'Meeting with the *Ad Hoc* Committee', 18 January 1958, Hoffman Papers.
23. For more on the Labour government's attitudes towards Europe, see John W. Young, *Britain and European Unity, 1945–99* (Basingstoke: Macmillan, 2000), pp. 16–24.
24. Victor Gollancz to Bertrand Russell, 12 June 1947, Victor Gollancz Papers, Modern Records Centre, Warwick University.
25. Morgan Phillips to Labour MPs, 21 April 1948, International Department, Labour Party Papers, National Museum of Labour History, Manchester.
26. Anonymous, 'The Labour Party and the European Movement', 31 May 1949, Labour Party Papers.
27. See Aldrich, 'OSS, CIA and European Unity', 196.

28. See Denis Healey, report on Consultative Assembly of Council of Europe, 10–23 August 1949, Labour Party Papers; Denis Healey, report on Second Session of the Consultative Assembly of Council of Europe, 7–28 August 1950, Labour Party Papers.
29. Arthur Bax, 'Press Conference', 8 June 1950, Hugh Dalton Papers, British Library of Political and Economic Science, London.
30. See Tom Braden to Allen Dulles, 28 December 1949, Dulles Papers.
31. William Donovan to European leaders, 20 December 1949, Dulles Papers.
32. See Aldrich, 'OSS, CIA and European Unity', 200–1.
33. Cuttings from *New York Times*, 21 February 1950, ACUE Papers.
34. 'News from the ACUE', 19 June 1950, Dulles Papers.
35. See, for example, Richard Coudenhove-Kalergi to Allen Dulles, 30 November 1948, Dulles Papers.
36. See, for example, Joseph Retinger to Duncan Sandys, 18 November 1949, Retinger Papers.
37. Joseph Retinger to Duncan Sandys, 12 March 1950, Retinger Papers.
38. Joseph Retinger to Duncan Sandys, 31 March 1950, Retinger Papers.
39. Braden interview.
40. Tom Braden to Walter Bedell Smith, 26 June 1950, Walter Bedell Smith Papers, Dwight D. Eisenhower Library, Abilene, Kansas.
41. Tom Braden to G. H. A. Clowes, 7 July 1950, Dulles Papers.
42. Anonymous, 'Work at Strasbourg, August-September 1950', 26 September 1950, ACUE Papers.
43. ACUE Executive Committee minutes, 26 September 1950, ACUE Papers.
44. William P. Durkee, ACUE Annual Report, 16 March 1951, ACUE Papers.
45. Tom Braden to Allen Dulles, 27 August 1950, Dulles Papers.
46. ACUE preliminary meeting minutes, 5 January 1949, Dulles Papers.
47. Tom Braden to Walter Washington, 4 January 1951, Dulles Papers.
48. William Durkee, ACUE annual report, May 1952, ACUE Papers.
49. See Rebattet, 'The European Movement', pp. 143–4, 162–6.
50. ACUE Executive Committee minutes, 20 January 1950, ACUE Papers.
51. Tom Braden, 'Activities of the American Committee on United Europe', April 1950, ACUE Papers. 'In attempting to ascertain the influence and practicability of Mackay's proposals, the Executive Director has asked many opinions', reported Braden. Among those approached were Harold Butler and Lord Layton.
52. Tom Braden to G. H. A. Clowes, 7 July 1950, Dulles Papers.
53. Durkee, ACUE annual report.
54. See 'The Mackay Plan', R. W. G. Mackay Papers, British Library of Political and Economic Science, London.
55. Tom Braden to Walter Washington, 4 January 1951, Dulles Papers.
56. Tom Braden, 'Activities of the American Committee on United Europe', April 1950, ACUE Papers; George S. Franklin Jr. to Walter Bedell Smith, 3

December 1951, Dulles Papers; William Durkee, Report to Directors of ACUE, no date [probably late 1951], ACUE Papers. Even Frank Wisner of the OPC remarked on Mackay's 'valuable contribution on behalf of European Unity'. Quoted in Aldrich, *Hidden Hand*, p. 350.

57. Anonymous, 'Work at Strasbourg, August–September 1950', 26 September 1950, ACUE Papers.
58. See Durkee, ACUE annual report.
59. Hugh Dalton to Clement Attlee, 10 September 1949, Dalton Papers.
60. Hugh Dalton, 'Council of Europe: Consultative Assembly', no date [probably 1951], Dalton Papers.
61. See Durkee, Report to Directors of ACUE.
62. See Durkee, ACUE annual report.
63. See Dorril, *MI6*, p. 469. For more detail on EYC, see Aldrich, *Hidden Hand*, pp. 360–2.
64. See Allan Hovey Jr., 'London Report', 20 April 1957, Hoffman Papers.
65. See Dorril, *MI6*, p. 469.
66. John Blumgart, 'Report to Directors of ACUE', April 1958, Hoffman Papers.
67. Anonymous, 'Meeting with Geoffrey de Freitas at House of Commons', 30 July 1957, Hoffman Papers.
68. See, for example, Brian Goddard to Joseph Retinger, 29 May 1953, Retinger Papers.
69. John Blumgart, 'European Programs: Adult Activities', 15 April 1957, Hoffman Papers.
70. See Hovey, 'London Report'.
71. See Blumgart, 'Report to Directors of ACUE'.
72. See Allan Hovey Jr., 'Britain and Europe Study', 24 February 1958, Hoffman Papers.
73. Blumgart, 'Report to Directors of ACUE'.
74. Blumgart, 'European Programs'. ACUE also had links to the Political and Economic Planning group, a kind of British version of the Council on Foreign Relations with a strong interest in European union. See John Blumgart, 'Talks with Kermit Gordon and Shepard Stone', 20 June 1957, Hoffman Papers.
75. See, for example, Winston Churchill to William Donovan, 4 June 1949, Dulles Papers.
76. See Aldrich, 'OSS, CIA and European Unity', 186.
77. See, for example, Hugh Dalton to Ernest Bevin, 21 August 1950, Dalton Papers, in which he complains about the isolation of the Labour delegation at Strasbourg due to 'the Federalist and phrase-mongering tendencies here'.
78. Anonymous, 'ACUE, Hoffman-Benton trip, July 19–August 9 1957, arrangements as of July 12, 1957', Hoffman Papers.
79. Quoted in Stephen Howe, 'Labour and international affairs', in Duncan Tanner, Pat Thane and Nick Tiratsoo (eds), *Labour's First Century* (Cambridge University Press, 2000), p. 132.

80. C. D. Jackson quoted in Alden Hatch, *HRH Prince Bernhard of the Netherlands: An Authorized Biography* (London: Harrap, 1962), p. 213.
81. See Hatch, *Prince Bernhard*, pp. 214–15; John Pomian (ed.), *Joseph Retinger: Memoirs of an Eminence Grise* (Brighton: Sussex University, 1972), pp. 250–1.
82. Colin Gubbins to Hugh Gaitskell, 27 June 1952, Hugh Gaitskell Papers, University College London.
83. Meeting in Paris minutes, 25 September 1952, Gaitskell Papers.
84. Prince Bernhard to Walter Bedell Smith, 19 February 1953, C. D. Jackson Papers, Dwight D. Eisenhower Library, Abilene, Kansas. See also Joseph Retinger, 'Bilderberg Meetings', April 1962, RO 5464 Grant No. 560–0341, Ford Foundation Papers, New York, which reveals attempts by Retinger and Bernhard to interest members of the outgoing Democratic administration, in particular Averell Harriman, in the document.
85. Walter Bedell Smith to C. D. Jackson, 9 July 1953, Jackson Papers.
86. C. D. Jackson to Prince Bernhard, 15 July 1953, Jackson Papers.
87. C. D. Jackson to Ann Whitman, 19 November 1954, Jackson Papers.
88. John Coleman to C. D. Jackson, 25 November 1953, Jackson Papers.
89. 'European–American relations. European Committee – Report No. 2', Gaitskell Papers.
90. John C. Hughes to C. D. Jackson, 10 February 1954, Jackson Papers.
91. John Coleman to C. D. Jackson, 17 March 1954, Jackson Papers; Prince Bernhard to Hugh Gaitskell, 13 April 1954, Gaitskell Papers.
92. See Hatch, *Prince Bernhard*, p. 212.
93. C. D. Jackson to Walter Bedell Smith, 7 January 1955, Jackson Papers.
94. John H. Ferguson to Edward Littlejohn, 17 August 1954, Jackson Papers.
95. C. D. Jackson to Edward Littlejohn, 5 August 1954, Jackson Papers.
96. C. D. Jackson to Ann Whitman, 19 November 1954, Jackson Papers. These comments are echoed in Jackson's later description of Retinger to Alden Hatch as 'a very difficult, very opinionated man who would not take no for an answer and often achieved his purpose by very devious means'. Quoted in Hatch, *Prince Bernhard*, pp. 213–14.
97. Prince Bernhard to Dwight Eisenhower, 30 October 1954, Jackson Papers.
98. Ann Whitman to C. D. Jackson, 20 November 1954, Jackson Papers; Dwight Eisenhower to Prince Bernhard, 23 November 1954, Jackson Papers.
99. Prince Bernhard to C. D. Jackson, 29 November 1954, Jackson Papers.
100. Joseph Retinger to Joseph E. Johnson, 28 May 1955, Retinger Papers. ACUE officials appear to have had similar reservations about Retinger's role in the campaign for European unity. In 1957, when discussions were being held to establish an informal group of leading European federalists to discuss the future direction of the European Movement, John Blumgart noted that Bernhard's assistant 'had his own conception of the character and composition of the *ad hoc* committee, and wanted to run away with the ball'. Blumgart, 'Meeting with Mr Hoffman'.

101. C. D. Jackson to Edward Littlejohn, 5 August 1954, Jackson Papers. 'It does mean, however', Jackson continued, 'that in certain endeavors, and where there is major cleavage between the British and the Americans, he [Retinger] should be handled carefully'.
102. Dwight D. Eisenhower to Prince Bernhard, 23 November 1954, Jackson Papers; C. D. Jackson to Ann Whitman, 19 November 1954, Jackson Papers.
103. See meeting in Paris minutes, 6 December 1954, Gaitskell Papers.
104. C. D. Jackson to Walter Bedell Smith, 7 January 1955, Jackson Papers.
105. C. D. Jackson to Ann Whitman, 26 January 1955, Jackson Papers.
106. Joseph M. McDaniel Jr. to Joseph Johnson, 15 April 1955, RO 421 Grant No. 55–79, Ford Foundation Papers.
107. Philip M. Williams (ed.), *The Diary of Hugh Gaitskell, 1945–56* (London: Jonathan Cape, 1983), p. 516, fn. 36.
108. Meeting in Paris minutes, 6 December 1954, Gaitskell Papers.
109. Sam Watson to Hugh Gaitskell, 4 May 1954, Sam Watson Papers, Durham County Record Office, Durham.
110. Denis Healey to Hugh Gaitskell, 21 May 1958, Gaitskell Papers.
111. Hugh Gaitskell to Victor Cavendish-Bentinck, 11 March 1958, Gaitskell Papers.
112. Joseph Retinger to Hugh Gaitskell, 24 January 1958, Gaitskell Papers.
113. Steering Committee meeting minutes, 12 July 1956, Gaitskell Papers.
114. Hugh Gaitskell to Denis Healey, 8 March 1954, Gaitskell Papers.
115. Hugh Gaitskell to Joseph Retinger, 1 February 1954, Gaitskell Papers.
116. Paul Rykens to Hugh Gaitskell, 18 May 1954, Gaitskell Papers; Paul Rykens to Oliver Franks, 18 May 1954, Gaitskell Papers.
117. David Rockefeller to Hugh Gaitskell, 12 July 1954, Gaitskell Papers. Gaitskell received a similar letter from C. D. Jackson. C. D. Jackson to Hugh Gaitskell, 23 June 1954, Gaitskell Papers.
118. Denis Healey, *The Time of My Life* (London: Michael Joseph, 1989), p. 196.
119. Ibid.
120. C. D. Jackson to Allen Dulles, 6 August 1953, Jackson Papers.
121. See, for example, Paul Rykens, 'Europe–America Group: Contributions received from 1952 to 31 March 1955', RO 421 Grant No. 55–79, Ford Foundation Papers.
122. See Dorril, *MI6*, p. 458.
123. C. D. Jackson to Ann Whitman, 19 November 1954, Jackson Papers.
124. C. D. Jackson, diary log, May 29–31 1954, Jackson Papers.
125. Hatch, *Prince Bernhard*, p. 217.
126. Jackson, diary log.
127. See Hatch, *Prince Bernhard*, pp. 218, 222.
128. Ibid., p. 222.
129. See Pomian, *Joseph Retinger*, p. 256; Michael Heilperin, 'The Fifth Bilder-

berg Conference (St Simon's Island, Georgia, 14–17 February, 1957)', 23 February 1957, Jackson Papers.

130. Heilperin, 'Fifth Bilderberg Conference'. See also Denis Healey, 'Nationalism and neutralism in the Western Community', Jackson Papers.

131. Heilperin, 'Fifth Bilderberg Conference'. See also Denis Healey, 'The diplomacy of liberation', Jackson Papers.

132. Heilperin, 'Fifth Bilderberg Conference'.

133. C. D. Jackson, notes of discussion at St Simon's Island, February 1957, Jackson Papers.

134. C. D. Jackson to Henry Luce et al., 19 February 1957, Jackson Papers.

135. Denis Healey, 'Living with Khrushschev', August 1958, Gaitskell Papers.

136. 'HG's paper – sent to Retinger on 13 May 1954', Gaitskell Papers.

137. See Lawrence Black, '"The Bitterest Enemies of Communism": Labour revisionists, Atlanticism and the Cold War', *Contemporary British History* 15.3 (2001), 49. Sir Anthony Buzzard, former head of Naval Intelligence, was another ISS founder who attended Bilderberg.

138. See Black, '"Bitterest Enemies"'.

139. See Hatch, *Prince Bernhard*, p. 218.

140. See, particularly, Kees van der Pijl, *Transnational Classes and International Relations* (London: Routledge, 1998). A useful summary of the transnational thesis is provided in Kees van der Pijl, 'Transnational class formation and state forms', in Stephen Gill and James M. Mittelman (eds), *Innovation and Transformation in International Studies* (Cambridge University Press, 1997), pp. 118–33.

141. See Kees van der Pijl, *The Making of an Atlantic Ruling Class* (London: Verso, 1984). Another illuminating discussion of Bilderberg from an 'IR' perspective can be found in Stephen Gill, *American Hegemony and the Trilateral Commission* (Cambridge University Press, 1990), chap. 6.

8

The Uses of *Encounter*

When in 1967 the news broke in the American and British press that the Congress for Cultural Freedom had been covertly financed by the CIA, it was the organisation's English-language magazine, *Encounter*, which attracted the most vitriolic denunciations. Launched in 1953 in London under the joint editorship of established British poet Stephen Spender and young New York intellectual Irving Kristol, this monthly, literary–political periodical had rapidly developed a reputation as one of the best, if not *the* best, 'highbrow' journals in the English-speaking world. The revelation that such a prestigious intellectual forum had been secretly subsidised by the CIA – rumours to this effect had circulated for years but had always been vehemently denied by those involved – shocked and disgusted many younger British and American writers, who interpreted it as damning proof of not only the immorality of the CIA but also the ideological bankruptcy of the previous generation of non-communist left intellectuals. The latter defended themselves by arguing that the CCF's source of funding was immaterial, as *Encounter* had always enjoyed complete editorial independence of its sponsor.[1]

This claim was regarded with scepticism at the time and has been challenged repeatedly since, most recently – and convincingly – by Frances Stonor Saunders, who demonstrates in *Who Paid the Piper?* that *Encounter*'s editors were in fact subjected to constant pressure from the CCF's officers, particularly Michael Josselson, and that on at least two occasions articles due to be published in the magazine were pulled due to objections from the CIA. Saunders also reveals the extent of British collusion in the deception. While individuals such as Spender might have been genuinely 'unwitting', many others were well aware of the secret US government backing thanks to their connections with either the Information Research Department or MI6, both of which had helped the CIA plan and set up *Encounter* in the first place (and maintained an interest in the venture thereafter, IRD by placing staff in the magazine's offices and SIS by covertly paying for the British editor's salary). Indeed, *Encounter* emerges from Saunders's account as very much a joint, Anglo–American intelligence operation.[2]

The aim of this chapter is not to defend *Encounter* against charges that it was editorially beholden to the CIA – the evidence Saunders produces on that score is conclusive – but rather to explore further her theme of British collusion. The focus will be less on intelligence operatives, however, than on intellectuals, in particular two groups of British non-communist left intellectuals with whom *Encounter* was associated, that is Modernist Bloomsbury *literati* like Spender and those revisionist Labour Party thinkers, such as Anthony Crosland, who drew close to the magazine during the late 1950s. Why did such intellectuals have anything to do with a journal they either knew was CIA-sponsored or about which they must at least have entertained strong suspicions? Or, to put the question another way, what did they get out of their association with it? What were the *uses* of *Encounter*?

THE BRITISH EDITOR

The story of *Encounter*'s founding has been told at length several times before, so will not be related again here.[3] One point worth emphasising, however is that far from being an alien imposition on Britain's Cold War intellectuals by the CIA, the magazine was largely designed by British *literati*. As noted earlier, George Orwell's friend and successor as literary editor of *Tribune*, T. R. Fyvel, was discussing with various potential British and American collaborators the possibility of launching a new 'Anglo–American left-of-centre' publication, to be called the *Transatlantic*, as early as the summer of 1951.[4] Meanwhile, Spender used his position as an officer of the British Society for Cultural Freedom to pressurise the CCF's Parisian headquarters into terminating its support for Michael Goodwin's *Twentieth Century* and starting up a new literary journal in the style of the defunct *Horizon*, with him as editor.[5] Spender was still pursuing this idea independently in the spring of 1953, corresponding with his friend, the American poet and 'New Critic' Allen Tate, about the possibility of co-editing an Anglo–American 'little magazine', when the Congress approached him with the proposal that became *Encounter*. Initially, the plan was to base the publication in Paris and target it primarily at an Asian audience (François Bondy, director of the CCF's publications programme, had just returned from a tour of the Indian sub-continent and Far East greatly concerned about the growth of neutralist and fellow-travelling sentiment in those regions).[6] This was not enough, however, to satisfy Spender's literary colleagues in the British Society for Cultural Freedom, Fyvel, Fredric Warburg and Malcolm Muggeridge, who travelled to Paris calling for the projected magazine to be published instead in London.[7] Uncharacteristically, Michael Josselson gave in to these demands; whether he was persuaded by the force of the British group's argument or, more likely, received instructions from the CIA, is unclear. Either way, Britain's literary intellectuals had served notice that they fully intended having their say in the new magazine: *Encounter* was to be their project, too.[8]

Although he gave off the air of 'a kindly, absent-minded uncle', in fact no one had a clearer idea of the kind of publication he wanted *Encounter* to be – and not be – than Stephen Spender.[9] One feature of Spender's editorial vision present from the outset was his desire to avoid the appearance of serving merely as a mouthpiece for the CCF: to be accepted by literary intellectuals, his new magazine needed to have a 'personality' or 'character' of its own. His thinking on this score seems to have been guided by the recent experience of the Ford Foundation, whose attempts to launch an American literary journal aimed at a Euro-pean market, *Perspectives USA*, had foundered because the publication was perceived as so obviously an institutional fabrication.[10] (Indeed, it was almost as if *Perspectives* acted as a kind of negative template for *Encounter*: when the question of what title the CCF's new English-language magazine should have was being discussed in the summer of 1953, an early suggestion, *Outlook*, was dropped because it reminded the editors too much of 'that miserable Ford Foundation journal').[11] When in November 1953 Sidney Hook raised the possibility at a meeting of the CCF's Executive Committee of *Encounter* doing more to publicise its sponsor's principles and programme, Muggeridge 'argued against making the magazine overtly an organ of the Congress, because that would destroy its effectiveness'. Speaking after Muggeridge, Spender argued strongly that the more the CCF was seen not to meddle in the affairs of its magazines, the more European intellectuals would respect it.[12] Not for the last time, the British poet had subtly equated the cause of cultural freedom with his own editorial independence.

An allied concern of Spender's was that the new magazine should avoid any hint of Cold War propaganda. British intellectuals would

16 Stephen Spender, poet, editor of *Encounter* and CIA 'unwitting asset'.
(Photograph by Ida Kar, National Portrait Gallery, London)

'simply refuse to write for us', he told the CCF's Executive Committee, if they perceived *Encounter* as 'a subsidised American magazine [created] for the purpose of putting across the American version of the Cold War'. It was not that he objected to pro-American material per se; indeed, he was all in favour of 'positive', 'constructive' pieces written from an American point of view. What he did not want to see in *Encounter* was the 'negative', 'nagging', '"How we hate Stalin" kind of articles' that appeared in such US publications as *The New Leader*.[13] Anti-communist polemics would not only strike the wrong note in Britain, where intellectuals were less preoccupied with communism than in America; they would actually be counter-productive, because they would provoke suspicion of the CCF's motives in promoting the cause of cultural freedom. Far better, therefore, for *Encounter* to concentrate on the positive promotion of cultural standards and leave its readers to work out the political implications for themselves. '[W]e must speak for Culture', explained Spender, 'if we wish to plead the case for cultural freedom'.[14]

Finally, and again clearly linked to his other arguments, Spender urged that *Encounter* be allowed to build up a firm base of support for itself in Britain before attempting to create an international profile. Only when the magazine had established a sense of community between itself and British intellectuals, he insisted, would it have sufficient 'authenticity' and 'credibility' to command the respect of Asian readers.[15]

Spender's advocacy of his editorial vision was not limited to speaking out at CCF meetings. It also involved mounting a personal campaign against his American co-editor, Kristol, similar to that he had conducted against Michael Goodwin two years earlier. Although Kristol was clearly well qualified for the post – after his spell at *The New Leader* he had helped to edit the American Jewish Committee's brilliant new organ, *Commentary* – he was ten years younger and considerably less well-known than the famous Thirties poet Spender.[16] Although the editorial partnership between this unlikely pairing of MacSpaunDay and City College at first appeared to work reasonably well – under the terms of a division of labour worked out in the summer of 1953, the American editor was to take responsibility for the magazine's political coverage, and leave the cultural side entirely to his British colleague – it was not long before personal relations began to sour. Within months of the appearance in October 1953 of the first issue – which included Kristol's greatest coup as editor of *Encounter*, Leslie A. Fiedler's controversial essay on the American atom spies Julius and Ethel Rosenberg[17] – Spender was writing to Michael Josselson in Paris to complain that his American co-editor was selecting for publication precisely the kind of negative, anti-communist polemic he had warned against. Besides offending the political sensibilities of the magazine's British readers, these pieces – most of which originated, Spender noted, from 'Irving's clique of friends at *Commentary* and *The New Leader*' – were for the most part very poorly written ('mangled, chopped up and generally messed about'), giving the impression of having been 'dictated by a committee of tough Americans'.[18]

> In the long run the magazine will eventually be killed off by the boredom of articles about politics which are really a kind of back-street slanging in Brooklyn between different groups all of whose surnames are Rosenberg: Republican Rosenbergs, Democrat Rosenbergs, anxious to distinguish themselves from THE Rosenbergs.[19]

By March 1954 Spender's dissatisfaction with Kristol's performance had expanded to include his editorial style ('my dear co-editor's ... love of chopping things up keeps me awake at nights'), his reluctance to seek professional advice on such technical matters as typography and various alleged personality defects, including negativity and uncommunicative-ness.[20] For an apparently 'sweet' and '*distrait*' character, Spender went after Kristol with a surprising degree of ruthlessness.[21]

Spender's campaign against Kristol clearly succeeded in damaging the American's standing in the eyes of the CCF, as it was not long before moves were made to replace him with another American editor (although, as is discussed below, Michael Josselson had additional reasons for wanting rid of him). However, the clearest evidence that Spender's efforts to turn *Encounter* into an overwhelmingly cultural, British venture were having some effect is available in the form of the magazine itself. A content analysis of issues from its first two years of existence carried out by British researcher Jeremy Howard has revealed that, whereas only 18 'exclusively political contributions' appeared in this period, there were 37 pieces 'about general cultural issues ..., 24 short stories and no less than 99 poems'. Moreover, 'among the cultural contributions, the British literary establishment dominated', with Americans and Asians 'conspicuous by their absence'.[22] Indeed, as Howard also notes, by 1955 the magazine appeared pretty much to have abandoned its original mission of appealing primarily to Asian readers.[23]

Ironically, the single most talked-about article published during this time, the one which (as Irving Kristol put it) 'allowed us to "break through" our previous circle of readers', was an essay by Nancy Mitford about the cultural mores of 'The English Aristocracy' expounding the previously obscure academic theory of 'U and non-U'.[24] According to Kristol, the CCF's officers in Paris were perplexed by British readers' predilection for such frivolous fare.[25]

This bemusement was shared by Kristol's erstwhile colleagues at the American Committee for Cultural Freedom in New York, who were dismayed by the direction its parent organisation's new English-language organ appeared to be taking. There had been voices raised against *Encounter* in New York from the beginning, mainly belonging to magazine editors such as Elliot Cohen of *Commentary*, who perceived the CCF publication as a rival to their own.[26] Some New York intellectuals criticised the new magazine from a left-wing perspective: in 1954 *Dissent*, the organ of such diehard radicals as Irving Howe, printed a letter by Harold Rosenberg which, it claimed, *Encounter* had attempted to suppress (a charge emphatically denied by Kristol) attacking Fiedler's piece on the Rosenbergs.[27] (Incidentally, Sidney Hook suspected that the editors of *Partisan Review* only published Howe's famous protest against the conservative mood of the 1950s, 'This Age of Conformity', which contained barbs aimed at, *inter alia*, Hook himself, Lionel Trilling and Kristol, because they had failed 'to get money from various Foundations, from the Congress or from the Committee.... Kristol is singled out especially since they regard *Encounter* as a special threat to *PR*'.)[28] That said, the main criticism of the CCF's periodical was the more familiar, hardline anti-communist refrain that it was not tackling the challenge of Stalinism with sufficient vigour. There was not 'a single fighting anti-Communist magazine in Britain', Sol Levitas (editor, of course, of another competitor magazine largely ignored by the CCF) told Irving Brown in January 1954, 'and that includes *Encounter*, too'.[29] Himself the veteran – and victor – of several editorial faction fights, Levitas had a pretty good idea what was going on in London. The reason *Encounter* had 'become a "Greenwich Village", esoteric magazine', he explained to Josselson a year later, was that 'Spender dominates [it] completely'.[30] As in earlier, similar disputes, it was up to the unfortunate Sidney Hook to put the ACCF's case to its parent organisation. 'Members of the American Committee who read *Encounter* regard it as a "*belletristic*" [sic] organ', he informed a meeting of the CCF's Executive Committee in January 1955. 'They think that *Encounter* ought to carry material of general political significance even if it doesn't take a definite political point of view.' Few of the other Committee members agreed, however. 'I am very glad that [*Encounter*] does not have the aspect of certain American magazines', Nicolas Nabokov retorted, 'because I do not think that it would be read, if it were to take these aspects'. Sensing the general support of the meeting, Spender cunningly seized the opportunity to restate his editorial vision:

> Now, my conception of *Encounter* is that ... [it] ought to be a debate ... carried on in good faith between American opinion and European opinion, leaving out the whole cold-war aspect of the thing.... It is simply too dangerous for us to publish anything in the nature of propaganda.[31]

A final piece of evidence that – at least at this early stage – Spender was succeeding in his attempts to dictate the editorial direction of *Encounter* is provided by the British critical reception of the magazine. Much as with the first attempts of the CCF to establish a presence in Britain, initial reactions to the appearance of *Encounter* were predominantly negative. The 'police-review of American-occupied countries' was how *The Times* columnist 'Atticus' described it. 'We were ... criticised for being "official-looking", impersonal and too "anti-Communist"', Spender recalled in 1955. 'In effect, we were accused of bad faith.'[32] Gradually, however, at the same time that the New York intellectuals were becoming increasingly dissatisfied with the magazine, their British counterparts were growing more receptive. The transformation of the *Spectator*'s attitude is illustrative. Reviewing the first issue of *Encounter* in October 1953, essayist Anthony Hartley claimed to have detected 'something of the pomposity of official culture' in it, dismissed the Fiedler article as 'ignoble' and concluded, 'It would be a pity if *Encounter* ... were to become a mere weapon in the Cold War'. A year later, the same reviewer was more kindly disposed towards the new magazine, remarking, for example, that the 'literary side of it' had 'perked up considerably'. In August 1955 'Pharos' gave *Encounter* the *Spectator*'s seal of critical approval, declaring it 'one of the very few monthlies of generalised intellectual interest in Britain today'.[33] These changes in critical reception were accompanied by other salutary developments: a steady rise in circulation – by 1955 sales stood at 14,000, exceptionally high for an intellectual review – and a growing number of contributions from British writers who had previously hung back. Most important, though, in Spender's opinion, was *Encounter*'s success in achieving 'a reputation for good faith'.[34] Evidently the British editor's strategy of downplaying the magazine's institutional origins, avoiding the appearance of political propaganda and maximising its British connections was working.

BLOOMSBURY VERSUS THE ANGRY YOUNG MEN

Cultural historians writing about a variety of countries in the early Cold War period have noticed a tendency amongst local intellectuals involved in the US Cultural Cold War effort to use American patronage in domestic projects which had no immediately obvious relevance to the anti-communist struggle. This tendency was particularly pronounced in the Congress for Cultural Freedom's magazine-publishing programme. According to literary historian John McClaren, *Quadrant*, the CCF's Australian organ, was deployed by 'cultural conservatives' in a local culture war with 'radical nationalists' grouped around rival journal *Overland*. To be sure, Cold War ideological positions were taken in this contest, but the main issue at stake was not so much global geopolitics as the future shape of Australian literary culture.[35] Anti-communism was even less of a concern in India where, according to Margery Sabin, intellectuals associated with the CCF publication *Quest* were preoccupied 'by internal cultural aspirations of little interest to their foreign sponsors'.[36] Indeed, the concept of 'cultural freedom' itself acquired a different meaning in an Indian context, where intellectuals such as *Quest*'s editor Nissim Ezekial invoked it in 'a specifically Indian project of internal "opposition to authority"'.[37] Not only did this project have little to do with American Cold War interests, Indian intellectuals turned the discourse of cultural freedom back against those 'Western liberals who seemed overeager to endorse indigenous Indian traditions when they seemed to serve their anti-Communist politics'.[38] What is being suggested here is that British intellectuals also succeeded, to a certain extent, in appropriating *Encounter* from the CCF and using it in ways unintended by the CIA. Moreover, in a manoeuvre similar to that performed by Ezekial, Stephen Spender employed the rhetoric of cultural freedom *against* his patrons, specifically as a kind of discursive smokescreen for this act of appropriation.

How, then, did British intellectuals use the cultural space cleared for them by Spender in *Encounter*? For scholars at British universities, the magazine appears to have served as a point of access to a wider, public audience beyond the confines of their academic discipline. Perhaps the most notable example of this kind of use being made of *Encounter* is provided by Hugh Trevor-Roper. Although he had led British opposition to the Congress for Cultural Freedom in 1950, the Oxford historian soon became a frequent contributor to, indeed supporter of, the CCF's English-language organ. His best-known piece published during the 1950s was a scathing critique of Arnold Toynbee's gloomy treatise on the self-destructive urges of European civilisation, *Study of History* (so scathing, in fact, that it was only printed after extensive consultations with *Encounter*'s lawyers).[39] For an academic such as Trevor-Roper who also aspired to the status of public intellectual, *Encounter* was the ideal publishing venue. It had a much greater circulation than any scholarly journal, yet, unlike the newspapers, published 5,000-word essays. 'I liked *Encounter* because writing for it suited me', he later recalled. 'I wanted to express my views and it expressed them for me.'[40] Such a pragmatic attitude was probably not unique amongst *Encounter*'s academic contributors.

However, it was literary intellectuals – or, to be more precise, a particular group of writers who had established their literary reputations before or during the 1930s and who in the 1940s were to be found editing or writing for *Horizon* – who made the most use of *Encounter*. The evidence that Spender conceived of the CCF's new magazine as a platform for those Bloomsbury *literati* who had been deprived of one when *Horizon* folded is abundant. To begin with, there is the con- temporary testimony of his colleague Kristol, who noticed that Spender moved 'within a small literary–artistic clique' made up of members of 'the older literary generation (Cyril Connolly, etc.)'.[41] Similarly, while the majority of British reviewers preferred *Encounter*'s cultural to its political side, a number remarked adversely on the age profile of its literary contributors. 'The culture, whose freedom we are defending, is genuine', A. J. P. Taylor wrote in the *Listener*, 'but it seems to have been going for a very long time and it is getting a little thin on top'. '*The Dial* created reputations', A. Alvarez reminded readers of the *New Statesman*, '*Encounter* merely uses ready-made ones'.[42] This impression of 'establishment' domination is born out by Jeremy Howard's content analysis of the magazine's early issues. 'In the first two years', Howard found, 'W. H. Auden wrote three articles, Spender three, P. G. Wodehouse two, Herbert Read two, and Christopher Isherwood, Robert Graves and Kenneth Tynan one each.' The short stories and, particularly, poetry which appeared reflected a similar editorial bias, 'with Edith Sitwell, C. Day Lewis, ... Spender and W. H. Auden all making frequent contributions'.[43] Finally, there is the retrospective comment of such participants as Fredric Warburg, who in his memoirs frankly admitted that his 'personal objective right from the start' in helping to create *Encounter* was to 'fill the gap left by the lamentable death of Cyril Connolly's brilliant *Horizon*'.[44]

It was not merely a matter of whose work *Encounter* printed; equally significant was who got left out. At the same time that Spender was using *Encounter* to bolster the cultural power of the metropolitan avant-garde-turned-establishment, new, anti-Modernist, provincial impulses were making their presence felt in British literary life. Leavisite literary criticism, a body of critical theory and practice which de-emphasised those elements of Modernism which Bloomsbury was most inclined to privilege – cosmopolitanism, experimentalism, 'art-for-art's sake', alienation – was assisting in the institutionalisation of English studies at the 'red-brick' universities. Meanwhile, the poets of the 'Movement' – Thom Gunn, Donald Davie, Philip Larkin – were winning growing critical attention by writing a form of verse which owed less to Modernist poetics than more 'traditional', 'English' structures and methods.[45] With the very rare exception, neither Leavisite critics nor Movement poets were welcomed in the pages of *Encounter*. In the face of these challenges to established literary authority, the magazine consistently championed Modernist poetic conventions, if not explicitly in critical essays then implicitly in the Audenesque verses it printed, while at the same time taking passing potshots at provincial and academic intellectual culture.[46]

The greatest threat to the cultural capital of Bloomsbury, however, came not from the poets of the Movement but from its novelists and dramatists, the so-called Angry Young Men. The books of Kingsley Amis and plays of John Osborne, with their provincial settings, working or lower-middle-class heroes and deliberate formal simplicity, constituted a clear rebuke to the dominant literary culture, characterised by Leslie Fiedler (ironically enough in the pages of *Encounter* itself) as 'a blend of homosexual sensibility, upper-class aloofness, liberal politics and avant-garde literary devices'. Indeed, it is possible to interpret the writing of the Angry Young Man as precisely about, to use Fiedler's words again, 'the comedy of his relationship to the writers of the '30s (who are not only a generation but a class away from him)'. Fiedler assumed that the cultural rebellion of the Angry Young Men was bound to succeed, because the 'world of wealth and leisure' they were seeking to replace had 'become quite unreal'.[47] This judgement, though, was premature: Bloomsbury still existed – thanks in part to the injection of patronage recently provided by the CCF – and, furthermore, had not lost its capacity for defusing threats to its hegemony by incorporating or 'recuperating' them. For their part, the Angry Young Men were not, as they themselves were prepared to admit, immune to the trappings of establishment recognition.[48] The scene was set for a complex and fraught cultural encounter which had many parallels with the confrontation taking place simultaneously across the Atlantic between the New York intellectuals and the Beat movement in the pages of *Partisan Review*.[49]

After opting initially for a strategy of simply ignoring the Angry Young Men, in 1957 the editors of *Encounter* appear to have toyed with the notion of promoting them. In October of that year, the magazine published extracts from two essays shortly to appear in a collection of Movement writing, *Declaration*, under the ironic heading 'This Scepter'd Isle'. Kenneth Tynan's contribution took the form of a letter addressed to a young friend about to graduate from Oxford offering advice on how to achieve literary success in 1950s Britain: conform politically with the 'middle-aged Swing to the Right'; avoid 'bad taste' and 'vulgarity', for a writer accused of these things will be 'an outcast for life'; adopt a patronising attitude to anything popular or American.[50] Whereas Tynan's tone was mordantly satirical, John Osborne's was savagely indignant. The 'idiocies' of British politicians were 'no longer funny' after the H-Bomb test on Christmas Island – 'the most debased criminal swindle in British history' – because they were 'not merely dangerous', they were 'murderous'. British veneration of the monarchy was a form of 'national [pig]-swill', British theatre was the 'Old Ladies' Home in the Haymarket' and so on.[51] In addition to lambasting such failings in the national culture, both pieces also offered pointers to a better future, Tynan identifying the jazz scene as containing the potential for a more spontaneous, tolerant and egalitarian society, and Osborne hymning the working-class world of his East End upbringing.

'We have suddenly got involved with the Angry Young Men', wrote Irving Kristol to Leslie Fiedler, shortly after the Tynan and Osborne essays appeared, 'and we should like to publish something detached about them, before people begin to gossip'.[52] Fiedler's essay about 'The Un-Angry Young Men' came out a few months later, but it proved to be less concerned with the rebelliousness of the British Movement

273

writers per se than the comparative conservatism of the latest generation of American intellectuals. Having flirted with the Angry Young Men, *Encounter*'s editors seem now to have gone off them – the negative response of the magazine's readership to the 'Scepter'd Isle' experiment might well have been a factor in this[53] – and the next article to deal with them did not appear until April 1959. In an essay commissioned by Spender, 'Revolt and Commitment', the twenty-five-year-old novelist and contributor to *Declaration*, Stuart Holroyd, appeared to turn his back on the Movement by dismissing 'most of our revolutionaries today' as 'class-conscious reactionaries with an axe to grind'. Rather than engaging in such acts of 'negative revolt', Holroyd pledged himself to a politics of positive 'commitment' and 'responsibility' – the same words, in fact, used by Spender and other intellectuals involved in the Congress for Cultural Freedom to describe their own politics of Cold War engagement.[54]

The final episode in *Encounter*'s short-lived romance with the Angry Young Men was the publication in July 1960 of an essay by Kingsley Amis, 'Lone Voices: View of the "Fifties"'. Although undeniably bad-tempered – among the targets of Amis's excoriating wit were American sociology, the advertising industry and the recently-expanded British higher education system – 'Lone voices' was not 'Angry'. Indeed, it explicitly rejected the use of any such label to categorise Amis's past fiction, demanding instead that his writing be read as 'a work of art' rather than 'a purée of trends and attitudes'. The Angry Young Men were, Amis suggested, a 1950s 'trend' which had 'encouraged a philistine, paraphrasing, digest-compiling attitude to literature'.[55]

Amis's deliberate distancing of himself from the Movement/Angry Young Men and affirmation of an art-for-art's sake aesthetic (which occurred, perhaps not coincidentally, not long after his somewhat belated renunciation of Stalinism) signalled a general move within British literary culture at the beginning of the 1960s away from the anti-Modernist mood of the mid-1950s towards a rejuvenated Modernism. The anti-establishment provincial revolt had failed; Spender and his Bloomsbury coterie, using the apparatus and rhetoric of the American Cultural Cold War effort in ways for which they were not originally designed, had headed it off. This is not to say, though, that the British *literati*'s subtle act of appropriation was also one of opposition, as was the case in India. Indeed, the Modernism they were helping to defend was itself a highly Americanised construct, consisting as it did mainly of critical theories borrowed from the New York intellectuals and New Critics, and a canon of texts that, in poetry for example, ran from T. S. Eliot and Ezra Pound to Robert Lowell and John Berryman. For that matter, the very category of 'Modernism' promulgated in British academe was, arguably, in large part an invention of American literary critics writing in the early Cold War period.[56] In this sense, then, the covert patronage of the CIA did work to uphold American dominance, but in a far more complex and *mediated* process than notions of 'Americanisation' or US 'cultural imperialism' would lead to one to suppose.

THE AMERICAN EDITOR

Confronted by the obvious ambition of the British editor to employ *Encounter* for domestic literary projects that, on the surface at least, had little to do with the Cold War, Michael Josselson began to have second thoughts about the cultural strategy he had been pursuing since taking control of the Congress for Cultural Freedom from Arthur Koestler in 1950. This is not to say he went over to the hardline camp of the New York intellectuals, whose doctrinaire, purist anti-communism remained a source of inconvenience and irritation for him for the rest of the decade. However, the excessively cultural drift of *Encounter* under Spender's influence did force him to consider ways of re-establishing American control over the magazine and inserting more explicitly political themes into it. The obvious way of doing this was through the American-owned slot on the editorial board, a position which Josselson clearly viewed as crucial not only to the operation of *Encounter* but to the CCF's pro-gramme as a whole. Eventually, the unusual degree of personal interest he showed in this post paid off, when it was filled in 1958 by Melvin Lasky, a 'witting' CIA agent who fully shared his vision of how the magazine ought to be run. Before then, however, Josselson was to experience problems with the American editorship of a sort typical of the CIA's relationship with the US non-communist left generally.

Although Spender frequently complained to Paris that Irving Kristol was filling *Encounter*'s pages with anti-communist, American material, in fact the opposite was true: it was the British, cultural side that domi-nated during the period of Kristol's editorship. In part, this might have been the consequence of the British editor's relentless campaigning against his American colleague. However, there is also evidence that Kristol naturally sympathised with aspects of Spender's editorial vision. As early as October 1953, he was writing to Josselson to advise him

275

against drawing attention to the CCF's sponsorship of *Encounter*, as it was 'fatal for a magazine in England ... to give any impression of [being] a "house organ"'.[57] He was similarly keen to defend the first issue against charges that it had featured too many 'Big Literary Names', arguing that such an approach was necessary in order to capture the attention of British and Asian writers. 'We here in London ... can better judge the situation than you can in Paris', he told Josselson, in words reminiscent of other British-based American NCL-ers reporting to their bosses, such as David Williams of the Union for Democratic Action and William Gausmann of the Economic Cooperation Agency.[58] As his habit of wearing a bowler hat to *Encounter*'s office illustrated, Kristol had, if in small part only, 'gone native'.

Josselson was infuriated by this development, berating the American editor in a manner which betrayed a disturbing disregard for *Encounter*'s editorial independence. 'We are not publishing cultural magazines with a capital C', he admonished Kristol in 1955. 'A good editor can't have a supercilious attitude and judge all contributions in terms of his own omniscience.'[59] If these and other pronouncements in the same vein by Josselson are shocking for the degree of external interference in *Encounter*'s affairs they reveal, no less remarkable is the determination shown on Kristol's side of the correspondence to protect his editorial freedom from Paris. 'I have a very clear idea of what the Congress wants, and of how one should go about getting it', he told Josselson. 'But I can't operate efficiently with the Paris office breathing down my neck, sending editorial directives, etc.'.[60] Or again:

> Perhaps I'm deluding myself, but I really think that in *Encounter* the Congress has hold of something far more important than even you realise.... Potentially, we have it in us to become, in a few months, *the* English-language cultural periodical.... [I]f I'm wrong, then you ought to get yourself another editor. But you've got to give us time and editorial freedom to achieve this....[61]

This frequent invocation of editorial freedom, the same rhetorical trump-card played by Spender at CCF Executive Committee meetings in Paris, shows that Kristol was quite adept at negotiating the patronage relationship with institutional sponsors (a skill learned, presumably, in the course of his spell at the American Jewish Committee's *Commentary*). It also backs up his later claims that he was not 'witting' of the US government's secret stake in *Encounter*.

Among Josselson's many gripes about Kristol's editorial performance in London was his alleged lack of interest in British Labour politics. One of *Encounter*'s main purposes, the CCF's Executive Director reminded the American editor (much as he had Michael Goodwin of *The Twentieth Century* two years earlier), was to combat the baleful influence on Britain's left-wing intellectuals of Kingsley Martin's *New Statesman*. Yet, under Kristol, the magazine had conspicuously failed to speak out on such matters as the Labour Party's apparent readiness to appease communist China. Kristol's response to Josselson's criticism was characteristically robust. 'This Labour Party fixation (sometimes even a *New Statesman and Nation*-fixation) is quite absurd', he told Josselson.

> We are not a substitute for a sensible Social-Democratic weekly and can't try to act as one. We cannot save the Labour Party from itself – that is beyond our powers. What we can do is to create a certain kind of intellectual–cultural milieu, which would in turn have far-reaching, but indirect, effects. [62]

As part of this effort to create a distinctive 'intellectual-cultural milieu', early in 1955 Kristol instituted occasional editorial dinners to which he invited such Labour intellectuals as Denis Healey and Anthony Crosland. Both subsequently served *Encounter* as important sources of advice – at a May 1956 dinner, for instance, Healey made 'some excellent suggestions for specific articles' – and, as is discussed below, contributions.[63] Evidently, Kristol had not lost the interest in the Labour right he had displayed whilst working as *The New Leader*'s London correspondent. In this respect, then, Josselson's charges were unfair.

That said, the guest-lists for the *Encounter* dinners were not restricted to Labour intellectuals. Rather, they represented a broad cross-section of British Cold War intellectual life – with the exception, of course, of the Bevanites and a noticeable bias towards individuals with intelligence connections – including as they did the likes of such conservatives as Michael Oakeshott.[64] In part, this reflected a preference of Kristol's for a broad, 'front' strategy in the Cultural Cold War of the sort advocated by James Burnham in 1950 and incarnated in the American Committee for Cultural Freedom, as opposed to the non-communist left orientation favoured by the CCF. However, it was not merely a question of tactics. Like Burnham (perhaps not coincidentally another ex-Trotskyist), Kristol had by the early 1950s grown thoroughly disaffected from liberalism – witness his infamous 1952 *Commentary* essay in which he appeared to pin the blame for McCarthyism on 'Commibut' American liberals – and was growing increasingly fascinated by conservatism. If anything, his move to *Encounter* appears to have accelerated this process, as it brought him into contact with a conservative tradition of far greater intellectual coherence and self-confidence than he had encountered in the US. Not only did he prefer mixing socially in conservative circles – Spender's literary friends, he later testified, were 'simply not my kind of people' as 'there was never any serious intellectual or political talk at their parties, just malicious, witty ... gossip', while even the company of 'right-wing Labourites' began to pall as he 'found their socialist beliefs ... ever more questionable' – he also 'took some satisfaction in publishing a few article by some of the younger, more gifted British Tories' such as Peregrine Worsthorne, Colin Welch and Henry Fairlie.[65] It was not, then, that Kristol was obsessed with negative anti-communism, as Spender and some left-wing New York intellectuals charged. Indeed, anti-communism as an intellectual project had ceased being of much interest to him. It was rather that he now perceived himself as a 'neo-conservative', whose main political concern was with critiquing 'the fundamental assumptions of contemporary liberalism'.[66]

This, of course, was the opposite of the CCF's main objective, which was precisely to defend western liberalism against communism. By 1955 Michael Josselson had had enough. 'I will not take time out to list all my grievances against Irving', he told Sidney Hook. 'Nor will I list all the efforts we here have made to try to put him on the right path.'[67] In April Kristol was summoned to Paris and given notice that he was going to be fired as American editor of *Encounter*. Soundings taken on both sides of the Atlantic had already produced a clear favourite for his replacement, the former one-man editor of *politics* and, more recently, *New Yorker* columnist Dwight Macdonald.[68] Spender was predictably delighted by these developments. 'I think the chance of having DM [*sic*] is the most amazing piece of good luck and should be seized', he urged Josselson.[69] Although some members of the American non-communist left, most notably Arthur Schlesinger Jr., shared this enthusiasm – Macdonald still had intellectual 'vitality and sparkle', he assured Josselson, but there had been a 'mellowing process' since his radical days[70] – the reaction of the anti-communist 'soreheads' on the ACCF was less favourable.[71] 'All of us are very disturbed by the fact that this exhibitionist may become the spokesman for us', Sol Levitas told Irving Brown, in the hope that the AFL operative might use his influence with the CIA to prevent Macdonald's appointment.[72]

Visiting New York in June to interview Macdonald, Josselson appears to have developed similar misgivings. The former anarchist was, he decided, a 'lone wolf type' who might treat *Encounter* as his 'own personal journal like *politics*' and 'resent any suggestions or intervention from the Congress'.[73] After returning to Europe a shaken Josselson tried, unsuccessfully, to patch things up with Kristol, who was understandably embittered by the treatment he had received at the hands of his employers.[74] The American editorship was by now a major quandary for the CCF's Executive Director. 'Either one of them is a headache', he told Hook in August, referring to the budding neo-conservative Kristol and incorrigible maverick Macdonald, 'though each one is a different kind of headache'.[75] The issue was still unsettled by September, when the Milan Future of Freedom conference witnessed an intense behind-the-scenes struggle between supporters of the rival candidates led by Schlesinger and Sidney Hook.[76] Eventually a compromise solution was worked out whereby Macdonald would join *Encounter* for one year only as a 'contributing editor' and Kristol stay on in his post on a kind of probationary basis.[77]

Macdonald immediately provided Josselson with evidence of the wisdom of this decision in the shape of a report on the Future of Freedom conference he had been commissioned to write for *Encounter*. 'No Miracle in Milan' was so unflattering and irreverent a portrait of the CCF that it was only published in December 1955, following a prolonged period of tortuous editorial negotiation with Macdonald, as 'a dissenting opinion' from a hastily written substitute piece by Edward Shils.[78] After this inauspicious start, it is perhaps not surprising that Macdonald's year-long spell at *Encounter*, which began in June 1956, was not considered a great success. Writing to Kristol after Macdonald's return to the US, Josselson listed the contributing editor's failings: despite being paid at over the Congress's normal rates, he had not written 'a single first-rate article'; an expensive trip to Egypt in the wake of the Suez crisis produced 'one of the worst pieces of reportage of all times' while other expeditions to France and Italy yielded nothing at all; 'then he wrote two exhibitionist articles about his Marxist days, over which certain people, who are models of moderation, almost left the Congress'. It was in light of these experiences that Josselson instructed Kristol not to ask for any contributions other than book reviews from Macdonald after his departure from London.[79]

Unfortunately this injunction did not come in time to prevent the submission by Macdonald of 'America! America!', an article describing his feelings on returning to his native New York after his sojourn in

Europe, and a particularly savage statement of his highbrow abhorrence for American 'mass-cult' not dissimilar to the Angry Young Men's attacks on British culture (indeed, Kristol described it as 'John Osborne-ish').[80] The story of the suppression of this piece has been told several times before, most recently by Frances Stonor Saunders, who persuasively argues that the CIA was directly involved in *Encounter*'s decision not to publish it.[81] Something missing from her account, however, is the fact that the controversy surrounding 'America! America!' did not end with its rejection. Macdonald sent the article to *The Twentieth Century* and *Dissent* with a note explaining how *Encounter* had turned it down after coming under pressure from 'the front-office Metternichs' in the CCF, and both journals – the former perhaps still smarting at having been passed over by Paris in favour of *Encounter* and the latter living up to its reputation as the focus of left-wing opposition to the Congress within the New York intellectual community – immediately accepted it.[82] When the piece and accompanying explanation appeared in *Dissent*, Josselson immediately launched a damage-limitation exercise, instructing Spender to try and persuade Macdonald at least to tone down the prefatory note before *The Twentieth Century* published it, and Kristol to rein in the resulting 'conversation and gossip' among the New York '*literati*'.[83] Although Macdonald did agree to the revision of the preface, word of his *Dissent* commentary had already got out in London. Norman Birnbaum, an American sociologist teaching at the London School of Economics, quoted it in its entirety in a public letter of protest to the CCF, which was published in the organ of the embryonic British New Left, *Universities and Left Review*. 'What the Congress ... has done', Birnbaum wrote, 'is to give evidence for the widely held view that it is more interested in ideological apologetics than in the substance of the great spiritual issues of our time'.[84] Again, Macdonald was persuaded to join in the attempt at damage limitation, writing to the '*ULR*' to dissociate himself from Birnbaum's remarks. His communication appeared alongside letters from Kristol and Spender, Nicolas Nabokov and Birnbaum, who wished 'to apologise for jumping to conclusions'.[85] The row subsequently petered out.

However, the damage had already been done. Ironically, it was Stephen Spender who was most upset by this demonstration of the CIA's inability to control transatlantic intellectual discourse completely. Having sent Macdonald a 'hysterical-bitchy' letter after the appearance of the *Dissent* note, which concluded with a wild denunciation of the New York intellectual community – 'To me there something a bit nauseating about the kind of internecine recriminations between you and old colleagues ... that fill the back pages of *Dissent*. At your age surely you ought to be free of having to squabble with "Paul" and "Harold" about whether or not you like kitsch' – Spender followed up the *ULR*'s publication of Birnbaum's protest to the CCF with a more measured assessment of the harm done to *Encounter*'s reputation by the 'America! America!' row.[86] 'Irving and I have tried to make this magazine as good as we possibly can', he told Macdonald, 'and put a tremendous amount of work and devotion into it'. However,

> We have always been surrounded by people who are glad to main-
> tain that we are a pressure group for promoting American policies.
> This is, in fact, the deduction drawn from your *Dissent* letter....
> What you have done is to exploit the confused situation about your
> article ... in order to lend colour to the talk against us....

Spender's tactic of undermining the conservative Kristol in order to obtain a more cooperative American co-editor from the left wing of the New York intellectual community had blown up in his face: Macdonald was so jealous of his intellectual freedom that he was unwilling to adopt the same pragmatic attitude towards the CCF's patronage as British intellectuals. The result of the row he caused was to draw attention to the institutional, political and American origins of *Encounter*, precisely the opposite of Spender's vision for the magazine.

From Josselson's point of view, the editorial situation at *Encounter*, long a source of nagging concern to him, was just about to take a dramatic turn for the better. In July 1958 the obstreperous Kristol suddenly announced that he was leaving London to take up the editor-ship of the New York periodical, *The Reporter*. Better still, Melvin Lasky, who after being readmitted to Congress circles following his indiscreet performance at Berlin in 1950, had grown increasingly close to Josselson, indicated his willingness to leave Berlin and *Der Monat* for London and *Encounter*. 'A long dreamed-of consummation has come true', Sidney Hook wrote to Josselson, on learning that Lasky had accepted the American co-editorship. The British welcome for the former US Army combat historian was typically frosty. Isaiah Berlin once talked about him in Hook's presence 'as if he were under the impression that Mel was still at HICOG [the US High Commission for Germany]'. ('It is as if someone were to believe that Berlin is still working for the British Embassy or Foreign Office!', Hook observed wryly.)[87] According to the departing editor Kristol, Spender (for whom Berlin was a powerful intellectual influence) was similarly 'unhappy at having an *"apparachnik"* (for so he regards Mel) foisted on him'.[88] Nonetheless, Lasky enjoyed one incalculable advantage Kristol never had: the full support of Paris. Hence, when Spender began trying to turn Josselson against him, complaining for instance about his 'lack of openness in dealing with colleagues', he met with a far less sympathetic response than before.[89] In return for this loyalty, Lasky strove to make the magazine more political and topical, as Josselson had always wished, for example increasing its coverage of African and 'Third World' affairs; he also performed a function similar to the Lovestoneites Jack Carney and Joseph Godson, by reporting regularly to his boss on political developments in London. Sensing he was losing the battle to dominate *Encounter*, Spender grumbled about 'becoming more and more flooded out by the sociologists and the politicos', and being treated as 'a "useful" connection who is kept on because he can occasionally get Stravinsky, Auden or Eliot'.[90] Josselson, though, turned a deaf ear. After five years' struggle, the American co-editorship was at last in a safe pair of hands.

GAITSKELLITES VERSUS BEVANITES

Although Lasky never quite shed the cloud of suspicion surrounding him – he was, he himself admitted, perceived as the 'shadowy, managerial type' at *Encounter* – he nonetheless gradually earned the grudging respect of British intellectuals as (in the words of A. Alvarez) 'a tougher and more accomplished journalist than either Spender or Kristol'.[91] Under his editorship *Encounter*'s reputation continued to grow. By 1963, its circulation stood at an unprecedented 34,000.[92] The increasing marginality of the British co-editor did not seem to matter: the magazine's relationship with Bloomsbury was now less important than it had been in the 1950s. These developments partly reflected the new degree of control the CIA exerted over editorial policy. Also significant, however, was Lasky's success in brokering closer relations with political intellectuals on the British non-communist left, in particular the revisionists of the Labour Party, which meant that *Encounter* was now deployed in an internal struggle between rival groups of British socialists, much as it had been used earlier in factional battles between literary movements.

Although Kristol had been in touch with the likes of Denis Healey and Anthony Crosland, it was Lasky, naturally more inclined to social democracy than his neo-conservative predecessor, who transformed *Encounter* into a Gaitskellite organ. His courting of the Labour revisionists, which was reminiscent of his networking with German Social Democrats during his days at *Der Monat*, was deliberate, persistent and highly effective.[93] In 1960, for instance, he was in frequent social contact with Hugh Gaitskell (who, incidentally, was already friendly with Stephen Spender), lunching with him and Sol Levitas, inviting him to an *Encounter* reception for Mary McCarthy and entertaining him at his London flat on Thanksgiving Day.[94] He also made a particular point of sending the Labour politician the galleys of articles which he thought might interest him.[95] The American editor – and witting CIA agent – even undertook, at Gaitskell's request, to write the text of a message to the Congress for Cultural Freedom on the occasion of its tenth anniversary, purportedly from the Labour Party leader himself. 'I have been much impressed with the international intellectual cooperation which the Congress for Cultural Freedom has built up over the years through its programme of conferences and seminars and through the periodicals it sponsors', read Lasky's draft of Gaitskell's message. 'May the next ten years witness the flourishing of those ideals of liberty which we share in common.'[96]

Again, however, the relationship cut both ways. Like the CCF, the Gaitskellites themselves had long been on the look-out for an organ which they could use to counter the left-wing influences of *Tribune* and the *New Statesman*. The solidly revisionist and Atlanticist *Socialist Commentary* was useful, but its readership was limited, and vestigial traces of its allegiance to ethical, 'Nelsonite' socialism made it appear slightly 'eccentric' in the eyes of mainstream Labourites.[97] Efforts to transform the Glaswegian weekly, *Forward*, into a Gaitskellite mouthpiece (with financial backing indirectly provided by David Dubinsky's ILGWU) had also ended in disappointment, the publication folding in 1960.[98] Yet the need for a theoretical forum had never been greater. In 1959 the Labour Party had suffered its third successive General Election defeat, then overwhelmingly rejected Gaitskell's attempt to modernise its programme by revising Clause IV – the clause committing it to nationalisation – of its constitution. The revisionists, it seemed, were losing the argument to labourism, the traditional socialist culture of the British labour movement. Hence the appeal of a receptive venue like *Encounter*, with its fashionable reputation and unusually large audience. The Gaitskellites were not being duped. Their association with the CCF's English-language magazine was 'instrumental'.[99]

It was with regard to Labour's domestic programme, rather than an issue with more self-evident implications for American strategic interests, such as European unity or nuclear disarmament (although, under Lasky's editorship, the magazine did have plenty to say about these matters as well),[100] that *Encounter's* relationship with the Gaitskellites was at its most efficacious. Appropriately enough, it was Anthony Crosland, excerpts from whose revisionist manifesto, *The Future of Socialism*, had appeared in the magazine earlier in the decade, who set the ball rolling. In February 1959, he used a report on a CCF seminar in Vienna as an occasion to lay out his own proposals for greater worker participation in management, a concern which typified his general interest in planning and social equality as opposed to ownership.[101] This was followed in September 1959 by an even more obvious intervention in the ideological disputes then raging within the Labour Party by the economic editor of the *Observer*. In 'A deadlock on the left', Andrew Shonfield registered his disappointment that 'the "new thinking" of the younger generation of socialists', in particular Anthony Crosland's 'distinguished' *Future of Socialism*, had not had more of an 'effect on the intellectual process of the party', and predicted that 'until capitalism is explicitly accepted by the Labour Party ... it will be hard to remove the doctrinal confusion which at present impoverishes the thinking of the British Left'.[102] Finally, in January 1960, D. W. Brogan, the highly respected observer of Anglo–American affairs, in a meditation on the current predicament of the 'North-Atlantic left' prompted by a memorandum on the subject by Arthur Schlesinger Jr., wrote of the British Labour movement's need to come to terms with postwar affluence and confront the possibility it 'may have to repent its doctrinal commitment to State Socialism'.[103]

This was but the dress rehearsal for the main event, which began in March 1960 with the publication by *Encounter* of Crosland's revisionist position paper, 'The Future of the Left'. Crosland began by sounding the now familiar theme that Labour's defeat the previous year was due to the 'exceptionally rapid increase in living standards' which had occurred during the 1950s, and that the major challenge now facing the Party was therefore 'to adapt itself ... to the realities of social change and to present itself to the electorate in a mid-twentieth-century guise'. The furore over nationalisation which had engulfed Labour in the wake of Gaitskell's attempt to revise Clause IV was a distraction from this task: the Party's leadership had in fact long accepted the permanence of 'the mixed economy', while the 'revisionism' attacked as a dangerous novelty by the 'older Party stalwart' and some 'middle-class Socialists' was actually a

284

17 Anthony Crosland, theoretician of Labour revisionism and British friend of the Congress for Cultural Freedom. (By Permission of People's History Museum)

venerable intellectual tradition dating back to the previous century. If it was not its stance on nationalisation, then, which really distinguished Labour from the Conservatives, what was it? Crosland ended the piece by listing the defining characteristics of his vision of 'mid-twentieth-century' socialism: a concern with social welfare and the equitable distribution of economic opportunity, particularly with regard to inheritance; a desire to create the 'classless society' by, for example, the introduction of comprehensive education; a belief in racial equality; and a commitment to democratic planning, particularly 'town and country planning'. 'If British Socialism succeeded in adapting itself and its doctrines to the mid-twentieth century', Crosland concluded, 'it will still find plenty of genuine battles left to fight. Besides, it might even get back into power, and have a chance to win them.'[104]

Perhaps not surprisingly, this radical statement of the revisionist case did not go unchallenged. In the next issue of *Encounter*, the long-standing contributor Richard Crossman – who was perhaps not far from Crosland's mind when he referred to middle-class socialists 'to whom … militancy and attachment to dogma are psychologically necessary'[105] – delivered a stinging riposte to 'The Future of the Left', accusing its author of 'Bohemian flippancy and economic punditry'. If anything required revision, suggested the Vice-Chairman of the Labour National Executive Committee, it was not Clause IV – in fact a far more flexible and reasonable statement of aims than the revisionists painted it – rather it was the botched job of nationalisation done by the Attlee government, which had resulted not in true public ownership but in various state monopolies. The other assumptions of revisionism, about, for example, the permanence of affluence and the inevitability of the international triumph of social democracy, were equally questionable, overlooking as they did signs of approaching economic crisis and the productive superiority of Soviet industry. In the face of this uncertain future, Labour should do a real job of opposition and 'stand by its principles'. Finally, Crossman accused Crosland and the other revisionists of reopening old Labour wounds by raising the nationalisation question so soon after the shocking electoral defeat of 1959.[106]

Melvin Lasky was delighted by this outbreak of doctrinal warfare in the pages of *Encounter* and set about trying to maximise its political impact, sending proofs of the Crossman piece to Gaitskell with the observation that it was due to be published around the time of the next NEC meeting.[107] The outcome of the resulting '*Encounter*–Crossman splash', which attracted considerable press attention,[108] was, Lasky believed, beneficial not only for the magazine – it made a 'solid impact on the

Labour Party' and 'established *Encounter* as a journal interested in their kind of problems' – but also for the revisionists themselves, as it helped 'rally the moderate forces flocking to Gaitskell'.[109] Denis Healey, for example, with whom Lasky talked after the NEC meeting, 'remarked that the Crossman [article] was a "very poor performance" showing only how "soft" and "weak-minded" that faction had become, and considered that the article really played a role in "exposing their hand"'. Similarly, Gaitskell himself told Spender (as Lasky reported to Josselson) 'that he thought *Encounter* had been playing "a very constructive role" in this whole affair, and he personally was pleased with it'.[110] Lasky even suspected that Crossman's forced resignation from the Shadow Cabinet was due to Gaitskell's reading of the advance proofs of his article.[111]

Crossman's piece also provoked a number of responses in *Encounter* itself, from Mark Abrams, Daniel Bell, Michael Foot, Patrick Gordon-Walker and Mark Bonham Carter.[112] However, it was left to Anthony Crosland to have 'Some last words on the Labour controversy' in the October 1960 issue. Most of this article was given over to a meticulous refutation of Crossman's analysis of the international situation, in particular the state of the Soviet economy, and a critique of his plans for renationalisation. The Coventry MP's Cassandra-like warnings of impending crisis were, Crosland suggested, typical of a certain kind of doctrinal millennialism common on the left wing of the Labour movement. The most important passages of the article, however, were those in which the leading Gaitskellite intellectual, now hitting his stride polemically, restated the 'sort of policies which a radical, progressive, revisionist Socialist party would stand for'. These included, besides the commitments he had specified in his previous piece, consumer protection laws, the expansion of technological education, the liberalisation of laws on homosexuality and immigration, and an effective programme of foreign aid. Now that ordinary people were at last being released 'from the bondage of material deprivation', Crosland declared, it was up to the leaders of the left 'to nurture and articulate' their 'more imaginative, idealistic aspirations'.[113]

As had become his custom, Lasky sent advance proofs of Crosland's article to Gaitskell, describing it, with some justification, as 'a very effective last polemical word.... Even Dick C. will be hard put to wriggle out of some of the telling arguments'.[114] The Labour leader agreed. '[I]t is a most effective and impressive piece of work', he replied. 'I am very glad it is coming out so soon.'[115] Just how valuable *Encounter* had become to the Gaitskellites Lasky learned when, shortly after Crosland's piece had appeared, he attended the Labour Party Conference in Scarborough. 'Gaitskell has been very glad of our support', he reported to CCF headquarters.

> I also found in all of the center and right-wing groups enormous friendly feeling for *Encounter*. When some of our articles were even mentioned on the debating floor of the conference, we received much kudos about the 'plug'. In any event, I learned that the magazine is taken most seriously and closely followed by both friends and critics.[116]

Thanks to his excellent connections with the Labour leadership, Lasky was well placed the following year to observe Gaitskell's eventual triumph over the Bevanites on the question of nuclear defence policy. 'I was glad to note in my recent chat with R. H. S. Crossman, that the recent Gaitskell victory has also registered itself on the mood of the ... left of the Labour Party', he informed Josselson. 'In fact, now that the perspective for a left-wing victory has been cut off, there should be more disintegration in those circles.'[117] This prediction was soon proved correct. Not even Gaitskell's untimely death in 1963 prevented the eventual capitulation of the Labour left, always on the back foot intellectually in its contest with the revisionists, to the Gaitskellite ascendancy. Hence, when a newly unified Labour Party eventually achieved election under Harold Wilson in 1964, Lasky was able to boast to Daniel Bell, 'We are all pleased to have so many of our friends in the new government'.[118]

When details of *Encounter*'s covert sponsorship by the CIA emerged in 1967, it was noticeable that British intellectuals were, on the whole, less ready to condemn the magazine and its secretive patron than were their American counterparts. Hugh Trevor-Roper, for example, admitted candidly that he had 'always assumed' there was 'some connection between *Encounter* and the CIA through the Congress for Cultural Freedom' but that 'this conviction ... never prevented [him] from writing' for the magazine.[119] British literary intellectuals were, with one or two exceptions, similarly pragmatic. The CIA clearly had 'too much money' and generally had done 'more harm than good', thought Stuart Hampshire. 'Therefore any aid that it might have given in the past to *Encounter* is reckoned to be a net gain.'[120] Political intellectuals on the right wing of the British Labour Party took the same line. 'I later discovered that the Congress for Cultural Freedom, like *Encounter* magazine, was financed by the CIA', wrote Denis Healey in his memoirs; 'both nevertheless made a useful contribution to the quality of Western life'.[121] According to Roy Jenkins, a good friend to *Encounter* and Lasky, 'We had all known that it had been heavily subsidised from American sources, and it did not seem to me to be worse that these should turn out to be a US government agency rather than, as I had vaguely understood, a Cincinnati gin distiller'.[122]

The argument here is not that this insouciance about *Encounter*'s covert connections is morally justified; rather, it is that the magazine's British collaborators clearly felt very little sense of having been duped or betrayed as a result of their revelation. In part, this reflects the unusual degree of cooperation and consensus which existed between intellectuals and intelligence in early Cold War Britain, the consequence of shared class backgrounds and the recent experience of mobilisation in a total war effort. It also had much to do with the basic ideological sympathy many British leftists felt for anti-communist US foreign policy goals, as well as a vaguer sense of Anglo–American intellectual community springing not only from a shared language but also a common philosophical heritage of pragmatism and empiricism.[123] Most important, though, was the simple fact that, to put it perhaps rather crudely, British intellectuals used *Encounter* as much as it used them. Initially, it was Bloomsbury *literati* who employed the magazine in a local culture war which bore little obvious relevance to the CIA's Cultural Cold War objectives. Afterwards, when the Agency had succeeded in establishing a greater degree of control over the operation under a new American editor, it was the Gaitskellites' turn in their battle with the Labour left. 'It is not enough to read ... *Encounter* as an unmediated expression of US ideology', as one British scholar has written. 'Rather it represented an ongoing, complex negotiation of European and American concerns and needs.'[124]

This should not be taken as meaning, however, that *Encounter* represented a defeat for the CIA's campaign on the British left. Indeed, it should be counted as one the Agency's greatest successes. After all, the effect of the magazine's deployment in the contest between Bloomsbury and the Angry Young Men was, circuitously, to reinforce American cultural dominance. Similarly, in the political realm, once the American editorship had changed hands from Kristol to Lasky and the emphasis had shifted from the early, ex-communist, proto-'neo-conservative' project of the CCF to the more positive, social democratic/liberal enterprise of the mid-1950s, *Encounter* proved brilliantly successful at identifying itself with the right wing of the Labour Party. Not only did the US have an obvious political and economic interest in hastening the European left's move from socialism to social democracy, Lasky's alliance with the Labour revisionists over matters of domestic political economy also opened the door to his exercising influence on, as he put it to John Hunt of the CCF, 'the more burning issues of the H-Bomb, neutralism, NATO, and the like'.[125] Ultimately, Lasky's greatest achievement was in creating, to use Kristol's phrase, 'a certain kind of intellectual–cultural milieu' on the British left in which American and European interests came to appear as if they were identical. If, as T. J. Lears put it recently when explaining possible historical applications of Gramsci's theory of hegemony, 'the essence of the concept is not manipulation, but legitimisation', a process whereby 'the ideas ... of dominant groups are validated in public discourse [and] those of subordinate groups are not', then *Encounter*'s influence on the Cold War British left might justly be described as hegemonic.[126]

NOTES

1. For more on 'the revelation', see Ivan Yates, 'The *Encounter* affair', *Observer* 14 May 1967.
2. See Frances Stonor Saunders, *Who Paid the Piper? The CIA and the Cultural Cold War* (London: Granta, 1999), especially chaps. 12 and 19.
3. See Saunders, *Who Paid the Piper?*, pp. 166–77; Peter Coleman, *The Liberal Conspiracy: The Congress for Cultural Freedom and the Struggle for the Mind of Postwar Europe* (New York: Free Press, 1989), pp. 59–61; Jeremy P. Howard, 'A political history of the magazine *Encounter*, 1953–67', Ph.D. thesis, Oxford (1993), pp. 34–51; Hugh Wilford, *The New York Intellectuals: From Vanguard to Institution* (Manchester University Press, 1995), pp. 217–21.
4. T. R. Fyvel to Arthur Schlesinger Jr., 10 June 1951, Arthur M. Schlesinger Jr., Papers, John F. Kennedy Memorial Library, Boston; T. R. Fyvel to Irving Brown, 4 August 1951, Irving Brown Papers, George Meany Memorial Archives, Silver Spring, Maryland.
5. See chap. 6.
6. Stephen Spender to Allen Tate, 20 February 1953, Allen Tate Papers, Firestone Library, Princeton University; American Committee for Cultural Freedom Executive Committee minutes, 30 January 1953, American Committee for Cultural Freedom Papers, Tamiment Institute Library, New York University.
7. For recollections of this meeting by the three British participants, see T. R.

Fyvel, 'Remembering Fred Warburg: A London publisher and his times', *Encounter* 54.2 (August 1982), 36; Malcolm Muggeridge, 'When I hear the word "Gun" I reach for my culture', *New Statesman* 19 May 1967; Fredric Warburg, *All Authors Are Equal: The Publishing Life of Fredric Warburg, 1936–71* (London: Hutchinson, 1973), pp. 156–7.

8. This fact was demonstrated again when Irving Kristol arrived in London in the summer of 1953 to discover Warburg, whose firm had undertaken the printing and distribution of the new magazine, apparently trying to usurp control of the editorial process as well. Irving Kristol to Fredric Warburg, no date, Congress for Cultural Freedom Papers, Joseph Regenstein Library, University of Chicago. Josselson instructed Kristol not to accept the accommodation offered him by Warburg but to make temporary use of the British Society for Cultural Freedom offices instead. Even then, he was advised to be 'careful' of Society officer Jasper Ridley, 'a close friend of Warburg' who was 'likely to repeat to Warburg everything' Kristol might say. Michael Josselson to Irving Kristol, 12 May 1953, CCF Papers.

9. Dwight Macdonald to Michael Josselson, 12 February, no year [probably 1958], CCF Papers.

10. See Hugh Wilford, 'Winning hearts and minds: American cultural strategies in the Cold War', *Borderlines* 1 (1994), 315–26.

11. Irving Kristol to Stephen Spender, 25 March 1953, ACCF Papers.

12. CCF Executive Committee minutes, 26 November 1953, CCF Papers.

13. CCF Executive Committee minutes, 26 November 1953, CCF Papers; Stephen Spender to Michael Josselson, 22 October 1953, CCF Papers.

14. Stephen Spender, 'The editors' reflections on *Encounter*', no date [probably 1955], ACCF Papers.

15. Ibid.

16. See Irving Kristol, *Neoconservatism: The Autobiography of an Idea* (New York: Free Press, 1995), pp. 21–5.

17. Leslie Fiedler, 'A postscript to the Rosenberg case', *Encounter* 1.1 (October 1953), 12–21.

18. Stephen Spender to Michael Josselson, 22 January, no year [probably 1954], CCF Papers.

19. Stephen Spender to Allen Tate, 26 January, no year, Tate Papers.

20. Stephen Spender to Michael Josselson, 31 March, no year [probably 1954], CCF Papers; Stephen Spender to Michael Josselson, no date [probably spring 1954], CCF Papers; Stephen Spender to Irving Kristol, 24 April, no year [probably 1954], CCF Papers.

21. Dwight Macdonald to Michael Josselson, 12 February, no year [probably 1958], CCF Papers.

22. See Howard, 'Political history of *Encounter*', p. 69.

23. See ibid., pp. 74–83.

24. Nancy Mitford, 'The English aristocracy', *Encounter* 5.3 (September 1955), 5–12; Irving Kristol to Michael Josselson, 1 October 1955, CCF Papers.

25. See Kristol, *Neoconservatism*, p. 23.
26. ACCF Executive Committee minutes, 28 January 1953, ACCF Papers.
27. See Harold Rosenberg, *The Tradition of the New* (London: Paladin, 1970), pp. 204–6; Irving Kristol to Harold Rosenberg, 17 November 1955, Dwight Macdonald Papers, Sterling Memorial Library, Yale University.
28. Sidney Hook to Michael Josselson, no date [probably 1953], Brown Papers. This act revealed *PR*'s editors to be 'disgusting opportunists and morally rotten to the core', Hook concluded.
29. Sol Levitas to Irving Brown, 30 November 1954, Brown Papers.
30. Sol Levitas to Michael Josselson, 18 January 1955, CCF Papers.
31. CCF Executive Committee minutes, 25 January 1955, ACCF Papers.
32. Spender, 'Editors' reflections on *Encounter*'.
33. Anthony Hartley, review of *Encounter*, *Spectator* 9 October 1953; Anthony Hartley, review of *Encounter*, *Spectator* 22 January 1954; 'Pharos', 'A spectator's notebook', *Spectator* 12 August 1955.
34. Spender, 'Editors' reflections on *Encounter*'.
35. See John McLaren, *Writing in Hope and Fear: Literature as Politics in Postwar Australia* (Cambridge University Press, 1996), especially chaps. 4–5.
36. Margery Sabin, 'The politics of cultural freedom: India in the nineteen fifties', *Raritan* 14.4 (Spring 1995), 47. This is an extremely stimulating and suggestive article.
37. Ibid., 50.
38. Ibid., 59–60.
39. Hugh Trevor-Roper, 'Arnold Toynbee's Millennium', *Encounter* 8.6 (June 1957), 14–28; Irving Kristol to Hugh Trevor-Roper, no date [probably 1957], *Encounter* Papers, Boston University.
40. Hugh Trevor-Roper, interview with Frances Stonor Saunders, London, 11 July 1994.
41. Irving Kristol to Sidney Hook, 17 June 1955, Sidney Hook Papers, Hoover Institution, Stanford University.
42. A. Alvarez, 'The light is dark enough', *New Statesman* 29 December 1961.
43. See Howard, 'Political history of *Encounter*', pp. 69–70.
44. See Warburg, *All Authors Are Equal*, p. 156.
45. My analysis here is heavily indebted to the brilliant work by Alan Sinfield, *Literature, Politics and Culture in Postwar Britain* (London: Athlone Press, 1997).
46. See, for example, Stephen Spender, 'On literary movements', *Encounter* 1.2 (November 1953), 66-8, in which Spender lambasts the 'rebellion of the Lower Middle Brows'.
47. Leslie Fielder, 'The un-Angry Young Men', *Encounter* 10.1 (January 1958), 9.
48. See, for example, Colin Wilson, 'The writer and publicity', *Encounter* 13.5 (November 1959), 8–13.
49. See Wilford, *New York Intellectuals*, pp. 123–8. Like the Movement writers, the Beats reached back to earlier, 'indigenous' literary traditions (such as, for

example, the poetry of Walt Whitman) in an attempt to create a non-Modernist aesthetic; were courted by the metropolitan cultural establishment (in their case, the New York intellectuals or, more precisely, the editors of *Partisan Review*); and were eventually rejected, Norman Podhoretz's infamous anti-Beat polemic in *PR*, 'The know-nothing bohemians', performing a not dissimilar function to Stuart Holroyd's *Encounter* essay. Ultimately, however, the Beats would prove to be a more enduring and influential literary movement than the Angry Young Men.

50. Kenneth Tynan, 'Letter to a young man', *Encounter* 9.4 (October 1957), 19–23.

51. John Osborne, 'And they call it cricket', *Encounter* 9.4 (October 1957), 23–30.

52. Irving Kristol to Leslie Fiedler, 18 October 1957, *Encounter* Papers.

53. Subsequent issues of the magazine contained numerous critical letters about the Tynan and Osborne pieces.

54. Stuart Holroyd, 'Revolt and commitment: Thoughts at twenty-five', *Encounter* 12.5 (April 1959), 23–7.

55. Kingsley Amis, 'Lone voices: View of the "Fifties"', *Encounter* 15.1 (July 1960), 6–11.

56. See Sinfield, *Literature, Politics and Culture*, chap. 9.

57. Irving Kristol to Michael Josselson, 28 October 1953, CCF Papers.

58. Irving Kristol to Michael Josselson, 16 September, no year, CCF Papers.

59. Michael Josselson to Irving Kristol, 1 December 1955, CCF Papers.

60. Irving Kristol to Michael Josselson, 15 September, no year, CCF Papers.

61. Irving Kristol to Michael Josselson, 16 September, no year, CCF Papers.

62. Irving Kristol to Michael Josselson, no date [probably February 1955], CCF Papers.

63. Irving Kristol to Michael Josselson, 14 May 1956, CCF Papers.

64. Irving Kristol to Michael Josselson, 8 February 1955, CCF Papers.

65. Kristol, *Neoconservatism*, pp. 23–4, 482.

66. Ibid., p. 485; Irving Kristol to Harold Rosenberg, 30 December 1955, *Encounter* Papers. See Gary Dorrien, *The Neoconservative Mind: Politics, Culture and the War of Ideology* (Philadelphia: Temple University Press, 1993), chap. 3.

67. Michael Josselson to Sidney Hook, 19 August 1955, Hook Papers.

68. See, for example, Michael Josselson to Isaiah Berlin, 18 July 1955, CCF Papers. Among other names suggested as possible replacements for Kristol were Richard Rovere, H. Stuart Hughes and Alfred Kazin. At one point the possibility of appointing T. R. Fyvel as a temporary 'American' editor was considered. Michael Josselson to Sidney Hook, 19 August 1955, Hook Papers.

69. Stephen Spender to Michael Josselson, 30 March 1955, CCF Papers.

70. Arthur Schlesinger Jr. to Michael Josselson, 23 July 1955, CCF Papers.

71. Nicolas Nabokov to Arthur Schlesinger Jr., 7 February 1955, CCF Papers.

In this letter, Nabokov predicted that 'the soreheads might, if they got wind of [Macdonald's appointment], fire a nuclear weapon at Paris'.

72. Sol Levitas to Irving Brown, 11 July 1955, Brown Papers. Although Kristol had been criticised previously for having been '"softened up" by Spender in his capacity as an agent of the Cold War', there was also some sympathy for him personally. 'Simply put, nice people don't do this kind of job with Josselson telling all kinds of stories, Spender bleating his irritations to anybody who'll listen – and Kristol unable to defend himself', Abba Lerner told Sidney Hook. Abba Lerner to Sidney Hook, 5 July 1955, Hook Papers.

73. Dwight Macdonald to Stephen Spender, 30 June 1955, Macdonald Papers.

74. Irving Kristol to Sidney Hook, 26 August 1955, Hook Papers.

75. Michael Josselson to Sidney Hook, 19 August 1955, Hook Papers.

76. See Saunders, *Who Paid the Piper?*, p. 310.

77. Michael Josselson to Malcolm Muggeridge, 19 September 1955, CCF Papers.

78. Edward Shils, 'Letter from Milan: The end of ideology', *Encounter* 5.5 (November 1955), 52–8; Dwight Macdonald, 'No miracle in Milan', *Encounter* 5.6 (December 1955), 68–74.

79. Michael Josselson to Irving Kristol, 31 October 1958, Michael Josselson Papers, Harry Ransom Humanities Research Center, University of Texas at Austin.

80. Irving Kristol to Dwight Macdonald, 17 April 1958, Macdonald Papers.

81. See Saunders, *Who Paid the Piper?*, chap. 19.

82. Quoted in Norman Birnbaum, 'An open letter to the Congress for Cultural Freedom', November 1958, Macdonald Papers.

83. Michael Josselson to Irving Kristol, 31 October 1958, Josselson Papers.

84. Birnbaum, 'Open letter to Congress for Cultural Freedom'.

85. Norman Birnbaum to *Universities and Left Review*, no date [probably January 1959], Macdonald Papers.

86. Dwight Macdonald to Bernard Wall, 4 December 1958, Macdonald Papers; Stephen Spender to Dwight Macdonald, 28 November 1958, Macdonald Papers.

87. Sidney Hook to Michael Josselson, 22 July 1958, Hook Papers.

88. Irving Kristol to Sidney Hook, 17 July 1958, Hook Papers.

89. Stephen Spender to Michael Josselson, 12 November 1962, Josselson Papers.

90. Stephen Spender to Michael Josselson, 7 June 1961, Josselson Papers; Stephen Spender to Michael Josselson, 18 November 1962, Josselson Papers.

91. Melvin Lasky to Stephen Spender, 13 November 1962, Josselson Papers; A. Alvarez, 'Light is dark enough'.

92. See Coleman, *Liberal Conspiracy*, p. 185.

93. For more on Lasky and *Der Monat*, see Michael Hochgeschwender, *Freiheit in der Offensive? Der Kongress für kulterelle Beziehungen und die Deutschen* (Munich: Oldenbourg, 1998); Marko Martin, *Orwell, Koestler und all die anderen: Melvin J. Lasky und Der Monat* (Assendorf: MUT, 1999); Giles Scott-Smith, '"A Radical Democratic Political Offensive": Melvin J. Lasky,

Der Monat and the Congress for Cultural Freedom', *Journal of Contemporary History* 35 (2000), 262–79.

94. See chap. 4; Melvin Lasky to Hugh Gaitskell, 2 March 1960, Hugh Gaitskell Papers, University College London; Hugh Gaitskell to Melvin Lasky, 22 November 1960, Gaitskell Papers.

95. See, for example, Melvin Lasky to Hugh Gaitskell, no date, Gaitskell Papers, enclosing a copy of an article by Henry Fairlie and advance proofs of a piece by David Marquand.

96. Melvin Lasky, 'Proposed message from Hugh Gaitskell', Gaitskell Papers. 'Thank you so much for your help in drafting a message for the Congress for Cultural Freedom', Gaitskell wrote to Lasky. 'This is exactly what I wanted.' Hugh Gaitskell to Melvin Lasky, 16 March 1960, Gaitskell Papers.

97. Radhika Desai, *Intellectuals and Socialism: 'Social Democrats' and the British Labour Party* (London: Lawrence and Wishart, 1994), p. 85.

98. Giora Goodman, '"Who is anti-American?": The British left and the United States, 1945–56", Ph.D. dissertation, University College London (1996), pp. 260–1.

99. David Marquand, quoted in Desai, *Intellectuals and Socialism*, p. 86.

100. See Howard, 'Political history of *Encounter*', pp. 159–63, 169–73.

101. Anthony Crosland, 'What does the worker want?', *Encounter* 12.2 (February 1959), 10–17.

102. Andrew Shonfield, 'A deadlock on the left', *Encounter* 13.3 (September 1959), 11, 19.

103. D. W. Brogan, 'The future is behind us? On the North Atlantic left', *Encounter* 14.1 (January 1960), 70.

104. Anthony Crosland, 'The future of the left', *Encounter* 14.3 (March 1960), 3–12. The article was accompanied by an appendix detailing how continental European socialist parties were modernising their programmes. 'A spectre is haunting Europe', Crosland suggested, playfully alluding to Marx, 'the spectre of Revisionism'. An interest in revisionist continental socialism, particularly that of the German SPD, was a common feature of *Encounter* in this period. See, for example, F. R. Allemann, 'Farewell to Marx', *Encounter* 14.3 (March 1960), 67–9.

105. See Crosland, 'Future of the left', 7.

106. R. H. S. Crossman, 'The spectre of revisionism: A reply to Crosland', *Encounter* 14.4 (April 1960), 24–8.

107. Melvin Lasky to Hugh Gaitskell, no date, Gaitskell Papers.

108. See the excerpts from the *Spectator*, *New Statesman*, and *Guardian* reproduced in *Encounter* 15.5 (November 1960), 86–7.

109. Melvin Lasky to Michael Josselson, 14 March 1960, CCF Papers.

110. Melvin Lasky to Michael Josselson, 18 March 1960, CCF Papers

111. Melvin Lasky to Michael Josselson, 14 March 1960, CCF Papers.

112. Mark Abrams, *Encounter* 14.5 (May 1960), 57–9; Daniel Bell, *Encounter*

14.5 (May 1960), 59–61; Michael Foot, *Encounter* 15.1 (July 1960), 69–71; Patrick Gordon-Walker, *Encounter* 15.1 (July 1960), 71–2; Mark Bonham Carter, *Encounter* 15.2 (August 1960), 69–71.
113. Anthony Crosland, 'On the left again: Some last words on the Labour controversy', *Encounter* 15.4 (October 1960), 3–12.
114. Melvin Lasky to Hugh Gaitskell, 13 September 1960, Gaitskell Papers.
115. Hugh Gaitskell to Melvin Lasky, 15 September 1960, Gaitskell Papers.
116. Melvin Lasky to John Hunt, 11 October 1960, CCF Papers.
117. Melvin Lasky to Michael Josselson, 21 June 1961, *Encounter* Papers.
118. Quoted in Saunders, *Who Paid the Piper?*, p. 331.
119. Hugh Trevor-Roper to Melvin Lasky, no date, *Encounter* Papers.
120. Stuart Hampshire to Melvin Lasky, 8 June 1966, *Encounter* Papers.
121. Denis Healey, *The Time of My Life* (London: Michael Joseph), p. 195.
122. Roy Jenkins, *A Life at the Centre* (London: Macmillan, 1991), p. 118.
123. See Volker R. Berghahn, *America and the Intellectual Cold Wars in Europe: Shepard Stone Between Philanthropy, Academy and Diplomacy* (Princeton University Press, 2001), pp. 290–4.
124. Wilford, *New York Intellectuals*, p. 236.
125. Melvin Lasky to John Hunt, 11 October 1960, CCF Papers.
126. T. J. Lears, 'The concept of cultural hegemony: Problems and possibilities', *American Historical Review* 90 (1985), 574.

Conclusion

The Gaitskellite victory in 1961 that Melvin Lasky reported to Michael Josselson was in large part the work of the Campaign for Democratic Socialism (CDS), a pressure group organised by young revisionist activists the previous year to mobilise support for the Labour Party leadership's multilateralist position on nuclear disarmament. The considerable financial reserves at the disposal of the CDS, which enabled it to maintain offices with a full-time staff, publish a regular newsletter and pay the expenses of local campaigners, gave rise to speculation on the Labour left about the source of its funding.[1] Suspicions that the CIA was in the background were stimulated by the fact that William Rodgers, Chairman of its six-person Executive Committee, once reported that the organisation had received 'a large sum from a source who wished to remain anonymous'.[2]

Later, however, it emerged that the CDS's mysterious benefactor was the British restaurateur Charles Forte, founder of Trust-House Forte: 'THF, not CIA', in the words of Robin Ramsay and Stephen Dorril.[3] Jack Diamond, Labour MP for Gloucester, Treasurer of the Fabian Society and a generous patron of revisionist projects (Anthony Crosland was among the recipients of his largesse), had taken it upon himself to raise funds for the new initiative from sympathetic British businessmen and industrialists.[4] At a dinner thrown at the Café Royal in March 1961, ostensibly for the benefit of the now defunct revisionist weekly *Forward*, Forte 'started the ball rolling' (as Diamond reported to Hugh Gaitskell) 'by offering to provide £3,250', exactly half of the sum needed to run the CDS for the following year. Other guests followed suit, and the remainder was made up by a combination of small subscriptions and further gifts solicited by Diamond from the land-owner Henry Walston and retailer Alan Sainsbury, both of whom had previously given to

Forward. 'There is no question, therefore', Diamond assured Gaitskell (who had addressed the dinner, then retired discreetly before the fund-raising began), 'but that the necessary money is assured for the time being'.[5]

The CDS, the documents show, was not a CIA front; like the Bilderberg Group, its funds in fact came from local sources. That said, it is not hard to see why the organisation should have attracted the suspicion of the Labour left, considering the furtive manner in which the money was raised and the élite character of its donors – again, both characteristics of Bilderberg. Also, whereas there is nothing to suggest CIA involvement, there is one fragment of evidence pointing towards possible British intelligence backing. In February 1961 Diamond told Gaitskell that Victor Rothschild – the principal 'fence' for covert British subsidies to *Encounter* during the late 1950s – 'has helped us to the tune of £2,250'.[6] Perhaps, then, it was a case of THF *and SIS*, not CIA.

Evidently, then, it would not do to pin the blame – or credit, depending on one's ideological perspective – for such developments as the eventual victory of Gaitskellism over Bevanism on the external agency of the CIA. To do so is to lapse into the binary logic of the Cold War itself, according to which all left-wing advances within the British labour movement were the result of outside interference from Moscow, and right-wing Washington. Far more important were the domestic roots of these impulses, which in the case of the Labour right can be traced at least as far back as the 1930s, to the anti-communism of Ernest Bevin, the revisionism of Evan Durbin and the anti-Stalinism of George Orwell. Nor, for that matter, was exposure to American influence a novel development of the 1950s: all three sections of the British non-communist left – Labour politicians, trade unionists and literary intellectuals – enjoyed pre-existing transatlantic contacts which were entirely spontaneous, non-official and private. Finally, it would be unwise to underestimate the role of the British secret state in the Cold War struggle for hearts and minds, in particular the contribution of the Information Research Department, whose existence predated that of the Office of Policy Coordination, and which was extremely active on the British left. Far from being dupes of Whitehall, IRD's leftists collaborators were eager, indeed sometimes *over*-eager, allies in the Cold War.

Compared with the consensual, even intimate relationship which prevailed between the secret services and non-communist left in Britain, the CIA's relations with the US NCL – so crucial to the success of the American Cold War covert operations – were surprisingly poor. Having invented many of the organisational weapons with which the covert Cold War was to be waged in the first place, the Agency's leftist agents, mainly ex-communist trade unionists and intellectuals from New York, thought that they knew rather better than the intelligence professionals how to fight the Soviet Union and, consequently, often competed for control of operations on the European left. This was, it is true, a battle that was usually won by the officials, thanks to their possession of the purse-strings. Hence the change in the ideological emphasis of CIA/NCL operations that many commentators have detected in the early 1950s, as the narrow anti-communism of the AFL's Lovestoneite Free Trade Union Committee and the New York intellectuals' American Committee for Cultural Freedom began to be replaced by the more positive, liberal political values advocated by the ex-socialists and New Deal-ers of the CIO and Americans for Democratic Action (a development attended by its own share of irony, considering that these tendencies had been overwhelmed by Cold War anti-communism during the late 1940s). However, the CIA's victory over the private anti-communists only came after long and bruising conflicts, which naturally did little to enhance operational efficiency. Moreover, the influence of the hardliners was never entirely eliminated, with the Lovestoneites and New York intellectuals carrying on their activities throughout the decade, much to the consternation of most Agency bosses. Consequently, while there is a great deal of truth in recent accounts of the American Cultural Cold War effort which depict it as representing the internationalisation of New Deal-style corporatism, it would be a mistake to ignore the persistence of a radical, working-class *anti*-statist ideology, which later would mutate into neo-conservatism.[7]

These internal contradictions in the American campaign, combined with several peculiar local factors, explain why its impact on the ground in Britain was so uneven. The most conspicuous failure was the continuing resistance of the Labour Party leadership to proposals for European federation. True, some younger revisionists were converted; but Gaitskell's 'thousand years of history' speech in 1962 dramatically demonstrated the defeat of pro-European modernisers by the forces of labourism. Much the same was true of American efforts to convert Britain's factory workers to the productivity gospel. Long-established workplace habits and attitudes created a formidable barrier to the importation of American concepts and practices. Even in the case of those operations which appear at first sight to have been unqualified successes, such as the Congress for Cultural Freedom and its magazine *Encounter*, a closer inspection reveals more mixed results. British intellectuals only cooperated with such ventures when they realised they stood to get something out of them. The popularity of *Encounter* was, in this sense, a measure of the CIA's failure fully to control it. Finally, the state of ideological obedience which the US had apparently imposed on the British left by the early 1960s proved, of course, illusory. Although the by now ageing members of the 1930s 'Old Left' generation remained, for the most part, dependable allies, the young radicals of the 'New Left' rebelled against what they perceived as 'American imperialism', denouncing amongst its many 'crimes' the CIA's clandestine financing of such ventures as the CCF. Judged from the vantage point of the late 1960s, then, covert operations on the British left appeared to have done the US more harm than good, as they retrospectively discredited the American cause in the early years of the Cold War.

Such a judgement, though, fails to take account of the more subtle – some commentators would say insidious – long-term effects of the CIA campaign. The main one of these in the cultural sphere was the reinforcement of the literary authority of Modernist, internationalist intellectuals at the expense of anti-Modernist, cultural nationalists. As well as helping to shore up the Bloomsbury establishment, this process indirectly supported American cultural power which, in the postwar period, was becoming increasingly identified with Modernism and internationalism.

Meanwhile, in the more obviously political world of Labour Party intellectuals, covert US support not only helped expose such revisionists as Anthony Crosland to American sociological influences, it also provided the Gaitskellites with important institutional backing in their doctrinal war of position with the Bevanites. Again, it is possible to interpret this conflict as one between internationalists and nationalists, with Bevan and his followers trying, unsuccessfully, to formulate a left-wing politics of British resistance to growing American preponderance. The Gaitskellites' internationalism, however, was a very different project from the vision of global transformation which had inspired the left immediately after the Second World War. Just as talk of a Third Force had given way to the concept of an Anglo–American non-communist left, so the internationalist aspirations of the Labour right had gradually narrowed to Atlanticism. In the final reckoning, it was probably the artificial stimulation of this diminished form of internationalism – something, of course, further encouraged by the semi-secretive Bilderberg meetings – which was the CIA's most signal success in Britain, for it helped bring the British left more firmly within America's political and economic

300

sphere of influence. In this sense, perhaps, it is possible to talk of a Cold War American hegemony.

This is very far, however, from the scenario posited in the imagery of 'Washington gold', hoodwinking and dupes, puppet masters and marionettes. It might well have been the case that the CIA tried to call the tune; but the piper did not always play it, nor the audience always dance to it.

NOTES

1. Richard Fletcher, 'How CIA money took the teeth out of British socialism', in Philip Agee and Louis Wolf (eds), *Dirty Work: The CIA in Western Europe* (London: Zed Books, 1978), p. 197.
2. Quoted in Stephen Dorril and Robin Ramsay, *Smear! Wilson and the Secret State* (London; Fourth Estate, 1991), p. 27.
3. Ibid.
4. Brian Brivati, *Hugh Gaitskell* (London: Richard Cohen Books, 1996), p. 384.
5. Jack Diamond to Hugh Gaitskell, 7 March 1961, Hugh Gaitskell Papers, University College London.
6. Jack Diamond to Hugh Gaitskell, 17 February 1961, Gaitskell Papers.
7. See, for example, Giles Scott-Smith, *The Politics of Apolitical Culture: The Congress for Cultural Freedom, the CIA and Postwar American Hegemony* (London: Routledge, 2002).

References

PRIMARY SOURCES

Manuscript collections: United States

*Archives of Labor and Urban Affairs, Walter P. Reuther Library,
Wayne State University, Detroit*
Congress of Industrial Organizations, Washington DC Office Papers
United Automobile Workers International Affairs Department, Reuther
    and Carliner Files, 1955–63
United Automobile Workers President's Office, Walter P. Reuther Papers
Victor G. Reuther Papers
William C. Gausmann Papers

Dwight D. Eisenhower Library, Abilene, Kansas
C. D. Jackson Papers
United States President's Committee on International Information Activi-
    ties (Jackson Committee) Records, 1950–53
Walter Bedell Smith Papers
White House Office, National Security Council Staff Papers, 1948–61,
    Psychological Strategy Board Central File Series
White House Office, National Security Council Staff Papers, 1948–61,
    Operations Coordinating Board Secretariat Series

Columbia University Rare Books and Manuscripts Collection
Frank Altschul Papers
Lionel Trilling Papers
Meyer Schapiro Papers

Firestone Library, Princeton University
Allen Tate Papers

George Meany Memorial Archives, Silver Spring, Maryland
Irving Brown Papers
Jay Lovestone Papers

Ford Foundation, New York
Ford Foundation Papers

Harry S. Truman Library, Independence, Missouri
Paul G. Hoffman Papers
Psychological Strategy Board Files, 1951–53

Harry Ransom Humanities Research Center, University of Texas at Austin
Michael Josselson Papers
Nicolas Nabokov Papers

Hoover Institution, Stanford University
Bertram D. Wolfe Papers
James Burnham Papers
Jay Lovestone Papers
Sidney Hook Papers

John F. Kennedy Library, Boston
Arthur M. Schlesinger Jr. Papers

Joseph Regenstein Library, University of Chicago
Congress for Cultural Freedom Papers

Lauinger Library, Georgetown University
American Committee on United Europe Papers

Mugar Memorial Library, Boston University
Encounter Papers

National Archives, Washington DC
Records of Department of Labor, Record Group (RG) 174
Records of Department of State, RG 59

Records of Foreign Service Posts of the Department of State, RG 84
Records of United States Foreign Assistance Agencies, RG 469
Records of United States Information Agency, RG 306

Seeley G. Mudd Library, Princeton University
Allen W. Dulles Papers
George F. Kennan Papers

Sterling Memorial Library, Yale University
Dwight Macdonald Papers

Tamiment Institute Library, New York University
American Committee for Cultural Freedom Papers
American Socialist Party (Daniel Bell) Papers
James Oneal Papers
Social Democratic Federation Papers

Manuscript collections: United Kingdom

British Library of Political and Economic Science, London
Hugh Chevins Papers
Hugh Dalton Papers
R. W. G. Mackay Papers

Durham County Record Office, Durham
Sam Watson Papers

Edinburgh University Library
Arthur Koestler Papers

Modern Records Centre, Warwick University
Richard Crossman Papers
Socialist Vanguard Papers
Trades Union Congress Papers
Victor Gollancz Papers

National Museum of Labour History, Manchester
Labour Party International Department Papers

Polish Library, London
Joseph Retinger Papers

Public Record Office, London
Foreign Office, FO 1110
Ministry of Labour, LAB 13

University College London
Hugh Gaitskell Papers
George Orwell Papers

Microfilms

Americans for Democratic Action Papers, Cambridge University Library

Freedom of Information Act requests

Gerald Miller, 'Office of Policy Coordination, 1948–52', CIA Historical
    Study (February 1973)
Samuel D. Berger FBI file
James Burnham FBI file
Joseph Godson FBI file
Sidney Hook FBI file
Samuel M. Levitas FBI file

Personal interviews

Daniel Bell, 13 November 1995, Cambridge MA
Thomas W. Braden, 18 June 2001, Woodbridge VA
Geoffrey Goodman, 1 September 2000, London
Myron Kolatch, 15 July 1998, New York City
Irving Kristol, 14 July 1999, Washington DC
Melvin J. Lasky, 13 August 1997, Rusper, Sussex
Mitchel Levitas, 16 July 1998, New York City
Cord Meyer, 25 June 1997, Washington DC
Jasper Ridley, 7 January 1999, London
Paul Sakwa, 21 June 1997, Washington DC
Arthur M. Schlesinger Jr., 15 July 1998, New York City
Herbert Weiner, 20 June 2001, Washington DC
David C. Williams, 18 June 1997, Friendship Heights MD

Oral history collections

Samuel D. Berger, interview by Terry Anderson, 18 April 1978, Indiana University Oral History Research Project

Herbert Weiner, interview by Roger Schrader, 18 June 1991, Labor Diplomacy Oral History Project

Published documents, reports, diaries and memoirs

Alsop, Joseph W., *I've Seen the Best of It: Memoirs* (New York: Norton, 1989).

Brown, George, *In My Way* (London: Gollancz, 1971).

Citrine, Walter, *Men and Work: The Autobiography of Lord Citrine* (London: Hutchinson, 1964).

Davison, Peter (ed.), *The Complete Works of George Orwell, Volume 17: I Belong to the Left, 1945* (London: Secker and Warburg, 1998).

Davison, Peter (ed.), *The Complete Works of George Orwell, Volume 20: Our Job is to Make Life Worth Living, 1949–50* (London: Secker and Warburg, 1998).

Feinberg, Barry and Kasrils, Ronald (eds), *Bertrand Russell's America, Volume 2: 1945–70* (London: Allen and Unwin, 1983).

Fyvel, T. R., *George Orwell: A Personal Memoir* (London: Weidenfeld, 1982).

Healey, Denis, *The Time of My Life* (London: Michael Joseph, 1989).

Hook, Sidney, *Out of Step: An Unquiet Life in the Twentieth Century* (New York: Harper and Row, 1987).

Jenkins, Roy, *A Life at the Centre* (London: Macmillan, 1991).

Kaiser, Philip M., *Journeying Far and Wide: A Political and Diplomatic Memoir* (New York: Charles Scribner's Sons, 1992).

Kienzle, Don and Bowie, Thomas (eds), *Historical Lessons of Labor Diplomacy: A Seminar Report in Washington DC, April 27 1995* (Washington DC: Friedrich-Ebert-Stiftung, 1995).

Kristol, Irving, *Neoconservatism: The Autobiography of an Idea* (New York: Free Press, 1995).

Mayhew, Christopher, *Time To Explain* (London: Hutchinson, 1987).

Mayhew, Christopher, *A War of Words: A Cold War Witness* (London: I. B. Tauris, 1998).

Meyer, Cord, *Facing Reality: From World Federalism to the CIA* (New York: Harper and Row, 1980).

Morgan, Janet (ed.), *The Backbench Diaries of Richard Crossman* (London: Hamish Hamilton, 1981).

Pomian, John (ed.), *Joseph Retinger: Memoirs of an Eminence Grise* (Brighton: Sussex University, 1972).

Thorne, C. Thomas, Jr., and Patterson, David S. (eds), *Foreign Relations of the United States, 1945–50: Emergence of the Intelligence Establishment* (Washington DC: US Government Printing Office, 1996).

Warburg, Fredric, *All Authors Are Equal: The Publishing Life of Fredric Warburg, 1936–71* (London: Hutchinson, 1973).

Williams, Philip M. (ed.), *The Diary of Hugh Gaitskell, 1945–56* (London: Jonathan Cape, 1983).

Winstone, Ruth (ed.), *Tony Benn, Years of Hope: Diaries, Letters and Papers, 1940–62* (London: Hutchinson, 1995).

SECONDARY SOURCES

Books and theses

Aldrich, Richard J., *The Hidden Hand: Britain, America and Cold War Secret Intelligence* (London: John Murray, 2001).

Ayer, Douglas Richard, 'American liberalism and British socialism in a Cold War world, 1945–51', Ph.D. thesis, Stanford University (1983).

Berger, Graenum, *A Not So Silent Envoy: A Biography of Ambassador Samuel David Berger* (New Rochelle, NY: John Washburn Bleeker Hampton Publishing Co., 1992).

Berghahn, Volker R., *America and the Intellectual Cold Wars in Europe: Shepard Stone Between Philanthropy, Academy and Diplomacy* (Princeton University Press, 2001).

Bergonzi, Bernard, *Wartime and Aftermath: English Literature and its Background, 1939–60* (Oxford University Press, 1993).

Brick, Howard, *Daniel Bell and the Decline of Intellectual Radicalism: Social Theory and Political Reconciliation in the 1940s* (Madison: University of Wisconsin Press, 1986).

Brivati, Brian, *Hugh Gaitskell* (London: Richard Cohen Books, 1996).

Carew, Anthony, *Labour under the Marshall Plan: The Politics of Productivity and the Marketing of Management Science* (Manchester University Press, 1987).

Carew, Anthony, *Walter Reuther* (Manchester University Press, 1993).

Cesarani, David, *Arthur Koestler: The Homeless Mind* (London: William Heineman, 1998).

Chester, Eric Thomas, *Covert Network: Progressives, the International Rescue Committee and the CIA* (New York: M. E. Sharpe, 1995).

Coleman, Peter, *The Liberal Conspiracy: The Congress for Cultural Freedom and the Struggle for the Mind of Postwar Europe* (New York: Free Press, 1989).

Cooney, Terry A., *The Rise of the New York Intellectuals: Partisan Review and Its Circle, 1934–45* (Madison: University of Wisconsin Press, 1986).

Crick, Bernard, *George Orwell: A Life* (London: Secker and Warburg, 1980).

Dell, Edmund, *A Strange Eventful History: Democratic Socialism in Britain* (London: HarperCollins, 2000).

Desai, Radhika, *Intellectuals and Socialism: 'Social Democrats' and the British Labour Party* (London: Lawrence and Wishart, 1994).

Dorrien, Gary, *The Neoconservative Mind: Politics, Culture and the War of Ideology* (Philadelphia: Temple University Press, 1993).

Dorril, Stephen, *MI6: Fifty Years of Special Operations* (London: Fourth Estate, 2000).

Dorril, Stephen and Ramsay, Robin, *Smear! Wilson and the Secret State* (London: Fourth Estate, 1991).

Durbin, Elizabeth, *New Jerusalems: The Labour Party and the Economics of Democratic Socialism* (London: Routledge and Kegan Paul, 1985).

Fillippelli, Ronald L., *American Labor and Postwar Italy, 1943–53* (Stanford University Press, 1989).

Gelderman, Carol, *Mary McCarthy: A Life* (New York: St Martin's Press, 1988).

Gilbert, James, *Writers and Partisans: A History of Literary Radicalism in America* (New York: Wiley, 1968).

Gill, Stephen, *American Hegemony and the Trilateral Commission* (Cambridge University Press, 1990).

Gillon, Steven M., *Politics and Vision: The ADA and American Liberalism, 1947–85* (Oxford University Press, 1987).

Gleason, Abbot, *Totalitarianism: The Inner History of the Cold War* (Oxford University Press, 1995).

Goodman, Giora, '"Who is anti-American?": The British left and the United States, 1945–56', Ph.D. dissertation, University College London (1996).

Gramsci, Antonio, *Selections from the Prison Notebooks* (London: Lawrence and Wishart, 1971).

Grémion, Pierre, *Intelligence De L'Anti-communisme: Le Congrès pour la liberté de la culture à Paris (1950–75)* (Paris: Fayard, 1995).

Grose, Peter, *Operation Rollback: America's Secret War Behind the Iron Curtain* (Boston: Houghton Mifflin, 2000).

Hamilton, Iain, *Koestler: A Biography* (London: Secker and Warburg, 1982).

Hatch, Alden, *HRH Prince Bernhard of the Netherlands: An Authorized Biography* (London: Harrap, 1962).

Hinds, Lynn Boyd and Windt, Theodore Otto, Jr., *The Cold War as Rhetoric: The Beginnings, 1945–50* (New York: Praeger, 1991).

Hitchens, Christopher, *Orwell's Victory* (London: Penguin, 2002).

Hixson, Walter L., *Parting the Curtain: Propaganda, Culture and the Cold War, 1945–61* (New York: St Martin's Press, 1997).

Hochgeschwender, Michael, *Freiheit in der Offensive? Der Kongress für kulturelle Beziehungen und die Deutschen* (Munich: Oldenbourg, 1998).

Howard, Jeremy P., 'A political history of the magazine *Encounter*, 1953–67', Ph.D. thesis, Oxford (1994).

Jumonville, Neil, *Critical Crossings: The New York Intellectuals in Post-war America* (Berkeley: University of California Press, 1991).

Kessler, Paul, 'History of *The New Leader*', thesis, Columbia University (1949), Tamiment Institute Library, New York University.

Khong, Yuen Foong, *Analogies at War: Korea, Munich, Dien Bien Phu and the Vietnam Decision of 1965* (Princeton University Press, 1992).

Lasch, Christopher, *The Agony of the American Left* (New York: Vintage, 1968).

Lashmar, Paul and Oliver, James, *Britain's Secret Propaganda War, 1948–77* (Stroud: Sutton, 1998).

Levenstein, Harvey A., *Communism, Anticommunism and the CIO* (Westport, CT: Greenwood, 1981).

Lewy, Guenter, *The Cause That Failed: Communism in American Political Life* (Oxford University Press, 1990).

Lichtenstein, Nelson, *The Most Dangerous Man in Detroit: Walter Reuther and the Fate of American Labor* (New York: Basic Books, 1995).

Liebich, André, *From the Other Shore: Russian Social Democracy after 1921* (Harvard University Press, 1997).

309

Lucas, Scott, *Freedom's War: The US Crusade Against the Soviet Union, 1945–56* (Manchester University Press, 1999).

Lundestad, Geir, *'Empire' by Integration: The United States and European Integration, 1945–97* (Oxford University Press, 1998).

McLaren, John, *Writing in Hope and Fear: Literature as Politics in Post-war Australia* (Cambridge University Press, 1996).

Macshane, Denis, *International Labour and the Origins of the Cold War* (Oxford: Clarendon Press, 1992).

Mangold, Tom, *Cold Warrior: James Jesus Angleton, the CIA's Master Spy Hunter* (New York: Simon and Schuster, 1991).

Martin, Marko, *Orwell, Koestler und all die anderen: Melvin J. Lasky und Der Monat* (Assendorf: MUT, 1999).

Medhurst, Martin, J. and Brands, H. W. (eds), *Critical Reflections on the Cold War: Linking Rhetoric and History* (College Station: Texas A&M University Press, 2000).

Medhurst, Martin J., Ivie, Robert L., Wander, Philip and Scott, Robert L., *Cold War Rhetoric: Strategy, Metaphor and Ideology* (East Lansing: Michigan State University Press, 1997).

Minkin, Lewis, *The Contentious Alliance: Trade Unions and the Labour Party* (Edinburgh University Press, 1991).

Morgan, Ted, *A Covert Life. Jay Lovestone: Communist, Anti-Communist and Spymaster* (New York: Random House, 1999).

Oliver, James, 'Britain and the covert war of words: The Information Research Department and sponsored publishing', MA thesis, University of Kent (1995).

O'Neill, William L., *A Better World. The Great Schism: Stalinism and the American Intellectuals* (New York: Simon and Schuster, 1982).

Paterson, Thomas G., *Meeting the Communist Threat: Truman to Reagan* (Oxford University Press, 1988).

Pelling, Henry, *America and the British Left: From Bright to Bevan* (London: Adam and Charles Black, 1956).

Pijl, Kees van der, *The Making of an Atlantic Ruling Class* (London: Verso, 1984).

Pijl, Kees van der, *Transnational Classes and International Relations* (London: Routledge, 1998).

Pimlott, Ben, *Labour and the Left in the 1930s* (Cambridge University Press, 1977).

Pisani, Sallie, *The CIA and the Marshall Plan* (Edinburgh University Press, 1991).

Radosh, Ronald, *American Labor and United States Foreign Policy* (New York: Random House, 1969).

Ranelagh, John, *The Agency: The Rise and Decline of the CIA* (Sevenoaks: Sceptre, 1998).

Rathbun, Ben, *The Point Man: Irving Brown and the Deadly Post-1945 Struggle for Europe and Africa* (London: Minerva, 1996).

Rebattet, F. X., 'The European Movement, 1945–53: A study in national and international non-governmental organisations working for European unity', Ph.D. thesis, Oxford (1962).

Romero, Federico, *The United States and the European Trade Union Movement, 1944–51* (Chapel Hill: University of North Carolina Press, 1992).

Ronson, Jon, *Them: Adventures with Extremists* (Basingstoke and Oxford: Picador, 2001).

Rosenberg, Harold, *The Tradition of the New* (London: Paladin, 1970).

Roth, Philip, *I Married a Communist* (New York: Random House, 1998).

Saunders, Frances Stonor, *Who Paid the Piper? The CIA and the Cultural Cold War* (London: Granta, 1999).

Saville, John, *The Politics of Continuity: British Foreign Policy and the Labour Government* (London: Verso, 1993).

Schrecker, Ellen, *Many Are the Crimes: McCarthyism in America* (Princeton University Press, 1998).

Scott-Smith, Giles, *The Politics of Apolitical Culture: The Congress for Cultural Freedom, the CIA and Postwar American Hegemony* (London: Routledge, 2002).

Shaw, Tony, *British Cinema and the Cold War: The State, Propaganda and Consensus* (London: I. B. Tauris, 2001).

Shelden, Michael, *Friends of Promise: Cyril Connolly and the World of Horizon* (London: Hamish Hamilton, 1989).

Silverman, Victor, *Imagining Internationalism in American and British Labor, 1939–49* (Urbana: University of Illinois Press, 2000).

Sinfield, Alan, *Literature, Politics and Culture in Postwar Britain* (London: Athlone Press, 1997).

Smant, Kevin J., *How Great the Triumph: James Burnham, Anticommunism and the Conservative Movement* (Lanham, NY: University Press of America, 1992).

Sumner, Gregory D., *Dwight Macdonald and the politics Circle: The Challenge of Cosmopolitan Democracy* (Ithaca, NY: Cornell University Press, 1996).

Taft, Philip, *Defending Freedom: American Labor and Foreign Affairs* (Los Angeles: Nash, 1973).

311

Taylor, Robert, *The TUC: From the General Strike to New Unionism* (Basingstoke: Palgrave, 2000).

Theakston, Kevin, *The Labour Party and Whitehall* (London: Routledge, 1992).

Thomas, Evan, *The Very Best Men. Four Who Dared: The Early Years of the CIA* (New York: Simon and Schuster, 1995).

Vickers, Rhiannon, *Manipulating Hegemony: State Power, Labour and the Marshall Plan in Britain* (Basingstoke: Macmillan, 2000).

Wagnleitner, Reinhold, *Coca-Colonization and the Cold War: The Cultural Mission of the United States in Austria after the Second World War* (Chapel Hill: University of North Carolina Press, 1994).

Wald, Alan M., *The New York Intellectuals: The Rise and Decline of the Anti-Stalinist Left from the 1930s to the 1980s* (Chapel Hill: University of North Carolina Press, 1987).

Warren, Frank A., *Noble Abstractions: American Liberal Intellectuals and World War II* (Columbus: Ohio State University Press, 1999).

Weiler, Peter, *British Labor and the Cold War* (Stanford University Press, 1988).

Weiler, Peter, *Ernest Bevin* (Manchester University Press, 1993).

Wilford, Hugh, *The New York Intellectuals: From Vanguard to Institution* (Manchester University Press, 1995).

Young, Hugo, *This Blessed Plot: Britain and Europe from Churchill to Blair* (Basingstoke: Macmillan, 1998).

Young, John W., *Britain and European Unity, 1945–99* (Basingstoke: Macmillan, 2000).

Zieger, Robert H., *The CIO, 1935–55* (Chapel Hill: University of North Carolina Press, 1995).

Zurcher, Arnold J., *The Struggle to Unite Europe, 1940–58* (Westport, CT: Greenwood Press, 1975).

ARTICLES AND PAPERS

For references to articles which appeared in *The New Leader* and *Encounter*, please see footnotes.

Aldrich, Richard J., 'OSS, CIA and European Unity: The American Committee on United Europe', *Diplomacy and Statecraft* 8 (1997), 184–227.

Alvarez, A., 'The light is dark enough', *New Statesman* 29 December 1961.

Anonymous, obituary, Joseph Godson, *The Times* 6 September 1986.

Anstey, Caroline, 'The projection of British socialism: Foreign Office publicity and American opinion, 1945–50', *Journal of Contemporary History* 19 (1984), 417–51.

Bell, Daniel, Letter to the editor, *New York Times Book Review* 3 May 1987.

Beloff, Max, 'L'avvenire della liberta', *Spectator* 30 September 1955.

Black, Lawrence, 'Social democracy as a way of life: Fellowship and the Socialist Union, 1951–59', *Twentieth Century British History* 10 (1999), 499–539.

Black, Lawrence, '"The Bitterest Enemies of Communism": Labour revisionists, Atlanticism and the Cold War', *Contemporary British History* 15.3 (2001), 26–62.

Braden, Thomas W., 'I'm glad the CIA is "immoral"', *Saturday Evening Post* 20 May 1967.

Brooke, Stephen, 'Atlantic crossing? American views of capitalism and British socialist thought, 1932–62', *Twentieth Century British History* 2 (1991), 107–36.

Campbell, Duncan, 'The FO and the eggheads', *New Statesman* 27 February 1981.

Carew, Anthony, 'Conflict within the ICFTU: Anti-communism and anti-colonialism in the 1950s', *International Review of Social History* 41 (1996), 147–81.

Carew, Anthony, 'The American labor movement in Fizzland: The Free Trade Union Committee and the CIA', *Labor History* 39 (1998), 25–42.

Carruthers, Susan L., 'Cold War captives: Narratives of captivity and early Cold War culture in America', unpublished paper, workshop on 'Cold War Cultures and Societies', 25 March 2000, Warwick University.

Copeland, Miles, 'James Burnham', *National Review* 11 September 1987.

Crick, Bernard, 'Why are radicals so eager to give up one of their own?', *Independent on Sunday* 14 July 1996.

Dorril, Stephen, 'The puppet masters', *Guardian* 18 August 1995.

Fishman, Nina, 'The phoney Cold War in British trade unions', *Contemporary British History* 15.3 (2001), 83–104.

Fletcher, Richard, 'Who were *they* travelling with?', in Fred Hirsch and Richard Fletcher (eds), *The CIA and the Labour Movement* (Nottingham: Spokesman Books, 1977), pp. 51–71.

Fletcher, Richard, 'How CIA money took the teeth out of British socialism', in Philip Agee and Louis Wolf (eds), *Dirty Work: The CIA in Western Europe* (London: Zed Press, 1978), pp. 188–200.

Fletcher, Richard J., 'British propaganda since World War II: A case study', *Media, Culture and Society* 4 (1982), 97–109.

Hartley, Anthony, Review of *Encounter*, *Spectator* 9 October 1953.

Hartley, Anthony, Review of *Encounter*, *Spectator* 22 January 1954.

Hitchens, Christopher, 'Was Orwell a snitch?', *The Nation* 14 December 1998.

Hogan, Michael J., 'The Marshall Plan', in Charles S. Maier (ed.), *The Cold War in Europe: Era of a Divided Continent* (Princeton, NJ: Markus Wiener Publishers, 1996), pp. 203–40.

Hook, Sidney and Beichman, Arnold, Letter to the editor, *New York Times Book Review* 25 March 1984.

Howe, Irving, 'How *Partisan Review* goes to war', *New International* 13 (1947), 109–11.

Howe, Stephen. 'Labour and international affairs', in Duncan Tanner, Pat Thane and Nick Tiratsoo (eds), *Labour's First Century* (Cambridge University Press, 2000), pp. 119–50.

Kirby, Dianne, 'Divinely sanctioned: The Anglo–American Cold War alliance and the defence of western civilization and Christianity, 1945–48', *Journal of Contemporary History* 35 (2000), 385–412.

Kofas, Jon V., 'US foreign policy and the World Federation of Trade Unions, 1944–48', *Diplomatic History* 26 (2002), 21–60.

Lears, T. J., 'The concept of cultural hegemony: Problems and possibilities', *American Historical Review* 90 (1985), 567–93.

Lichtenstein, Nelson, 'From corporatism to collective bargaining: Organized labor and the eclipse of social democracy in the postwar era', in Steve Fraser and Gary Gerstle (eds), *The Rise and Fall of the New Deal Order, 1930–80* (Princeton University Press, 1989), pp. 122–52.

Liebich, André, 'Mensheviks wage the Cold War', *Journal of Contemporary History* 30 (1995), 247–64.

Lucas, W. Scott and Morris, C. J., 'A very British crusade: The Information Research Department and the beginning of the Cold War', in Richard J. Aldrich (ed.), *British Intelligence, Strategy and the Cold War, 1945–51* (London: Routledge, 1992), pp. 85–110.

Lundestad, Geir, 'Empire by invitation: The United States and western Europe, 1945–52', *Journal of Peace Research* 23 (1986), 263–77.

Maier, Charles S., 'The politics of productivity: Foundations of American international economic policy after World War II', in Charles S. Maier (ed.), *The Cold War in Europe: Era of a Divided Continent* (Princeton, NJ: Markus Wiener Publishers, 1996), pp. 169–201.

Muggeridge, Malcolm. 'When I hear the word "Gun" I reach for my culture', *New Statesman* 19 May 1967.

Newsinger, John, 'George Orwell and Searchlight: A radical initiative on the home front', *Socialist History* 9 (1996), 55–81.

Newsinger, John, 'George Orwell and the IRD', *Lobster* 38 (1999), 9–12.

Newsinger, John, 'The American connection: George Orwell, "literary Trotskyism" and the New York intellectuals', *Labour History Review* 64 (1999), 23–43.

Niebuhr, Elisabeth, 'An interview with Mary McCarthy', *Paris Review* 27 (1962), 58–94.

Norton-Taylor, Richard and Milne, Seumas, 'Orwell offered blacklist', *Guardian* 11 July 1996.

'Pharos', 'A spectator's notebook', *Spectator* 12 August 1955.

Pijl, Kees van der, 'Transnational class formation and state forms', in Stephen Gill and James M. Mittelman (eds), *Innovation and Trans-formation in International Studies* (Cambridge University Press, 1997), pp. 118–33.

Ramsay, Robin, 'The clandestine caucus: Anti-socialist campaigns and operations in the British labour movement since the war', *Lobster* special issue.

Rudgers, David F., 'The origins of covert action', *Journal of Contemporary History* 35 (2000), 249–62.

Russell, Bertrand, Letter to the editor, *Guardian* 26 March 1956.

Sabin, Margery, 'The politics of cultural freedom: India in the nineteen fifties', *Raritan* 14.4 (1995), 45–65.

Schneer, Jonathan, 'Hopes deferred or shattered: The British Labour left and the Third Force movement, 1945–49', *Journal of Modern History* 56 (1984), 197–226.

Scott-Smith, Giles, '"A Radical Democratic Political Offensive": Melvin J. Lasky, *Der Monat* and the Congress for Cultural Freedom', *Journal of Contemporary History* 35 (2000), 263–80.

Shaw, Tony, 'The Information Research Department of the British Foreign Office and the Korean War, 1950–53', *Journal of Contemporary History* 34 (1999), 263–81.

Shelden, Michael and Johnston, Philip, 'Socialist icon who became Big Brother', *Daily Telegraph* 22 June 1998.

Smith, Lyn, 'Covert British propaganda: The Information Research Department, 1947–77', *Millennium: Journal of International Studies* 9 (1980), 67–83.

Smith, Raymond, 'Ernest Bevin, British officials and British Soviet policy, 1945–47', in Anne Deighton (ed.), *Britain and the First Cold War* (London: Macmillan, 1990), pp. 32–52.

'Special correspondent', 'Food for thought at Milan congress', *Guardian* 20 September 1955.

Stevens, Richard, 'Cold War politics: Communism and anti-communism in the trade unions', in Alan Campbell, Nina Fishman and John McIlroy (eds), *British Trade Unions and Industrial Politics, Volume 1: The Postwar Compromise, 1945–64* (Aldershot: Ashgate Press, 1999), pp. 168–91.

Tiratsoo, Nick, '"What you need is a Harvard": The American influence on British management education', in Terry Gourvish and Nick Tiratsoo (eds), *Missionaries and Managers: American Influences on European Management Education, 1945–60* (Manchester University Press, 1998), pp. 140–56.

Trevor-Roper, Hugh, 'Ex-Communist v. Communist', *Guardian* 10 July 1950.

Utley, Tom, 'Orwell is revealed in role of state informer', *Daily Telegraph* 12 July 1996.

Warner, Michael, 'Origins of the Congress for Cultural Freedom, 1949–50', *Studies in Intelligence* 38 (1995), 89–98.

Wilentz, Sean, 'Socialism', in Richard Wightman Fox and James T. Kloppenberg (eds), *A Companion to American Thought* (Cambridge, MA: Blackwell, 1995), pp. 637–41.

Wilford, Hugh, 'An Oasis: The New York Intellectuals in the late 1940s', *Journal of American Studies* 28 (1994), 209–23.

Wilford, Hugh, 'Winning hearts and minds: American cultural strategies in the Cold War', *Borderlines* 1 (1994), 315–26.

Wilford, Hugh, 'The Information Research Department: Britain's secret Cold War weapon revealed', *Review of International Studies* 24 (1998), 353–69.

Wynne-Jones, Ros, 'Orwell's little list leaves the left gasping for more', *Independent on Sunday* 14 July 1996.

Yates, Ivan, 'The *Encounter* affair', *Observer* 14 May 1967.

Index

317

Daily Herald, 23, 174
Daily Mirror, 180
Daily Telegraph, 61, 162, 167, 172, 198
Daily Worker, 92, 174
Dallin, David, 124, 126, 127, 128–9, 130
Dalton, Hugh, 6, 26, 55, 237
Darlington, C.D., 60
Davie, Donald, 272
Davies, Joseph E., 125, 131
Day Lewis, Cecil, 8, 272
Deakin, Arthur, 40, 66–7, 94, 177, 179, 180, 181
Debs, Eugene, 6
Declaration, 273, 274
Democrat, The, 169
Democratic Party, 12
Detroit, 170, 184
Dewey, John, 131
Dial, The, 271
Diamond, Jack, 297, 298
Dissent, 110, 268, 280, 281
Donachy, Frank, 174
Donovan, General William 'Wild Bill', 83, 89, 93, 99, 134, 227, 228, 229, 231, 232, 233, 234, 236
Dorril, Stephen, 52, 297
Douglas-Hamilton, Lord Malcolm, 67, 68, 69
Dubinsky, David, 11, 93, 98–9, 124, 179, 283
Dufty, William (Bill), 19, 24
Dulles, Allen W., 83, 84, 85, 87, 98, 103, 112, 132, 134, 136, 174, 181, 182, 227, 228, 232, 233, 236, 249
Dulles, John Foster, 84, 89
Durbin, Evan, 6, 7, 249, 298

Eastman, Max, 110, 112, 124
Economic Cooperation Agency (ECA), 72, 73, 97, 159, 168, 169, 170, 171, 173, 174, 184, 228, 233, 276
Economist, The, 226, 240
Economist Intelligence Unit (EIU), 240–41
Edwards, Bob, 68
Edwards, Sheffield, 96
Einstein, Albert, 212

Eisenhower, Dwight D., 57, 87, 228, 245, 247, 250, 254; Eisenhower administration, 84, 134, 243
Eisler, Gerhart, 102
Electrical Trades Union, 67
Eliot, T.S., 196, 275
Elliot, Air Chief Marshall William, 252
Elmgrant Trust, 19
Emergency Civil Liberties Committee (ECLC), 212–13
Emmet, Christopher, 69
Encounter, 5, 135, 141, 142, 182, 193, 194, 203, 210, 212, 218, 262–96, 298, 299–300
English-Speaking Union (ESU), 175, 181–2
Enoch, Jean, 106
Ericsson, Peter, 145, 147
Erlich, Henryk, 125
Etter, Willard, 93, 95, 96
Europe-America Groups (EAG), 30–34, 102
European Economic Community (EEC), 225, 241
European League for Economic Cooperation (ELEC), 228
European Movement (EM), 226, 227–30, 231, 232–3, 235, 236, 239–40, 241, 242, 248
European Parliamentary Union (EPU), 227, 235, 241
European Recovery Program (ERP), 167–8
European Unity (pamphlet), 231, 232, 235
European Youth Campaign (EYC), 239, 240
Evans, Lincoln, 177
Ezekial, Nissim, 270

FBI (Federal Bureau of Investigation), 92, 137, 213
Fairlie, Henry, 278
Farfield Foundation, 103, 107, 108, 109, 112
Farrell, James T., 110, 112, 206, 213–14
Faulkner, Katherine B., 212
Feather, Vic, 66, 67, 68, 146, 175

320

Pound, Ezra, 275
Pravda, 145
Princeton University, 212
Progressive Citizens of America
  (PCA)/Progressive Party, 22, 23, 38,
  131, 132
Psychological Strategy Board (PSB), 91,
  181, 182
Public Record Office (PRO), 60

Quadrant, 270
Quest, 270
Quill, Mike, 130

Radio Free Europe, 87
Radio Liberty, 87
Rahv, Philip, 9, 32, 33
Ramsay, Robin, 297
Randolph, A. Philip, 143
Rank, J. Arthur, 70
Read, Herbert, 28, 196, 197, 271
Rebattet, Georges, 233
Red Fascism, 127
Redgrave, Michael, 197
Rees, Richard, 62
Reisel, Victor, 130
Reporter, The, 281
Republicans, 176
Retinger, Joseph, 227–8, 230, 232–3,
  234, 239, 242–3, 244, 245, 247, 248,
  249, 250, 254
Reuther, Victor, 97, 98, 161, 170, 171
Reuther, Walter, 12, 39, 97, 98, 145,
  161, 162, 170, 180
Rhodes/Milner 'Round Table', 254–5
Ridley, Jasper, 208–9
Robens, Alfred, 177, 248
Rockefeller, David, 244, 249
Rockefeller Foundation, 247
Rodgers, William (Bill), 6, 225, 226,
  297
Rome, 51
Roosevelt, Eleanor, 177
Roosevelt, Franklin D., 6, 7, 12, 22, 41
Rosenberg, Ethel, 266
Rosenberg, Harold, 268
Rosenberg, Julius, 266
Rosenberg spy ring, 213
Rothschild, Victor, 298

Rougemont, Denis de, 217
Rousset, David, 205
Rusk, Dean, 247
Russell, Bertrand, 28–9, 30, 57, 64,
  102, 112, 137, 195, 202, 210–17
Russian Communist Party, 144
Rykens, Paul, 242, 249, 250

SAK, 93
Sabin, Margery, 270
Saillant, Louis, 37, 40
Sainsbury, Alan, 297–8
St Antony's College, Oxford, 202–3, 204
St Simon's Island: conference (1957),
  251–2
Sakwa, Paul, 182
Sandys, Duncan, 228, 232–3, 236
Sartre, Jean-Paul, 106
Saunders, Frances Stonor, 2, 61, 122,
  123, 262–3, 280
Scandinavia, 198
Scarborough, 288
Scheu, Frederick, 140
Schlesinger, Arthur M. Jr., 88, 110–11,
  112, 135, 137, 195, 206, 217, 278,
  279, 284
Schonfield, Andrew, 284
Schrecker, Ellen, 125, 130, 131
Schwarz, Solomon, 126
Second World War, 4, 5, 9, 11, 12, 13,
  17, 22, 27, 40, 55, 62, 63, 74, 87,
  128, 158, 181, 231
Secret Intelligence Service (SIS) *see* MI6
Secret Vote, 52
Service, John Stewart, 132
Seton-Watson, Hugh, 197, 202
Shachtmanites, 8
Sheffield Peace Congress, 169
Sheridan, Leslie, 58, 66
Shils, Edward, 279
Shub, David, 139
Singapore, 199
Sitwell, Edith, 272
Slater, Humphrey, 29
Smith, C.A., 67, 69
Smith, Gerald L.K., 133
Smith, Lyn, 54
Smith, Walter Bedell, 68, 91, 98–9, *100*,
  101, 181, 229, 243, 247